RON THOMSON

RON THOMSON

WW II WRECKS OF THE KWAJALEIN AND TRUK LAGOONS

WW II WRECKS OF THE KWAJALEIN AND TRUK LAGOONS

Dan E. Bailey

North Valley Diver Publications

PUBLISHED BY
North Valley Diver Publications
P.O. Box 991413
Redding, California 96099

Copyright © 1989 by Dan E. Bailey
All rights reserved. No part of the contents of this book may be reproduced or transmitted in any form or any means without the written permission of the publisher.

Publisher's Cataloging in Publication Data

Bailey, Dan E.
WW II Wrecks Of The Kwajalein and Truk Lagoons.
Includes Bibliography
Includes Index
1. World War, 1939–1945, Marshall Islands, Kwajalein Atoll
2. World War, 1939–1945, Micronesia (Federated States), Truk
3. Shipwrecks, Marshall Islands, Kwajalein Atoll
4. Shipwrecks, Micronesia (Federated States), Truk
5. Kwajalein Atoll (Marshall Islands), History
6. Truk (Micronesia), History
I. Title
Second Printing 1989, Revised
D767.99.M3 B35 1989 940.54/599683 82-63006
ISBN 0–911615–02–4 Softcover
ISBN 0–911615–01–6 Hardcover

Printed by:

KOKE PRINTING COMPANY
P.O. Box 2686 – 725 McKinley Street
Eugene, Oregon 97402

To Irene and Ed

CONTENTS

	Page
Preface	ix
Introduction	x
Explanatory Notes	xi

PART 1 — KWAJALEIN

	Page
Kwajalein Today	1
The Japanese Occupation Of Kwajalein	5
Initial Carrier Strikes (February 1, 1942)	7
Further Preliminaries And The Assault Of Kwajalein	12
The Wrecks Of The Kwajalein Lagoon	21
Southern Atoll Shipwrecks	23
The AKIBASAN MARU	23
The ASAKAZE MARU	24
The CHOKO MARU	26
The IKUTA MARU	27
The O-Buoy Wreck	28
The PRINZ EUGEN	29
The SHINSHO MARU	32
The TATEYAMA MARU	32
The U. S. Army Concrete Barge	34
The G-Buoy Wreck	35
The Kwajalein Ski Area Wreck	35
The Ski Area Dolphin Wreck	35
The N-Buoy Wreck	35
The DR Wreck	35
The N-East Wreck	36
The O-Buoy Submarine Chaser	36
The Gugegwe Island Wrecks	37
The Shell Island Wrecks	38
The Phantom Maru	38
The Bigej Coastal Tanker	40
The South Pass Wreck	41
The SHONAN MARU NO. 6	41
The Ships Of Eller Island	45
Southern Atoll Aircraft Wrecks	47
The Navy PV-1 Ventura	47
The OS2U Kingfisher Scout Planes	47
The AAF Transport Plane	48
The Ebeye Seaplanes	48
The Bigej Island Fighter-Bomber	51
Northern Atoll Shipwrecks	53
The RO 60	53
The EIKO MARU NO. 2	55
The KEMBU MARU	58
The TAKUNAN MARU NO. 7	62
The West Reef Aircraft Wrecks	63
The Mellu Island Landing Craft	66

PART II — TRUK

	Page
The Truk Lagoon Today	67
Mysterious Truk	72
Truk Naval Operations	72
Truk Army Operations	78
Australian Reconaissance And Bombing Attacks	79
The Photographic Overflight	80
The Fast Carrier Strikes On Truk (February 16-17, 1944)	84
Initial B-24 Attacks On Truk	111
Truk Revisited (Fast Carrier Strikes Of April 29-30, 1944)	112
Further B-24 Attacks And B-29 Experimental Raids	119
The British Carrier Attack (June 14-15, 1945)	120
The Japanese Surrender	120
Task Group 50.9 Battle Report	121
Convoy No. 3206	123

	Page
The Wrecks Of The Truk Lagoon	125
Shipwrecks	129
The AIKOKU MARU	129
The AKAGI MARU	132
The AMAGISAN MARU	133
CH 29	135
The FUJIKAWA MARU	135
The FUJISAN MARU	138
The FUMITSUKI	141
The GOSEI MARU	142
The "Gun High" Wreck	143
GYORAITEI NO. 10	143
The HANAKAWA MARU	143
The HAKUSHUN MARU	145
The HEIAN MARU	145
The HINO MARU NO. 2	147
The HOKI MARU	148
The HOKUYO MARU	149
The HOYO MARU	149
The I 169	150
The KATSURAGISAN MARU	153
The KENSHO MARU	154
The KIKUKAWA MARU	155
The KIYOSUMI MARU	155
The KOTOHIRA MARU	157
The Lighter	157
The MATSUTAN MARU	158
The MINSEI MARU	158
The MOMOKAWA MARU	158
The NAGANO MARU	159
The NAKA	160
The NIPPO MARU	161
The OITE	165
The OJIMA	166
PATROL BOAT NO. 34	166
The REIYO MARU	168
The RIO DE JANEIRO MARU	169
The SAN FRANCISCO MARU	171
The SANKISAN MARU	172
The SAPPORO MARU	174
The SEIKO MARU	174
The SHINKOKU MARU	176
SPECIAL SUBCHASERS NOS. 38, 46, and 66	179
The TACHIKAZE	180
The TAIHO MARU	180
The TAIJUN MARU	181
The TAIKICHI MARU	181
The TONAN MARU NO. 3	182
The Tugboat Wrecks	183
The UNKAI MARU NO. 6	184
The YAMAGIRI MARU	185
The YUBAE MARU	187
Aircraft Wrecks	189
The Zeke Fighter Wrecks	189
The Judy Dive Bomber Wreck	191
The Betty Bomber Wreck	191
The Emily Flying-Boat Wreck	192
The Kate Torpedo-Bomber Wreck	194
Appendices	195
Bibliography	203
Index	205

LIST OF ILLUSTRATIONS

MAPS	Page
Kwajalein Atoll	2
ENTERPRISE VB–6 Bombing Attack Against Japanese Shipping Kwajalein Island Anchorage – February 1, 1942 – 0720–0800 h	8
ENTERPRISE VS–6 Report – Japanese Ship Disposition Kwajalein Anchorage February 1, 1942 0745 h	9
ENTERPRISE VT–6 TBD Bombing And Torpedo Attack On Shipping Kwajalein Anchorage – February 1, 1942	10
Wreck Location Map – South End of Kwajalein Lagoon	22
Wreck Locations – North and central sections of Gugegwe Island	38
DD HARRISON Action Report – Engagement Of Enemy Tanker	40
Wreck Location Map – North End Of Kwajalein Lagoon	52
Truk Lagoon And Kuop Atoll	68
Ship Disposition – 4 February 1944 – Combined Fleet Anchorage	82
Ship Disposition – 4 February 1944 – Fourth Fleet Anchorage	83
Disposition of Bomber Aircraft – Moen No. 1 Airfield	102
ESSEX Air Group 9 Shipping Target Summary Dog-Day-Minus-One And Dog-Day – February 16 and 17, 1944	107
Truk Lagoon Wreck Location Map – Combined Fleet Warship And Repair Anchorage	126
Truk Lagoon Wreck Location Map – Uman Island Anchorages	127
Truk Lagoon Wreck Location Map – Fourth Fleet Anchorage And Vicinity	128
Truk Lagoon Aircraft Wrecks	188

SHIP DRAWINGS

KATORI, TOKIWA, YASUKUNI MARU, TOA MARU	11
AKIBASAN MARU	23
ASAKAZE MARU	24
CHOKO MARU	25
IKUTA MARU	26
SHOEI MARU	28
SHINSHO MARU, TATEYAMA MARU	32
NO. 1 Class Submarine Chaser	36
RO–60	53
AKITSUSHIMA	86
HIKAWA MARU NO. 2	104
AMAGISAN MARU	133
CH 29, FUJIKAWA MARU	135
FUMITSUKI	141
GOSEI MARU	142
GYORAITEI NO. 10, HANAKAWA MARU	143
HOKI MARU	148
HOKUYO MARU	149
I 169	150
KATSURAGISAN MARU	153
KENSHO MARU	154
KIYOSUMI MARU	155
MOMOKAWA MARU	158
NAGANO MARU	159
NAKA	160
NIPPO MARU	161
OITE	165
SUTSUKI	166
SEIKO MARU	174
SHINKOKU MARU	176
TACHIKAZE	180
TAIJUN MARU	181
UNKAI MARU NO. 6	184
YAMAGIRI MARU	185
YUBAE MARU	187

PREFACE

Following the publishing of the first edition of <u>WW II Wrecks Of The Kwajalein And Truk Lagoons</u> in 1982, several new shipwrecks have been found at both Truk and Kwajalein. In addition, much new historical data has surfaced from subsequent research which fills in areas where information was sparse previously. I want to thank Neil Hurley, Bill Remick, Bevan Jacobs, Mary Taylor, and Bob Hampton in particular for their contributions and suggestions. A significant contributor of information for this book was Francis A. Raven. Francis or "Frank," as he was known to friends, had been involved in World War II as a cryptanalyst working on solving enciphered Japanese codes under the command and direction of Joseph J. Rochefort. They were part of the Combat Intelligence Unit whose mission was to learn as much as possible about the operations and disposition of the Japanese naval and merchant vessels through radio communications intelligence. Frank was a main contributor in solving coded messages which produced "MAGIC" or "ULTRA" information. He was an expert in the field of cryptanalysis and the Japanese language and was a great help in solving some ship identification problems and the nuances in the Japanese ship names. He also alerted me to the presence of files that had been compiled from cryptanalysis on Japanese ships that were still classified. Frank always insisted on anonymity and would not stand for any credit being given to him. It as only after Frank passed away and I had read the book, <u>The Puzzle Palace</u>, which alluded to his role in the National Security Agency (NSA) that I began to understand his reluctance for recognition.

The writing and production of this revised edition was influenced by my desire to document all new information along with the aircraft action reports and intelligence files in order to provide the reader with the most complete description and history of these wrecks as possible. Some of this information has only been recently declassified following a 40-year classification period. The text from the first edition has almost completely been revised and supplemented with new information in this second edition. Many new photographs and drawings have also been incorporated which I feel add a great deal to the book.

D.E.B.
Redding, California 1989

INTRODUCTION

My love of wreck diving was a natural transition from the fascination I'd developed about ships which began at a very early age when I first was able to read and began accumulating magazines and pocket books dealing with anything having to do with warships. Having been brought up in an inland area, I had little or no contact with the ocean and certainly no opportunities to do any wreck diving. It wasn't until 1969 when I went to work for GTE Sylvania on Roi-Namur in the Kwajalein Atoll that I was exposed to scuba diving. Roi-Namur had been a Japanese World War II Island base and some ships had been sunk in the lagoon nearby. I found myself listening very intently to members of the local scuba club, the Roi-Namur Dolphins, discussing their dives on the shipwrecks. Several divers had "artifacts" they had recovered; these were not much (a few medicine bottles of various sizes, shapes, and colors from the pharmacy of one of the ships, a number of bronze porthole covers, a few pieces of china, and some fire-blackened, coral-covered bronze items), but they were all treasures in my eyes. I also looked over some underwater photos of some of the shipwrecks; there was something about the huge deck guns and the doorways leading to rooms within the ships just waiting to be explored that intrigued me and got me convinced that I had to start concentrating on getting myself ready for the upcoming scuba course. I was hooked.

The Roi-Namur Dolphins Scuba Club was formed under the direction of Ed Schiele who was the first and only instructor in the club for many years. Ed's love for diving and his long hours spent in the classroom and pool training sessions were responsible for giving hundreds of people the opportunity to enjoy scuba diving. I remember several instances while taking the scuba course of climbing out of the pool almost completely exhausted at one a.m. after sessions of 4 to 6 hours. The scuba course in those days was structured to not only teach you the fundamentals, but to practice all aspects of safety and at the same time whip the students into peak shape. Because the safety record of the club was under close scrutiny and diving practices were monitored closely by the army command, it was felt that the divers would be allowed only one mistake before having diving discontinued for everyone on the atoll.

Many of the members of the scuba club were very personable and their enthusiasm and contributions to my diving enjoyment were considerable. My introduction to wreck diving occurred shortly after completing the scuba course. My dive partner, Pete Gyrich, and I were supposed to explore the exterior of a Japanese shipwreck; I had mentioned to him that I was apprehensive about entering the interior of the ship with so little diving experience. Following a descent to the deck of the wreck, Pete unhesitatingly entered through a doorway into the interior. After having the "buddy system" rule that you are to stay close to your dive partner drilled into me in the scuba course, I had no choice but to follow. We ended up making a complete tour of the interior of the wreck from bow to stern. I didn't remember what I saw following the dive; I had been concentrating very hard on just following my dive partner. All my anxieties about going inside shipwrecks disappeared with this dive. The wreck diving, the deep black coral dives, and our shark encounter adventures added to the close associations developed between the members of the Dolphins. I shall never forget Jerry Travis, Bernie Pociask, Dave Edwards, Wally Oshima, Lionel Kaawaloa, Joe Schmidt, Fred Kirk, Russ Campi, Gary Schilling, Bill Smith, Mike Wells, and others that I was able to spend many memorable dives with.

During the work week, we often had the opportunity to dive during the lunch break. Even though we had to rush somewhat, it was possible to get a 30- to 40-minute dive in. I want to acknowledge Len Woronoff, who got me interested and on the right track in underwater photography and my other lunch-time dive partners at Roi-Namur, Joe Castelli, Rudy Nemkovsky, and Harry Fitzpatrick.

After awhile, I began making frequent weekend trips to Kwajalein Island on the southern end of the atoll for diving trips. I became acquainted at this time with Jim Lawson and Ron Barnett, two of the most experienced and knowledgeable wreck divers in the Kwajalein Scuba Club. Jim Lawson was a wealth of information on the Kwajalein wrecks. Visiting Jim at his room in the bachelor quarters was an experience; the room was filled with items he had recovered from the wrecks including a 4-foot-high ship's whistle, a ship's telegraph, bronze lanterns, porthole covers, and boxes of china. In addition, he had buckets of acid strung out all over the floor with artifacts being cleaned in them. Ron Barnett and Jim had been to Truk and while exposing me to the Kwajalein wrecks, both of them told me enough about what they had seen at Truk to convince me that I wanted to mount a diving expedition there. The lure of wreck diving was firmly established amongst many of the divers and I was able to organize three groups to make diving trips to Truk within a year before completing my first tour on Kwajalein.

At Truk, I was fortunate to meet and dive with Kimiuo Aisek, the manager of the Blue Lagoon Dive Shop. I found his diving experience on the wrecks to be invaluable and his knowledge and stories of the ships sunk there added much to my trips to the Truk Lagoon. I always enjoy returning to Truk and visiting with Kimiuo; I consider him a valued friend.

On my second tour for Sylvania beginning in 1974, I concentrated mostly on diving the wrecks at the Kwajalein Island end of the atoll and was fortunate to team up with such avid wreck divers as Charlie Wakefield, Bob Boatman, Rod Vincent, and Ron Sargent. After these divers left site, I spent many enjoyable dives with Gordon Alcantra and started diving regularly with Frank Cataldo and Theron Anders. I am particularly grateful to Theron who not only put up with my phobia for wreck diving, but also go me interested in reef diving and photographing fish along with all types of coral and marine life.

Over the years as I learned more and more about the wrecks, I was encouraged by divers I had contact with and others who had seen my collection of underwater photos to document all my wreck diving information into a book. This book is a summation of all the historical and present-day data I've accumulated from numerous sources plus observations I've made while diving on the wrecks of the Kwajalein and Truk Lagoons. It is my hope to share with the reader the rewarding experiences I've had while diving, including the thrill of discovery and exploration and the mystery, beauty, and lure of the wrecks themselves.

EXPLANATORY NOTES

Miscellaneous Abbreviations/Glossary

AA — Anti-Aircraft
AP — Armor Piercing (bombs)
ASP — Anti-Submarine Patrol
Bogie — Unidentified Aircraft
CAP — Combat Air Patrol
CD — Coastal Defense
CinC — Commander-in-Chief
CincPac — Commander-in-Chief Pacific
DP — Dual Purpose
GP — General Purpose (bombs)
JANAC — Joint Army-Navy Assessment Committee
JICPOA — Joint Intelligence Center, Pacific Ocean Areas
Mitsubishi — Name often given to any Japanese plane that dropped bombs.
R.D.F. — Radio Direction Finding
SAP — Semi-Armor Piercing (bombs)
Sortie — Single plane launch from carrier on an operational mission.
TG — Task Group
TF — Task Force
Zero — Name often given to any single-engine Japanese fighter plane

Ship's Names

The Hepburn romanized version of Japanese ship's names derived from kanji are used primarily in the text. The Kokutai version is also noted in the Technical Summaries under the category "Other Names."

Ship Types (Glossary of Type Designations)

AE	Auxiliary Cruiser
AF	Provisions Storeship
AG	Miscellaneous Auxiliary
AGS	Surveying Ship
AH	Hospital Ship
XAH	Converted Hospital Ship
AK	Cargo Ship
AM	Minesweeper
AMc	Minesweeper, Coastal
AO	Fuel Oil Tanker (Oiler)
AP	Personnel Transport
APS	Submarine Transport
APV	Aircraft Transport
XAPV	Converted Aircraft Transport
AR	Repair Ship
ARC	Cable Layer
ARS	Salvage Vessel
XARS	Converted Salvage Vessel
AS	Submarine Tender
XAS	Converted Submarine Tender
AT	Unidentified Transport
AV	Seaplane Tender
XAV	Converted Submarine Tender
BB	Battleship
CA	Heavy Cruiser
CH	Submarine Chaser
CHa	Auxiliary Sub-Chaser
CL	Light Cruiser
CL(T)	Training Cruiser
XCL	Auxiliary Cruiser
CM	Minelayer
XCM	Converted Minelayer
CMc	Minelayer, Coastal
CV	Aircraft Carrier
CVE	Aircraft Carrier Escort
CVL	Light Aircraft Carrier
CVS	Seaplane Carrier
DD	Destroyer
DE	Destroyer Escort
DM	Destroyer Minelayer
LSV	Landing Craft Carrier
PC	Submarine Chaser, Large
XPC	Converted Sub-Chaser
PF	Patrol Escort or Frigate
PG	Gunboat
XPG	Converted Gunboat
PR	River Gunboat
PT	Motor Torpedo Boat
SCS	Submarine Chaser, Small
SM	Submarine Minelayer
SS	Submarine
TB	Torpedo Boat
YN	Net-Tender
XYN	Converted Net-Tender
YP	Patrol Vessel

Configuration Sequence

The relative position and numbers of kingposts and masts in relation to the smokestack or funnel is very important in determining the classification and identity of merchantmen vessels. No attempt is made to classify warships in this manner. The mast (M), funnel (F), and kingpost (K) configuration given in the Technical Summaries represents the sequence that exists aboard the ship between the bow and the stern.

Gross Tonnage/Displacement

The relative size of a merchant ship is represented by its gross tonnage. This refers to the cubical capacity of the interior of a ship where each ton represents a unit of 100 cubic feet. Warships are characterized by their displacement where a ton symbolizes the volume of weight of 2,240 pounds of water displaced by the ship and contents of equal weight.

Dimensions

Dimensions are given in the Technical Summary in feet in the format Length/Beam/Draft. The lengths shown are waterline lengths except when noted as being overall lengths (o.a.). The waterline lengths are considered to be approximately the same as the "between perpendicular" (b.p.) or registered lengths given in Lloyd's Register of Shipping. The beam is the width of the ship at its widest point. The draft or depth of water a ship draws is given for the fully-loaded condition if known.

Machinery

Included in this category are the number of shafts, screws, and types of engines. Horsepower figures are given when known. The most common nominal horsepower (NHP) figures have been taken from Lloyd's Register of Shipping. Indicated horsepower (iHP) figures represent the horsepower that the engine develops as measured by the pressure on the cylinders during the stroke with no allowance made for

EXPLANATORY NOTES (Continued)

friction. Shaft or brake horsepower (SHP or BHP respectively) figures represent the actual twisting power given to the shaft and measured by a brake. The name of the engine's manufacturer is given when different from the builder of the ship's hull. Engines are assumed to be located amidships unless otherwise noted (i.e., located aft).

Speed
The maximum speed of the vessel is given in knots in the warship Technical Summaries.

Radius
The radius figures are approximate and are estimates based on the normal or most economical operating speeds of the vessels, their fuel-carrying capacity, and their machinery.

Complement
The complement figures are approximate for the number of passengers that the ships could carry plus the officers and crew manning the ships.

Armament
The numbers and types of guns placed aboard and numbers of any torpedo tubes, depth charges, and depth charge throwers are given when known in the warship Technical Summaries. Aircraft carried aboard the ship are listed also.

Building Information
Data listed under this category includes the year built, the commercial or naval builder of the hull, and the location of the shipbuiding yard.

The building of Japanese warships and merchantmen was mostly influenced by designs and engineering features of British ships. These ships were often built better than the originally designed ship as the Japanese often used their ingenuity to improve on them by extending ideas and in the case of many warships, evolving a better designed ship through the development of subsequent classes.

The following is a sample list of the Romanized names of various shipbuilding companies or yards and the approximate translation of what the names mean in English:

- Mitsubishi Zosensho K.K. (Mitsubishi Shipbuilding Co., Ltd.)
- Osaka Tekkosho K.K. (Osaka Iron Works Co., Ltd.)
- Kawasaki Jyuko Co. (Kawasaki Heavy Industries Co.)
- Kawasaki Senshu Works (Kawasaki Shipping Works)
- Tsurumi Seietsu Zosensho (Tsurumi Iron Works Shipbuilding Co.)
- Sasebo Kaigun Kosho (Sasebo Navy Yard)

Ship Owners
Merchant ships requisitioned by the Japanese Navy to be utilized in the war effort were owned by numerous shipping companies, both large and small. Glossary of terms:

- Bussan – Production or products.
- Goshi Kaisha – Partnership or association of members with limited liability as well as those with unlimited liability.
- Kabushiki Kaisha (K.K.) – Joint Stock Co., Ltd., (consisting only of shareholders with limited liability).
- Kaisha – Company.
- Kiodo – Mutual.
- Kisen – Steamship.
- Kyodo – Mutual.
- Maru – Merchant Ship.
- Nippon – Japan; Japanese.
- Shoji – Commercial.
- Shosen – Merchant Vessel.
- Taiyo – Ocean.
- Unyu – Transport.
- Yusen – Mail Steamship.

The English translation is sometimes merely an approximate indication of the meaning of the name. The following list of Japanese owners is given with an explanation of what the company stands for:

- Asahi Sekiyu K.K. (Asahi Petroleum Co., Ltd.)
- Baba Shoji K.K. (Baba Commerce Co., Ltd.)
- Hamane Shoten K.K. (Hamane Commerce Co., ltd.)
- Hokkaido Tanko Kisen K.K. (Hokkaido Coal & Collier Steamship Co., Ltd.)
- Ishihara Sangyo Kaiun Kaisha (Ishihara Industries Shipping Co., Ltd.)
- Kita Nippon Kisen K.K. (Northern Japan Steamship Co., Ltd.)
- Kobe Sanbashi K. K. (Kobe Pier Co., Ltd.)
- Kokusai Kisen K.K. (Kokuyo Whaling Co., Ltd.)
- Kyokuyo Hogei K.K. (Kokuyo Whaling Co., Ltd.)
- Mitsubishi Jukogyo K.K. (Mitsubishi Heavy Industries Co., Ltd.)
- Nagai Unyu Goshi K.K. (Nagai Transportation Co., Ltd.)
- Nippon Yusen Kisen Kaisha (Japan Mail Steamship Co., Ltd.)
- Nippon Suisan K.K. (Japan Marine Products Co., Ltd.)
- Okitori Godo Gyogyo Kaisha (Okitori Amalgamated Fishing Co., Ltd.)
- Osaka Shosen Kaisha (Osaka Merchant Shipping Co., Ltd.)
- Taiyo Kogyo K.K. (Taiyo Engineering Industries Co., Ltd.)
- Teikoku Senpahu K.K. (Teikoku Shipping Co., Ltd)
- Toa Kaiun K.K. (Toa Marine Transportation Co., Ltd.)

Japanese Planes
(Allied Code Name – Japanese Name & Designation)

- ALF – Kawanishi E7K, Navy Type 94 Reconnaissance Seaplane.
- BETTY – Mitsubishi G4M1/G4M3 Navy Type 1 Attack Bomber.
- CLAUDE – Mitsubishi A5M Navy Type 96 Carrier Fighter.
- DAVE – Nakajima E8N, Navy Type 95 Reconnaissance Seaplane.
- DINAH – Mitsubishi Ki-46, Army Type 100 Command Reconnaissance Plane.
- EMILY – Kawanishi H8K, Navy Type 2 Flying-Boat.
- HAP/HAMP – Mitsubishi A6M3 (ZEKE Variant), Navy Type 0 Carrier Fighter Model 32.
- IRVING – Nakajima J1N1–C,R, Navy Type 2 Reconnaissance Plane or J1N1–S, Navy Night Fighter Gekko.

JAKE – Aichi E13A, Navy Type 0 Reconnaissance Seaplane.
JILL – Nakajima B6N, Navy Carrier Attack Bomber Tenzan.
JUDY – Yokosuka D4Y, Navy Carrier Bomber Suisei.
KATE – Nakajima B5N, Navy Type 97 Carrier Attack Bomber.
MAVIS – Kawanishi H6K, Navy Type 97 Flying-Boat.
NELL – Mitsubishi G3M Navy Type 96 Medium Attack Bomber.
NICK – Kawasaki Ki-45 KAI, Army Type 2 Two-seat Fighter Toryu.
OSCAR – Nakajima Ki-43, Army Type 1 Fighter Hayabusa.
PETE – Mitsubishi F1M, Navy Type 0 Observation Seaplane.
RUFE – Nakajima A6M2-N, Navy Type 2 Fighter Seaplane.
SALLY – Mitsubishi Ki-21, Army Type 97 Heavy Bomber.
TOJO – Nakajima Ki-44, Army Type 2 Single-seat Fighter Shoki.
TONY – Kawasaki Ki-61, Army Type 3 Fighter Hien.
TOPSY – Mitsubishi Ki-57, Army Type 100 Transport.
VAL – Aichi D3A Carrier Bomber.
ZEKE – Mitsubishi A6M, Navy Type 0 Carrier Fighter Reisen (Zero).

U.S. Plane Squadron/Unit Designations

VB	Dive Bomber
VBF	Fighter Bomber
VF	Fighter
VFN	Night Fighter
VOS	Scout Observation
VS	Scout
VT	Torpedo Bomber

U.S. Plane Types

A-29	Navy-USAAF two-engine bomber, the Lockheed Hudson.
B-24	Army four-engine bomber, the Consolidated Liberator.
B-25	Army two-engine bomber, the North American Mitchell.
B-29	Army four-engine bomber, the Boeing SuperFortress.
F4U	Navy single-engine fighter, the Chance-Vought Corsair.
F6F	Navy single engine fighter, the Grumman Hellcat.
OS2U	Navy single engine observation-scout seaplane, the Chance-Vought Kingfisher.
PBY	Navy two engine long-range maritime reconnaissance amphibian flying-boat, the Consolidated Model 28 Catalina.
PB4Y	Navy-Marine four-engine bomber, the Consolidated Liberator.
PV-1	Navy two-engine bomber, the Lockheed Ventura.
SB2C	Navy single-engine dive bomber, the Curtis Helldiver.
SBD	Navy single-engine dive bomber, the Douglas Dauntless.
TBD	Navy single-engine torpedo bomber, the Douglas Devastator.
TBF	Navy single-engine torpedo bomber, the Grumman Avenger.

PART I

KWAJALEIN

Kwajalein Today

The Kwajalein Atoll, located 2,400 miles southwest of Hawaii, is the site of the U.S. Army's missile range now known as USAKA (U.S. Army Kwajalein Atoll) and is currently the home of nearly 2,700 scientists, engineers, technicians, and support personnel. This base is part of the Western Test Range. The islands are leased from the Marshallese; over $22 million annually is funnelled to the Government and local populace. Radar and optical sensors are positioned on the islands of Roi-Namur, Meck, Kwajalein Island itself, and some of the smaller peripheral islands to track missiles launched from Vandenberg Air Force Base and other Pacific sites and record data that is used in the development of advanced IRBM/ICBM missile systems and that will serve as a data base for anti-ballistic missile defense system technology. Much of this work now supports the SDI or Star Wars programs and testing concepts for new space weapons technologies will begin in 1990. The American population is expected to double by that time.

Kwajalein Island is the largest island within the atoll (900 acres) and supports a large community living in bachelor quarter barracks, Seabee-built family houses and a multitude of trailers. A large mixture of people live and work here including Filipino-Americans, Hawaiians, and Americans from all over the continental United States. Many of the Marshallese themselves work for the missile range and they are transported from Ebeye, where the majority of the Marshallese population live (nearly 10,000 people), to Kwajalein Island on work days. Many defense contractor companies are represented including GTE Sylvania, RCA, Lincoln Laboratory, Pan American World Services, General Electric, McDonnell Douglas, and Lockheed. It is expected that several others companies will be coming on island as the SDI testing program is expanded. Kwajalein Island is closed to the general public and special permission is needed from the Army to arrange any kind of visit. People coming to Kwajalein on a work assignment arrive and depart by either C-141 Military Airlift Command Jets or by Continental Air Micronesia. Supplies and mail are brought to the islands in the same manner and by sea trains arriving 1–2 times a month. Most shopping is done in the military exchange facility (Macys) or in the Ten-Ten store. There is one food market on the island (Surfway) and one night-club/restaurant (the Yokwe-Yuk Club).

With only a limited land area, anyone can go from one side of the island to the other in minutes by the common mode of transportation, the bicycle. Because most island residents have to wait between six months to a year between leaves or vacations, many sports and recreational activities, several TV stations, and movies have been made available to keep people occupied. Besides the softball, volleyball, and basketball leagues for both men and women, boats are available for water sports such as sailing, scuba diving and snorkeling, fishing, and water skiing. Windsurfing is now a popular new sport. The Kwajalein Scuba Club has a large membership and has diver training courses in progress several times a year. This club has to be one of the most active scuba clubs in existence and members are actively involved in wreck diving, shell and coral collecting, and underwater photography.

Kwajalein Island was the site of an important historical amphibious assault in 1944 where 20,000 U.S. troops were put ashore to take the island from its defenders giving the U.S. Forces an important foothold in the drive towards the homeland islands of the Japanese. The island now has only a Japanese shrine for war dead, a few monuments, and crumbling cement pillboxes as reminders of the battle that took place there. The reality of war becomes much easier to visualize after diving on the wrecks within the lagoon and seeing the ships loaded with war materials and the damage they sustained when sunk.

Forty-four miles north of Kwajalein Island lies the island of Roi-Namur which was originally two separate islands, but the reef separating them was filled in and the islands joined. This island is now the home

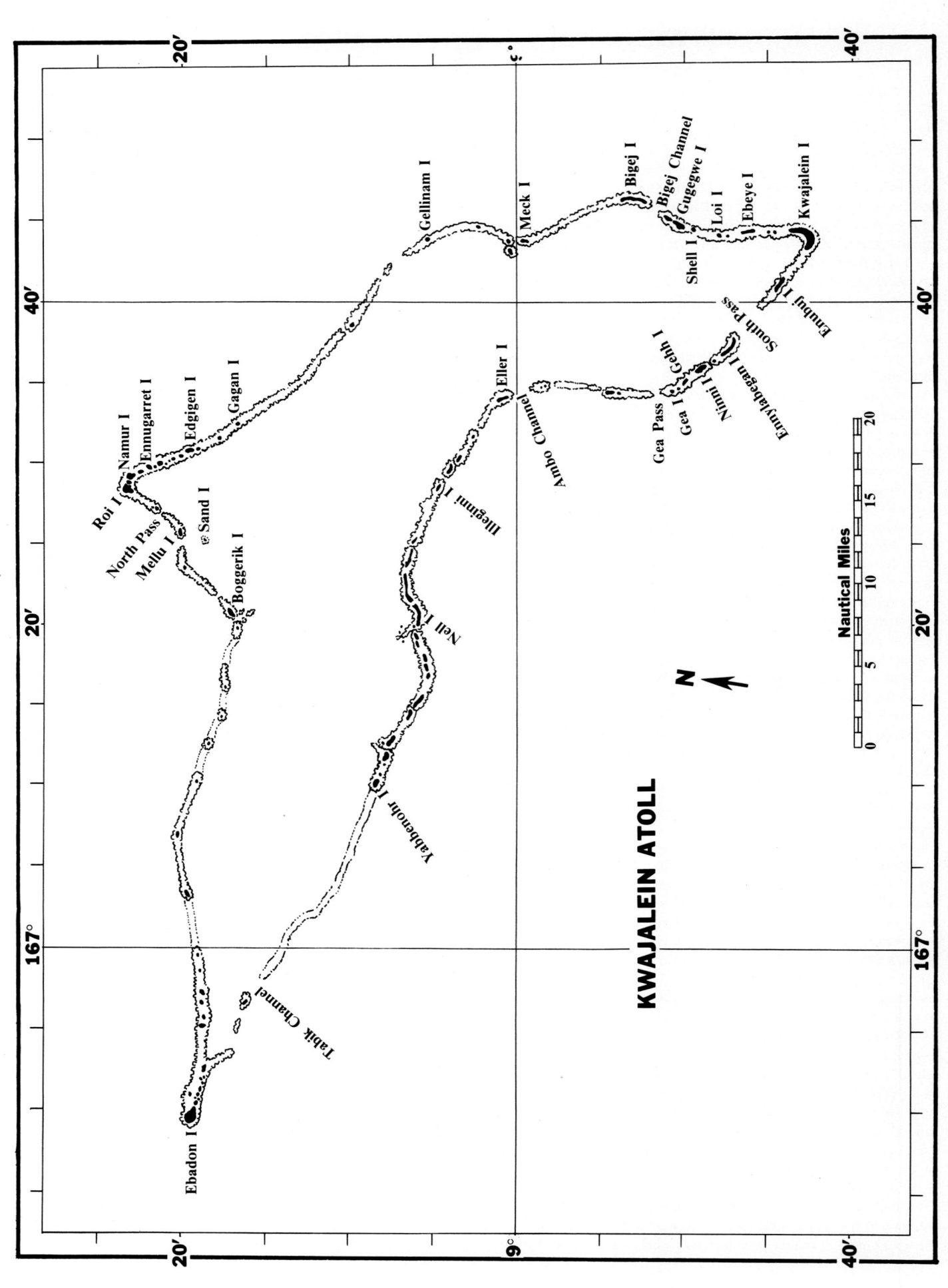

Kwajalein Island (Kwajalein Atoll, Marshall Islands).

–U.S. Army Photo

Roi-Namur and east reef islands (Kwajalein Atoll, Marshall Islands).

—*U.S. Army Photo*

for approximately 300 men affectionately named "Roi-Rats" on bachelor status. The airstrip, living quarters, mess hall, store (Gimbles), club, and most recreational facilities are located on Roi while the majority of the work areas are on Namur. Men and women living on Kwajalein and working on Roi-Namur commute daily on Shorts aircraft. Intricate state-of-the-art missile tracking instrumentation radars, including ALCOR, ALTAIR, and TRADEX, are located on Roi-Namur as part of the Kiernan Reentry Measurements Site (KREMS).

Roi-Namur is also home to the Roi-Namur Dolphins Scuba Club with a membership of between 30 and 50 divers. The members of this small club also actively follow the same pursuits as the Kwajalein Scuba Club.

Many of the WW II Japanese installations on the island of Roi-Namur have been left standing and are preserved for residents and visitors to see. Several large cement blockhouses that had been used by the Japanese for munitions and fuel storage loom high above the flat ground; most of them are used today for storage of equipment and materials. The picturesque air headquarters building on Roi is the standout monument testifying to the furious battle that was raged on the island. Large craters in the cement roof show evidence of bomb damage while the walls exhibit naval projectile and bullet holes from guns of many sizes. A sightseeing tour around the island will turn up many strategically-placed pillboxes that once held coastal defense guns. There are several personnel bomb shelters still remaining also.

The large 127mm twin-mount dual purpose gun and parapet installation can be still found on Roi with the barrels of the gun still pointing towards North Pass. Just off the runway on the northeast side of Roi, the remnants of a corroded landing craft lies in the shallows on the reef. Some of the pillboxes which were once covered by the dense foliage have had the jungle cleared away; many on the Namur side of the island are still hidden by the heavy growth. Just 50 yards from the ALCOR radar is the remains of a Japanese hospital. Built with a corrugated tin roof, the hospital is completely covered by the thick foliage. Inside are some large gas cannisters, an examination table, and several sheets of X-ray film strung out over the floor.

Much of the war-related wreckage that littered the island has been bulldozed onto the reef where the rusting remains are constantly being washed by the tide. Beachcombing around the island often produces interesting finds such as dog tags, coins, bottles, knives, and ammunition of various types. A special ordnance removal unit is available to handle any live ammunition found.

Evidence of the assault and occupation of the islands along both the east and west reefs that flank Roi-Namur can be found. Obella Island on the east reef has remains of several landing craft on its beaches lagoon-side, and an American M–5 light tank lies in the shallows just off Ennuemennet Island. The site of the preliminary landing on Mellu Island on the west reef is still recognizable by the large amount of discarded equipment lying in the jungle.

The Japanese Occupation Of Kwajalein

Located in the central part of the Ralik Chain of islands in the Marshalls, Kwajalein is one of 33 atolls and is the largest atoll in the world with a circumference of nearly 190 miles encompassing a lagoon with an area of approximately 850 square miles. The largest of the islands are Roi-Namur to the north, Ebadon to the west, and Kwajalein Island located at the southern extremity of the atoll. The islands are very flat with their tops rising only a few feet above sea level. Non-inhabited islands are thickly covered with jungle-like growth.

Originally colonized by Spain in the 19th century, these islands were later taken over by Germany who lost them to the Japanese in 1914 during the outbreak of World War I. Kwajalein was placed under a mandate to the Japanese under a grant from the League of Nations in 1920. A civilian administration was established and Japanese citizens were brought in to begin developing the economy. During the 1930s, they began building roads, towns, railways, supply facilities, and by 1934 had a chain of airfields and seaplane bases that extended from Palau to Saipan and from Truk to Kwajalein and Wotje.

Unknown to American war planners, the Japanese had begun a systematic military buildup of the Marshall Islands beginning in November 1940. On 15 January 1941, the 6th Base Force and the 24th Koku Sentai (Air Flotilla) were activated as the defense force for the Marshalls and were deployed two months later. Once the fall of the Philippines, Malaya, and the Dutch Indies had been accomplished, the strategic plan dictated that the primary effort of the Japanese would be directed toward a southward thrust through New Britain, the Solomons, and New Hebrides to Australia and New Zealand. The bases in the Marshalls bases were envisioned by the Japanese military planners to be used as a defensive screen to prevent the enemy from making flanking attacks on their forces participating in that offensive thrust. The Marshalls bases would also serve as the center of a self-supporting defensive system in conjunction with Truk in the Carolines and Saipan in the Marianas. A planned drive by Japanese forces staged through the Marshalls southward to Samoa and Fiji would add more supporting defensive bases to further protect the Marshalls bases themselves and those in the newly occupied Gilbert Islands. Plans were made for Japanese task forces to use the Marshalls as a staging point for the assembly and deployment of air and naval forces preparing to raid Allied bases and to oppose any counter operations against them. By extending their air and sea power from the Marshalls and other South Pacific bases, the Japanese figured to close American supply lines or at least force them south of their normal supply routes. These bases were used in the initial attack operations in the Central Pacific Ocean Area. The submarine expeditionary force that participated in the Wake Island invasion operation and those that attacked Pearl Harbor originated from Kwajalein. The initial bombing attacks against Wake Island on December 8, 1941 were flown from Roi Island and Wotje and the amphibious task force assault troops that later overran the marine defenders on the island belonged to the Marshall's garrison. The forces participating in the mopping up operations in the Gilbert Islands, Howland Island, and Baker Island were all staged through the Marshalls. The Marshalls were also designated to be used for bases for submarines operating in the Central Pacific Ocean Area and for the forces conducting reconnaissance and raiding activities against the Hawaiian Islands and Midway Island. The strategic location of the Marshalls played an important role in their use as a relay supply base for the Wake and Gilbert Islands areas. The construction of extensive fixed fortifications before or during the early stages of the war was not attempted. Efforts were limited to the establishment of beach defenses intended to annihilate the enemy attempting an amphibious assault on the beaches.

Kwajalein figured largely in the planning of the offensive phase of the Japanese war effort and had become the most important base in the Marshalls. Kwajalein Island was developed into a land relay base and became the naval base headquarters for the 6th Base Force under the command of Admiral Shigeyoshi's 4th Mandate Fleet based at Truk. The main fleet anchorage was north of Kwajalein Island extending along the east side of the lagoon to a point opposite Loi Island. Three passes provided entrance into the lagoon. Most Japanese ships approaching Kwajalein used the Gea channel, located nine miles northwest of Kwajalein Island between Gea and Ninni islands. South Pass was a secondary access used mostly by smaller vessels. The wide and shallow Bigej Channel, almost always filled with swells, provided good access for small vessels. A 1,600-foot pier was constructed near the north end of Kwajalein Island where loading facilities and approximately 120 buildings including barracks, warehouses, repair shops, and utility facilities associated with the supply base were built. In addition to the base force headquarters, the 61st Guard Unit, a communications unit, a sub base unit, a branch installation of the civil engineering department, a naval stores department, and a transportation department were established. Both naval and army military units were garrisoned on Kwajalein Island. The breakdown of the individual naval units included the 6th Base Force Headquarters (80 men), the 61st Guard Unit (1,500 men), the 6th Communication Unit (400 men), the 6th Sub Base Unit (200 men), and miscellaneous facilities, munitions, transportation and intendance units (520 men) for a total of 2,700 men. Army units included the 1st Mobile Amphibious Brigade and elements of the 1st South Seas Detachment totaling 3,900 men. Both the navy and army units were commanded by Rear Admiral Akiyama Monzo, commander of the 6th Base Force.

Ennubuj (Carlson) Island was a communication and administration center. A two-tower radio station was built near the center of the island with 4–5 large buildings and 5 or more smaller ones.

At Ebeye Island, north of Kwajalein Island along the reef, the Japanese had established a permanent base installation for two squadron units of scout seaplanes composed of the large Mavis flying-boats and one fighter seaplane unit. These were part of the 952nd Air Group which was organized on 1 November 1942. Construction of facilities had started in 1940 and included a seaplane ramp, one receiving and one sending radio station, storehouses for ammunition, and fuel storage. One or more of the seaplanes usually acted as air cover for ships leaving Kwajalein, and they were also known to work with patrol vessels searching for prowling American submarines.

Extensive small boat repair facilities including two piers, two marine railways, repair shops and warehouses were built on Gugegwe Island. Escort vessels were often congregated in the lagoon off the island. Ships leaving the atoll via Gea or South passes were usually accompanied by three to five of the escort vessels. Patrols were continually being conducted outside these passes.

Bigej Island was used by the Japanese to store munitions including large supplies of bombs, torpedoes, mines, and etc. Nine large heavy concrete buildings were constructed for storage. A narrow gauge railway track connected the buildings with the two piers which were served by a marine railway.

A central base for land-based aircraft in the Marshalls was completed at Roi Island which included an airfield with three intersecting runways. The Chitose Kokutai (752nd Naval Air Group) of the 24th Air Flotilla, equipped with Nell bombers and Claude fighters, was based at Roi and Taroa Islands. Units from the Southeast Area Fleet were also based at Roi; this included planes from the 753rd Air Group of the 23rd Air Flotilla. The Roi Island air organization was known as the Southeast District Air Depot 2nd Branch. Its function was to supply and repair planes in the Marshall and Gilbert Islands area. Roi-Namur was under the command of Rear Admiral Yamada Michiyuki, commander of the 24th Air Flotilla. Subordinate organizations included a detachment of the Naval 61st Guard Unit (400 men), the Air Force or "Yamada Unit" (1,500 men), the construction unit or "Tomomura Section of the Hagiwara Unit" (800 men), the Air Depot or "Todaki Unit" (200 men), and the Naval Stores Department and others (20 men). There were a total of 2,920 men assigned to Roi-Namur, 1,900 navy and 1,100 civil employees (of which 150–200 were Korean). Facilities on Roi included a heavy concrete constructed air headquarters building, an air operations building, a large hangar, power plant, and both fighter and bomber revetments. Two grid-type radars were positioned on the west side of the island. The lagoon south of Roi-Namur served a a secondary fleet anchorage and a considerable amount of naval stores and shipping facilities were located on Namur Island. There were nearly 150 buildings on Namur including barracks, mess halls, garages, fuel and munitions storage bunkers, generator plant warehouses, a hospital, a communications facility, and etc. Regular patrols of small craft were maintained off North Pass.

The Japanese constructed an important radio station consisting of a large "T" shaped, two-story, concrete building with three large towers on Ennubirr island, located about one and one-half miles south-southeast of Roi-Namur. This radio station complex was similar to those constructed by the Japanese on Jaluit and Taroa.

The Naval Air Force 24th Air Flotilla came under the operational command of the CinC of the 4th Fleet. It functioned as a component unit of the 11th Air Fleet in conjunction with the advance of the 11th Air Fleet headquarters into the Rabaul area. The primary purpose of this organization was to enhance the mobility of the air strength as much as possible and make it possible to transfer and concentrate air strength as the occasion demanded in the Central and South Pacific front, which included the areas adjacent to the Solomons and the Central Pacific Ocean Area. The 24th Air Flotilla was transferred back to the Empire in December 1942. At this time the 22nd Air Flotilla advanced to the Marshall Islands in its place and engaged in operations. There were a total of 41 transports assigned to the 6th Base Force at Kwajalein, the 5th Base Force at Saipan, the 4th Base Force at Truk, and the 3rd Base Force at Palau which were constantly being used to transfer supplies and men from Japan to these island bases. Other vessels were assigned to the 6th Base Force with specific roles in serving as a defensive force for the Marshalls. These craft served as picket boats, patrol craft for submarine defense, convoy escorts, minelayers or minesweepers, and net tenders. The following vessels were assigned to the 6th Base Force in the early months of the war:

Gunboat Division 8	DAIDO MARU, IKUTA MARU, NAGATA MARU.
Minesweeper Division 16 (Kwajalein)	SHOWA MARU NO. 7, SHOWA MARU NO. 8, TAMA MARU NO. 3, TAMA MARU NO. 5.
Sub-Chaser Division 62	Net-tender KATSURA MARU, CHs TAKUNAN MARU NO. 6, TAKUNAN MARU NO. 7.
Sub-Chaser Division 63 (Jaluit)	Net-tender KOTOBUKI MARU NO. 3, CHs SHONAN MARU NO. 3, FUMI MARU NO. 3.
Sub-Chaser Division 64 (Wotje)	Net-tender KASHIMA MARU, CHs SHONAN MARU NO. 10, SHONAN MARU NO. 11.
Sub-Chaser Division 65 (Wotje)	Net-tender UJI MARU, CHs KYO MARU NO. 6, KYO MARU NO. 7.
Gunboats	HAKKAISAN MARU, KATORI MARU, TOYOTSU MARU SANTO MARU.

Guard units for the defense of the islands were also established throughout the Marshalls. These units were allocated as follows:

ORGANIZATION	LOCATION
61st Guard Unit	Kwajalein, Roi Islands
62nd Guard Unit	Emidj (Jaluit)
63rd Guard Unit	Taroa (Maloelap)
64th Guard Unit	Wotje
66th Guard Unit	Mille

Sub-Chaser Division 62 was disbanded on 15 February 1943. The TAKUNAN MARU NO. 7 and KATSURA MARU were then assigned to the 63rd Guard Unit.

The sub base unit established at Kwajalein was the 6th Submarine Fleet. This organization was under the command of Vice Admiral Shimuzu. It was composed of the following units:

Light Cruiser	KATORI (Flagship)
Submarine Squadron 1	Sub-tender HEIAN MARU, I 15–26
Submarine Squadron 2	Sub-tender SANTOS MARU, I 1–7 and one other.
Submarine Squadron 3	Sub-tender YASUKUNI MARU, I 8, I 69–75

Just prior to the invasion of the Gilbert Islands by U.S. forces, the American fast carrier raids coupled with mounting Japanese losses forced the Japanese to adopt a new operational policy. This new joint Army-Navy strategy was termed "A-Go" and called for action to delay the American's drive through the Central and Southeast Pacific areas as long as possible while developing a counteroffensive to destroy the enemy fleet in a decisive battle. Kwajalein, like other bases, would have its defenses reinforced and strengthened and an extensive fortification plan began. Japanese strategy had been switched from offensive to defensive in nature.

Initial Carrier Strikes (February 1, 1942)

The disastrous attack on Pearl Harbor in December 1941 forced the U.S. Pacific Fleet to undertake a defensive strategy. With the knowledge that the Gilbert Islands had fallen, Wake Island was under attack, and Japanese submarines were operating between Hawaii and the mainland, the war plan became one of retaining what bases the U.S. had until forces could be built up. The surviving Pacific Fleet forces of carriers, cruisers, and destroyers would be used to protect Wake, Johnston, Palmyra, and the Hawaiian Islands, prevent Japanese expansion into Fiji and the Samoas, and to keep intact sea communications between the west coast of the United States and south to the Panama Canal to New Zealand and Australia. It was feared that the mighty Japanese forces which had attacked Oahu would return to bomb Pearl Harbor Navy Yard installations that had been neglected previously, raid Midway and the Aleutians, and mount an amphibious offensive against Samoa. Intelligence had shown that the Japanese offensive forces attacking Wake Island had originated from the Marshalls or Caroline Islands (Truk) to take Samoa. To prevent this, fast carrier task forces would have to be used for the tactical offensive mission of raiding advanced bases where Japanese attacks could originate. With Japanese air raids on Rabaul by planes flying from Truk on January 6, and shelling of the U.S. naval station in Samoa on January 11, 1942, coupled with reports that the enemy was massing ships at Truk for an offensive against Fiji, it was time to act to prevent the Japanese from expanding further. Admiral Chester W. Nimitz, the new Pacific Fleet Commander, felt there were two important goals to accomplish. The first was to protect Midway which was strategically located as a guard to Hawaii's approaches from the west; secondly, to maintain a line of contact with Australia from Hawaii through Samoa and Fiji. The only weapons Nimitz had available were the carriers YORKTOWN and ENTERPRISE (the SARATOGA had taken a torpedo hit from a submarine and would be lost for five months). The course of action chosen was to first reinforce Samoa then follow with an air raid against Wake and the Gilbert and Marshall Island bases.

Initial plans excluded Kwajalein from attack, but after U.S.S. DOLPHIN made a reconnaissance of the Marshalls and reported that Kwajalein Atoll held the most enemy shipping and the greatest concentration of air power, the decision was made to attack there also. Responsibilities were divided amongst two task forces. Task Force 8 was split into three groups. The first, consisting of the carrier ENTERPRISE under Admiral "Bull" Halsey accompanied by three destroyers, would direct air raids on Roi and Kwajalein Islands in the Kwajalein Atoll, Wotje, and Taroa Island in the Maloelap Atoll. The second group, commanded by Rear Admiral Spruance in heavy cruiser NORTHAMPTON, accompanied by SALT LAKE CITY and a destroyer would bombard Wotje; and Captain Shock in the cruiser CHESTER along with two destroyers would bombard Maloelap. The second task force (TF 17), consisting of the carrier YORKTOWN under the command of Rear Admiral Fletcher, accompanied by the light cruisers ST. LOUIS and LOUISVILLE and four destroyers, would launch strikes against Jaluit and Mille in the southern Marshalls and Makin, newly occupied by the Japanese, in the Gilberts. A fleet oiler would accompany each force for fueling at sea. These initial raids deep into the Japanese-held islands could potentially be a very hazardous undertaking as little was known of the geography of the islands and the true strength of enemy forces.

Admiral Halsey directed his ENTERPRISE to a position between Wotje and Ailuk Atolls about 155 miles from Kwajalein on February 1, 1942, and commenced launching pre-dawn fighter planes strikes on Wotje and Maloelap and combination dive- and torpedo-bomber strikes on the Kwajalein Atoll. Air Group 6's first strike group from ENTERPRISE consisted of nine torpedo bombers (TBD Devastators) that would make high altitude bombing attacks against the seaplane base at Ebeye and shipping targets in the naval anchorage at the southern end of the lagoon off Kwajalein Island, and 36 SBD dive bombers led by Air Group 6's Commander Howard L. Young who was personally going to lead the SBDs against the Roi airfield and installations at the northern end of the atoll. Six F4Fs were launched to provide CAP over the ENTERPRISE. In addition, 12 more F4Fs were launched to carry out strafing and light bombing attacks against the airfields at Wotje and Taroa. Because the only maps of the attack area available were of primitive charts from the Wilkes Exploring Expedition of 1840, the Roi attack group was delayed in finding its target allowing the Japanese to prepare its AA defenses and get planes into the air to intercept the attacking aircraft. The 17 SBDs of Scouting 6 were the first to attack at 0700 h after climbing to 15,000 feet and then glide bombing at a shallow angle to make their drops on the airfield. The unprotected SBDs with no fighter escorts were able to cause considerable damage at Roi hitting several planes on the ground despite being fired upon by Claude fighters either already airborne or taking off while the SBDs were completing their dives. Three dive bombers of Scouting 6 were lost to the Japanese fighters or AA batteries including the plane of the squadron's skipper, Lt. Commander H.L. Hopping. As a result of the failure of the dive bombers to neutralize the Roi airfield or destroy all the operational planes at the cost of three planes lost, the attack was not considered successful.

The torpedo bombers (VTBs) had in the meantime been busy in glide bombing attacks against the shipping at the Kwajalein anchorage. Four ships in a row at the outer periphery of a large group of ships were hit including the AO TOA MARU which was the furthermost in the row to the east. A second row of ships almost parallel to the first to the south included (from west to east) a large AK, the minelayer (ex-cruiser) TOKIWA, the sub-tender YASUKUNI MARU and another large AK. The TOKIWA (described as an "old classic 4-stack BB") received at least one direct hit, the YASUKUNI MARU a near miss which damaged the vessel, and the last AK closest to Ebeye (possibly SHINHEI MARU) was reported to have received six direct hits. The VTBs left the main group of ships and continued to the east where several ships were attacked close to the east reef islands. A gunboat and an AK in the lagoon at Bigej Island both headed into the shallows on the west side of the island. A 5-plane section scored only two near misses on the AK. A large AK just to the northwest of Shell Island was attacked by 7 VTBs; three near misses resulted. Bombs dropped on another large AK west of North Loi fell short. Two four-engine seaplanes at Ebeye were damaged. Buildings forming a compound near the center of Kwajalein Island received direct hits from another 3-plane section.

While orbiting above the foray at Roi, Commander Young heard reports from the TBDs attacking Kwajalein of targets in the lagoon. Ship targets were the primary objective of the Bombing 6 SBDs, so he ordered the planes to break off the attack on Roi and divert to the Kwajalein anchorage to utilize their 500-lb bomb loads. Three SBDs from Scouting 6 followed. Several large ships were seen at anchor in the lagoon including three tankers or aft-engine cargo ships, a large transport, a light cruiser, the old cruiser-minelayer TOKIWA, a cluster of seven submarines, and numerous small harbor craft, picket boats, or sub-chasers. The leading SBDs picked out the training cruiser KATORI and three pilots claimed hits. The cruiser was returning fire from both heavy and light AA guns. The other SBDs picked different targets including the "large transport" (the 507-foot long, 11,930-ton sub-tender YASUKUNI MARU) and pilots reported hits on the tankers, several cargo ships, and two submarines. It appeared to the pilots that the instantaneous fused bombs exploding on contact were not doing the job; delayed fuses would have been more effective instead, allowing them to explode deep inside the ships. Following release of their bomb

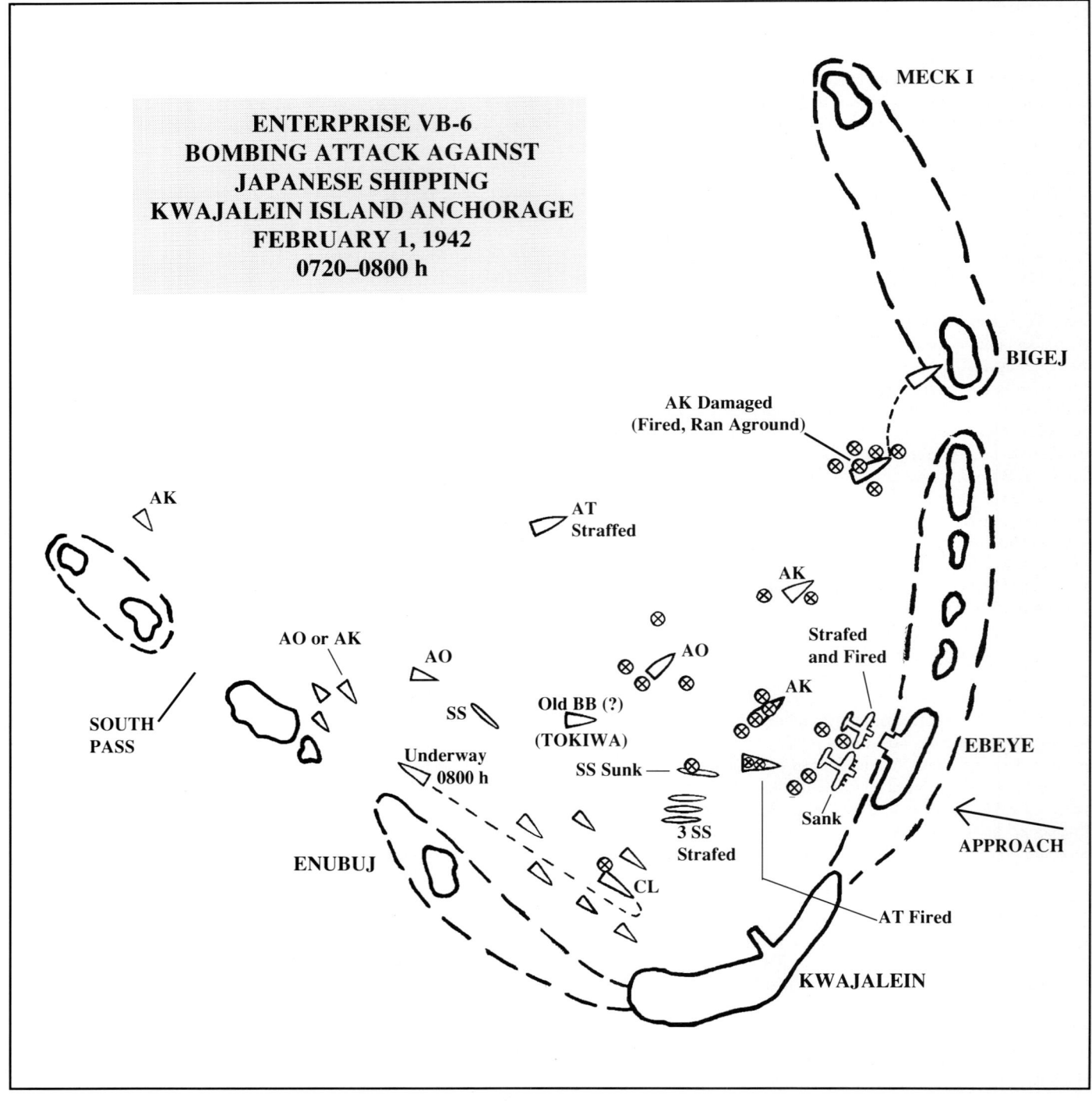

loads, the planes swept low across the harbor area where one pilot strafed a launch furiously racing from shore towards one of the anchored ships. When the hands aboard the launch spotted the aircraft approaching, they all prudently dove over the side, leaving the launch turning in circles. A cluster of three submarines in a row were strafed along with several other ships, radio installations, and other shore facilities. At nearby Ebeye Island, two Mavis flying-boats spotted moored near the shore were strafed and sunk. In addition, four buildings on Gugegwe Island and two small storehouses on Kwajalein Island were destroyed.

Upon arrival off the Bigej Channel at 0905 h with their 2,000-lb torpedoes, the Torpedo 6 planes immediately encountered 5- or 3-inch AA from ships and ground installations. The pilots reported about 10 larger ships anchored in parallel lines lying approximately east to west with AOs in the northernmost line, AK and ATs in the next line.

Several of the ships were burning and smoking heavily. Some "light vessels of tender-type" were anchored close into the island and there were about a dozen patrol-type vessels maneuvering around the lagoon to the north of the AO line. A cruiser (the KATORI), with bomb damage clearly visible, had gotten underway and was trying to flee towards South Pass to the open sea. According to the plan of attack, the first plane would take the first large vessel to the east while the following planes were to assume large ship target objectives working toward the west in rotation. The last 3-plane section would concentrate on the KATORI. In their approach, it was necessary for the planes to pass over numerous small vessels of PG-types and skirt beached vessels along the east reef of the lagoon. Intense machine gun fire was coming from all of these vessels; the larger ships were using pompons and 3- or 5-inch AA guns. The planes closed in to within 4–500 yards range before releasing their torpedoes and then zoomed over their targets and

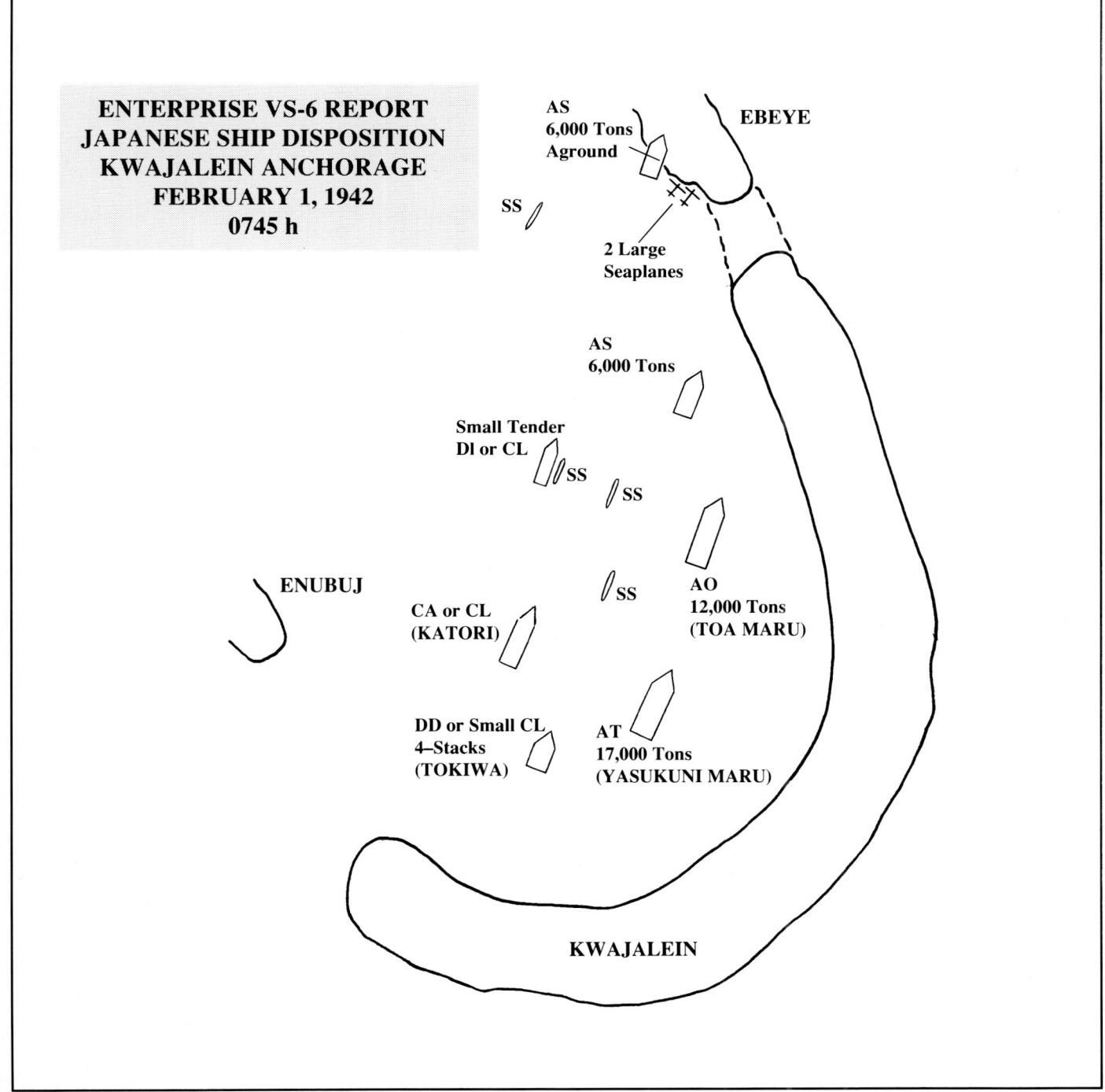

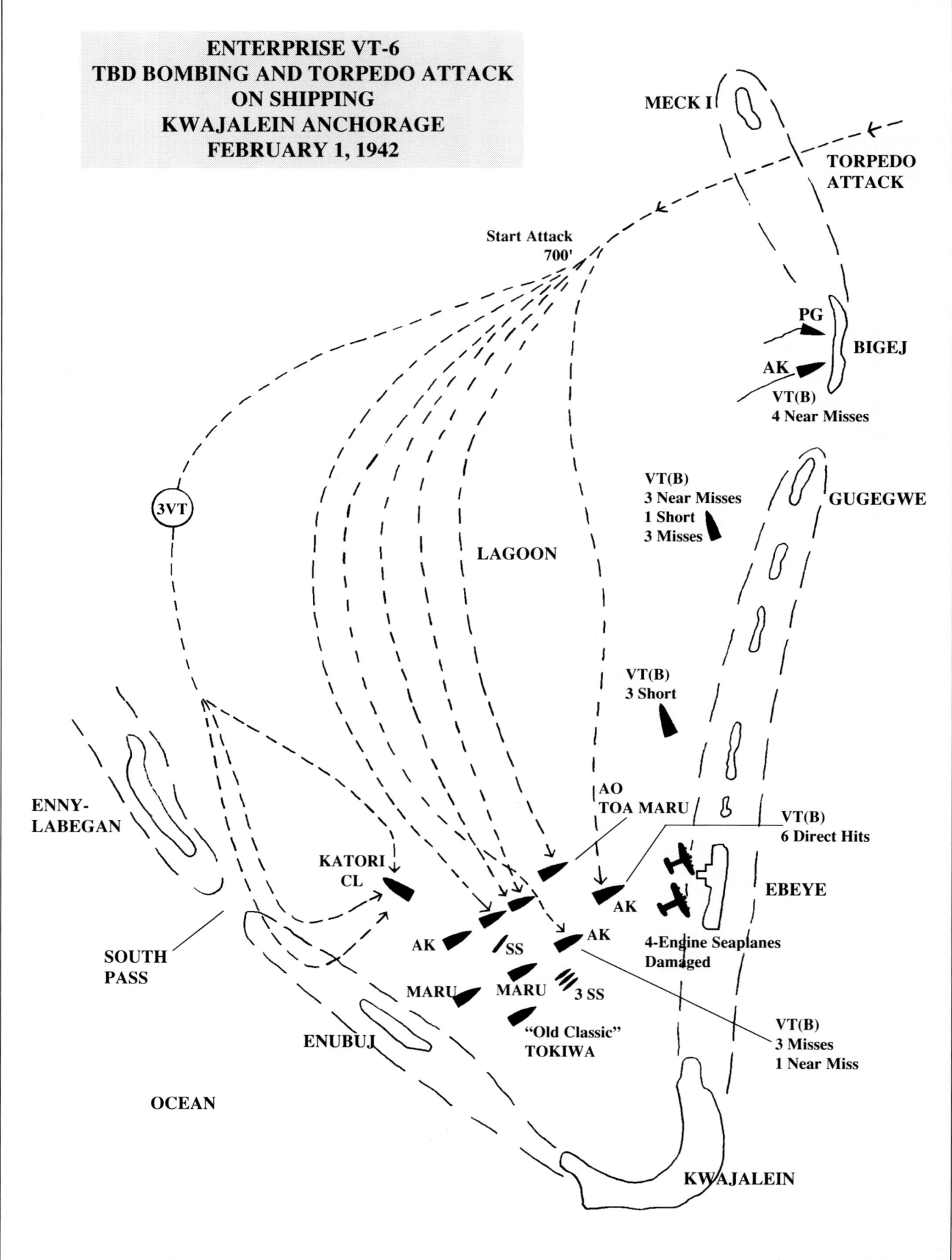

banked sharply away to the east. Planes with targets in the second line had to drop their torpedoes after maneuvering over or through the first line before retiring. Anti-aircraft fire was intense and sustained but haphazardly controlled as it appeared that the second line of ships were firing into the first line and shore AA was firing into all ships. A hit was made on the tanker TOA MARU in the first line and the sub-tender YASUKUNI MARU in the second line. The pilots noted that as a result of the previous dive and glide bombing attacks that these two ships and one other were already damaged and listing with large pools of oil spreading about them on the surface of the water. The three planes attacking the KATORI attempted to "box in" the CL, dropping their torpedoes off each beam of the the ship. One torpedo was seen to "premature," exploding short of the CL. Another appeared to hit her and explode. The KATORI stopped dead in the water and started settling down by the bow. As the planes retired, the YASUKUNI MARU was seen down by the stern but was underway and appeared to be heading towards shore possibly intent on beaching herself to prevent sinking in deep water. The TOA MARU and two other AOs had large quantities of oil on the water on the north side of them. One other auxiliary was already beached.

It appears that despite optimistic claims no submarine or surface craft, with the possible exception of some small harbor craft, were sunk by the ENTERPRISE planes at Kwajalein. Post-war Japanese records list on the following ships as damaged:

SHIP'S NAME	TYPE	TONNAGE	DAMAGE EXTENT
YASUKUNI MARU	XAS	11,933	HEAVY
SHINHEI MARU	AK	6,700	HEAVY
TOA MARU	AO	10,050	HEAVY
HOYO MARU	AK	2,930	HEAVY
KANTO MARU *	XAPV	8,606	LIGHT
TOKIWA	CM	9,700	MEDIUM
KATORI	CL(T)	5,890	UNKNOWN
I 23	SS	2,198	UNKNOWN

* Possibly damaged at Wotje.

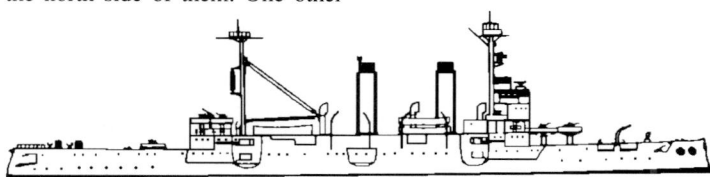

TOKIWA configured as a minelayer. Originally built as an armored cruiser (9,700 tons, 408 feet long) in 1896, the ship was a member of the battle fleet and served in the Russo-Japanese War. She was rebuilt as a minelayer in 1922 and carried up to 500 Type 5 mines.

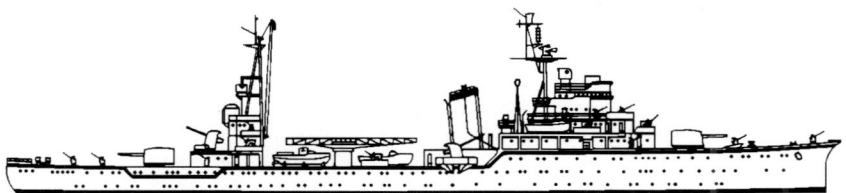

KATORI – Classified as a training cruiser, she served as the flagship for the Sixth Submarine Fleet at Kwajalein and later at Truk.

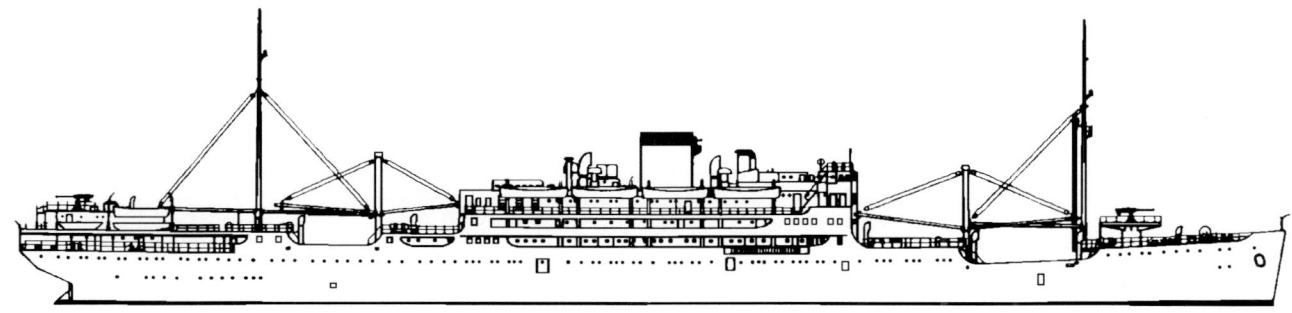

YASUKUNI MARU – Built in 1930 as a passenger liner for the Japanese shipping company Nippon Yusen K.K., the ship was requisitioned by the Japanese Navy in 1940, converted to a submarine tender, and assigned to the Sixth Submarine Fleet.

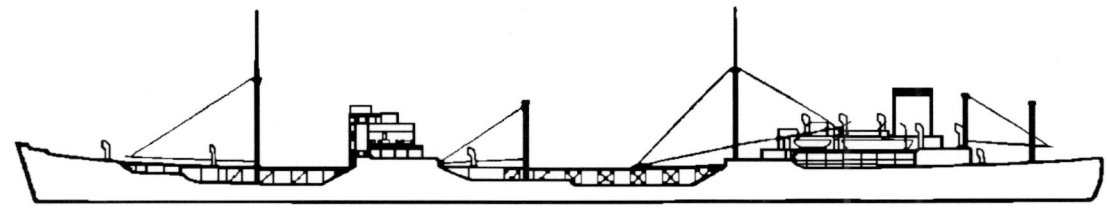

TOA MARU – This fleet tanker survived the February 1942 attacks at Kwajalein and was later sunk north of Ponape on November 25, 1943 by U.S. Submarine SEARAVEN.

Further Preliminaries And The Assault of Kwajalein (November 1943 – February 1944)

Following the successful operations in the Coral Sea, at Midway, in the Aleutians and Guadalcanal and with an Allied offensive in full swing against the islands and airfields of Bougainville and the Bismarks including Rabaul during the last few months of 1943, plans were being laid for an American thrust into the Gilberts and Marshalls. It had become clear that as the United states expanded its sea power, the network of naval air bases in Micronesia would pose a dangerous threat to any westward advance from Pearl Harbor. Nimitz's CincPac strategic planners also reasoned these bases could be as valuable to Allied forces advancing towards Japan as they had been to the Japanese in their offensive thrusts. The best way to acquire needed airfields quickly was to take them from the Japanese. As a result, a joint offensive through the Gilberts, Marshalls, and Carolines was planned at the same time as a push through the Bismark Archipelago. This would protect Allied forces in the southwest Pacific from a flank attack, make the enemy divide his forces, and deceive the Japanese as to the planned route to his homeland.

The carrier strikes against Rabaul in November 1943 had cost the Japanese dearly. In addition to the fleet units and other shipping sunk or damaged, the Japanese Navy and Army had lost tremendous numbers of aircraft in its defense. Many of these planes were reinforcements sent from Marshall and Gilbert Island bases to support Rabaul. The carriers of the Japanese Combined Fleet were low on planes which prevented Admiral Koga from committing his carriers to the defense of the islands and without carriers, Koga dared not send his cruisers and battleships. Operation GALVANIC was put into effect for the occupation of Makin, Tarawa, and Abemama in the Gilbert Islands. Photographic coverage needed for planning an assault on Kwajalein could be obtained after these islands were taken and their air bases used for long-range reconnaissance flights. The Gilberts operation was completed by the end of November 1943. The Japanese were caught flat-footed by the first amphibious assault on the Gilberts. They had shifted their Combined Fleet units southward when U.S. forces landed at Empress Augusta Bay in Bougainville and they were unable to join Fourth Fleet units at Kwajalein in repelling the landing forces in the Gilberts. Light cruisers ISUZU and NAKA were sent from Truk to pick up troops in Ponape to reinforce Tarawa, but Tarawa had fallen by the time they reached Kwajalein. The cruiser NAGARA arrived at Kwajalein on December 1st with more troops. Other fleet units consisting of heavy cruisers CHOKAI, SUZUYA, and KUMANO, light cruiser NOSHIRO, and several destroyers also arrived too late to support the Japanese garrisons in the Gilberts and departed Kwajalein on December 3rd.

The next offensive after the completion of the Gilberts operation was a fast carrier strike against Kwajalein and Wotje scheduled for December 4th. This strike was designed to lessen Japanese resistance to the upcoming invasion of the Kwajalein Atoll by destroying enemy merchant shipping and warships found in the lagoon, eliminating enemy air opposition and providing photographic coverage of beaches and installations. The force designated for this operation was divided into two sub groups, Task Group 50.1 under Rear Admiral Pownall and Task Group 50.3 under Rear Admiral Montgomery. The composition of these groups were as follows:

TG 50.1 (Rear Admiral Pownall)
Carriers:	LEXINGTON, YORKTOWN
Light Carrier:	COWPENS
Heavy Cruisers:	BALTIMORE, MINNEAPOLIS, NEW ORLEANS, SAN FRANCISCO
Light Cruiser:	OAKLAND
Destroyers:	BULLARD, CHAUNCEY, KIDD, LAVALLETTE, NICHOLAS, TAYLOR

TG 50.3 (Rear Admiral Montgomery)
Carriers:	ENTERPRISE, ESSEX
Light Carrier:	BELLEAU WOOD
Heavy Cruiser:	PORTLAND
Light Cruisers:	MOBILE, SAN DIEGO, SAN JUAN, SANTA FE
Destroyers:	ERBEN, FLETCHER, HALE, JENKINS, RADFORD

The operational air plan was devised by Admiral Pownall and was oriented towards a cautious and defensive posture. LEXINGTON and ESSEX planes were assigned shipping and aircraft in the Roi Island area. The air groups of YORKTOWN and ENTERPRISE were assigned to Tabik anchorage about 30 miles from Roi near the northwest end of the atoll and the Kwajalein area, respectively. The attack planes were all subject to the Air Group Commander of LEXINGTON's Air Group 16. The COWPENS and BELLEAU WOOD air groups would be kept in reserve strictly for defensive purposes, and nearly one-third of the large carrier's fighters launched would be withheld to serve as CAP over the Task Group. Air Group 16's skipper, Commander Ernest M. Snowden, had urged a fighter sweep over the atoll prior to the bombing strikes but was turned down by Pownall who reasoned that the Task Force would not surprise the Japanese and would most likely be attacked.

The task force, with the two carrier groups of TF 50 separated by about 12 miles, reached its launching position east-southeast of Rongerik Atoll about 118 miles north of the Roi airfield on December 4th. Launching of planes was begun at 0626 h and 45 minutes later 249 planes from the four air groups had rendezvoused separately and were proceeding towards the atoll. Numbers of strike planes launched from the carriers were as follows: LEXINGTON, 72; YORKTOWN, 59; ENTERPRISE, 53; ESSEX, 65. BELLEAU WOOD and COWPENS launched their first CAP of the day. The Japanese radars picked up the attack groups 50 miles out and Japanese pilots were alerted and began racing for their planes. The attack groups, flying at 14,000 feet, arrived over Roi about 0755 h where "one NATORI class CL, and one large 8–10,000-ton AK" were seen at anchor with another 10 small "inter-island steamers and lighters" scattered about the anchorage. Shortly afterward another NATORI class CL was observed underway inside the lagoon 6–10 miles further south on a course towards Roi. These vessels were the ISUZU and the 6,816-ton KEMBU MARU anchored at Roi; the CL proceeding towards Roi was the NAGARA. The plane crews identified the CLs correctly as NATORI class units.

The planes from Air Group 6 (ENTERPRISE) were directed to break off and proceed to Kwajalein Island and report on conditions there and Air Group 5 (YORKTOWN) was directed to proceed westward and to reconnoiter the area in the vicinity of Tabik Island. Twelve VF-5 planes were left to provide high cover for the Air Group 16 (LEXINGTON) planes which were to attack Roi. At this time, 2VB and 2VT of Air Group 9 (ESSEX) accompanied by 2VF were detached to perform photographic missions. No enemy aircraft had been encountered in the air from 25,000 to 15,000 feet; however, as the 12 VF-16 planes which were initiating the strafing attacks on the airfield approached the field, they found Japanese fighters and bombers taking off and the field literally packed with medium bombers. Many planes were seen with their props turning over and others were taxiing and taking off in a cloud of coral dust. Only one strafing run was accomplished by the 12VF as approximately 30 enemy fighters which had just taken off from the Roi airfield were encountered at altitudes from 1,000 to 6,000 feet. The 12 F6Fs destroyed three Bettys on the ground but then had their hands full in combatting the Japanese fighters. In the ensuing engagement, 17 Zekes, 1 Hap, 1 Oscar, and 1 Betty were shot down in the air. The higher altitude fighter support did not join in the foray as radio communication was not possible (failed VHF radio sets) and the VF-16 planes were forced to flee from the vicinity. If the three fighter groups over Roi could have coordinated their efforts in gaining control of the air, destruction of the estimated 40 to 60 Bettys left undamaged on the ground probably would have been effected.

The LEXINGTON's 24 SBDs and 18 TBFs with their 12 F6F cover initiated a coordinated attack on the three ships in the northern part of the lagoon. The attack surprised the CL ISUZU at anchor and the TBFs made their initial torpedo drops which scored two hits. The first torpedo hit the stern on the starboard side just abaft of the mainmast. Pilots reported this hit caused two definite explosions, one at the position of the hit and the second extending from the extreme stern and around to the port side. Approximately two minutes later, a second torpedo hit was scored abaft of amidships along the starboard side. Despite the damage incurred, the ISUZU's crew managed to get the CL underway within a few minutes and began making 3–5 knots in a series of circles to starboard. Apparently the ship had no steerage control following the stern torpedo hit. The CL was observed to be leaving a broad trail of oil which covered the entire area where it had been circling. Five more torpedoes were dropped on the crippled CL; two passed ahead of the ship with one missing only by 5–10 feet, one ran erratically to the right, and two failed to run. Thirteen SBDs split up to make both dive- and glide-bombing attacks on the CL with 1,000-lb GP bombs. All bombs dropped from dives missed the ship. The glide bombing attack was successful as the planes scored four hits and three near misses. Three of the hits were clustered near the aft gun

–National Archives Photo

Light cruiser ISUZU is under bombing attack. Ennuebing Island is in the background. Smoke column from the right side of the photo is from the KEMBU MARU.

mount and the fourth was closer to the stern. The hits were crippling to the CL but not fatal as the instantaneous and .1 second fused GP bombs caused serious exterior damage but did not penetrate to the bowels of the ship. During the bombing runs against the ISUZU, the ship was firing at its attackers with medium and light AA. One plane from the second division of dive bombers was hit by AA fire as it pulled out of its dive at low altitude; the plane was observed to roll over onto its back and crash into the lagoon.

The NAGARA was attacked by VB-16 planes while making a run to the north. The CL received three bomb hits, one just aft of the bridge superstructure, one alongside the aft stack, and the last near the catapult aft. The ship, now afire and smoking heavily, reduced its speed from 12 knots to dead in the water. Pilots observed that a part of the port side had been blown off and the area near the aft stack had been partially demolished. The CL was reported to be heavily damaged. Five VTs from LEXINGTON also chose the NAGARA as their target. The CL was found 10–12 miles south of Roi and appeared to he heading towards two ship passages (either North or Mellu Passes). The ship had been slowed to 10 knots after being hit by VB-16 planes. The VTs made their torpedo drops between 275 and 350 feet altitude, scoring one hit amidships on the port side. The CL turned her bow into the last three torpedoes dropped and was able to "comb" them. The remaining large ship, the KEMBU MARU, was anchored about 1/2 mile north of the ISUZU. Eight SBDs attacked the ship scoring hits just aft of the bow gun, along the port side opposite the No. 2 hold, on the starboard side of the bridge, and one directly in the center of the hold aft of the stack. The ship was enveloped in flames following the attack with black smoke billowing several thousand feet into the air. Four VTs dropped torpedoes from 300–350 feet altitude on the ship scoring two hits on the starboard side, one forward and one abaft of amidships. The SBDs strafed a vessel estimated at 75 feet long near the mouth of Mellu Pass (TAKUNAN MARU NO. 7-author). It was seen smoking upon retirement. As the VT planes were retiring, three came under attack by enemy planes. Two were fired at by Zekes and the other by a Val. In every instance, the Japanese planes pulled away and broke off their attacks without closing to an effective kill range.

The Tabik anchorage was reported empty by the commander of Air Group 5 and at 0810 h, was directed with his group to Kwajalein Island. ESSEX's strike planes (22VF, 24VB and 19VT), which had been circling above Roi at 13,000 feet, were then ordered to split forces to attack the airfield and shipping targets. Since all the TBFs carried torpedoes, they were ordered to attack the enemy CLs while the dive bombers were ordered to allocate half their number against the airfield and half against the ships. Each group was escorted by F6Fs which strafed ahead of the dive bombers or torpedo planes. ISUZU was attacked by 6VT with one hit being observed, but the resulting explosion was small. The ISUZU's steering was damaged. She was cruising in high speed circles near Ennuebing Island near North Pass with her rudder jammed when the next attack by 13VB began but they were able to score only one direct hit and many near misses. The NAGARA was attacked by 12VTs which observed one hit. Again, the torpedoes exhibited erratic performances. Two torpedoes obviously stuck in the bottom in their initial dives as discolored water and bubbles were observed there. One torpedo ran in an almost opposite course after hitting the water. Several torpedo wakes were seen to run to the side of the cruiser with no resulting explosions. The KEMBU MARU, which by now was on fire, was attacked by one SBD which missed the ship. The airfield and installations were attacked by 7VB and 4VF. Three fires were started in the hangar area east of the runways. Several Bettys were strafed but none were observed to burn.

The VT photographic plane obtained good verticals of Roi Island and the atoll from 12,000 feet 10 miles on either side of the island. One VB got the same coverage from 1,200 feet but the other was attacked by 4 Zekes and in attempting to lose them was able to snap only a few pictures. Photos taken showed some 40 airplanes on the Roi airfield which were left virtually undamaged. The plane's camouflage was effective as they blended very well with the field and were thought to be undetected by most attacking planes except at very low altitudes.

–Naval Operational Archives Photo
After suffering damage from multiple bomb hits and a torpedo, the light cruiser NAGARA is still underway while on fire and smoking heavily aft and amidships.

When last seen, the KEMBU MARU had blown up in a tremendous explosion which sent columns of smoke 10,000 feet into the air. The aircraft action reports indicated that the pilots believed that the ship had contained munitions or aviation fuel as the resulting fire and explosion indicated such a cargo. The southernmost cruiser, the NAGARA, was afire amidships on the port side and was making about four knots. The ISUZU was smoking, burning, and practically dead in the water. Both cruisers were able to make emergency repairs and escape. The TAKUNAN MARU NO. 7, on fire and smoking, entered the lagoon through Mellu Pass where she later sank.

While the attacks on the northern end of the atoll were still continuing, aircraft from YORKTOWN and ENTERPRISE had proceeded southward to the Kwajalein Island anchorage where a large number of ships had been reported. The pilots estimated that there were from 9 to 12 large cargo ships between 5,000 and 12,000 tons plus another 10 to 15 smaller ships anchored in the lagoon close to Kwajalein Island. One large DD was reported and a submarine seen tied up to a tender in the lagoon off the northeastern tip of Kwajalein Island. A CL was later seen in this same area underway and attempting to leave the anchorage. No enemy air opposition was encountered over the target, but intense, heavy and accurate AA was reported as the VB and VT planes began their attacks about 0835 h.

The 24 YORKTOWN SBDs sighted the shipping and approaches were made down to 12,000 feet before commencing their dives. The planes dove from west to east with pullouts from 2,500 to 1,500 feet. The ships under attack were reported to be dead at anchor and took no evasive action. Only one or two had steam up and it was evident that the Japanese were completely surprised. The ships were strafed during the dives and the rear seat gunners strafed during pullouts. The ASAKAZE MARU was hit by two 1,000-lb bombs aft of the midship superstructure and on the starboard quarter. Fire and smoke resulted and the ship began settling by the stern. The second target, estimated at 4,000 tons was hit by a 1,000-lb SAP bomb along the starboard side aft of amidships. The bomb was observed to go completely through the AK before exploding. The ship raised up considerably at the time of the explosion. This was probably the TATEYAMA MARU. The final hit obtained by the VB planes was on another AK estimated at 4,000 tons. The ship was hit directly amidships; debris flew through the air and fire with heavy smoke resulted. The final results for VB-5 included 4 hits, 15 near misses, two release failures, one bomb not observed, and one plane did not dive.

YORKTOWN's torpedo bombers (17 planes) had circled to the south waiting for the VB planes to commence their attack. An AK spotted near Ebeye Island at this time was seen to be smoking slightly with no apparent damage visible. The planes approached the ships from between 10–14,000 feet before making a high-speed let-down to between 6–8,000 feet. Then a 60 degree dive was begun on approach on the beam of the selected targets with a point of aim approximately 1,000 yards short of the ship. The TBFs would start their initial pull-out at approximately 1,500 feet such that the planes would end up in a 20 degree dive at 300–310 knots at 200 feet altitude. The 2,000-lb bombs with 4–5 second delay times were dropped as the water line of the target ship passed under the nose of the plane. After the actual release was made at about 150 feet altitude, the planes would immediately zoom up and away to clear the masts of the ship. A direct hit and a near miss off the starboard bow were made on a "6,500-ton AK of the KOGYO MARU class." This was the 6,517-ton ASAKAZE MARU. The TATEYAMA MARU, anchored close to the ASAKAZE MARU, was the target of two VT planes which scored near misses off the starboard bow and quarter. The CHOKO MARU, anchored at the western edge of the group of ships was rocked by a near miss. A ship described as a "YOMEI MARU class AK" (2,861 tons, M–F–M configuration) near the center of the anchorage received a near miss (this appreass to be the 3,083-ton SHOEI MARU-author). Further hits were scored on two "HOKO MARU class AKs" (1,514-ton, aft-engine configurations) in the east central part of the anchorage. A large AK, described as an "ARATAMA MARU class AK" (6,780 tons) was hit; this ship, located at the northwest end of the ship group, was the 6,776-ton YAMASHIMO MARU which later was reported by the Japanese as having suffered minor damage. The 6,938-ton FUJIKAWA MARU was also reported to have received a direct hit. The final hits reported were on a "CHILE MARU class AK" (5,860 tons, M–F–M configuration) and a "MANKO MARU class AK" (4,472 tons, M–K–F–M configuration). This second ship was likely the 4,319-ton MIKAGE MARU NO. 18 which was heavily damaged.

The YORKTOWN VF planes (19 F6Fs) escorting the VB and VT planes on their runs strafed ships in the Kwajalein anchorage and then looked for other targets. One 4-plane division strafed the radio station on Enubuj Island and then proceeded further up the west coast where three small picket or patrol boats were sighted. The F6Fs made 15 strafing runs on these boats located west of Lagan and Eller Islands leaving one of the vessels smoking. One Japanese float plane ("probably a Pete") was shot down in flames by the VF-5 flight leader. Another 4-plane section, which had been escorting the VT planes, observed numerous seaplanes on the ramp at Ebeye Island and in the adjacent lagoon. Joined by 4 more F6Fs which had been escorting the VB planes during their dives, they set afire six float planes on the ramp and parking apron and another three moored in the lagoon nearby. The majority of these planes appeared to be Jakes; only three planes were not burning following the strafing attacks. One VF-5 plane was apparently hit by AA fire. The pilot was seen to parachute from his plane and land in the water about one mile east of Ebeye Island. Another VF-5 division was jumped by 18 or more Zekes while returning

–Naval Operational Archives Photo

Attacking planes encounter large group of ships at the Kwajalein Island Anchorage. Ship at the right is the CHOKO MARU. At left center is the "K-2" cluster of ships (barge in left foreground, TATEYAMA MARU in center, and ASAKAZE MARU to the rear). The ship behind the ASAKAZE MARU in between the aft-engine HOKO or GOSEI MARU class vessels is probably the SHOEI MARU.

–Naval Operational Archives Photo

The 6,796-ton YAMASHIMO MARU receives a near miss off the starboard quarter and a second bomb bursts well off the stern. The next large ship to the right and behind is the FUJIKAWA MARU which is also under attack.

—Naval Operational Archives Photo

The 4,319-ton MIKAGE MARU NO. 18, appearing undamaged, lies at anchor in foreground. The CHOKO MARU (right) has been hit and is on fire and smoking. A large column of smoke is rising from the ASAKAZE MARU (center); the TATEYAMA MARU lying along its port side is smoking also.

to its rendezvous point. Enemy tactics were characterized as expert and one F6F was shot down and seen to crash in the sea.

Twelve ENTERPRISE TBFs, each loaded with four 500-lb bombs scored 6–7 hits on four ships. No locations of the target shipping was given in the aircraft action reports. The first target was an AK estimated at 6–8,000 tons. Four bombs dropped in a train scored a direct hit on the bow and a 30-foot miss off the starboard bow. A second AK, also estimated at 6–8,000 tons, was hit on the starboard side just forward of amidships. The last pair of ships attacked appear to have been the ASAKAZE and TATEYAMA MARUs. The reports describe a 6–8,000 ton AK with a 4,000-ton AK along the port side of the larger ship. Bomb hits on each set the ships on fire with heavy clouds of brown smoke being emitted. In attacks against shipping, two ENTERPRISE SBDs attacked an AK (estimated at 10,000 tons or more) at anchor on the west side of the Kwajalein anchorage. Dropping from an altitude of 1,700 feet, one 1,000-lb bomb hit just aft of amidships and the other was a near miss off the starboard quarter. The ship was reported to have broken in two and sunk. A 5,000-ton AK just to the south of the previous ship attacked was hit by two bombs on the stern. The ship started smoking but no fire could be observed. The next targets were the ASAKAZE MARU and the TATEYAMA MARU which were described as a "10,000-ton AK with a 6,000-ton AK alongside on the west side of the anchorage." The TATEYAMA MARU was hit twice along the port side, once just aft of amidships and the other near the stern. Two hits along the centerline of the ship near the stern produced fierce fires aboard the ASAKAZE MARU. The ship blew up and sank. An 8,000-ton AK at anchor near the north center of the anchorage was the target of 2 SBDs which hit the ship once on the starboard side aft of amidships; the second bomb missed 30 feet off the port quarter. The ship was observed to be down by the stern when the planes retired (probably FUJIKAWA MARU-author). Along the east side of the anchorage, a 7,000-ton AK was attacked by 3 SBDs which scored one hit amidships on the starboard side and one near miss of the starboard side that buckled its plates. The third bomb was a miss off the stern. This vessel was reported to have sunk later. Two SBDs picked out a 7,000-ton AK near the center of the anchorage, scoring one hit on the starboard side just aft of amidships and a miss off the port quarter. The ship began smoking but no fire could be observed. The final ship attacked was an 8,000-ton AK on the east side of the anchorage. A single SBD missed with its bomb.

Two VT-6 photo planes were tasked to provide vertical photo coverage of the atoll from 5,000 feet. Interpretation of photos taken showed seven large AKs of over 5,000 tons with approximately 20 smaller vessels of various types in the Kwajalein Island anchorage. One AK in the center of a large oil slick was sinking with its fantail already under water. At the right edge of the oil slick, another AK was seen low in the water with a slight starboard list. These last three descriptions appear to be of the K-2 group of ships with the capsized vessel actually a barge that had been anchored close by. Further to the east of this group, an AK leaving an oil slick was slightly down by its stern. The photo interpretation report noted that large oil slicks in the anchorage area may have indicated the loss of other vessels prior to when the photos were taken.

The F6Fs launched from ENTERPRISE encountered 20 Zekes at Roi Island or in the vicinity after arriving over the target at 0830 h; nine Bettys were observed 45 minutes later parked or landing on the airfield there. The fighters accounted for three confirmed kills and several probables. At Ebeye Island, five Emilys (actually Mavis flying-boats-author) were spotted moored in the water opposite the island along with 1–2 Dave float bi-planes. Approximately 20 Jakes and Rufes were parked on the ramp and apron of the seaplane base. Eight VF planes strafed the Mavis flying-boats leaving three on fire in the water near the ramp. Six of the Jakes or Rufes were set on fire by another 7-plane division. Eight F6Fs left 2–3 Daves located in the water near the beach and on the seaplane ramp on fire from their strafing runs.

A landing strip with taxiways and a dispersal area under construction was spotted on Kwajalein Island. Heavy caliber AA, which was described as accurate as to altitude but inaccurate as to range, was observed coming from known AA installations on the Kwajalein target charts plus other areas along the shore south of the new airstrip.

In assessing the success of the air strikes, poor communications prevented the air strike coordinator from organizing more attacks on the airfield at Roi where most aircraft on the ground and the runways themselves were left intact. The results of the bombing attacks against shipping was poor considering the number of bombs dropped. The Mark 13 torpedoes carried by the TBFs had not worked well; cameras aboard the planes confirmed that many of the torpedoes turned right, porpoised, ran erratically or hit the bottom of the lagoon. Many of the torpedoes were apparently duds and some explosions that resembled hits were probably prematures. Torpedoes were not dropped on any of the ships concentrated at the southern anchorage off Kwajalein Island where they had been successfully used in February 1942. American and Japanese assessments of the attacks against shipping listed the KEMBU, TAKUNAN NO. 7, ASAKAZE, CHOKO, and the TATEYAMA MARUs as sunk and the ISUZU, NAGARA, refrigerated storeship KINEZAKI, FUJIKAWA MARU, MIKAGE MARU NO. 18, EIKO MARU NO. 2, and the YAMASHIMO MARU damaged. The heavily damaged EIKO MARU NO. 2 may have been at the southern anchorage when she was attacked and damaged as no sign of the vessel can be seen in action photos taken over the Roi anchorage on December 4th.

The operational plan called for a second strike at noon and more strikes the following day. However, shortly before noon, enemy Kates and Betty bombers launched a series of counter attacks on the U.S. carriers, hampering launch and recovery of the Wotje strike aircraft. It was believed that these planes were flown from Roi. These counter attacks continued through the night at which time LEXINGTON took a torpedo hit near the stern. After considering the risk to his task force and the limited success achieved allowing important enemy naval craft and airplanes to escape, Admiral Pownall decided to retire his forces.

The decision making for planning an assault on the Marshalls was influenced by military principles requiring the taking of an atoll with a bomber airstrip which could be used for advanced area U.S. air operations against Japanese bases. Photographs taken during the carrier strikes of December 4th showed a bomber strip nearly completed on Kwajalein Island. Maloelap, Wotje, Mille, and Jaluit had airfields and were all strongly defended like Kwajalein, but since Kwajalein was the most important atoll in the Japanese outer defensive perimeter and acted as the main distribution center for all Marshall Island activities, it was decided to mount landings there. A "leap-frogging" strategy was planned which called for the neutralization of air power on Maloelap, Wotje, Mille and Jaluit. It was also decided to take lightly defended Majuro and make use of its lagoon anchorage to establish a fleet base. The target date for Operation "FLINTLOCK," the occupation of both Kwajalein and Majuro Atolls, was set for January 31, 1944. Nearly a month of intensive bombing and strafing attacks by land-based aircraft of the Seventh Air Force flying from new Gilbert Island bases followed. The purpose of these operations would be to obtain photographic coverage of the Japanese bases, attack enemy shipping and to eliminate enemy air opposition from the five important air bases before the Kwajalein operation.

During a nighttime attack on 19 December, a single PBY sunk the SHOEI MARU in the Kwajalein Island anchorage. Reconnaissance photographs taken over Kwajalein on January 9th showed 10 medium-sized and 14 small craft at anchor. On January 12th, Navy PB4Ys were sent to bomb Roi and attack the shipping previously spotted. The IKUTA MARU was a victim of the bombing attacks.

In the month of January, nearly 200 tons of bombs were dropped on the five important air bases in the Marshalls including Roi Island. Mille and Jaluit bases were almost completely destroyed and the Japanese air power and bases in Maloelap and Wotje were effectively neutralized. The final neutralization attacks were left up to the naval task force and were planned for January 29, two days before the amphibious assault was to begin on Kwajalein. This force was given the mission of obtaining and maintaining control of the air in the Marshalls opening the way for the assault and capture of Kwajalein. The air plan for these pre-invasion strikes would start with simultaneous attacks against the Roi, Taroa (Maloelap Atoll), and Wotje airfields. Admiral Nimitz had reorganized his fast carriers under a new commander, Admiral Pete Mitscher. The old Task Force 50 was re-designated Task Force 58 with four carrier task groups as follows:

TG 58.1
Carriers: BELLEAU WOOD, ENTERPRISE, YORKTOWN

TG 58.2
Carriers: CABOT, ESSEX, INTREPID

TG 58.3
Carriers: BUNKER HILL, COWPENS, MONTEREY

TG 58.4
Carriers: LANGLEY, PRINCETON, SARATOGA

Admiral Montgomery's Task Group 58.2 planes were assigned specific missions: (1) to attain and maintain control of the air in the northern sectors of the Kwajalein Atoll; (2) to destroy defensive installations in the Roi-Namur area; (3) to provide photographic reconnaissance of beaches and defenses for Commander Northern Attack Force, in advance of the landings; and (4) to provide direct air support for the assault and landing operations of the Fourth Marines. The air operations on the 29th of January began with a dawn fighter sweep which would pave the way for scheduled successive bombing strikes throughout the day, initially on air installations and later against other defense positions. Continuous CAP over the target would be scheduled to maintain control of the air.

The Japanese radars picked up the incoming fighter sweep and some 27 enemy fighters were aloft when the planes arrived over target. Some F4Fs and F6Fs broke off to engage the enemy planes while others made repeated strafing runs on the Roi airfield, hammering the single-engine planes on the ground first and then the larger Betty bombers. CABOT's planes claimed 12 enemy planes shot down in the air with five probables. Another 22–24 single-engine planes and 15–18 Bettys were destroyed in strafing attacks. ESSEX planes destroyed 4 Zekes, 3 Hamps, 1 Oscar, and 1 Kate in the air and another 26–28 single-engine and 23–25 twin-engine bombers on the ground while losing 1 F6F and 1 TBF over the target. INTREPID launched its first strike, a composite mix of F6Fs for cover and SBDs carrying one 500-lb and two 250-lb bombs each at 0630 h, whose mission was to bomb AA positions on Roi. The F6Fs found no enemy aircraft in the air or on the ground due to heavy smoke over the target area resulting from the fighter sweeps previously. The planes were able to concentrate on bombing and strafing AA positions and it was believed that most of these positions were knocked out by this strike. The first CAP (12 F6Fs) from INTREPID shot down 6 Betty bombers and one transport (Topsy) but lost one F6F from AA fire off Roi between 0800–1030 h. The pilot was seen in the water, but was not recovered. A strike composed of 17 TBFs loaded with 2,000-lb bombs with fighter cover was launched at 0815 h to bomb the runways at Roi. All bombs hit the target while the F6F cover strafed the area and destroyed 2 Bettys, 1 Val, and 2 Zekes on the ground and sank a small ship in the lagoon by strafing. The 872-ton converted net-tender UJI MARU was sunk on this date near Roi-Namur and may be the vessel described. The 6 Bettys shot down by INTREPID's F6Fs were the last Japanese aircraft seen in the air over the target at 0830 h. American aircraft had seized command of the air and had destroyed most of the nearly 100 planes that had been based on Roi while losing 1VT and 4VF. The bombing strikes continued during the day against the airfield, AA positions, ammunition storage areas, and buildings. Several fighters continued strafing the aircraft on the ground and others strafed the AK EIKO MARU NO. 2 in the lagoon anchorage. During INTREPID's last CAP of the day from 1630 to 1830 h, the EIKO MARU NO 2 was strafed again and at 1800 h, the commander of VF-6 spotted for the Battleship North Carolina, which shelled and finally sank the ship.

Attacks on Kwajalein and Ebeye Islands on January 29th were carried out by Admiral Sherman's Task Group 58.3 planes simultaneously with the attacks at Roi at the northern end of the atoll. BUNKER HILL launched 20VF for the initial strike on the southern part of the atoll. The pilots observed "one large AK, one medium AK, and 11 small inter-island cargo vessels" that were either anchored or

—Naval Operational Archives Photo

Columns of smoke rise from aircraft parked in dispersal areas on Roi Island, 1/29/44. Several installations on Roi and Namur (left center) islands have been hit and are on fire also.

getting underway towards Bigej Channel off Kwajalein. Several small vessels were set afire and left smoking; none were confirmed sunk. At Ebeye Island, 5–7 float planes were moored on the lagoon side. Three float planes (two Jakes and a Dave) were parked on the seaplane ramp and apron; two and possibly three of these were damaged. The pilots reported that the camouflage painting of the apron was effective and this was reflected in their estimates of the planes there which varied from 2 to 8. The BUNKER HILL VB and VT planes joined those of MONTEREY in making day-long bombing strikes against aircraft, aircraft installations, AA positions and buildings while fighters escorted bombers, flew separate patrols over the target, and maintained CAP. The bombers dropped 100-lb GP bombs on the runway and seaplane ramp on Ebeye and 100-lb fragmentation bombs on the peripheral areas. Eight Rufe float planes were shot up on the water at Ebeye and assorted shipping in the lagoon were strafed. The VT planes reported three hits and four near misses on a 400-foot AK. This was most likely the AKIBASAN MARU. The pilots and crews reported one direct hit on the stern, one on the starboard side amidships, and one hit on the bow forward of the bridge. The ship was left burning and smoking extensively with its well deck awash. It was settling astern and listing to starboard. Several small craft and one escort vessel were strafed. The BUNKER HILL fighters continued strafing attacks against shipping and land targets through out the morning and into the afternoon. Eight planes expended 1,500 rounds of .50 caliber ammunition on several barges and a small AK in a convoy at the lagoon entrance to Bigej Island. Another four planes fired 2,000 rounds at an escort vessel off Ninni Island. This escort vessel was steaming down the west side of the atoll towards Gea Pass, just off Ninni Island. Fires started aboard the vessel twice and it seemed to go out of control, but it was still under way as the planes left. The large AK (AKIBASAN MARU-author) off Kwajalein was attacked again. Its AA guns were silenced in the strafing attacks and a fire was started aboard. The U.S. planes flew against continuous and intense AA fire initially and 1 F6F and 3 TBFs from BUNKER HILL were lost. A retiring MONTEREY strike plane reported an enemy submarine on the surface bearing 240 degrees true, distance 20 miles from Kwajalein. It submerged immediately and ASP planes searched without results. An Air Intelligence Report derived from photos taken on the 29th by BUNKER HILL planes listed the following shipping in the lagoon off Kwajalein Island:

- 1 patrol craft, 175 feet long, was under way heading north.
- 1 AK, approximately 375 feet long, was dead in the water (AKIBASAN MARU-author).
- 10 small craft (approximately 90 feet long).
- 20–25 small craft (approximately 40 feet long).

Rear Admiral Ginder's Task Group 58.4 concentrated on facilities on Wotje where the field was empty of planes. Rear Admiral Reeve's TG 58.1 planes delivered eight strikes against Taroa where they destroyed five single-engined planes and 32 Bettys on the airfield and then concentrated on the base installations. The fighter cover destroyed 13 enemy fighters in the air.

During the night, as TG 58.2 was proceeding on a northerly course north and east of Ujae Atoll, the destroyer BURNS engaged four Japanese auxiliary ships at 0200 h. The convoy was reported to consist of two medium sized and two small sized ships, one of which was believed to be a tanker. All ships were sunk or set ablaze from end to end. BURNS reported several life boats filled with survivors. ESSEX

–Naval Operational Archives Photo
The unfinished airstrip, taxiways, and the main pier are visible on Kwajalein Island under attack in January 1944, prior to the amphibious assault and landings on the island.

launched a special flight to observe the night action described. The plane reported two wooden hulls of about 100 feet in length burning and dead in the water with numerous oil slicks. It saw no trace of any survivors. These vessels are believed to have included the 78-ton picket boat NICHIEI MARU, the 36-ton picket boat HOKOKU MARU NO. 2, and the 562-ton cargo ship PARAN MARU.

On the 30th of January, the TG 58.3 flattops moved northwest to take Engebi Island and Eniwetok under attack. The carriers of TG 58.2 joined with a surface force; the air strikes were coordinated with battleships SOUTH DAKOTA and ALABAMA along with the cruiser INDIANAPOLIS and four DDs which had left formation to carry out the prescribed bombardment plan for Roi-Namur and nearby islands in conjunction with battleship NORTH CAROLINA and two DDs already on station. Task Group 58.1, which had been engaged in attacking Taroa the day before, launched a series of strikes on Kwajalein and Ebeye Islands. Several of these were coordinated with surface bombardment by the battleships INDIANA, WASHINGTON and MASSACHUSETTS to prepare for actual landings. The targets selected generally included aircraft on both islands, artillery positions, block houses, pillboxes, AA positions, command posts and other defense installations on the northern and western tips of Kwajalein Island. Added later were the small ships, picket boats, sampans, and barges in the lagoon. YORKTOWN planes sunk two small vessels or sampans; 10 others were strafed thoroughly and stopped. One landing barge loaded with 30–40 Japanese personnel was sunk and all aboard believed killed by the strafing. BELLEAU WOOD planes strafed several small craft in the lagoon, setting five on fire; a sixth was hit by a 500-lb GP bomb. Following strafing attacks on ammunition dumps on Bigej Island which caused two to erupt in tremendous explosions that sent flames 4,500 feet high, several vessels in the nearby lagoon were strafed including a 150-foot vessel, two smaller craft, and an AK which "momentarily caught fire in a number of places." ENTERPRISE F6Fs strafed boats in the lagoon setting five on fire also. These vessels included a 100-foot boat with two tall antennas mounted, a 75-foot schooner, a sampan, a 40-foot boat returning AA fire, and one other craft. A near miss by a 1,000-lb bomb on a barge 100 yards off the south western tip of Kwajalein Island by a VB-10 SBD turned the barge over and it sank. Several Japanese were observed aboard the barge. Other SBDs strafed the wharf area on Bigej Island where a small AK and five small boats were moored. Several were burning following the attacks. Three ENTERPRISE TBFs dropped 100-lb bombs on a small vessel in the lagoon scoring two hits.

On 31 January, the strikes continued against ships in the lagoon. YORKTOWN VF made 34 strafing runs on medium sized ships both underway and dead in the water. Four of these ships were set on fire and another eight were damaged. Oil slicks were observed on most vessels as they were stopped dead in the water. During attacks by BELLEAU WOOD planes on Gugegwe Island, one SBD scored a bomb hit on the pier next to a 175-foot schooner which turned over on its side. Strafing attacks by F6Fs from BELLEAU WOOD were made on eight ships tied up at both Gugegwe and Bigej Islands. One 300-foot AK caught fire and became enveloped by a big column of smoke. The crew was attempting to beach the ship as the last strafing run was being made. A second ship alongside a pier was set on fire. In strafing attacks against a 50-foot fishing boat and two small utility craft, fire broke out on one and a second began to list. The pilots noted a huge oil slick which marked where the planes had strafed a large AK the day before. Four more ships and piers on Kwajalein Island were also strafed. In addition to the shipping sunk or damaged by U.S. planes during the period 30–31 January, two small cargo ships, an oiler, and several small craft were spotted in the lagoon and reported sunk by naval surface units.

The Japanese commanding officer of Base Force No. 6 reported on damages suffered at Kwajalein on the 30th of January and included AKIBASAN MARU and PARAN MARU sunk; in addition, SHONAN MARU NO. 6 was reported to have been hit by a bomb and beached. The name of several other small ships were recovered from coded message traffic:

NAME	TYPE	TONNAGE
ASHITAKA MARU NO. 5	XPP	139
FUKUYOSHI MARU NO. 5	XPP	119
NICHIEI MARU	XPP	78
FUMI MARU	——	217
KOTOBUKI MARU NO. 3	AK	723

A list of Japanese naval vessels, extracted from a file of administrative orders, was captured later in the war on the island of Saipan. This list was corrected to April 1944 and had many of the vessels crossed out in red ink. Special Duty Sub-chasers (CHAs) NOs. 18, 19, 21, 25, 28, and 33 were all so marked.

Prior to the occupation of Roi-Namur, assault troops using LCI gunboats and LVTs made landings on minor islands Ennuebing and Mellu. The LVTs attempted to land on Mellu along the ocean side of the island where one capsized, drowning several marines. The rest of the LVTs had to enter the pass and land on the lagoon side. After these two islands were occupied, the LCIs, minesweepers, and other gunfire support ships entered North Pass and swept across the lagoon. Landings were completed by the Fourth Marine Division on the small islands on the western side adjoining Roi, making it safe for naval ships to enter into the lagoon via the passes from which artillery could be directed against the main objective. The three islands adjoining Namur on the eastern side of the reef were taken also. The troops waited a day while the Japanese were pounded further by more air strikes and artillery and then made the first landings on Roi and Namur on February 1st. The Japanese remaining from an original garrison of 3,700 men fell to the marines in 24 hours. The landings on Kwajalein, which held an army garrison of 4,000 enemy soldiers, had begun also and the island was secured by army troops of the Seventh Division four days later. Landings on Ebeye Island, which had a garrison of 400 well dug in Japanese troops, was begun on February 2nd and it was secured by the 4th. In conjunction with the occupation of Kwajalein Island and Ebeye, the smaller islands were to be secured on the eastern and western reefs. The western reef force objectives were to secure the islands from Ninni to Eller starting with the two islands flanking Gea Pass, Ninni and Gea. On February 6th, the five islands north of Gehh were secured with no enemy opposition.

Naval Operational Archives Photo
Harbor craft are tied to the main pier and clustered about the small boat basin on Kwajalein Island (January 30, 1944).

—Naval Operational Archives Photo
Strafing attacks against small craft near Kwajalein Island's main pier has left one smoking heavily and five others sinking or already sunk.

THE WRECKS OF THE KWAJALEIN LAGOON

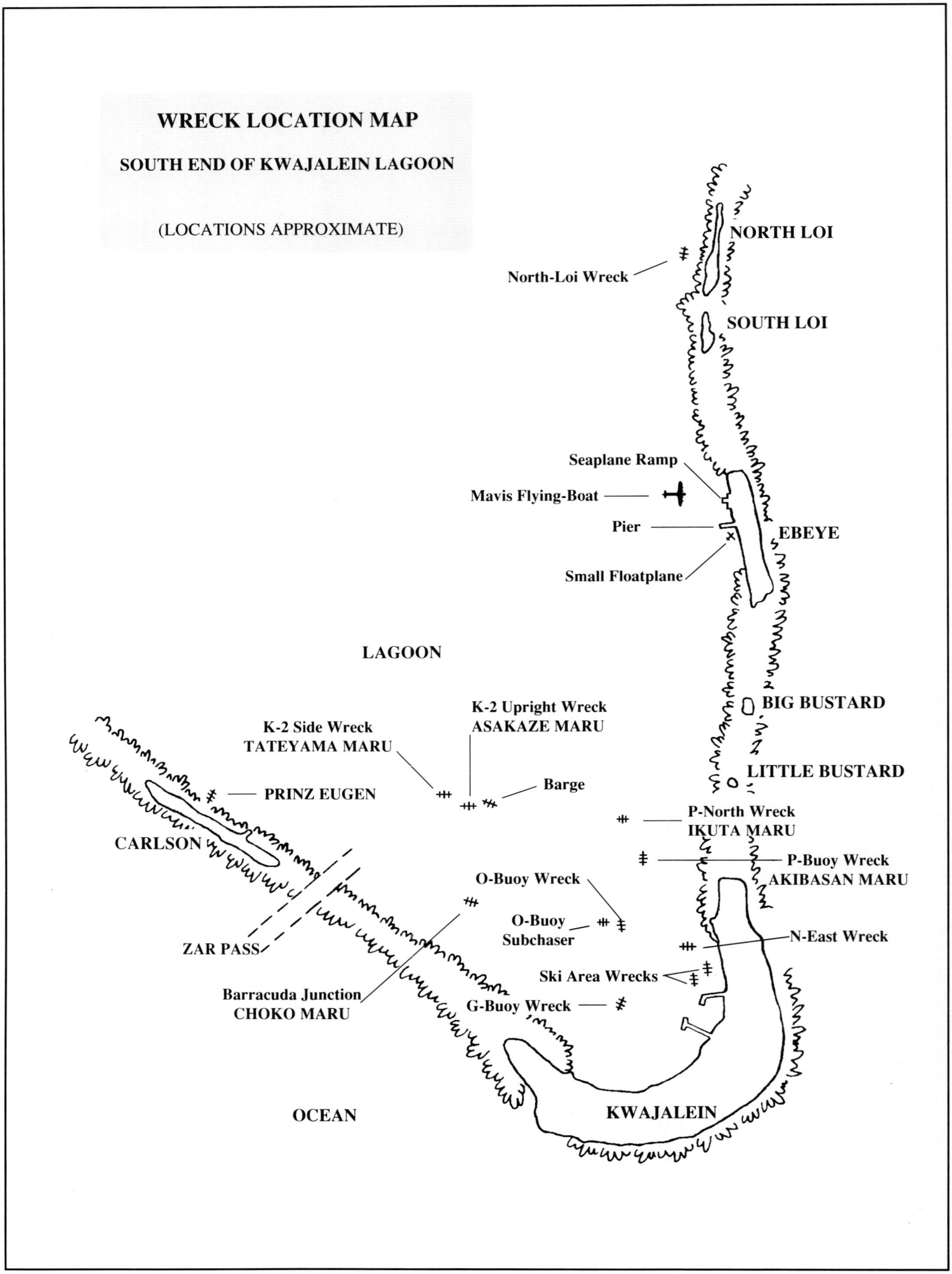

WRECK LOCATION MAP

SOUTH END OF KWAJALEIN LAGOON

(LOCATIONS APPROXIMATE)

- North-Loi Wreck
- NORTH LOI
- SOUTH LOI
- Seaplane Ramp
- Mavis Flying-Boat
- Pier
- Small Floatplane
- EBEYE
- LAGOON
- BIG BUSTARD
- LITTLE BUSTARD
- K-2 Side Wreck TATEYAMA MARU
- K-2 Upright Wreck ASAKAZE MARU
- PRINZ EUGEN
- Barge
- P-North Wreck IKUTA MARU
- P-Buoy Wreck AKIBASAN MARU
- CARLSON
- O-Buoy Wreck
- O-Buoy Subchaser
- N-East Wreck
- Ski Area Wrecks
- ZAR PASS
- Barracuda Junction CHOKO MARU
- G-Buoy Wreck
- OCEAN
- KWAJALEIN

SOUTHERN ATOLL SHIPWRECKS

The AKIBASAN MARU

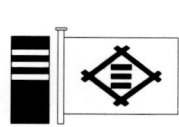 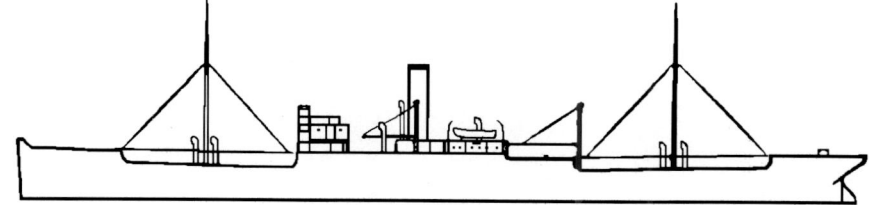

MITSUI BUSSAN KAISHA

ULTRA message intercepts provided U.S. Naval Intelligence with details of an attack on a convoy by U.S. Submarine POGY on December 5, 1943. The convoy was designated No. 4205 and consisted of Section A (YASUKUNI MARU, the AF IRAKO, and the escort MIKURA) and Section B (SOYO MARU, AKIBASAN MARU, and the escorts HIRADO and TAKUNAN MARU NO. 2) which left Truk for Yokosuka, Japan with Section B sailing five hours before Section A. At 1441 h on 7 Dec. 1943, the SOYO MARU was reported sunk and the AKIBASAN MARU damaged by torpedoes fired at them in position 13°30'N, 155°20'E (later found to be 152°09'E). The TAKUNAN MARU NO. 2 took over escort duties and apparently accompanied the damaged AKIBASAN MARU away from the scene of action and MIKURA was detached from Section A to assist in rescuing survivors. The AKIBASAN MARU was laid up at Truk until December 30 or later. A Japanese stevedore captured on 5 February 1944 off Kwajalein reported that the AKIBASAN MARU of about 5,000 tons arrived at Kwajalein from Truk on 29 January 1944. Between 0800 to 0900 h on 31 January, the ship received three direct hits from single-engine carrier planes and sank in five minutes, 4,000 meters from shore. The POW was working aboard the ship at the time of the bombing. The AKIBASAN MARU was most likely the ship described as a "medium AK" sunk in a skip bombing attack by TG 58.1 planes and BUNKER HILL (TG 58.2) on the date indicated.

The AKIBASAN MARU was probably the first Japanese shipwreck found in the Kwajalein Island anchorage following the introduction of scuba diving to the island. It was found in 1965 by dragging an anchor from a boat until it snagged on the superstructure of the wreck. Identification of the vessel was determined from kanji characters etched on the ship's bell and substantiated by information on the builder's plaque which was later recovered by divers.

The wreck of the AKIBASAN MARU lies about 400 to 500 yards from shore on a 160-foot bottom resting against two coral heads with her bow facing northeast. She is locally referred to as "P-Buoy," referring to the large buoy placed near the wreck by the U.S. Coast Guard. Because she is only a short ride away from the small boat marina, the AKIBASAN MARU is visited regularly by scuba divers and is probably the most popular of the wrecks in the lagoon.

You can't usually see the wreck from the surface of the lagoon as the visibility is limited due to the normally murky water. The first glimpse of the wreck a diver gets as he descends is usually of the huge smokestack with three wide strips of metal encircling it which is the stack insignia markings of the ship's merchant owner, Mitsui Bussan Kaisha. The depth to main deck level amidships is nearly 100 feet.

The three decks in the midship superstructure are fairly open due to the collapse of the wooden decks and ceilings. The floor of the rooms in the bridge are covered with a deep layer of muck and charred pieces of wood, giving strong evidence of a fire on board prior to the ships sinking. All kinds of china, some with the Mitsui house flag symbol on them, have been found along with myriads of bottles and other items such as keys, navigational instruments, guns, coins, and buttons.

The No. 2 hold just forward of the bridge contains seaplane wings and pontoons with kanji characters painted on them; these were probably replacement parts for the squadron of Mavis seaplanes stationed at the seaplane base on nearby Ebeye Island. This hold also contained many blue, green, and brown 16-inch saki bottles until they became a desirable diver collector's item.

The upper level of the No. 1 hold has piles of various types of Japanese beer bottles lying all over its extent at a depth of 135 feet. A pile of shoe soles is lying on the port side. The bottom level of this hold is at 150 feet and contains more bottles and remains of broken wooden crates.

The bow has the usual anchor winch and gun platform with a gun mount, but the deck gun itself is missing and it doesn't appear to be lying alongside the bow on the seabed below. The rooms in the forecastle served as crew's quarters. Remains of the partitions that separated the quarters can still be seen; many personal effects of the crewmembers have been found over the years by divers searching through the layer of muck in this area.

The superstructure extends aft of the bridge with the funnel positioned in its center and the engine room below. One compartment, with its wooden ceiling collapsed, contained a western style bathtub with its end chipped off by a large bomb. The bomb, which was finally removed by a bomb disposal group, had caromed off a ceiling support beam before hitting the tub and then ended up alongside the tub. Other nearby compartments were used for food and beer storage; the remains of canned foodstuffs and bottles are plentiful.

The small hold adjoining the engine room was used as a coal storage space. A large muck-covered pile of coal still remains. The No. 4 hold further aft contains many 50-gallon drums, lumber, metal serving pans, and an outboard motor. There is a large hole in the hull plates on the starboard side of this hold from either a skip-bomb or torpedo attack which caused the ship to sink.

Several depth charges were found on the fantail of the wreck at a depth of 100 feet; some were mounted on the deck and others had been jarred loose and were just lying about. It is very unusual for cargo ships to be carrying depth charges to be used against submarines. These have been removed by a bomb disposal unit in recent years. There is easy access to the rooms below deck in the stern where equipment and machinery used for steering control can be found.

The wreck of the AKIBASAN MARU serves well as an artificial reef drawing many types of fish. Large schools of jack and occasional rays, tuna, and sharks can be found in the vicinity. At various times, large concentrations of groupers can be found in the aft section of the wreck. Some spear fishing has been done here and Marshallese are often seen fishing from boats above the wreck.

TECHNICAL SUMMARY:

Type: Cargo
Configuration Sequence: M–K–F–K–M
Gross Tonnage: 4,607 tons
Dimensions: 375/50/24.5 feet
Machinery: Reciprocating engines, single screw, 496 NHP.
Radius: 15,000 miles at 11 knots.
Complement: 49 (crew), 2 (passengers)
Built: 1924 by Mitsui Bussan Kaisha, Tama
Owner: Mitsui Bussan Kaisha, Ltd.
Remarks: Two decks.

The large forward mast is shaped like a cross-tree – AKIBASAN MARU.

The ASAKAZE MARU

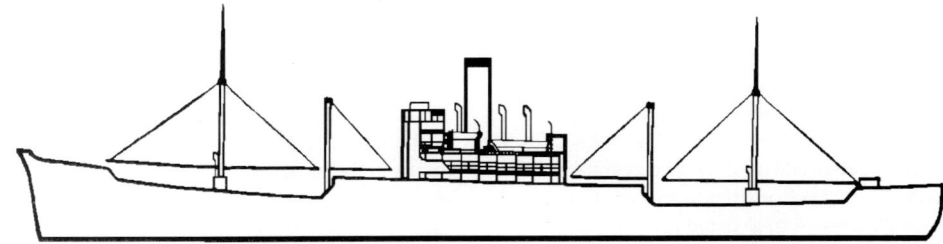

The ASAKAZE MARU was one of six large AKs amongst the approximately 30 vessels attacked by 24 SBDs, 17 TBFs, and 16 F6Fs on the morning of 4 December 1943. The pilots of the attacking planes correctly identified the ship as a KOGYO MARU class merchantmen and claimed a total of three 1,000-lb bomb hits on the vessel. Two explosions were seen aboard and as the planes retired, the ship was on fire and settling by the stern. A Japanese notebook captured on Kwajalein referred to the vessel having sunk five hours later.

The wreck of the ASAKAZE MARU was found by using a fathometer in 1965 on a 160-foot bottom in the Kwajalein Island anchorage. Divers conferred the name "K-2 Upright" to the wreck, referring to her upright disposition and location near the K-2 ship-channel buoy. To my knowledge, the identity of the wreck has not been confirmed although the configuration (M–K–F–K–M) and size of the vessel agree with that of the ASAKAZE MARU. I have made numerous attempts to find the name of the vessel on the hull near the bow and have searched the bridge and engine room for the shipbuilder's plaque, all with negative results. The ASAKAZE MARU was owned by Todai Kisen Kaisha but Yamashita Kisen Kaisha house flag symbols found on china and uniform buttons indicate a possible ownership change or use of the latter shipping company as a manager.

The ship has several gun platforms with the guns missing around the boat deck and cabin areas aft of the bridge. She was heavily armed at one time. Armament still found on the wreck includes a 3-inch bow gun and a wide-barreled machine gun on the starboard side of the wheelhouse.

Visible damage indicated that the ship was subjected to several bomb hits before sinking. The bomb which blew apart the stern was probably responsible for its sinking. Another bomb dropped through the skylight above into the engine room and exploded there rendering the area unsafe for divers due to the tangled catwalks, gratings, and machinery, many of which are hanging precariously and could easily fall. It appears that this bomb or possibly one other hit near the smokestack, leaving it canted over to the starboard side against the deck.

The large bridge and extensive cabin areas with two deck levels were gutted by fire prior to the ship sinking. The ship's helm and telegraph have long since been removed from the wheelhouse at the 90-foot level. A light source here will expose brilliant red sponge growth along the walls of the wheelhouse. Large rooms connected by

Goal-post kingpost (with top mast missing) has derricks and standing rigging still intact after over 40 years of submersion.

Corroded car found in hold of ASAKAZE MARU.

Diver swims toward coral encrusted bow gun and huge anchor winch.

long, spacious companionways run the length of the next deck below. China and some pots and pans have been found on the port side indicating that the galley may have been located here. The crew's quarters, latrines, bath areas, and some storage rooms can be found along the port side on the main deck level. There are entrances to a catwalk landing above the engine room at this level.

The No. 1 hold reportedly contains bags of cement or rice. The No. 2 hold, just forward of the bridge, is empty except for a paravane or aileron stored in the lower level of the hold on the starboard side at 130 feet. This object was used to sweep for and cut mine cables. Passage from the upper level of the hold can be made through corridors on each side of the ship with storage rooms to their sides underneath the midship superstructure to No. 3 hold. The forward space of this No. 3 hold was used for a storage area for beer and saki; many bottles, originally in crates, can be found here by searching under the deep layer of muck and debris. The aft section of the hold contains the outer shell of a small car with stacks of pipe around it plus other plumbing supplies. Large metal rice cooking kettles almost three feet in diameter can be found on the deck between the No. 3 and No. 4 holds. The No. 4 and No. 5 holds contain no cargo.

Diver swims alongside funnel which has fallen and now lies against the deck.

A large lighter can be found several hundred feet northeast of the wreck of the ASAKAZE MARU. This large barge was probably utilized in transporting cargo, water, or fuel between ship and shore. It was anchored and probably sunk at the same time as the ASAKAZE MARU on 4 December 1943.

TECHNICAL SUMMARY:

Type: Passenger-Cargo
Configuration Sequence: M–K–F–K–M
Gross Tonnage: 6,517 tons
Dimensions: 424.1/57.4/27.5 feet
Machinery: Two geared steam turbine engines (oil) built by Hitachi Seisa Kusha in Tokyo, single screw, 500 NHP.
Radius: 9,000 miles at 12 knots
Complement: 43 (crew), 6 (passengers)
Built: 1938 by Osaka Iron Works, Innoshima
Owner: Todai Kisen K.K., Osaka
Remarks: Two decks, cruiser stern.

The CHOKO MARU

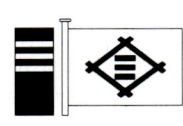

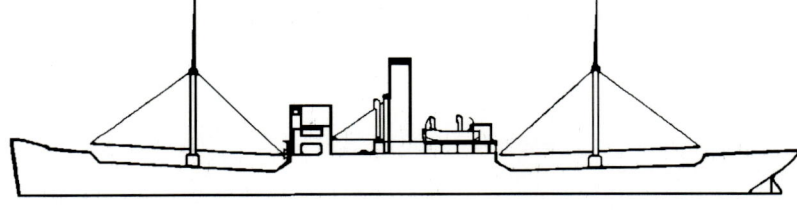

MITSUI BUSSAN KAISHA

The 3,516-ton transport CHOKO MARU was found in 1965 approximately two-thirds of the way from the Kwajalein Island small boat marina to Zar Pass which is just a few hundred yards east-southeast of Carlson Island. Kwajalein divers refer to the CHOKO MARU as the "Barracuda Junction" wreck due to some friendly barracuda which at one time inhabited the area. The wreck lies on her port side facing east towards Kwajalein on a 145-foot bottom.

The name of the ship in the Romanized Kokutai spelling, "TYOKO

MARU," can be found on the upside hull near the bow in 95 feet of water. A 3-inch deck gun and platform is mounted on the bow with its barrel pointing upward. The No. 1 hold contains many 50-gallon-sized barrels and many of them are strung out on the seabed where they've spilled out of the hold. The No. 2 hold forward of the bridge contains sections of pipe and lumber. The bridge superstructure is intact but shows evidence of having been swept by fire. Almost everything in the midship superstructure and bridge has slid to the bottom and lies under the deep layer of muck. The huge smokestack lying off to the side has the familiar three steel band stack markings designating the ship's owner as Mitsui Bussan Kaisha. China found aft of the bridge in a small compartment at main deck level also had house flag markings of the same shipping company. Lloyd's Register of Shipping lists Taiyo Kogyo K.K. as the owner at the time of registry; there most likely was an ownership change some time afterward.

Holds aft of the bridge are mostly empty but contain some barrels and sections of pipe. Many large turkey fish can be found around the upper exposed portion of the wreck usually somewhere between the bridge and the fantail. These fish aren't afraid of divers at all and are great subjects for underwater photographers. The stern has been damaged by bombs dropped by Task Force 50 carrier aircraft; the damage inflicted here evidently sank the ship. The rooms in the fantail are still intact. A large machine gun and several artillery shells are located here intermingled amongst some pots, pans, and ceramic cups and bottles. One day while trying to pry loose a ceramic bottle with a beautiful design and kanji characters painted on it, I found that I was bracing my knee against several artillery shells that could be unstable enough to explode with very little jarring.

The CHOKO MARU was attacked along with the TATEYAMA MARU and the ASAKAZE MARU on 4 December 1943 in the Kwajalein anchorage. The vessel was hit by 1,000- or 2,000-lb bombs and was obviously on fire extensively before sinking. Captured documents indicate the CHOKO MARU did not sink until 0440 h on 6 December, the following day.

TECHNICAL SUMMARY:

Other Name: TYOKO MARU (Kokutai spelling)
Type: Cargo
Configuration Sequence: M–K–F–M
Gross Tonnage: 3,516 tons
Dimensions: 340.5/48.2/22 feet
Machinery: Reciprocating with exhaust turbines (coal), single screw, 232 NHP.
Radius: 5,100 miles at 12 knots.
Complement: Unknown
Built: 1939 by Tama Sanbashi Co., Ltd., Tama
Owner: Taiyo Kogyo K.K. (?)

The IKUTA MARU

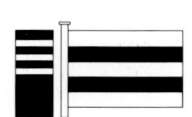

NIPPON YUSEN KAISHA

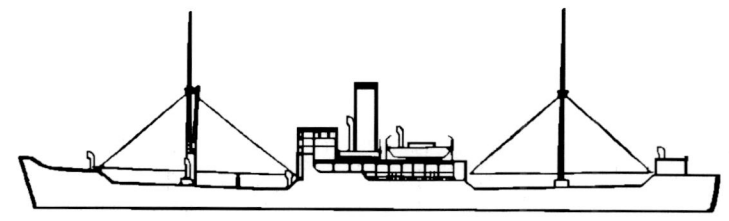

On 12 January 1944, eight U.S. Navy PB4Ys bombed Roi Island and then attacked shipping in the southern part of the lagoon. The planes were based at Abemama in the Gilbert Islands, four from VB-108 and four from VB-109; they were accompanied by two photo-reconnaissance planes. The bombers swept across the lagoon anchorage at 250 to 500 feet dropping five 500-lb bombs each. Damage was claimed to four medium freighters and two 150-foot ships which were all left burning from bomb hits and near misses. Shortly after the attack, a Japanese dispatch was intercepted and decoded which listed the 2,969-ton IKUTA MARU as being engaged by "nine B-24s" at 1243 h, and then sinking at 1429 h. Further information was obtained from the notebook of leading seaman captured in February 1944 on Kwajalein. It contained a note as follows: "January 12, 1944 – We had our tenth air attack. The IKUTA MARU was hit and set ablaze. At 1430 h, the magazine exploded and the ship sank. One plane hit on the ground and burned." The action reports of VB-108 and VB-109 indicate that two aircraft in the group had shrapnel in their tails but sustained no casualties.

The wreck of the IKUTA MARU was found in 1966 by dragging a weighted anchor until it snagged on the ship. Shortly thereafter, the ship's bell was recovered with the name of the vessel etched on its side, thus confirming its identity. Originally built by Nippon Yusen Kaisha for commercial cargo service, the IKUTA MARU was requisitioned by the Japanese Navy and converted for use as a gunboat. She was assigned to the Fourth Fleet and the 6th Base Force at Kwajalein where she operated almost exclusively in the Marshalls-Gilbert Islands area in 1943 and 1944.

Local divers at Kwajalein have designated the wreck as "P-North" as it lies several hundred yards to the north of P-Buoy. Dives to 150 feet or deeper are needed to explore this wreck as it lies on its port side on the lagoon bottom that ranges from 180-plus feet at the bow to 160 feet near the stern.

–*National Archives Photo*
U.S. Navy PB4Y can be seen at left following low-level bombing attack which left IKUTA MARU on fire and sinking.

There is a large gun on a platform mounted above the forecastle and two more amidships on each side of the ship forward of the midship superstructure. They are reported to be 12.7 cm (5-inch) guns which were most likely removed from older, decommissioned vessels before they were broken up. The two mid-ship guns are in their rest positions, trained forward. The bow gun points upward slightly to starboard. There is a pile of shell casings on the seabed below the bow gun. A machine gun has been seen on the bottom opposite the boat deck. The first hold aft contains a huge, square tank with valves mounted on it. This tank is similar to others seen in use for carrying water. The other holds were partially loaded with pipes, coal, and saki bottles. The stern is heavily damaged from one or more bomb hits. Items known recovered from the wreck include brass instruction plaques for the large guns, several hundred saki bottles, many bronze lanterns, various types of china, the ship's telegraph, and the builder's plaque.

TECHNICAL SUMMARY:

Type: Gunboat (Converted 1940)
Configuration Sequence: M–F–M
Gross Tonnage: 2,969 tons
Dimensions: 301.8/45.3/21.5 feet
Machinery: Reciprocating engines, single screw, 214 NHP.
Radius: 6,000 miles at 11 knots
Complement: Unknown
Built: 1936 by Mitsubishi Jukogyo K.K., Yokohama
Owner: Nippon Yusen K.K.
Kinkai Yusen K.K. (Previous)
Remarks: One deck, cruiser stern. This vessel was of modern design and was built in quantity by the Japanese.

The O-Buoy Wreck

This shipwreck was located in 1965 and is reported to be a medium sized (3,000- to 5,000-ton) cargo ship lying upside down on a 140-foot bottom. There is very little room to maneuver between the bottom and the upper superstructure and deck of the ship. This lack of clearance plus the potential danger from falling equipment and cargo has limited exploration a great deal. The wreck has not been buoyed for several years.

The ship was loaded with many types of munitions aboard when sunk. The seabed around the wreck is littered with mines, torpedoes, aircraft bombs and artillery shells. The forward deck of the ship is suspended over the top of a small car lying upright on the seabed with mines resting on the hood and underneath the running boards. An aircraft fuselage lies on the bottom alongside the wreck nearby. The forward hold contains lumber and some 50-gallon-sized barrels. The stern shows a great deal of damage and the entire wreck looks as if it were on fire for some time before sinking. The ship's propeller shaft along with the propeller and rudder have been separated from the rest of the wreck and are lying to the side due to a bomb hit.

The probable identity of the O-Buoy wreck is the 3,083-ton SHOEI MARU. The SHOEI MARU was anchored at Kwajalein after arriving on 19 December 1943, when about midnight, she was the target of a U.S. Navy PBY in a glide bombing attack on the ship from 400 feet. An unstated number of bombs were dropped and the ship left burning. Intercepted dispatches and P.O.W. reports confirmed her identity and established that the ship sunk between 0200 and 0230 h on the 20th before her cargo could be off-loaded. A coded intercept deleted the SHOEI MARU from the Japanese War Organization list on 25 January 1944.

TECHNICAL SUMMARY:

SHOEI MARU
Other Names: SHOYEI MARU
SYOEI MARU (Kokutai spelling)
MATSUE MARU (Internal Japanese designation)
GENERAL LUKIN
OAKWIN
WAR OASIS (Original)
Type: Cargo
Configuration Sequence: M–F–M
Gross Tonnage: 3,083 tons
Dimensions: 331.9/46.5/25.5 feet
Machinery: Reciprocating diesel engines, single screw, 429 NHP.
Radius: 9,600 miles at 10 knots.
Complement: Unknown
Built: 1919 by W. Gray & Co., W. Hartlepool, England
Owner: Towa Kisen K.K.
Shoyei Kisen K.K. (Previous)
Unknown (Original)

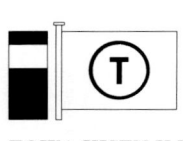

TOWA KISEN K.K.

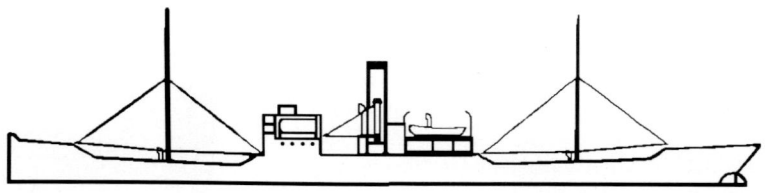

SHOEI MARU

The PRINZ EUGEN

The German heavy cruiser PRINZ EUGEN was named after the "The Liberator of Vienna," Prince Eugene of Savoy, who had been an 18th century officer of the Holy Roman Empire. Like most of the major German Fleet units in World War II, the PRINZ EUGEN was never allowed to fulfill her potential because of Adolf Hitler's reluctance and lack of enthusiasm for surface ship operations. Hitler had an expressed fear of ship sinkings and the loss of prestige to the Reich that would come with it.

The PRINZ EUGEN is mostly noted for its sortie with the 42,000-ton battleship BISMARK into the North Atlantic in May 1941 to make combined attacks on Allied shipping. After being spotted and trailed by British ships and aircraft, the two German ships were confronted by HMS HOOD and PRINCE OF WALES southwest of Iceland. The 860-foot-long battle cruiser HOOD had been the pride of Britain's Navy and the largest warship in the world for 21 years. She was armed with eight 15-inch guns. The PRINCE OF WALES was a modern 35,000-ton battleship armed with ten 14-inch guns. In a dawn confrontation, both sides opened fire simultaneously at a range of 13 miles. Initially, the German ships concentrated on the HOOD while the HOOD fired at the PRINZ EUGEN and the PRINCE OF WALES engaged the BISMARK. The first salvo by the PRINZ EUGEN fell short, but the second straddled the HOOD starting fires on the boat deck causing the 4-inch AA ammunition in the ready-use locker to start exploding. One or two more hits on HOOD followed in short order. The BISMARK was straddled and hit by the PRINCE OF WALES. Up to this time, Admiral Holland in HOOD had been engaging the enemy with his battleship oriented such that the rear turrets could not bear on the German ships. Just after the signal was made for both the HOOD and PRINCE OF WALES to alter course to port to bring the aft turrets into action, BISMARK straddled the HOOD with a broadside salvo. The HOOD was hidden to observers by a curtain of shell splashes. In this fifth minute since the engagement began, one of the shells evidently penetrated the light upper deck armor amidships to the HOOD's vitals below, exploded, and touched off the 4-inch followed by the 15-inch magazine. A column of flame shot up from the HOOD followed by a huge mushroom cloud of smoke resulting from the tremendous explosions that broke the back of the ship separating it into two pieces. The bow and stern portions reared up from the water towards the sky before sliding beneath the waves to the thousand fathom depth, taking with them all but three of the ship's complement of 1,500 men.

The order was then given for the PRINZ EUGEN to shift her fire toward the PRINCE OF WALES with BISMARK. In short order, the PRINCE OF WALES received three 8-inch hits from the PRINZ EUGEN and four 15-inch hits from the BISMARK, one of which penetrated the bridge killing everyone except the captain and one other officer. Captain Helmuth Brinkmann of the PRINZ EUGEN was ordering a torpedo attack on the PRINCE OF WALES when it turned away and extricated itself from the battle. The PRINZ EUGEN had nearly been hit by the HOOD, but luckily received no damage. Of the

–National Archives Photo

PRINZ EUGEN at anchor following its being turned over to the U.S. after World War II.

The capsized wreck of the PRINZ EUGEN. One of the screws has been removed and returned to Germany.

18 salvos fired by the PRINCE OF WALES during the 21-minute battle, three shells had hit the BISMARK. That evening, the PRINZ EUGEN was released to begin independent cruiser warfare operations while the BISMARK struck out alone to be pursued and chased by Britain's air and naval forces and sunk three days later with few survivors. The PRINCE OF WALES survived her encounter with the PRINZ EUGEN and BISMARK, but her end was soon to come. Sent to discourage Japanese expansion towards Singapore, she was sunk along with the BB HMS REPULSE by Japanese aircraft a few days after Pearl Harbor.

Following action with the BISMARK, engine problems on the PRINZ EUGEN cut short her shipping raids and the ship went to Brest, France in July 1941 for drydocking and overhaul. Her main gunnery control and damage control center were destroyed there during a bombing raid which killed 52 of her crew. Later in February 1942, the PRINZ EUGEN and battle cruisers GNEISENAU and SCHARNHORST, with destroyer and torpedo boat escorts and a Luftwaffe air cover, made a daring return dash to Germany through the English Channel. The British employed destroyers, patrol boats, aircraft, and coastal defense guns against the armada of German ships, but all attempts to destroy them were thwarted. While engaged in operations in Norwegian waters in late February 1942, the British submarine TRIDENT torpedoed the PRINZ EUGEN in the stern and she was stuck in Trondheim Fjord for nearly two months before temporary repairs could be made allowing her to be returned to Kiel for more complete repairs. At this time alterations were made to the stern and newly designed rudder was installed. During operations in 1944 supporting German ground forces engaging Russian forces in coastal areas near Lithuania and Latvia where she served as flagship for Baltic forces, the PRINZ EUGEN collided with the light cruiser LEIPZIG, necessitating having her bow replaced.

After surrendering to British forces in Copenhagen on 7 May 1945, the PRINZ EUGEN was taken to Germany and turned over to U.S. authorities. She then sailed for Boston and then to the Philadelphia Naval Shipyard with part of her German crew under U.S. supervision. At this time, plans were made for her to be used as a target ship in the Bikini atomic bomb tests and she was brought to the Pacific through the Panama Canal.

Along with two Japanese ships, the cruiser SAKAWA and the battleship NAGATO, and an assortment of old U.S. Navy ships including battleships PENNSYLVANIA and NEVADA, light carrier INDEPENDENCE, and cruisers SALT LAKE CITY and PENSACOLA, the PRINZ EUGEN served as a test bed for determination of the effects of atomic weapons. Designated IX-300, the PRINZ EUGEN survived an air burst followed by an underwater burst which produced radiation contamination aboard. Approximately 50 remaining ships still afloat following the tests were towed to

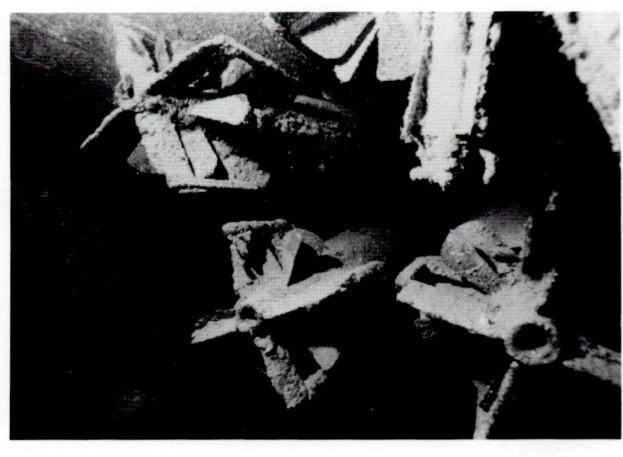

Torpedoes still remain their racks in a storage compartment.

The crosstree-shaped foretop structure of the PRINZ EUGEN lies crumpled against the sand bottom.

Kwajalein where they were anchored in the lagoon and inspected for radiation and bomb damage effects and for signs of leaks and flooding. Ammunition aboard the ships was off-loaded at this time.

Certain structures aboard the PRINZ EUGEN weakened over a period of time and what had been controllable small leaks turned into major flooding below decks. In order to prevent the cruiser from sinking and blocking the shipping lanes in the lagoon, tugboats attempted to beach the ship against Enubuj Island. The tugs pushing her towards the island lost control and the PRINZ EUGEN floundered stern first against the reef. Attempts at pulling her off the reef were futile. The ship developed a 35-degree list overnight and the following day, December 22, 1946, rolled over slowly on to its starboard side and capsized. The wreck was inspected by radiological safety teams and much contaminated debris was removed at this time. Another survey of the ship in 1970 indicated that a radiation hazard aboard no longer existed.

Many words have been written expressing sadness at the sight of this once beautiful warship lying upside down with only some of its screws and rudder exposed above water. Kwajalein divers feel differently. They are grateful that the PRINZ EUGEN didn't join the ranks of the other remaining ships used in the Bikini tests which were scuttled in deep water never to be seen again. Even though the PRINZ EUGEN is capsized, she offers the diver a rare opportunity for sightseeing and exploration of a major warship that had an interesting historical role in World War II. I feel fortunate for having been able to make many dives on this historic monument surrounded by the beauty of the reef and marine life of the Kwajalein Lagoon.

The boat trip to the PRINZ EUGEN takes only between 15 and 20 minutes from the Kwajalein small boat marina. Dive boats generally anchor the skeleton of a small wooden hulled wreck in 30 feet of water just opposite the screws of the PRINZ EUGEN on the leeward side. The hull of the shipwreck rests against the reef along the leeward starboard side; however, a small opening at the 90-foot level allows you to swim underneath the ship just forward of the bridge. Normally, divers swim around the stern to the forward section of the wreck. The wreck is progressively deeper as you go further towards the bow. You can swim under the bow at 110 feet.

When the PRINZ EUGEN rolled over and sank, it went over on its starboard side crunching the bridge and upper superstructure to the side against the bottom. Easy access to most of the ship is available all along the port side of the wreck. An open hatch in the center of the deck near the stern at 35 feet is an entrance to the crew's quarters and mess area. The crew's quarters contain lockers, cabinets and drawers for the personal effects of the crew; the remains of many bunks can still be found here. The mess area contains bowls, serving platters and pans. A narrow entrance way leads forward past a latrine area. The sinks, commodes and urinals take on an unusual appearance hanging upside down. As you follow the corridor leading to the central interior of the ship, lights with red glass covers that had been mounted along the ceiling lie below you every few feet. A large and what was undoubtedly a rather magnificent table hangs upside down in what appears to be the officer's mess. Dishes found on the wreck bearing the design of a black eagle were probably found nearby.

A great deal of machinery and fire fighting gear lie suspended on the deck of the ship. Amidships, much has fallen to the seabed including some dual AA guns and their mounts along with large dome-shaped structures which housed fire control equipment. It is difficult to find an entrance into the bridge as it is crumpled against the bottom of the lagoon. However, someone must have solved the problem as there are rumors of many interesting items being found and recovered from it.

The armament associated with that of a heavy cruiser is apparent everywhere. Two large turrets lie near the bottom with their twin 8-inch gun barrels half buried in the soft sand of the lagoon floor. The relatively large 4.1-inch guns and the dual- and quad-mounted AA guns are almost all still intact. The port side torpedo tubes have torpedoes in them. The torpedoes were transferred to the tubes on a rail system from torpedo storage compartments along the outside of the ship. Forward of the bridge and torpedo storage areas are several corridors, doorways, and rooms which served as officer's quarters. The bunks in these rooms are hanging upside down as they were attached to the floor. A beautiful chandelier was recovered from one of these rooms.

The interior structures of the ship are intact and it appears safe for exploration. Deep penetration into the interior of the ship involves working your way through a maze or corridors, doorways and rooms. This type of exploration dictates the use of safety lines and good underwater lights. I regret that I was unable to explore more of the interior of the wreck including the engine room prior to the death of two divers who were exploring deep inside; since then interior penetration of the wreck has been prohibited by the army command following this tragic accident.

TECHNICAL SUMMARY:

Type: German ADMIRAL HIPPER Class Heavy Cruiser
Displacement: 14,800 tons (design)
Dimensions: 654 (o.a.)/71/15 feet
Machinery: 4-shaft geared turbine engines (80,000 HP maximum) and diesel engines for generating electricity.
Speed: 32 knots
Radius: Unknown
Complement: 830
Armament: Eight 8-inch guns in 4 turrets, twelve 4.1-inch AA guns, twelve 37mm AA guns; twelve 21 inch torpedo tubes in groups of 3.
Built: 1936–38 at Krupp Germania Werft Yards, Kiel Commissioned August 1, 1940.

The SHINSHO MARU

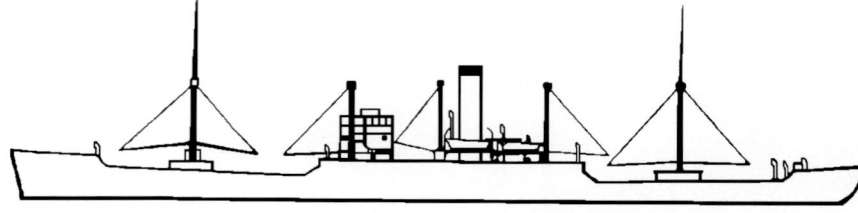

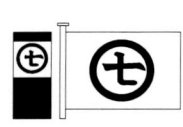

KURIBAYASHI SHOSEN KAISHA

While on patrol in the Marshalls on 9 July 1942, The U.S. submarine THRESHER spotted the 4,836-ton Motor Torpedo Boat Tender SHINSHO MARU off the southern tip of the Kwajalein Atoll. The ship was described as a 6,000-ton passenger-freighter with a Japanese ensign painted on her side amidships. She was zig-zagging toward the Gea Pass entrance to the lagoon on a base course of 030 degrees and at a speed of 12 knots. The THRESHER made a periscope attack on the ship, firing two torpedoes at her from a range of less than 1,500 yards with depth settings at 20 feet. The first torpedo was seen to hit 60 feet inside the bow and the second to hit 150 feet back from the stern. A few seconds after the second hit, a third and heavier explosion was also heard and felt aboard the submarine. The three explosions blew considerable wreckage up through and above the target. THRESHER dove deep following the attack but was spotted by a patrol plane which jolted the submarine with a depth bomb. After nearly two hours, more depth bombs were dropped close by. Strange buzzing noises were heard shortly thereafter, followed by loud scraping noises on the hull of the submarine. With a sudden jerk, the stern rose to a steep angle; the THRESHER had been snagged by a giant grapnel from a Japanese vessel on the surface. The submarine towed the vessel above for nearly 10 minutes like a fish on the end of a line. The grapnel finally shook loose but the Japanese then dropped several close depth charges which severely shook the submarine. Later the next day, the crew found that damage from the initial patrol plane attack had caused a small leak which constantly emitted a stream of bubbles. The Japanese had pinpointed the location of THRESHER by following the bubble trail on the smooth surface of the sea.

Three messages were intercepted which provide additional information:

(1) Message of 9 July (0750), originating by the Captain of the SHINSHO MARU, states that his ship is listing at a 30-degree angle and will soon sink.

(2) Message of 9 July (0800), also originated by the Captain of the SHINSHO MARU, states that his ship was sunk at 0800; part of the crew were rescued.

(3) Message of 9 July (1800), again from the Captain of the SHINSHO MARU, is a general report of the sinking of that vessel. Message states that the SHINSHO MARU was en route from Imieji to Ruotto (Jaluit to Roi-author) on 8 July. At 0630, July 9th, the SHINSHO MARU suddenly received a torpedo attack from an enemy submarine in ambush at 11 miles southwest of Kiiyo (Gea-author) Channel, Kwajalein Island. The engines were damaged and it was impossible to navigate. Gradually the ship was flooded and at the same time it began to list to starboard. No method at all to reclaim it. Finally the SHINSHO MARU sank at the scene of action at 0800.

The above information should end speculation that the SHINSHO MARU might be the large shipwreck rumored to have been spotted in the Bigej Island area from aircraft flying overhead. Although lost in deep water, the story of the attack and sinking of the ship plus the experiences of THRESHER add to the history of WW II and Kwajalein.

TECHNICAL SUMMARY:

Other Name: SINSYO MARU (Kokutai spelling)
Type: Motor Torpedo Boat Depot Ship (Converted 1941)
Configuration Sequence: M–K–K–F–K–M
Gross Tonnage: 4,836 tons
Dimensions: 373.1/50/29 feet
Machinery: Reciprocating engines, single screw, 322 NHP.
Radius: 11,500 miles at 12 knots.
Complement: Unknown (crew), 12 (passengers)
Built: 1936 by Mitsui Bussan Kaisha, Ltd., Tama
Owner: Kuribayashi Shosen Kaisha, Tokyo
Remarks: Two decks, cruiser stern, well decks.

The TATEYAMA MARU

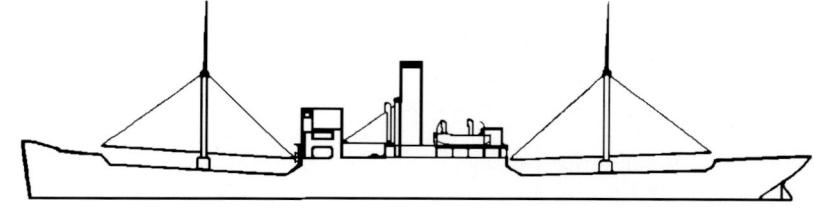

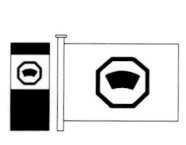

BABA SHOJI K.K.

My diving partner was about 15 feet behind me when he let out an underwater yell that sent chills down my spine. As I whirled around to face him, I was thinking that a shark must surely have bit him in two. He appeared all right, but he was rubbing his hand furiously against something on the exterior of the bridge of the wreck we were diving on. On this particular day in June 1972, we were diving on one of a

Diver stands on huge kingpost lying to its side (TATEYAMA MARU).

cluster of ships sunk near the K2 Buoy; this one was named "K2 Side" as it was the only ship in the cluster of wrecks located in this area that was lying on its side. My dive partner, Ron Barnett, was motioning for me to come to him and I immediately recognized the reason for his excitement. He had found one of the most sought after trophies in wreck diving, the ship builder's plaque. This plaque is usually placed on either the ship's bridge or engine room (or both) and contains information relating to the builder, location, and date the ship was built. The bronze plaque was covered with orange colored sponge growth and stood out clearly against the dark colored bridge superstructure on which it was mounted. We had no tools with us and if we were to return on this same day to the 110-foot depth at which we found the plaque on a non-decompression dive (Kwajalein divers are limited to making non-decompression dives only), we would have to terminate the present dive immediately and start accumulating some surface time. Several hours later, after collecting the necessary tools we would need, we returned to the wreck and removed the plaque. The identity of the wreck had always been a mystery and we were anxious to get a look at the information etched on it. In order to remove the sponge and coral growth covering the face of the plaque, it was placed in an acid bath. The cleaned plaque was identical to one that had been found in the engine room of the same wreck some years earlier. Due to some mis-information, the first plaque was believe to have been removed from a different wreck. With the date and building information found on the plaque in mind, I researched further and found that the 3,787-ton TATEYAMA MARU, which had been reported sunk at Kwajalein, had been built in 1937 by Mitsui Bussan Kaisha in Tama, Japan. This agreed with the data found on the plaque and the mystery identity of the wreck was solved.

The TATEYAMA MARU lies on its starboard side facing eastward. This wreck rests on a 135-foot bottom and is one of the most popular ships being dove on at Kwajalein. The wreck was buoyed normally with a plastic Japanese fishing float attached with stainless steel cable on the upper side near the rear hold at 85 feet. There is a gun platform mounted on the stern, but the gun was evidently removed prior to its sinking. The rear hold contains either 3- or 4.7-inch artillery shells banded together in clusters of fours. Some of these have spilled out of the hold onto the floor of the lagoon.

Entrance to the engine room can be made through open hatch covers. One of the ship's crewmembers had been caught here when the ship had been attacked. His grisly skeletal remains lie on the grating floor.

The huge smokestack lying off to the side appears to have no stack markings. The kingposts have strangely configured mushroom shaped ventilators at their tops and are not connected across the tops.

A large hole can be found on the starboard side aft of the bridge; this was probably caused by a bomb that had skipped into the side of the ship and caused its sinking. There are two deck levels below the wheelhouse that offer many "artifacts" to the divers that search through the deep muck. Most items are found near the bottom at 135 feet. The porthole covers from the wreck are highly prized by divers who work at removing them. They are unusual in design and are made with higher than usual quality bronze.

Forward of the bridge is the No. 2 hold which can be labeled a bottle collector's heaven. Here at 120 feet are stacks and layers of various types of beer bottles. One of the most prized bottles to be found was one with a warrior on a horse rearing up on its hind legs on its side. This was likely the same flying horse that you see on the labels of Kirin Beer today.

The No. 1 hold contains large metal tanks which were probably used to carry water. The presence of these tanks confirms why the TATEYAMA MARU was listed as a converted water carrier. The ship has a well deck (recessed one deck in depth, bordered by a railing), a fact not easily recognized unless you are really concentrating while diving on a wreck lying on its side. Forward near the bow, another bare gun platform is mounted.

Prisoner-of-war reports confirm that the TATEYAMA MARU was regularly assigned as a Marshall's supply ship. She was the target of YORKTOWN VB and VT planes on 4 December 1943 and was sunk by one or more 1,000- or 2,000-lb bomb hits and close misses. A POW diary lists the ship as having sunk shortly after the attacks by U.S. planes.

TECHNICAL SUMMARY:

Type: Cargo-Water Carrier
Configuration Sequence: M–K–F–M
Gross Tonnage: 3,787 tons.
Dimensions: 340.4/48.2/26.2 feet
Machinery: Diesel engines, single screw, 240 NHP.
Radius: 5,100 miles at 12 knots.
Complement: Unknown
Built: 1937 by Mitsui Bussan Kaisha, Ltd., Tama
Owner: Baba Shoji K.K.
Remarks: Two decks.

The U.S. Army Concrete Barge

Although not positively identified, the concrete-hulled vessel aground at Ennylabagen (Carlos) is one of four 4,338-ton B7-D1 supply barges used by the U.S. Army as floating warehouses in World War II. Concrete shipbuilding began late in World War I, and about 16 steamers were completed in the United States. The ships were not considered successful and either sank as a result of accidents or were permanently docked. As World War II approached, concrete shipbuilding was again proposed. The Maritime Commission agreed to have them built, partly out of a consideration of a potential shortage of steel, particularly steel plate; (greater than 70% of the weight of steel in a typical ship is plate) and partly to forestall building of wooden ships. The Commission contracted for 142 concrete vessels of which 104 were built, including twenty-four 4,700-ton steamers named after denizens of the concrete industry; twenty-two 2,500-ton barges named after elements; and four 4,388-ton barges named after minerals.

The barge at Ennylabagen seems to have suffered the fate of the majority of World War II concrete vessels as it appears to have been purposely put aground to serve as a breakwater. However, it has the distinction of being the largest American vessel sunk at Kwajalein. Possible candidates for the barge include: BCL-2569 AGATE, BCL-2570 CHROMITE, BCL-2571 MICA, and BCL-2572 GRANITE.

TECHNICAL SUMMARY:

Type: B7–D1 Concrete Barge
Configuration Sequence: M–???
Gross Tonnage: 4,388 tons
Dimensions: 366/54/35 feet
Machinery: None
Radius: Not applicable.
Complement: Unknown
Built: 1943 by Barrett and Hilp Belair Shipyard at South San Francisco, California
Owner: U. S. Army

Miscellaneous Small Wrecks

No positive identification has been made of several of the small vessels that have been found within the Kwajalein Lagoon. The names of many of the smaller craft reported to be lost are known, but their identities have not been correlated to any of the wrecks that have been located. Amongst the vessels reported lost at Kwajalein are several small watch/picket boats. Vessels of this type include the following: AIKOKU MARU (35 tons), PALAU MARU (35 tons), TAKEURA MARU (26 tons), and the YAMASHIRO MARU (38 tons). In most cases, the dates these vessels were lost are known, but little other information is available.

The G-Buoy Wreck

This small vessel found in 1966 probably served as a harbor craft. It lies on its port side facing north in about 80 feet of water. The 80-foot-long vessel lies several hundred yards from shore almost directly west of the Kwajalein small boat marina. There is no armament aboard; however, a small gun platform is mounted on the bow. The small holds and compartments are virtually empty and there is little to interest a diver. A fire gutted the vessel before it sank.

The Kwajalein Ski Area Wreck

Special permission is needed to dive on this wreck as it is located in a normally prohibitive diving area. It is a favorite attraction for night divers as it is located less than 100 yards from shore. This 80- to 100-foot long steel-hulled vessel has an extended type of bow configuration consistent with Japanese schooners. It was most likely utilized as a harbor craft, auxiliary, or picket boat. The wreck lies on its starboard side facing north in about 50 feet of water. The bridge house and stack are gone, either blown up or removed by dredging. A few lanterns, bottles, personal effects and other small artifacts have been found on the wreck. A gun platform is mounted on the bow; the gun had been removed prior to the vessel sinking. There is no other armament aboard.

The Ski Area Dolphin Wreck

Located about 200 feet farther out and slightly south from the above ski area wreck, the "Dolphin" wreck was found around 1975. The wreck is named after the large mooring buoy (or dolphin) used to moor barges in the ski area. The wreck is a small wooden vessel, perhaps 60 feet long facing the shore in about 60 feet of water. With its wooden ribs in varying states of decay, the wreck presents a jagged appearance with no recognizable rooms and few familiar features. This wreck is probably one of the small workboats seen partially submerged in BUNKER HILL photos taken on January 31, 1944.

The N-Buoy Wreck

Located in 1970, this small vessel is reported to be approximately 50 feet long lying upright on a 125-foot bottom. She supposedly has a wooden hull with a steel-plated keel and sports twin diesel engines. It is in poor shape with little of the framework structure remaining. The vessel was evidently sunk during strafing attacks as remaining superstructure and some of its aluminum porthole covers exhibit bullet holes. The wreck lies just north of N-Buoy.

The DR Wreck

Reportedly very similar to the N-buoy wreck, this vessel was found in 1971 in poor condition with much of it covered by sand.

The N-East Wreck

Lying in a designated work-boat area, diving access to this wreck is limited as special permission must be granted to dive the site. The vessel, which appears to be a 200-foot-long steel-hulled net-tender or converted sub-chaser, lies upright on the lagoon floor at a depth of 110 feet. The wreck was found in 1965 and is located a few hundred yards to the east of N-Buoy facing east.

A gun mount and platform have been placed on the bow. The forecastle below served as crew's quarters as remains of bunks and personal effects are located there. The forward hold is empty except for two or three barrels and a machine gun with its mount which must have been knocked loose from the deck or bridge area and fell into the hold. A large, aggressive grouper hung out in this area for a long time and delighted in scaring divers by making charges at them as they entered the hold.

A second machine gun, which appears identical to the one found in the forward hold, lies on its side of the deck forward of the bridge. It was originally mounted on top of the bridge. Only the framework of the midship superstructure remains due to the fires on board before sinking and the long immersion in salt water. The bridge has several small compartments with narrow passageways. The ship's wheel, telegraph, and other controls once located here had been removed by divers. Compartments or cabin areas extend below and aft of the bridge with the engine room located below main deck. Entrance to the engine room can be made through the port side doorway at deck level or from the aft hold by swimming over the top of a large unexploded bomb lying in midst of the narrow entrance. This rear hold contains many coils and rolls of ropes and cables. The stern is blown apart; this may be due to the ship's own depth charges, some of which are still lying about the stern and the bottom of the lagoon nearby.

There is considerable confusion as to the identity of the "N-East" and the "N-North" wrecks which according to Broadwater, <u>Kwajalein – Lagoon of Found Ships</u>, are similar type vessels. This confusion surrounds the net-tenders assigned to the Fourth Fleet and attached to the 6th Base Force at Kwajalein. One of these wrecks was thought to be the KASHIMA MARU previously, but newly released intelligence files now confirm that net-tender vessel was sunk at Wotje. These same files do confirm that the net-tender KOTOBUKI MARU NO. 3 as sunk at Kwajalein (see description under "The Bigej Coastal Tanker") and thus she is a candidate for the N-East or N-North wrecks. It is not known if the KOTOBUKI MARU NO. 3 has an aft-engine or mid-engine configuration (like N-East). Another net-tender, the UJI MARU (also with an unknown engine configuration) was reported sunk at 9°20'N, 167°29'E on 29 January 1944. This location is near Roi-Namur at the northern end of the atoll and there is an undiscovered shipwreck marked on the hydrographic charts there. The finding and exploration of this shipwreck plus more careful study of the "N-North" wreck by Kwajalein divers might be the key to unlocking this identity dilemma.

TECHNICAL SUMMARY:

UJI MARU
Other Name: UZI MARU
Type: Net Tender (Converted 1941)
Configuration Sequence: Unknown
Gross Tonnage: 872 tons
Dimensions: 185/?/? feet
Machinery: Unknown
Radius: Unknown
Complement: Unknown
Built: 1940
Owner: Unknown
Remarks: Assigned to 6th Base Force, Sub-Chaser Division No. 65.

The O-Buoy Submarine Chaser

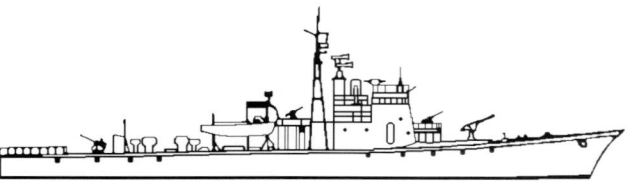

No. 1 Class Submarine Chaser

This sub-chaser was discovered by Bevan Jacobs, Phil Copeland, Mike Mouris, and Charles Zambon in 1983 and is one of the recent shipwreck finds in the Kwajalein Atoll. The wreck was found while towing divers at a 60-foot depth behind a boat in a search for the O-Buoy wreck. It lies in 120 feet of water, less than 50 yards due west of the O-Buoy wreck. The vessel is reported to be approximately 80 feet long with a wooden hull and single screw. No masts or kingposts are present. The stern and 60 feet of the hull is intact but the bow section of the wreck is strewn with piles of rubble, debris, and twisted metal. The superstructure has collapsed leaving the height of the remaining structure only 5 to 6 feet above the sand bottom. There is a machine gun that had been mounted to the deck lying next to the vessel's bow. The machine gun had been in use aboard as lots of spent ammo clips, holding 5–6 shells, lie about the wreck. Although there is no sign of any depth charges, a rack for holding them is mounted on the stern. It appears that the vessel had a single lifeboat or dingy aboard; the davits are still present. A searchlight has been found aboard as have a pistol and several rifles.

Divers have found the wreck to be a treasure house of artifacts. The bridge wheelhouse has collapsed to the starboard side out onto the sand. This has left open access to the radio room and many batteries, telegraph keys, headphones, radio and sounding equipment, and the compass have been located. The galley was apparently located just forward of the radio room where a crystal decanter and lots of "Fujikawa" blue and white-colored china was strewn about; none had the ship owner's flag symbol on them. Several musical instruments were found on board including a horn and large bamboo flute. There were many perfume, cold cream, and other types of decorative bottles found, most likely used for trading with the Marshallese. Jewelry and small jade pieces were collected, including a 6- to 8-inch tall statue of Hirohito. A sealed tube located on the wreck produced one of the most unusual finds I've heard of. Inside were 13 pornographic ink paintings.

–Photo by Bob Hampton
Remains of the crew can still be found aboard the subchaser.

TECHNICAL SUMMARY:

AUXILIARY SUBMARINE CHASERS NOs. 18, 21
Other Names: CHA 18, CHA 21
Type: Submarine Chaser (No. 1 Class)
Displacement: 130 tons
Dimensions: 85.33/18.33/6.5 feet
Machinery: 1-shaft geared diesel, 400 S.H.P.
Speed: 11 knots
Radius: 1,000 miles at 10 knots
Complement: 23
Armament: One 7.7mm machine gun; 22 depth charges.
Built: 1943 onwards. A total of 200 auxiliary submarine chasers of this class were built by shipyards specializing in fishing vessels. It is not known at which shipyards the individual vessels were built. The following is a list of the shipyards and number of vessels of this class built in each:

Fukuoka Shipbuilding Iron Works, Fukuoka	(10)
Fukushima Shipbuilding Co., Matsue	(13)
Funaya Shipbuilding Co., Hakodate	(7)
Goriki Shipbuilding Co., Ujiyamada	(12)
Hayashikawa Heavy Industrial Co., Shimonoseki	(20)
Ichikawa Shipbuilding Co., Ujiyamada	(16)
Jinen ShipbuildingIron Works, Moji	(12)
Koyanagi Shipbuilding Co., Shizuoka	(12)
Miho Shipbuilding Co., Shimuzu	(13)
Murakami Shipbuilding Co., Ishinomaki	(8)
Nishii Shipbuilding Co., Ujiyamada	(13)
Saga Shipbuilding Iron Works, Takaoka	(18)
Shikoku Dock Industrial Co., Takamatsu	(20)
Tokushima Shipbuilding Co., Tokushima	(3)
Yamanishi Shipbuilding Iron Works, Ishinomaki	(17)
Yokosuka Naval Dockyard, Yokosuka	(1)
Yonago Shipbuilding Co., Yonago	(6)

The wreck is littered with bottles, boots, batteries, and spent ammo dispersed about amongst the personal effects and human remains of the vessel's crew. Numerous wrist and pocket watches, gold and silver ribbed fountain pens, brass belt buckles, coins, chops (signature stamps), war medals, binoculars, naval caps with brass insignias, a coin purse with coins, and a bosun's whistle have been recovered. The vessel had a crew of 12 or more men as that many skulls are present aboard the wreck. The crew of the sub-chaser was overmatched by the firepower aboard the aircraft that attacked them. From the amount of spent ammo lying about and the damage to both the bow and stern, its obvious that they went down fighting.

The identity of the wreck had not been confirmed but it appears likely that it is one of the auxiliary submarine chasers, either CHA 18 or 21, lost on 30 January 1944 at a reported location of 8°42'N, 167°44'E.

The Gugegwe Island Wrecks

Planes from BELLEAU WOOD attacked eight ships near Gugegwe Island (known by American forces at the time as Berlin Island) and Bigej Island (known as Bennet) both on 30 and 31 January 1944. The action reports of 30 January described the strafing of a 150-foot ship off Bigej, two smaller craft (both of which were stopped dead in the water, one smoking) and an AK which momentarily caught fire in a number of places. A 500-lb bomb landed alongside a "175-foot schooner" which turned over on its side next to the Gugegwe pier. The planes made strafing attacks the following day on three craft near the pier at Gugegwe; these were described as a 50-foot fishing boat and two small utility craft. The pilots reported that a huge oil slick marked the spot where the planes had attacked "a large AK" the day before. An action photo taken of the area shows a mid-engine ship sunk upright just off the Gugegwe pier with only its two masts, its funnel, and a portion of the top of the bridge showing. A large oil slick enveloped the wreck and spread with the wind direction to the south. A two-masted craft, 50-plus feet long, lies at anchor less than 100 yards to the south-southwest. The last vessel in the picture is a larger mid-engine vessel a quarter of a mile out into the lagoon that is smoking from fires aboard and has a naval artillery shell exploding in the water just to the west of it. The wreck located about 30 yards directly off the pier is reported to be a small cargo vessel. It was blown up to clear access to the pier and no superstructure remains except for a 10-foot long section of the bow lying in 15 feet of water amongst widely scattered debris.

A second small wreck lies to the south of the Gugegwe pier wreck. It is a 60-foot long wooden vessel sunk upright in 60 feet of water with only two fuel tanks, the engine, and hull planking remaining. A nearly full case of small arms ammunition lies in the debris near the bow. Just forward of amidships, several blue-colored bottles with "Mineral Crystal Water" (in English) on their sides have been found along with a pile of 6-inch diameter round cobble stones that were used for ballast. A glass jar was recovered from the the wreck containing some Japanese sailor's sea shell collection. In 1978, four Samurai swords were located aft with the wood handles and sheaths intact; unfortunately, the blades had rusted away. An action photo from 4 December 1943 shows a small vessel anchored where this second wreck has been found. It was likely sunk on that date.

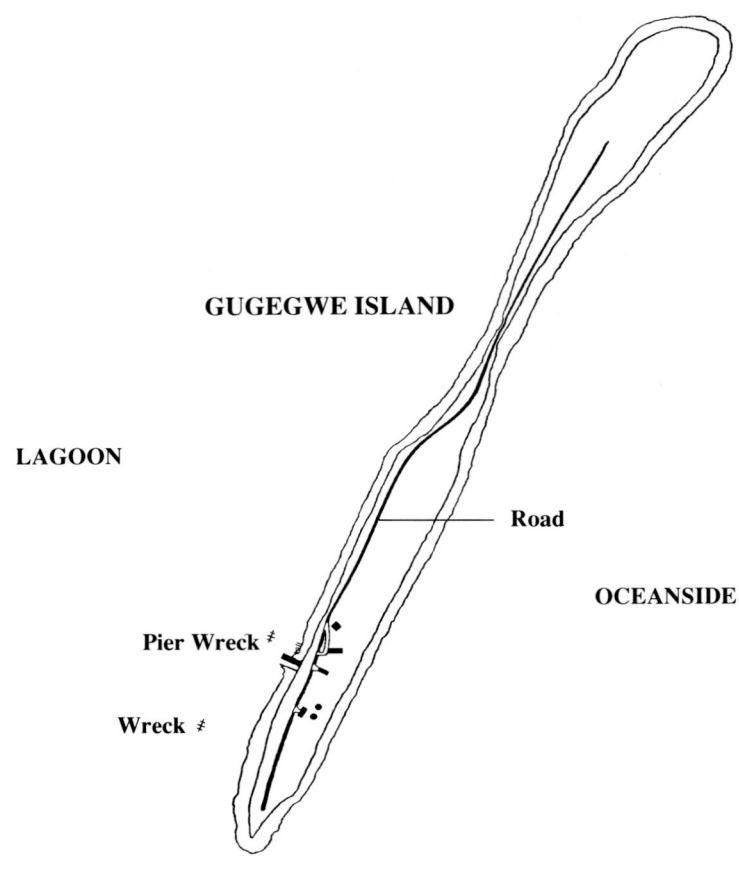

Wreck locations – north and central sections of Gugegwe Island.

The Shell Island Wrecks

The first wreck is located west-southwest of the pier on Shell (Ebwaj) Island. It lies upright on the lagoon bottom beyond the drop-off opposite the middle of the island in 110 feet of water. Photos taken on 31 January 1944 show the two-masted schooner-type vessel listing to the starboard and sinking. It was probably damaged and sunk by a combination of TF 58 aircraft and surface ships of the Southern Fire Support Group of Task Force 52. This vessel appears to be identical to the North Loi wreck. These craft were likely used as inter-island trading/supply vessels or fishing ketches. Both wrecks have two adjoining holds with offset circular hatches flanking their corners (two hatches are common with each hold, total of six). The holds are empty.

Another wreck is reported to be lying nearly 200 yards from shore in 130 feet of water almost directly to the west of the first. It is reported to be in good condition and approximately the same size as the other Shell Island wreck.

The Phantom Maru

The name "Phantom Maru" was given to this wreck because of the many unsuccessful attempts made by divers to search for and locate the vessel. It has a history of being found and then lost again. This 75- to 100-foot-long ship lies well out into the lagoon almost directly west of the northern tip of Loi Island. It was originally found during a fathometer search in 1967. The wreck lies upright on a 150-foot sandy bottom in an area where good visibility is the rule.

The superstructure is in good condition with the exception of the bow which has been bashed in and flattened. A machine gun is mounted on the bow. The vessel has one or two holds forward and amidships and an aft-engine configuration. The wheelhouse of the small bridge and crew's quarters are located near the stern. A second machine gun is reported to be located there. The wreck has been stripped of many brass artifacts and china. It appears that the vessel described was sunk along with several others in the southern Kwajalein lagoon between 29 January and 1 February 1944 by patrolling TF 58 aircraft and surface ship artillery. Not enough information is known about the ship to ascertain its identity. It is most likely one of the picket boats or auxiliary sub-chasers reported lost at Kwajalein.

–Naval Operational Archives Photo
Already damaged and smoking, a small ship off Gugegwe Island is being shelled by U.S. warships. A second vessel has been sunk just off the pier.

–Naval Operational Archives Photo
Photo taken by ENTERPRISE plane on 31 January 1944, 1600 h, shows small vessel listing and sinking southwest of the pier on Shell Island (southern section of Gugegwe Island).

The Bigej Coastal Tanker

On the morning of 31 January 1944, the cruiser SAN FRANCISCO and destroyer HARRISON were cruising off the southeast coast of Kwajalein Atoll as part of the Southern Support Group of Task Force 52. The SAN FRANCISCO was shelling Gugegwe Island while HARRISON was screening the CL about 4,000 yards to seaward. When a Japanese ship was spotted underway steaming north through the lagoon at 0846 h, the HARRISON was instructed to intercept the vessel described as a "coastal tanker of about 1,000 tons." The HARRISON sighted the enemy ship at 0853 h about 1,000 yards southwest of Bigej Island and opened fire at 6,000 yards range. The DD was forced to cease fire after two salvoes because the tanker dropped from sight behind the island. The HARRISON proceeded to the north of Bigej until the vessel was sighted once again. The observation plane from SAN FRANCISCO was in position to spot at this time and the HARRISON took the ship under fire again at 0912 h. The spotting plane reported at least three hits. A total of 153 rounds of 5-inch/38 AA ammunition were expended which were not effective in sinking the vessel quickly as they lacked penetration power, but the hits started fires along the whole length of the tanker. The target vessel offered no resistance and its crew attempted to beach it on the north tip

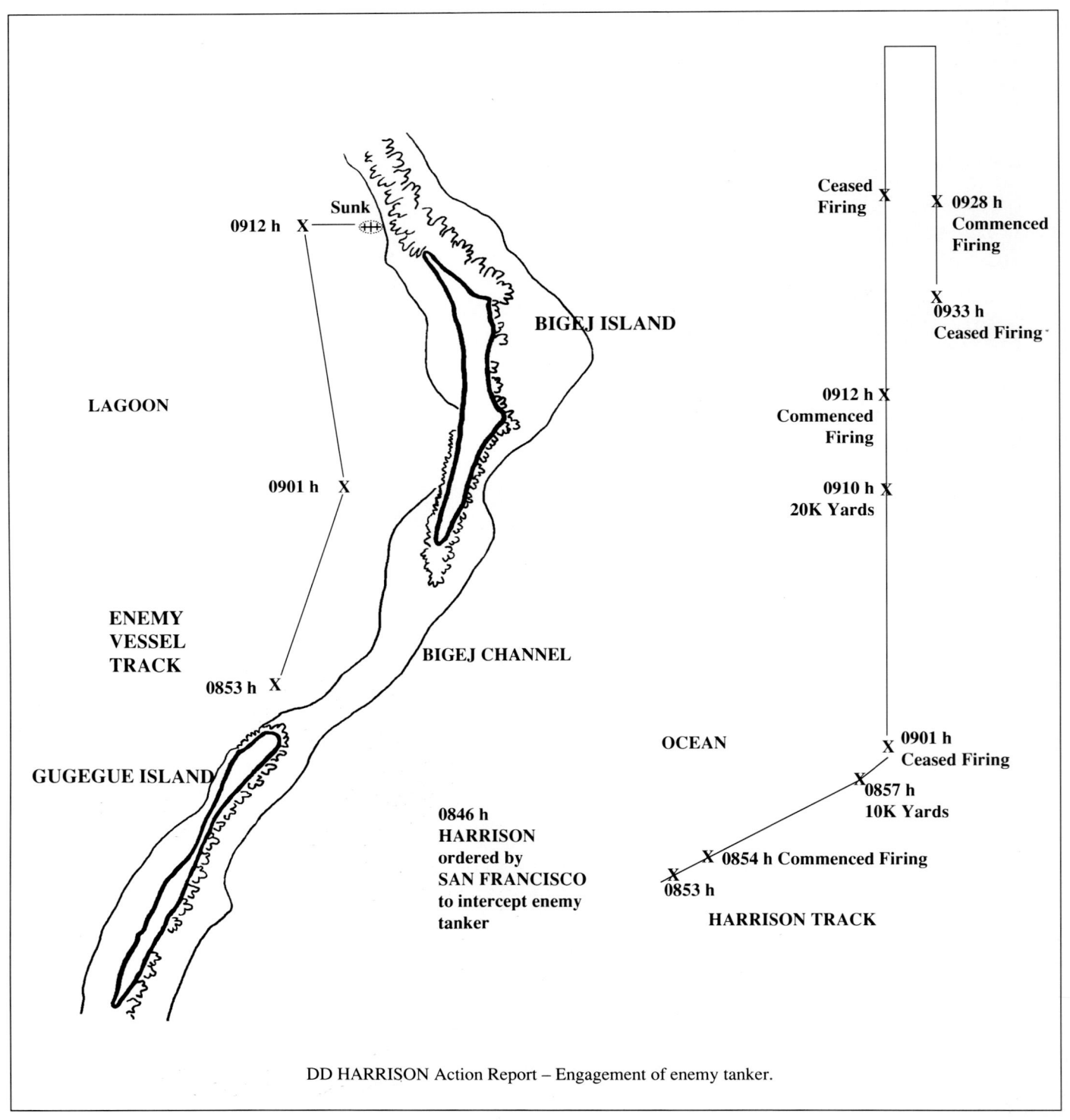

DD HARRISON Action Report – Engagement of enemy tanker.

of Bigej Island after the first hit. After firing was ceased at 0933 h, the tanker was observed to be smoking badly throughout, listing to starboard and sinking; her rigging was a mass of debris. The HARRISON returned to her screening position leaving the target vessel in a completely disabled condition. The tanker sank at 1039 h.

Few ships of the size described in the action above were afloat at Kwajalein by January 31st. The identification of the ship as a "coastal tanker" was probably based on its having an aft-engine configuration. Although not confirmed, it is believed that the vessel sunk by HARRISON was probably the 541-ton net-tender KATSURA MARU (known to have an aft-engine configuration) or possible the 723-ton KOTOBUKI MARU NO. 3, both of which were sunk on 31 January. It appears that a second ship, also with the name KATSURA MARU, was sunk at Eniwetok on the same day. The Eniwetok vessel, clearly shown in action photos, does not have an aft-engine configuration.

TECHNICAL SUMMARIES:

KATSURA MARU
Type: Net-Tender (Converted 1941)
Other Name: KATURA MARU (Kokutai spelling)
Configuration Sequence: Unknown
Gross Tonnage: 541 tons
Dimensions: 160/27.5/13.7 feet
Machinery: Aft-engines (oil), single screw, 80 NHP.
Radius: Unknown
Complement: Unknown
Built: 1938 by Sanoyasu Dock Goshi Kaisha, Osaka.
Owner: Setsuyo Syosen K.K.
Remarks: Assigned to 6th Base Force, Sub-Chaser Division No. 62.

KOTOBUKI MARU NO. 3
Type: Net-Tender (Converted 1941)
Configuration Sequence: Unknown
Gross Tonnage: 723 tons
Dimensions: 184/?/? feet
Machinery: Steam engines.
Built: 1936
Owner: Unknown
Remarks: Assigned to the 6th Base Force, Sub-Chaser Division 63. Sinking confirmed at Kwajalein by ULTRA information.

The South Pass Wreck

The latest Japanese wreck found at Kwajalein is nearly identical to the O-Buoy sub-chaser and is probably one of the 130-ton auxiliary sub-chasers, either CHA 18 or CHA 21, lost at Kwajalein. It was found in 1986 by Bevan Jacobs, Mike Mouris, Buck Jacobs, and Craig Wagner while searching for a spear fishing location along the west-side reef. The vessel is lying upright on the reef with her bow in 70 feet of water and the stern at 95 feet. Her location is approximately two-thirds of the way between the north end of Carlson and South Pass. The wreck is in better condition than that the O-Buoy sub-chaser wreck and is also 80 feet long, wooden hulled, and has a single screw. Oddly enough, the wheelhouse has also collapsed to the starboard side. Owing to the placement of the wreck against the sandy reef, searching for artifacts is very difficult as sand is replenished nearly as fast as one is able to clear it. The bow is most heavily covered with sand and the richest artifact areas corresponding to those which produced on the O-Buoy sub-chaser have hardly been explored. It appears that the vessel was on fire and driven towards the reef when it was attacked. Some human remains have been found aboard.

While not having been explored to the extent of the O-Buoy sub-chaser, this wreck has yielded additional "Fujikawa" china, brass locks and keys, swords, rifles, medicine bottles, many pieces of clothing, buttons, coins, and cases of unused machine gun shells. It is expected that divers for some years will be revealing her contents due to the rough water experienced on the west reef most of the year and to the sand shelf which refills every excavation with hourglass regularity.

The SHONAN MARU NO. 6

Long known to divers at Kwajalein as the Gehh tugboat wreck, the true identity of this vessel was not determined by clues found aboard the wreck, but instead by library research. In the early-1980's, former Kwajalein diver Neil Hurley found photographs of the wreck which clearly show it to be a SHONAN MARU-type with the number "42" painted on her side. It took a few more years before Neil found recently declassified documents which listed the identifying number 42 with SHONAN MARU NO. 6. The identity of the unknown wreck was solved; the vessel is the 356-ton auxiliary sub-chaser SHONAN MARU NO. 6.

The story of the SHONAN MARU NO. 6 involves aircraft, naval vessels, and infantry assault action, all of which revolve around tiny Gehh Island located just four islands north of Kwajalein Island on the western reef of the atoll. Built in 1938 as a commercial whaler, the SHONAN MARU NO. 6 was used as a whale killer in the South Pacific until June 1941. At that time, she was requisitioned by the Japanese Navy and underwent conversion to an auxiliary sub-chaser or "Tokusetsu Kusentei" (meaning "specially equipped sub-chaser"), by the Yokosuka Naval Arsenal. Among changes made to the 133-foot-long vessel was the addition of an 8cm gun and mount on the bow, the installation of a Type 92 7.7mm machine gun atop the bridge, and the fitting of a depth charge thrower and loading platform atop the main deck aft. Two depth charge dropping platforms were also installed on top of the fantail. In the ship's new role, she would have a complement of 38 crewmenbers. After the vessel was commissioned, she was assigned to the 4th Fleet and the 64th Guard Unit at Wotje. Her duties at this time were as follows:

(1) General patrol duty in the vicinity of Wotje with particular emphasis on anti-submarine (A/S) activities.
(2) Inspection of outlying islands within its area of cognizance, including occasional trips to Kwajalein, Jaluit, Majuro, etc. for supplies, refueling, and repairs.
(3) Escort duties to and from various islands of the Marshalls.

On January 30, 1944, circumstance found the SHONAN MARU NO. 6 at Kwajalein crossing the lagoon loaded with approximately 100 passengers and crew in an attempt to escape to another island in the lagoon or to Eniwetok. The passengers were most likely staff and service personnel from the base at Kwajalein Island. The vessel was disabled by bombing and strafing attacks by TF 58 planes and after it started to flood, the decision was made to beach the ship to give the passengers and crew a better chance of survival. As many of the men were scrambling over the side and wading the short distance to shore, another plane made a strafing run killing several in the shallow water. For the rest of the day, the survivors hid amongst the heavy brush and palm trees.

After night fell, some Japanese went back to the ship for food and supplies. At that time, they radioed the base at Kwajalein for assistance and a Daihatsu landing craft arrived later in the night with more supplies and weapons. During the night, some of the men slept ashore while others slept aboard the vessel.

The U.S.S. OVERTON and the MANLEY, both destroyer-transports, were tasked with the landing of troops to take Gea and Ninni Islands that flank Gea Pass. Once these islands were taken, the invasion fleet could enter the lagoon to perform amphibious assault operations safely. In the early morning darkness of the 31st, three platoons of the 7th Infantry Reconnaissance Troops in rubber boats attempted a landing on Ninni Island. Sea conditions were rough and visibility was poor, making identification of individual islands difficult. The Americans ended up landing on the north end of Gehh instead. While moving southeastward from the landing beach, the lead patrol almost immediately ran into six Japanese. In a short skirmish, four of the enemy were killed and the other two captured. The force pushed on across the island until they came upon the "beached ocean-going tug" and the landing craft. There were about a dozen dead Japanese floating in the water and more dead lying on the beach, all victims of the previous day's strafing attacks. The main body of Japanese had retreated inland after discovering that the Americans had landed but some were left aboard the tug. One Japanese was spotted aboard the vessel and an interpreter tried to persuade him to surrender. While this was going on, the commanding officer was sent a message informing him he was on the wrong island and was ordered to re-embark at once to the next island to the south. At this same time, four mortar men had found a small hut inland from the beach and upon investigating it were fired upon and forced to flee for safety with one man wounded. The mortar, mortar shells, and the rifle of the wounded man were left behind. As the troops were about to leave for Ninni, one of the Japanese "corpses" was found to be alive and conscious, though badly wounded. The Japanese indicated through an interpreter that there had been 50 men on the tug and pointed towards Ninni. As a result, it was assumed that most of the tug's crew had departed Gehh and only a 15 man infantry section with a single machine gun was left behind to guard the island and the tug while the rest of the force left for Ninni in six rubber boats accompanied by an LCVP. They arrived at 1130 h and by 1430 h had completely combed the island without finding any of the enemy.

The Ninni force was contacted at 1600 h that the guard force left behind was under heavy attack and that Japanese "were swarming all over the wrecked tug and the island." One infantryman was dead and another missing. No boats were available on Gehh or Ninni for retreat or reinforcement and the outnumbered troops were forced to remain where they were for the night. The destroyer OVERTON was directed to provide fire support before nightfall and took the lower part of the island and the tug under fire. Of the 57 rounds of 3-inch ammunition fired at the tug, three-quarters were direct hits and the rest near misses.

The large force of infantrymen did not attempt to land back on Gehh until the middle of the next day. Several of the landing barges got hung up on the reef and only one squad from the troop was put ashore to take over. They immediately reported an enemy force with two machine guns and that Japanese flags flew from a tall palm tree and the mast of the tug. As a result of these reports, the decision was made to not attempt further landings that day and the squad on the island set up a defensive position and waited until the next day for the remainder of the troops to arrive.

The surviving Japanese on Gehh had retreated to the island's center where they had formed a defensive position in a shallow trench by ringing it with a low coral rock parapet and then camouflaging it with a low-lying, elongated tent cover and palm fronds. In the morning of the third day of the operation, the rest of the 115 American troops landed on the north end of the island. Supported by searching fire from the OVERTON and four mortars, the three platoons advanced in a line until the left wing had reached that part of the island opposite the beached tugboat. At that point, the enemy opened up with heavy rifle and machine gun fire against the left center of the American force. The Japanese trench position was found to lie about 20 yards behind a long barren mound of earth, about five feet high and sloping at both ends. There were two machine guns in the trench which was now masked also by the dark shade of the tropical vegetation. When the troops reached the sides of the mound, the fire intensified and soon there was a battle raging with both sides firing rifles and machine guns. The Americans took several casualties. Heavy explosions rocked their positions and men were hit by steel fragments. This continued until a Japanese was seen rising from the top of a palm above the trench position and heaving something into the American lines. He was throwing the mortar shells which were left behind by the Americans two days before. The "tree bomber" was hastily dispatched and several other Japanese were killed in isolated actions, leaving only the Japanese in the trench. The troops began an all out assault on the trench with machine guns and grenades. As the Japanese manning the weapons in the trench were cut down, new gunners took their places and the bodies of the dead were stacked lengthwise across the front of the trench to provide more protection for those still inside. After nearly 40 grenades were thrown, the return fire reduced to a trickle. A bazooka team moved up and fired a rocket into the tent in the trench and the last two Japanese were flushed out. Machine guns quickly cut them down. Two more rockets were fired for good measure. The entire action had taken 45 minutes. When the troops examined the trench, they found 39 bullet-riddled corpses piled above the front of the trench plus another 26 in and around the position. Along the shore of the lagoon beach, 35 more Japanese dead were counted. When the troopers rowed out to the landing craft in rubber boats, 13 men were found dead; the tug held 12 more. Japanese losses totaled 114 killed and only 2 captured in the Gehh Island battle. The American troops lost 2 men and had 15 wounded.

Found on board the sub-chaser was a portfolio of approximately 75 secret Japanese hydrographic charts covering the Marshall and Caroline Islands, as well as selected charts of ports in the Bonins, the Marianas, and of major ports in Japan. In addition, other captured documents included a number of code books and recognition signals plus secret papers prepared by the Yokosuka Naval Arsenal documenting the vessel's conversion to an auxiliary sub-chaser. The material found aboard the vessel produced an intelligence windfall of incalculable value. The intelligence and navigational information detailing the lagoons and harbors of important Japanese bases was translated, redrafted and reproduced in short order. This data would be important to American ships participating in the CATCHPOLE operation against Eniwetok only 10 days later. Information on other areas in the Mandated Islands would be the first seen by the U.S. Hydrographic Office in over 100 years.

The wreck of the SHONAN MARU NO. 6 is easy to find as its 10- to 12-foot diameter boiler amidships protrudes above the water. The bow section is still recognizable in 3 to 4 feet of water but much of the rest of the vessel's hull has collapsed leaving twisted metal and debris lying on the seabed. The stern has somehow twisted around on the port side such that it now points in the same direction as the bow. The vessel's 4-bladed propeller lies against the bottom. The shelling by the OVERTON and the subsequent setting on fire of the vessel following removal of its charts and documents undoubtedly contributed

—Naval Operational Archives Photo

In photo taken by ENTERPRISE plane on January 31, 1944, American Troops (lower center of photo) have just landed and are making their way to the opposite side of Gehh Island to the beached landing craft and the SHONAN MARU NO. 6.

Converted sub-chaser SHONAN MARU NO. 6 and the Daihatsu Landing craft are beached on Gehh Island on January 31, 1944.

–Naval Operational Archives Photo

—Naval Operational Archives Photo
The SHONAN MARU NO. 6 was used as a commercial whaler before being requisitioned by the Japanese Navy. Note the harpoon gun on the bow and the stack markings of her owner, Nippon Suisan K.K.

to its poor condition today. Divers at one time found eight porthole rims lying free on the bottom around the wreck as the supporting structures had deteriorated. There is little of interest to see today; however, there may be artifacts beneath the wreckage. The remains of the Daihatsu landing craft are still present and a section can be seen above water also. It is my hope that the above narrative of the circumstances associated with the history of the SHONAN MARU NO. 6 will help the reader appreciate the significance of the wreck and the battle of Gehh Island.

TECHNICAL SUMMARY:

SHONAN MARU NO. 6
Other Name: SYONAN MARU NO. 6 (Kokutai spelling)
Type: Auxiliary Submarine Chaser (Converted), ex-Whaler
Configuration Sequence: M–F–M
Gross Tonnage: 356 tons
Dimensions: 133/27/15 feet
Machinery: Steam engines, single screw.
Radius: Unknown
Complement: 38
Built: 1938
Owner: Nippon Suisan K.K.

The Ships of Eller Island

February 6, 1944....this was a day when amphibious assault operations were in full swing on both the northern and the southern ends of the Kwajalein Atoll. The remaining Japanese shipping, now consisting of only small craft including picket boats, tugs, net-tenders, harbor craft, etc., was systematically being destroyed by patrolling aircraft and the guns of the American battleships, cruisers and destroyers. Three Japanese craft were spotted west of Legan and Eller Islands apparently attempting to escape; they were subjected to repeated bombing and strafing attacks by YORKTOWN planes and other air groups. The Japanese vessels made a run for the lagoon and apparently entered Ambo Channel before beaching their craft along the lagoon side of Eller Island. One or more of the vessels had been engaged in mine laying activities and were carrying a load of mines. Under continuous strafing attacks (YORKTOWN VT-5 planes made 15 strafing runs on the three boats), the Japanese decided to jettison their mines to prevent them from exploding aboard. At some point, the crewmen decided to take their chances ashore and 102 of them established a bivouac area and defensive positions around a Vicker's twin 40mm and a Navy Type 92 AA gun that they had removed from the beached vessels. Following a skirmish which lasted several hours, the Japanese were overcome by American LVTs, fire support from the destroyer HOEL, and infantry troops. The three vessels were then wired for demolition and blown up. The mines that had been jettisoned east of Eller Island were later reported removed by the U.S.S. REVENGE, group leader for the mine sweeping division which included YMS 383.

Today, these wrecks are visited very infrequently due to their being so far (24 miles) from Kwajalein Island up the western reef. The three wrecks lie almost in a line about 100 yards from shore where the reef drops off into deeper water. The southernmost wreck has two small sections sticking out of the water. This wreck appears to be a converted sub-chaser or a large picket boat-type craft lying on its starboard side. The ship lies at an angle against the reef with the stern propeller at 55 feet and the bow at 15 feet. There are open compartments within the interior of the vessel and exploration within has yielded

Diver looks over section of the southernmost wreck which rises steeply towards the surface.

Deck gun from one of the tugs sunk along Eller Island lies in the shallows.

some bottles, china, and even a small ship's telegraph. The vessel is in poor shape due to its demolition and heavy wave action. A smallish deck gun, heavily encrusted with hard fire coral, is mounted on the stern of the vessel. Once while trying to photograph the gun from below, I sank to the bottom along the stern railing where I was almost run over by a 10-foot-long nurse shark that exploded from its resting place beneath the hull in a cloud of sand. I had surprised the shark and just happened to have been blocking its only path to freedom. A second nurse shark of about 9 feet was later found lying against the side of the wreck amidships.

The second wreck lies approximately 500 yards north of the first. A portion of the bow and a part of the midship hull are exposed above the surface of the water. The ship lies on its starboard side and the winches located forward on the wreck with associated towing and cable handling gear indicate that this was once a tugboat. Ribbing from the ship's hull and other debris are scattered all around the stern; large fuel or ballast tanks lie amidships amongst the wreckage. The stern lies in about 30 feet of water and the bow in about 5 feet of water. No armament is visible on the wreck.

Approximately 150 yards further north, a second tug lies on its port side with its bow in 5 feet and stern in 40 feet of water. This tug also has two portions of the hull above water. It appears almost identical to the other tug. There is debris lying about all over the bottom near the bow and along the sides of the wreck. The bow gun and mount has fallen from the deck and lies on the bottom in shallow water. On our first visit to this wreck, we found a dark enclosed compartment inside the wreck which housed several large lobsters. We wasted no time in collecting same for dinner. On subsequent trips back to get more lobsters, we were thwarted by first a large moray eel which had either eaten or scared off the lobsters and secondly by an 8-foot nurse shark which had taken up residence with the lobsters.

A review of Japanese and U.S. assessments of shipping losses occurring on 6 February 1944 leads to some probable identities of these craft described above. The first vessel to the south is probably the 274-ton KIKYO MARU which is listed as a picket boat. The other two are most likely the 144- or 108-ton MEIHO MARU and the 135-ton FUJI MARU NO. 11. The MEIHO MARU is listed as a miscellaneous auxiliary and the FUJI MARU NO. 11 as a converted submarine chaser.

SOUTHERN ATOLL AIRCRAFT WRECKS

The Navy PV-1 Ventura

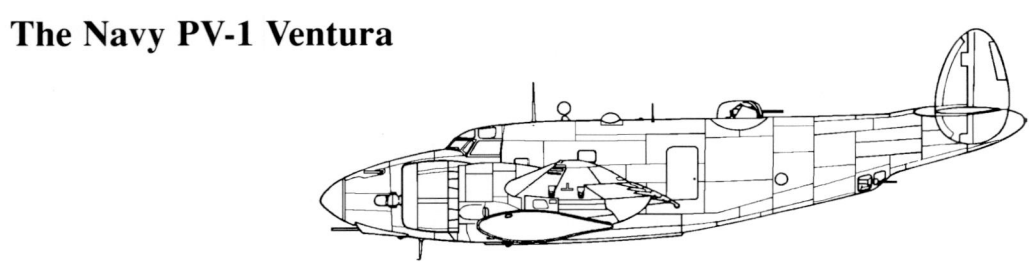

One day while boating along the west reef in 1967, Bill Remick and his father Harvey spotted a man-made object showing above water on the reef during a low tide. When they investigated, the remains of a twin-engine bomber were found in water from 2 to 20 feet deep. Metal structural pieces of the aircraft were strewn about the reef. The wreckage that had shown above water was a small turret sitting upright with two Browning .50 caliber machine guns still mounted. It was the size and shape of the turret and the Naval Bureau of Ordnance contract numbers on the electric gun chargers found on the weapons that lead to a tentative identification of the aircraft as a PV-1 Ventura. The exact location of the wreck cannot be remembered after all these years and searchers should concentrate in the area between north of Carlson Island and south of South Pass. Bill and his father removed the Brownings and later had a real interesting experience when the weapons (then disabled) were seized by customs agents when they tried to bring them into the U.S.

So little of the wreck likely remains today that positive identification of the aircraft type should center around the engines and propellers. PV-1's had a distinctive "paddle" propeller blade, much wider and shorter than standard propellers on similar aircraft. Serial numbers from identification plates on the engines also may allow researchers to identify the individual aircraft and possibly the date and cause of loss.

The PV-1 medium bomber was built as a land-based supplement to the PBY Catalinas for duty in the European and Pacific Theaters. This high-speed aircraft with a combat radius of 1,660 miles was used in sea patrol flights where it could carry 325- or 650-lb depth bombs or in strikes against land bases where 100-, 500-, or 1,000-lb bombs could be carried. When encountering Japanese fighter planes, it was known for outrunning them or if it couldn't, shooting them down. The plane carried a flight crew of 5–6 men and many aircraft were equipped with an ASD-1 radar housed in the nose.

Three PV-1 squadrons, VB-137, VB-142, and VB-144, began flying bombing attacks against Marshall Island bases from Tarawa after its capture by American forces in late 1943. The subject PV-1 may have been shot down over Kwajalein at that time or may have been lost later when VB-150 and VB-151 were operating from Kwajalein Island and VB-144 (July-September 1944) and then VB-133 (July 1944-early 1945) were deployed at Roi Island. These planes were utilized for sector searches, photo-reconnaissance, and frequent strikes against Japanese bases in the Marshalls while based in the Kwajalein Atoll.

Due to the generally inhospitable nature of the lagoon side of the west reef and the scarcity of "B" boats, the Remicks never returned to the wreck after salvaging the machine guns. Quite likely, the aircraft has set undisturbed since that time and may prove and interesting stop for divers in the future.

The OS2U Kingfisher Scout Planes

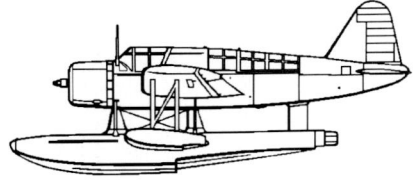

Two Kingfisher aircraft launched from U.S. naval ships were lost inside the lagoon in the southern end of the Kwajalein Atoll. It is not known if either plane was recovered. Its probable that both planes lie at the bottom of the lagoon and if so, these plane wrecks would be very interesting to discover and explore.

The first Kingfisher was launched from the cruiser U.S.S. MINNEAPOLIS on 1 February 1944 to spot for surface units bombarding Japanese installations on the islands. At approximately 1006 h, the plane flew into a line of fire from howitzers at Carlson Island firing on Japanese positions on Kwajalein and other islands. The plane was hit and was reported to have crashed at 1014 h nearly 3,000 to 4,000 yards east of Carlson Island. The plane was carrying an artillery spotter, Captain G.W. Tyson, and pilot Ensign W.J. Savers. Both men were lost in the crash.

The U.S.S. NEW MEXICO launched two Kingfisher spotting planes on the same day to relay topographical information and Japanese target locations to the battleship's gunners. One of them, piloted by Lt. Forney O. Fuqua with radioman 2nd Class Harrison D. Miller aboard, was hit by enemy AA fire at 1522 h over the lagoon. Fuqua was able to radio the ship: "Cockpit full of gasoline fumes....hit very badly....am making emergency landing...." Miller took over the controls and brought the damaged plane down towards the water where a landing was made but the plane overturned shortly after hitting the water. The American minesweeper YMS 383, operating inside the lagoon, rescued Miller who had gotten out of the plane and attached a line to the Kingfisher. The plane rapidly filled with water and sank with the pilot trapped inside the cockpit. The location of the plane when sunk was reported to be directly west of Loi Island.

The OS2U was classified as a single-engine, two-seat observation-scout float plane. The 33-foot, 10-inch long aircraft had a single float and could attain a maximum speed of 172 miles per hour. It was equipped with self-sealing fuel tanks and its crew was protected by 187-lbs of armor. It was utilized in a number of roles including spotting for naval gunfire, reconnaissance, anti-submarine patrol, attacks against shipping, and liaison. It could be operated from seaplane tenders, be catapult-launched from battleships and cruisers, or be deployed from shore bases. Armament consisted of one fixed forward-firing 0.3-inch Colt Browning machine gun with 500 rounds of ammunition and one flexible 0.3-inch gun with 600 rounds plus two 100-lb or 325-lb bombs.

The AAF Transport Plane

On July 23, 1944, an AAF transport plane took off from the airstrip on Kwajalein Island and crashed accidentally on the reef about one-half of the way between the northeastern tip of Kwajalein and Little Bustard. Eight officers and men were killed; no one escaped. Very little of the wreckage remains today due to the current and wave action in the shallow water. One landing gear is visible at low tide.

The Ebeye Seaplanes

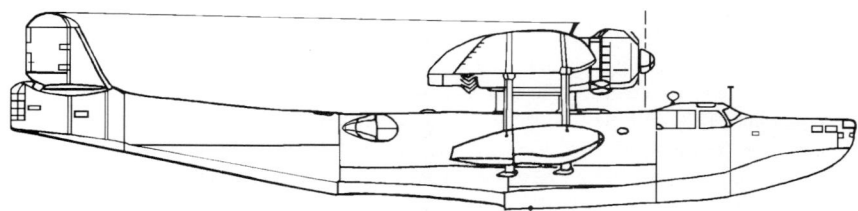

Mavis four-engine long range flying-boat.

Three large 4-engine Mavis flying boats (known as Kawanishi H6Ks) were located in 1965 by divers along the lagoon side of Ebeye Island. The first, and one best known to divers, is lying just north of the seaplane ramp along the drop-off into deeper water. This aircraft shows considerable damage due to the strafing and/or bombing attacks, but the body remains relatively intact. It is lying upside down on an 80-foot bottom. The tail section has been destroyed and the single parasol wing has separated from the struts on which it was mounted to the hull of the fuselage. The seaplane was moored when it was attacked and sunk; the mooring buoy is still attached to the underside hull of the aircraft but has been pulled down about 30 feet below the surface of the water. The tail section and aft third of the fuselage have been heavily damaged. There is little room for a diver to enter and maneuver within the interior of the aircraft. An elaborate high-backed seat and instrument panel can be seen in the cockpit when looking through the cabin windows from the exterior of the hull. The site of this wrecked flying-boat is a rather undesirable dive spot due to the raw sewage from nearby sewer pipe outlets.

The second Mavis reportedly lies on a 70-foot bottom directly offset from the center point between the seaplane ramp and the pier. It is also lying upside down and shows considerable structural damage. The third aircraft of this type lies just off the south end of Ebeye, also in 70 feet of water. It is reported to have been almost completely destroyed with little left intact.

Two of these Mavis flying-boats were likely the ones spotted and strafed repeatedly by ENTERPRISE planes during the initial attack on Kwajalein on February 1, 1942. The planes were reported to have been moored near shore in the aircraft action reports. The third Mavis was probably the one reported as afire from strafing attacks by YORKTOWN planes on December 4, 1943.

The Mavis flying-boats were characterized by their large size (80 feet long, 125-foot wing span, and 20-foot height) and design, which had been copied from American and French models. The large parasol wing with four engines was mounted above the hull on inverted-V struts and braced by parallel struts attached low on the hull and stretching to the half-span points on the wing. Known for its endurance, the aircraft had a normal 2,667 nautical mile and a maximum 3,656 nautical mile range. It had a maximum speed of 208 knots. Offensive armament could include up to two 800-kg (1,764-lb) torpedoes or up to 1,000-kg (2,205-lbs) of bombs attached to the parallel wing supporting struts. The defensive armament aboard the aircraft were in beam blisters which each contained a hand-held 7.7mm Type 92 machine gun, a turret housing in the bow with another Type 92 machine gun located immediately aft of the flight deck, and a flexible 20mm type 99 Model

–Naval Operational Archives Photo
Vertical photo of Ebeye Island shows Mavis flying-boat moored on lagoon side of the island on fire and 9 to 10 fighter seaplanes on the ramps and apron of the seaplane base. The hangar and repair shops appear undamaged.

1 cannon installed in the tail turret. The normal number of flight crew was nine; the modified transport versions carried a crew of eight and 10–18 passengers. Kawanishi Kokuki K.K. produced a total of 215 H6Ks between 1936 and 1943.

The Kawanishi H6K series of flying-boats were operated throughout the Pacific War as a long-range maritime reconnaissance aircraft, transport, and bomber. The Japanese Navy had 66 of these in operational service when the war began. The planes were used extensively in the Central and Southwest Pacific. Early in the war, these aircraft flew bombing missions against land targets in the Netherlands East Indies and at Rabaul. Losses in this role increased when Allied fighter aircraft were engaged as the Mavis lacked armor protection and self-sealing fuel tanks. The planes were soon withdrawn from bombing operations and restricted mainly to the maritime reconnaissance role. It proved to be invaluable with its long range capability in patrolling the vast expanses of the Pacific. The aircraft were also modified to perform transport duties. A version was developed with increased fuel tankage intended for military staff transport and use by the Kaiyo (Ocean) division of Dai Nippon Koku K.K. (Greater Japan Air Lines) for their Saigon-Bankok, Yokohama-Saipan-Palau-Timor, and Saipan-Truk-Ponape-Jaluit routes.

The remains of a single small float plane lies in shallow water near shore just about 50 yards south of the pier on Ebeye. The plane is in poor condition with its engine, wings, and pilot's seat intact but the rear portion of the fuselage aft of the single cockpit is missing. The type of plane is difficult to ascertain. Its likely that the single remaining seat and cockpit was the only one. If so, the plane was a Rufe float seaplane fighter (Nakajima A6M2-N). The Rufe was built for the

One of the Mitsubishi Kinsei fourteen-cylinder radial engines has separated from the Mavis and lies forward of the fuselage.

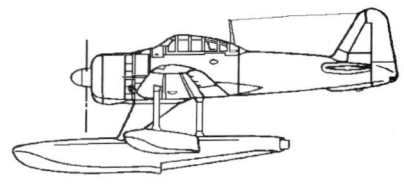

The Rufe Float Seaplane Fighter

Diver swims along wing of Kawanishi H6K Flying-boat (Mavis) towards pontoon, support structures, and guy wires.

Divers swim around nose section of large upside down Mavis seaplane off Ebeye Island.

Single-engine and single-seat float seaplane fighter in poor condition sunk in shallow water off Ebeye Island.

Japanese Navy to provide air cover during initial phases of amphibious landing operations and to serve on island bases where landing fields were not constructed. The Rufe's design was developed from that of the Zero fighter (Zeke) and a total of 327 were built by Nakajima Hikoki K.K. at Koizumi, Japan. It was armed with two wing-mounted 20mm cannon and two 7.7mm machine guns placed in the upper fuselage decking. It could carry two 60-kg (132-lb) bombs.

The Bigej Island Fighter-Bomber

On 1 February 1944, SAN FRANCISCO observers noted two "SBDs" diving on Bennet (Bigej) Island. The first "SBD" released several bombs causing a large explosion. The second, flying very close to the first, flew directly through the flames and smoke which extended several thousand feet into the air. The tail section of the second plane was seen to drop off as the plane emerged from the smoke and the aircraft tumbled end over end and crashed into the lagoon, sinking immediately. The observers reported that the plane was not on fire when it crashed.

The identity of the plane was established from the BELLEAU WOOD's aircraft action reports. The plane had been mis-identified as an SBD by the SAN FRANCISCO's observers: the two planes were actually F6Fs from Fighting Squadron 24 on a bombing support mission. The two fighter-bombers, piloted by Lt. Sours and Ensign Clem, strafed the north end of Bigej Island and then made a run on the ammunition dump in "area 342." The ammunition dump blew up as Clem's plane came down on it, spinning his plane into the lagoon with a shattered right wing and killing him.

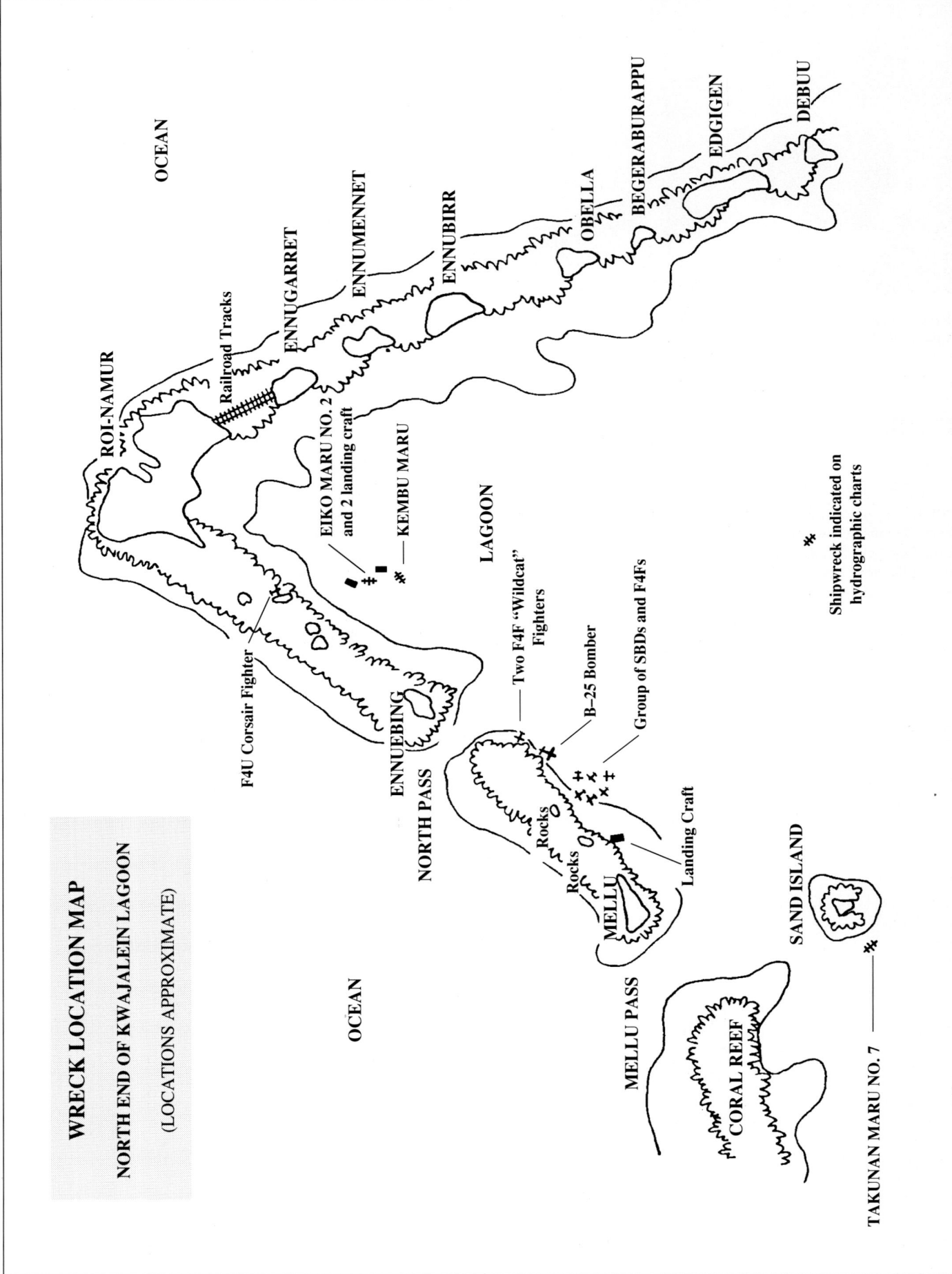

NORTHERN ATOLL WRECKS

The RO 60

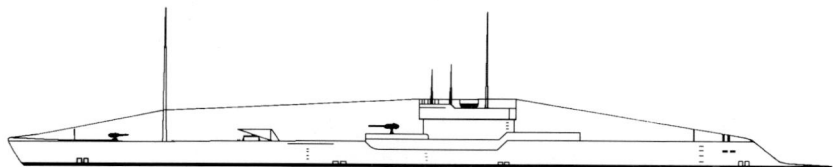

The shark was about 50 feet away swimming directly towards me. I was frozen with fear and a feeling of awe at the size of him. The massive tail was moving from side to side from far behind the head. I looked at the mouth of the shark to see if it was open or closed. I wanted it to be closed.

My snorkeling partner, Ken Fowler, and I had been sightseeing and searching for lobsters, shells, and bronze artifacts around the wreck of the RO 60, a Japanese submarine that had run aground on the reef. We were part of a party of six that had taken two Boston Whalers 14 miles from Roi-Namur to the site of the wreck of the submarine. We had earlier anchored our boats and swum against the current to the reef where we waded 200 yards to the forward section of the wreck. Part of the conditions we had accepted to allow us to make such a far trip out of the normal boating areas was the requirement that we had to contact the harbor control every hour and a half to let them know that we were O.K. It had come time to report in and Ken and I started towards the anchored Boston Whaler with the radio aboard. I was snorkeling in about three feet of water letting the current carry me towards the boats looking for bronze articles on the reef when I scanned ahead and saw the shark. I remember shaking my head and closing my eyes and saying to myself, "You really didn't see it; you're seeing things." The shark was no illusion! Its massive triangular-shaped head was nearly three feet wide. He appeared to be at least 15 feet long! I yelled to Ken in a very fastly-worded sentence that "There-is-a-huge-shark; get-to-the-boat-fast-but-don't-thrash-the-water." He needed little persuasion. When we got about 40 feet from the boat, I just had to stop and look again. Ken saw the great fish for the first time then. The shark was about 40 feet away and still swimming leisurely towards us. The sight of the shark plus my words, "I don't think we are going to make the boat" really spurred Ken into action and we both leaped out of the water like a pair of dolphins and dove into the bottom of the boat. The water on the surface was just choppy enough that we couldn't follow the whereabouts of the shark and when the other four members of our party snorkeled back to the boats later, the shark was gone. This period of time in the month of June was the height of shark activity in the atoll. Divers usually spot more numbers and more aggressive sharks during this part of the year. This particular summer, many huge sharks had been spotted including several monsters seen from aircraft flying between the islands. A couple of large sharks had been identified as tiger sharks, and I feel that the shark we saw near the wreck of the RO 60 was also a tiger. The sight of the great shark slowly swimming towards me in the shallow water with its huge tail moving to the sides is forever fixed in my memory.

The RO 60 was one of nine submarines (RO 60–68) of her class built by the Japanese between 1923 nad 1925. These 243-foot, 988-ton vessels did little to distinguish themselves during the war. The single ship, the AVP CASCO, sunk by RO 61 was the only vessel credited to any submarines in the RO 60 class. These old RO class submarines were highly vulnerable to attack. Besides having a practical safe diving depth of only 125 feet, the machinery was not reliable and the submarines most often couldn't stand up to the slightest concussion from depth charge attacks. Five of the RO 60 class submarines were lost during the war and the other four were scrapped.

The RO 60 must have grounded upon the reef due to a navigational error. A shallow water pass several hundred yards to the south of the wreck with a 15- to 20-foot high navigational marker must have been the intended route into the lagoon. The submarine, commanded by Lt. Commander Yasuo Fujimori, became stranded on the reef at 0200 h on December 9, 1941. The captain and entire crew were rescued by the submarine tender JINGEI at 1300 h.

Numerous 50-caliber bullets found lying on the reef amongst the wreckage indicate that the submarine was strafed either at the time of the attacks on the atoll or later when the U.S. forces occupied the atoll and someone felt that the torpedoes aboard posed a hazard. The submarine was blown in two when the torpedoes aboard blew up either due to set charges or the strafing attacks. The forward section lies near the center of the reef nearly 200 yards away from the stern section which still rests against the ocean side of the reef. The explosions which blew the submarine apart deposited parts of the vessel all over the reef. The conning tower lies nearly 150 yards away from the forward section; the deck gun lies another 50 yards away from it. Sheets of twisted metal lying in the shallow water act as hiding places for many lobsters (along with a few stray moray eels) and they can be collected easily. Very little remains intact in the 40-foot-long framework

Forward section of the RO 60 submarine lies in center of reef in shallow water.

Stern section lies on its starboard side against the reef where the submarine originally ran aground.

skeleton of the forward section. Many hatches, gauges, torpedo motors, and metal debris lie within its interior. Alongside are the remains of several torpedo tubes with the propellers of the exploded torpedoes still inside. Many interesting levers, gauges, handles, tools, and other bronze artifacts have been recovered from the wreck here.

The aft section of the RO 60 lies with its propellers and rudder up against the reef and its central portion pointing outwards to the ocean. It is fairly easy during low tide to climb to the top of the wreck where the wooden deck is still partially intact. Access to the interior is dangerous due to waves crashing against the wreck.

TECHNICAL SUMMARY:

Other Name: No 59 (Original)

Type: RO 60 Class (Vickers Type L4) Submarine
Displacement: 988 tons
Dimensions: 242.75/24.25/12.25 feet
Machinery: 2-shaft Vickers diesel and electric motors, 6,000 HP (diesel), 1,600 HP (electric).
Speed: 16 knots (diesel), 8 knots (electric).
Maximum Dive Depth: 195 feet
Radius: 5,500 miles at 10 knots (surface), 80 miles at 4 knots (electric).
Endurance Time: 20 days
Complement: 60
Armament: One 3-inch deck gun, 1 machine gun; six 21-inch bow torpedo tubes, 10 torpedoes.
Built: 1922 by Mitsubishi Zosensho, Kobe

The EIKO MARU NO. 2

My excitement increased as my dive partner, Harry Fitzpatrick, took his gloved hand and traced the outline of the hard-to-recognize lettering on the hull of the shipwreck we were diving on. Thoughts raced through my mind as I remembered the nearly 100 dives I'd made on this wreck without knowing its identity. Now at long last, by scraping and rubbing away marine growth that had been built up on the hull after 32 years of submersion, we were able to make out the letters E–I–K–O with the MARU suffix behind. We were making a dive alongside the hull near the bow section of the "1st Ship" as she is known to members of the Roi-Namur Dolphins. I had decided to make a concerted effort to find out the name of this ship that I had visited regularly over the previous four years. Clues to the vessel's identity were found on earlier dives when we recognized stack markings and found china with the flag symbol of the owner, Mitsui Bussan Kaisha, but now we finally knew the ship's name for certain.

The 3,535-ton transport EIKO MARU NO. 2 was heavily damaged and left floating low in the water by Task Force 50 carrier aircraft on the early morning raid on December 4, 1943. Photos of the Roi anchorage on that date do not show the EIKO MARU NO. 2 present at that time. She is anchored at Roi in pictures taken in January, however. It is my belief that the EIKO MARU NO. 2 was damaged at the Kwajalein Island anchorage and that she was towed to Roi possibly in preparation for being towed to Truk or back to Japan. There was indeed a decoded dispatch from the 4th Fleet command directing that the EIKO MARU NO. 2 or KENSHO MARU, which was damaged on 24 December, be towed to the Empire. The KENSHO MARU was towed as far as Truk. The EIKO MARU NO. 2 may have been too severely damaged to allow it to be towed. On 29 January, the battleship NORTH CAROLINA maneuvered to a point off the western coast of Roi to bombard certain shore installations on both Roi and Namur Islands. The EIKO MARU NO. 2 was spotted and at 1818 h was reported to have fired on the NORTH CAROLINA. The Japanese ship was taken under fire one minute later with the main battery at a range of 23,500 yards. A direct hit was observed on the second salvo and after the BB fired 16 more rounds, the ship was seen to receive hits on the bow and stern and was burning furiously. The ship was observed firing AA machine gun fire at the plane which was spotting for the BB. At 1850 h, the secondary battery opened fire at 17,000 yards and the ship was enveloped by large fires and explosions along her entire length. Fire was transferred to the shore installation objectives at that time. The following day, reports were received that the Japanese ship had sunk in the same location with only her masts above the water.

The wreck of the EIKO MARU NO. 2 is popular for diving due to its being sunk in fairly shallow water plus its close proximity to shore. Often, divers working on Roi-Namur would leave work at lunch time, ride their bikes to the marina, assemble their diving gear, make a short Boston Whaler boat ride to the wreck for a 30-minute dive, return, and get back to work in less than an hour and a half. Where else on earth can you dive on a shipwreck during your lunch break? The EIKO MARU NO. 2 has provided many memorable experiences to the divers at Roi-Namur who have come and gone over the years since diving became available there.

Another attraction of the wreck is the varied fish life that can be found at one time or another. When you first enter the water, you might draw several inquisitive barracuda to you or a passing shark or two. It is very disconcerting to get a feeling you are being watched causing you to turn around to look a barracuda in the eye, or rather the mouth, at a distance of 2 to 3 feet. In several instances also, groups of 3- to 4-foot-long black-barred grey sharks have made repeated passes at divers descending to the wreck below. I have found that sharks and barracudas normally stay away from the immediate vicinity of the wrecks. Encounters with them usually occur when you are first entering the water or when returning to the anchored boat above the wreck. Other fish life are attracted to the wreck and many angel and butterfly fishes can always be found there. I fondly remember a large batfish which would immediately swim over to us when we encountered him. He would follow us throughout our dives and always acted like a ham wanting his picture taken. Often both small and large rays of various types can be seen gliding by also. Turtles are often found near the wreck where they utilize the shelter afforded them.

Box of ready ammunition is positioned aft of bow gun on raised gun platform.

Divers attach another lift-bag in coordinated effort to raise heavy depth finder from the bottom of the lagoon.

A 3-inch deck gun is mounted on the bow at a depth of 50 feet. You can look over the edge of the bow railing here and see the anchor chain extending off into the blue haze towards a U.S. landing craft lying upright on the bottom of the lagoon below. The forecastle was used as a storage area for tools, hoses, ropes, and cables. The room can be entered from either of two doors, one on the starboard or one on the port side. After entering the room, you can take a "tour" by swimming forward, skirting the chain locker positioned in the forward center of the room, and return along the opposite side. There is just enough light to see where you are going but care must be taken not to stir up the deep muck on the floor as visibility can be lost easily. A large spare anchor is mounted against the bulkhead just below the starboard entrance to the forecastle.

The No. 1 hold contains piles of 50-gallon drums, most of which are crushed due to pressure. The plating on the port side of the hold has a large hole; it appears that this was the location of a hit by the large naval guns of the NORTH CAROLINA. Several motorized barges which had been connected together sank with the ship and lie across the No. 2 hold with two of them hanging over the port side down to the seabed. A large towing barge lies on the floor of the lagoon on the opposite side of the wreck.

The bridge was gutted by fire before the ship sunk. Bullet holes from strafing attacks are everywhere. The next deck below the wheelhouse served as a radio room. The scattered remains of all the radio equipment lies on the floor of the compartment. On one occasion, I made the mistake of getting between a 400- to 500-lb grouper that had been spooked by a diver approaching the room from the opposite side of the wreck and the only exit out. He just basically bulled me aside leaving me shaking like a leaf. These huge groupers were often seen around the wreck and tended to leave the area after encountering divers. The rooms at main deck level can be entered through two doors on the aft side of the superstructure. This area contained a pharmacy, latrine, and storage space; the partitions separating the individual areas are gone. The muck here is over a foot thick in most places and searchers have found hundreds of bottles, medicines enclosed in glass tubes, medical instruments, and an unopened case of serving platters with the Mitsui flag symbol on them.

The No. 3 hold can be entered just aft of the mid-ship superstructure. After swimming downward through steel hatch cover beams, you come to the first level of the hold which extends forward beneath the raised superstructure above. This area contains many interesting things including the remains of one of the ship's crew alongside a coal space. The skull has a bullet hole in the center of the forehead; he apparently committed hara-kiri by shooting himself with a rifle which was found lying nearby. He most likely figured that killing himself was the best way out after being trapped below decks with the ship on fire and sinking from the heavy bombardment being directed at the ship by the NORTH CAROLINA. Next to the large pile of coal, a 3-foot-long box was found which contained a mortar, an associated optical device, and several mortar shells. After bringing the box to the surface, a distinct hissing noise could be heard being emitted from the mortar shells. Army ordnance engineers took one look at the shells and decided that the box should be deep-sixed. Two spare propeller blades are mounted on the forward bulkhead in the hold. A corridor to the rear leads to the upper catwalk landing in the engine room. The bottom level of the hold interconnects with the No. 2 hold. Here lies a maze of 50-gallon drums, an air compressor on wheels, and several other kinds of other unidentifiable equipment beneath the drums.

Entrance to the engine room can also be made through a large hole probably caused by a bomb hit. The engine room is divided into an upper and lower section separated by a steel-meshed partition. Both levels contain numerous catwalks, controls, gauges, and etc. Caution has to be exercised in going to the lower level. There is very little space to move around in and it is almost pitch black here. By swimming slowly and carefully skirting the twisted metal and machinery, you can make your way to the port side and exit through a large hole in the hull which undoubtedly had a lot to do with the ship's sinking.

A compartment on the port side of the extended cabin area above the engine room served as a crew's mess. Many dishes, bottles, and cups and saucers of various types have been found here. To the rear of this eating area, there are narrow corridors leading to small rooms with ovens and sinks. Several small storage and supply rooms were built into the rear part of the cabin area containing several types of beer and saki bottles plus cooking utensils. The No. 4 hold lies just beyond and like the others, contains many 50-gallon drums.

The poop has two levels of crew's quarters and more storage compartments. In the lower level, the skeletal remains of several of the crew can be found, casualties of the bomb or naval shell which put a huge hole in the port side of the stern.

An interesting dive can be made to the bottom at 110 feet near the stern. Here, just below the counter-shaped stern is the huge propeller and rudder. This location is used by many divemasters of the Roi-Namur Dolphins Scuba Club in giving the required 100-foot checkout dives to new divers. While searching the bottom near the stern for artifacts one day, I found what appeared to be a ship's telegraph lying on the bottom. It had evidently been knocked over the side when the ship went down. After organizing a crew of six divers and as many float bags, the 300-lb "telegraph" was floated to the surface and towed ashore. After knocking away much of the coral growth that had accumulated over the years, it was found to actually be a sounding machine with a wound cable that could lower a weight to the bottom to check the depth of the water. A further search for artifacts near the stern area produced another U.S. landing craft about 50 yards away.

Following U.S. occupation of the atoll, the protruding masts of the ship were toppled along with the funnel as they were designated a menace to other ships. The funnel was blown at its base, causing it to fall over the starboard side where it now rests against the seabed.

Plaque recovered from binnacle of EIKO MARU NO. 2 shows trademark of Uraga Dock company indicating that the rudder stand and possibly the ship's hull were built by the company. Other information on the plaque reveals that the head office is in Tokyo with plants at Uraga and Yokohama. There is a serial number (2575) and the date stamped is June in the 14th year of the reign of Showa (which is the historical or eternal name of the emperor, Hirohito) or 1940.

Divers recovered official papers from the wreck at this time which identified it as the EIKO MARU NO. 2.

TECHNICAL SUMMARY:

Type: Cargo
Configuration Sequence: M–K–F–M
Gross Tonnage: 3,535 tons
Dimensions: 340/48/? feet
Machinery: Steam engines, single screw.
Radius: Unknown
Complement: Unknown
Built: 1940 by Tama Sanbashi Co., Ltd.
Owner: Mitsui Bussan Kaisha
    Taiyo Kogyo K.K. (previous)

The KEMBU MARU

My first opportunity to dive on the "2nd Ship" in the Roi-Namur anchorage came when I was asked to help attach a permanent buoy to the wreck. The location of the wreck had been marked with a temporary buoy after a visiting boat had found it with their depth finder. We found the temporary buoy approximately 500 yards southwest of the wreck of the EIKO MARU NO. 2. None of us knew what to expect as we descended following the temporary buoy line. The first thing I saw was a huge deck gun mounted on a platform on the bow of the upright wreck. A metal brace near the tip of the bow at 80 feet was picked for attaching the quarter-inch stainless steel cable that we would use for the permanent buoy line. We attached the cable to a plastic Japanese fishing float above on the surface. After we finished clamping the cable to the metal brace, my dive partner and I had a few minutes left for a cursory look at the rest of the ship. The deck aft of the forecastle was littered with piles of debris and twisted metal. A mast with a crosstree and several air scoop ventilators had been knocked over and were lying across the deck. We swam to the bridge and found walls caved in with huge metal support beams bowed inward. We were amazed and shocked at the destruction before us, but the biggest shock was yet to come. The whole rear section of the ship aft of the midship superstructure was gone. Nothing remained of the last 200 feet of the ship except for a pile of rubble on the lagoon floor. The metal ribbing and side hull plating plus the deck had been peeled back and were wrapped around the bridge. Amongst the side hull plates that were still intact, there were large buckles and upon examination, almost all the porthole rims showed cracks. It was pretty obvious that a tremendous explosion had occurred on board the vessel, and I felt that this must have been the ship documented by carrier pilots during their attacks on shipping in the Roi-Namur anchorage on December 4, 1943. At that time, the ship was described as "a large AK that had the appearance of an 8,000- to 10,000-ton cargo ship with high freeboard." After LEXINGTON planes had bombed and torpedoed the ship, it had become enveloped in fire and smoke along most of its topside. The vessel finally exploded with such force that debris was flung several thousand feet upwards and some pieces fell outside the lagoon. Columns of smoke were sent 10,000 feet into the air. The remainder of the ship sank.

Divers exploring the wreck often find that there is something in the water that produces burns. Usually they occur where straps, other scuba equipment, or clothes rub the skin. It appears that the natural body oils protect the skin from the caustic substance in the water and when these oils are rubbed away from an area on the skin, a burn results. I found that while diving on the wreck, my skin would start to tingle when I encountered the burning substance. The burns are not normally serious but in some cases did not go away for weeks. The caustic substance is present in the open water above the wreck and is really concentrated in the layers of silt and muck within the interior. The presence of this substance is probably the reason that few fish can be found in the wreck's vicinity. The only instance where a diver was seriously burned was when he removed a porthole rim and then dragged it with one arm through the deep muck. His arm had to be treated for second degree burns. Needless to say, we always took a shower with lots of soap after a dive on this wreck. Word spread about divers getting burned and from then on very little diving was done on the wreck. I feel that the burn-causing substance was probably the aviation gasoline that the ship was carrying when sunk.

As you approach the surface buoy to tie on the dive boat, the characteristic strong smell of fuel oil almost overwhelms you. No sign of the oil can be seen on the surface among the usual 1–2 foot waves. The deck gun below appears to be either a 5- or 6-inch variety mounted on a solid raised platform. Ammunition is stored beneath the gun. The heavy metal aft part of the gun platform has been bent directly downward due to a bomb exploding nearby or due to the explosion which sunk the ship. A small compartment to the left after you enter the port side entrance of the forecastle below served as a lantern locker and several have been found there. The large central room in the forecastle is almost barren; only a few cables and ropes were stored here. Some hand grenades and small arms ammunition can be found in one of the small storage compartments.

The No. 1 hold is empty except for a few pieces of lumber and two corroded cases of foodstuffs. A paravane or aileron used for sweeping mines and cutting their cables is lying on deck on the port side between the No. 1 and No. 2 holds. The No. 2 hold contains several 50-gallon drums which probably contained aviation gasoline for the planes on Roi.

The ship had a flying bridge and the ship's telegraph, wheel, rudderstand, and other equipment are lying on the deck almost completely covered by hardened muck containing the burn-producing substance. The ship's bell and two pairs of binoculars have been found here. A single room on the aft side of the wheelhouse served as a radio room and a pile of wiring and electronic equipment lies in a heap on the floor. Heavy bronze gun mounts lie on each side of the radio room on the upper deck. The guns are nowhere to be found and may have been blown off their mounts by the explosion. Rooms below the wheelhouse at the next deck level were probably the captain's quarters. A single urinal, bathtub, and remains of cabinets and drawers lie on the floor. The main deck compartments below can be entered through a single narrow entrance aft partially blocked by a 50-gallon drum with a 7-inch hole in its side. Once when starting to swim through this entrance, a huge moray eel stuck his head out of the hole in the barrel. His nasty disposition and full set of teeth discouraged us from entering the doorway. The entrance leads to a narrow passageway with compartments on the port side containing chop sticks, serving dishes, pots, and pans. The room opens up on the starboard side and was the location of the ship's mess. The roof has fallen such that there is only a couple of feet clearance between the roof and the deep layer of muck on the floor, leaving little room for a diver to maneuver.

The small hold aft of the midship superstructure contained more 50-gallon drums. Further aft, the two huge boilers are the only items you can identify amongst a veritable junkpile of silt-covered debris on

—National Archives Photo
Aircraft pulling away to right has just made a strafing run on the burning KEMBU MARU. Two smaller vessels can be seen at the left.

—Naval Operational Archives Photo
The KEMBU MARU explodes in the Roi-Namur anchorage. Namur Island is in the foreground.

the 125-foot seabed.

A fellow diver, Len Woronoff, and I decided to really put forth some effort to find out the identity of the wreck. While exploring a room one deck below the wheelhouse, we located a corroded strongbox. A few days later, we found a second strongbox in the radio room. We concentrated our efforts on the first strongbox, but attempts to remove it were in vain as it was fused to the wall and floor structure. The sides of the strongbox appeared to have been weakened due to the fire aboard and long-time immersion in salt water, so I decided to use a heavy hammer and chisel to break into it. After punching a 6-inch diameter hole in the side, I reached inside to find remains of several manuals or books. We salvaged as much as possible and took it ashore where we spent several hours separating the paper contents and laying them out to dry. The fire on board the ship had been so intense that the documents in the strongbox were burnt and singed around their outer edges. Our partial success with the first strongbox gave us the added incentive to work had at the recovery of the second. It turned out to be fused to the flooring also and it seemed impossible to recover the whole thing. I ended up using some steel bars to twist aside the riveted reinforcing straps enough to be able to reach inside where I found a single booklet about a half-inch thick containing nothing but 10 columns of 4-digit numbers.

It was some time before I had an opportunity to turn over the contents of the strongboxes to someone who could interpret what we'd found. The fragments of the documents found in the first strongbox included parts of three manual covers with the name of the ship printed in kanzi characters. The name was KEMBU MARU. The contents of the strongbox also included a collection of instruction, reference, and message coding manuals which may be indicative of those carried by merchantmen involved in fleet operations and support. A sampling of the manual titles are as follows:

Small Arms Manual For Civilians Working On Naval Vessels
Anti-Aircraft Gunnery Instruction
Action To Be Taken In Case Of Misfires
Manual Of Firing Instructions For Armed Merchant Vessels

完 — OWARI (END)

建 — KEM or KEN

武 — BU or MU

丸 — MARU

機 — KI

関 — KAN

配 — HAI

置 — CHI

Pieces of manual covers recovered from a strong box on "2nd Ship" at Roi-Namur provided the actual name of the ship, KEMBU MARU. The long strip at left translates to "Engine Displacement of KEMBU MARU." The other possible translations of the ship's name, KENBU, KEMMU, or KENMU were not used by the Japanese. References indicate that the KEMBU MARU was captured by the Japanese. The date, location, and circumstances of the capture are not known, nor is the previous name of the ship.

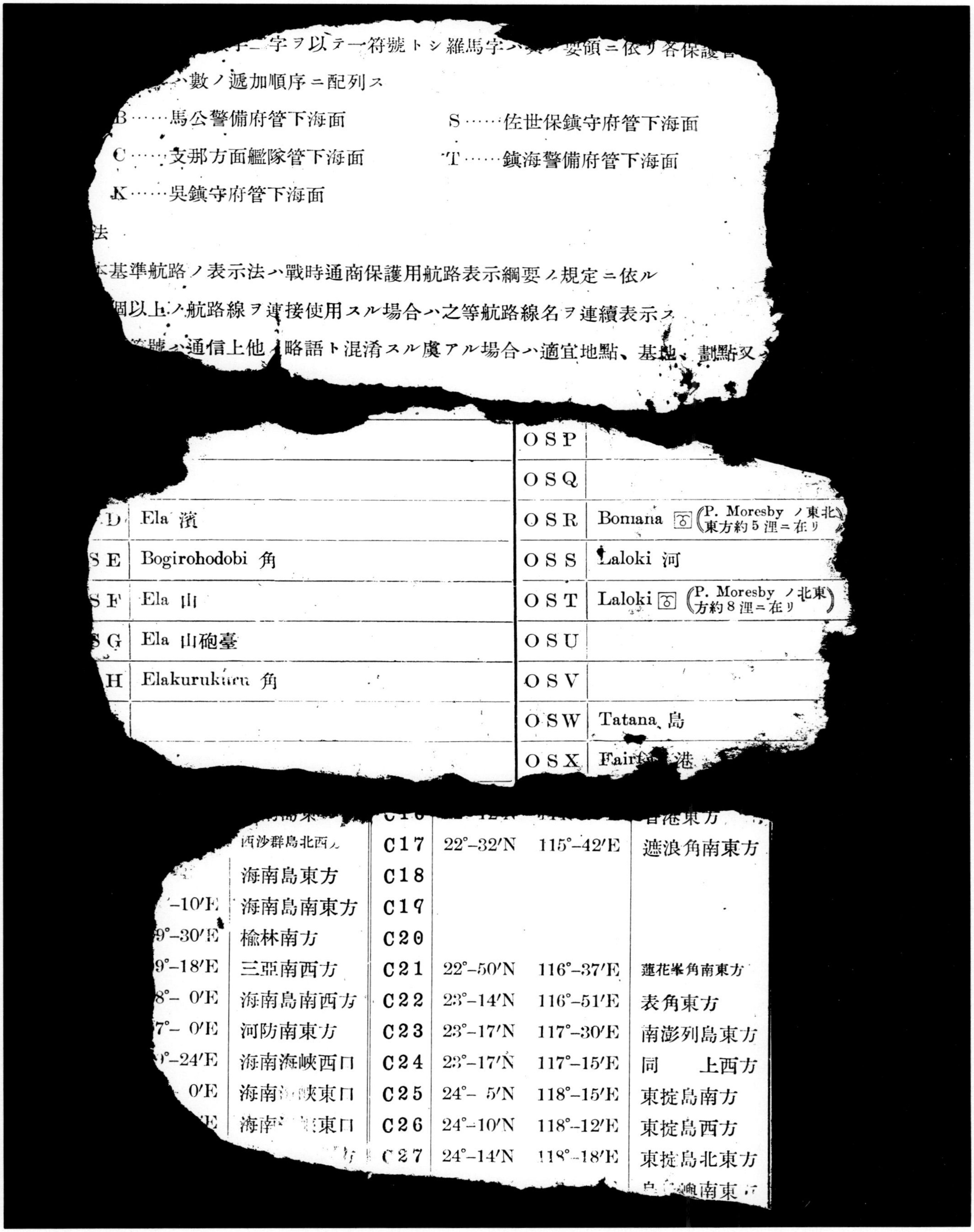

字ヲ以テ一符號トシ羅馬字ハ　要領ニ依リ各保護...
　　數ノ遞加順序ニ配列ス

B……馬公警備府管下海面　　　　S……佐世保鎮守府管下海面
C……支那方面艦隊管下海面　　　T……鎮海警備府管下海面
K……呉鎮守府管下海面

法

本基準航路ノ表示法ハ戰時通商保護用航路表示綱要ノ規定ニ依ル

個以上ノ航路線ヲ連接使用スル場合ハ之等航路線名ヲ連續表示ス

　　　　通信上他ノ略語ト混淆スル虞アル場合ハ適宜地點、基地、劃點又...

		OSP	
		OSQ	
D	Ela 濱	OSR	Bomana 〇 (P. Moresbyノ東北東方約5浬ニ在リ)
SE	Bogirohodobi 角	OSS	Laloki 河
SF	Ela 山	OST	Laloki 〇 (P. Moresbyノ北東方約8浬ニ在リ)
SG	Ela 山砲臺	OSU	
H	Elakurukuru 角	OSV	
		OSW	Tatana 島
		OSX	Fairfax 港

	島東	C16			香港東方
	西沙群島北西方	C17	22°–32′N	115°–42′E	遮浪角南東方
	海南島東方	C18			
–10′E	海南島南東方	C19			
9°–30′E	楡林南方	C20			
9°–18′E	三亞南西方	C21	22°–50′N	116°–37′E	蓮花峯角南東方
8°– 0′E	海南島南西方	C22	23°–14′N	116°–51′E	表角東方
7°– 0′E	河防南東方	C23	23°–17′N	117°–30′E	南澎列島東方
°–24′E	海南海峽西口	C24	23°–17′N	117°–15′E	同　　上西方
0′E	海南海峽東口	C25	24°– 5′N	118°–15′E	東掟島南方
	海南　峽東方	C26	24°–10′N	118°–12′E	東掟島西方
		C27	24°–14′N	118°–18′E	東掟島北東方

Fragments of documents found in strongbox aboard KEMBU MARU list identifier codes and locations of islands and other areas under specific naval district jurisdictions. Naval districts designated above include: **B** (Mako or Making in the Pescadore Islands), **C** (China), **K** (Kure), **S** (Sasebo), and **T** (Tinkai or Chinkai).

Large bow gun on platform – KEMBU MARU

Gunnery Instructions (for the deck gun)
Gunnery Manual Regarding Audio Detection Of Faults In Weapons.
Simplified Manual For Handling Of Torpedoes
Manual For Handling, Storage And Use Of Model 95 Depth
  Charges
Description Of Major Components, Outline Of Operation,
  And Methods Of Handling Depth Charges
Reference Document Concerning Depth Charge Engagements
  By Merchant Ships
Naval District Responsibility Chart (listing islands/ areas
  under specific naval district jurisdiction)
Navigational Instructions For Operation In The South China
  Sea
Instructions On Conduct Of Escort Ships In A Convoy
Tactical Methods Of Submarine Warfare As Opposed To
  Massive Naval Formations Against Enemy Shipping
Manual On Blackout Discipline Aboard Ship
U.S. Aircraft Recognition Manual
Instruction On Principles Of Defense

Instructions To Civilian Crew Members Of Ships Com-
  mandeered By The Navy Regarding Action To Be Taken
  In Combat Situations
Table Of Manning Requirements
Instructions On Semaphore
Brevity Codes

The code book found in the strongbox in the ship's radio room is thought to be the 4-digit code used by the Japanese to distribute information concerning the routes, timetables, and the origin and destination of convoys.

Reference documents indicate that the 6,816-ton KEMBU MARU was captured by the Japanese. No information is available regarding its previous history or circumstances under which it was captured. A gunsight telescope mounted on the forward deck gun had the following inscription:

G. S. Telescope X8
NEGRETTI & ZAMBRA
LONDON, 1917
No. 56

Markings on a lantern found included a "SEAHORSE" Great Britain trademark. The telescope (and gun itself) plus the lantern found aboard may be indicative that the ship was originally British.

TECHNICAL SUMMARY:

Other Name: TATEBU MARU
Type: Cargo
Configuration Sequence: M–F–M
Gross Tonnage: 6,816 tons
Dimensions: Unknown
Machinery: Unknown
Radius: Unknown
Complement: Unknown
Builder: Unknown
Owner: Unknown

The TAKUNAN MARU NO. 7

The wreck of the TAKUNAN MARU NO. 7 lies approximately 200 yards west of Sand Island along the west reef about three miles from Roi-Namur. Identification of the wreck has not been positively confirmed, but the location agrees with the sinking coordinates given by pilots of planes from LEXINGTON who sunk her and the combat photos which show the vessel on fire after entering the lagoon through Mellu Pass on the same date, December 4, 1943.

Originally a whaling vessel owned by the Japanese shipping company, Nippon Suisan Kaisha, the 343-ton TAKUNAN MARU NO. 7 was requisitioned by the Japanese Navy and converted into a submarine chaser in 1941. At the time of the outbreak of hostilities between the U.S. and Japan, she was assigned to Submarine Chaser Division 62 along with TAKUNAN MARU NO. 6 and net-tender KATSURA MARU with the 4th Mandate Fleet, 6th Base Force, at Kwajalein.

The wreck is unusual as almost all of the wooden hull and superstructure of the 135-foot-long vessel is gone, leaving only the engines, fuel tanks, and various equipment and debris lying on the sandy bottom of the lagoon at a depth of 90 feet. Several depth charges lie in the midst of the wreckage. Many bottles, navigational instruments, and other artifacts have been found on the seabed around the wreck. Two 6-foot-long anchors lie nearby.

TECHNICAL SUMMARY:

Type: Submarine Chaser (Converted 1941), ex-Whaler
Configuration Sequence: M–M–F
Gross Tonnage: 343 tons
Dimensions: 134.5/26.9/14 feet
Machinery: Aft-engines, single screw, 91 NHP
Radius: Unknown
Complement: Unknown
Built: 1937 by Osaka Iron Works, Ltd., Osaka
Owner: Nippon Suisan K.K., Tokyo
Remarks: Cruiser stern.

Diver inspects depth charges amongst wreckage of TAKUNAN MARU NO. 7

The West Reef Aircraft Wrecks

Of the many Japanese aircraft destroyed on the ground during the U.S. air strikes on Roi-Namur, very little remains of these planes except for some debris intermingled with other war-related wreckage which has been heaped off the southwest end of Roi Island into the shallows. The only recognizable portion of a Japanese aircraft is a wing section of a Val lying in about three feet of water off the end of the runway. Vals were used in the attack on Pearl Harbor and achieved considerable success in Japanese carrier operations against the Allies during the first 10 months of the war.

Several hundred yards from the end of the runway on Roi Island along the west reef lies the remains of an American-made F4U Corsair fighter plane. The aircraft crashed on the reef with tremendous force leaving it scattered in pieces in the shallow water adjacent to a coral head. It is not known whether the plane was lost during the fast carrier strikes on the atoll or if it was an operational loss following the capture of Roi-Namur. A squadron of corsairs, MAG-31, was based at Roi and deployed in conjunction with the Navy PV-1 Venturas which were involved in sector searches and bombing strikes against Japanese bases. In its day, the F4U was the finest carrier fighter used by the U.S. Navy. It was developed in 1938 and stayed in production for 11 years and was the last of the piston-engined fighters.

Further along the west reef from Roi-Namur between North Pass and Mellu Island, there are several types of partially-stripped U.S. World War II aircraft distributed on the bottom of the lagoon. The first of these aircraft lie just 50 yards from North Pass on a 90-foot bottom. Here, two Grumman F4F "Wildcat" fighters lie just a few yards apart along the drop-off into the lagoon. The engines and most of the instruments have been removed but the fuselages of the aircraft appear to be undamaged. During the war, the F4F was widely used against Japanese aircraft and proved to be a very capable and efficient interceptor. It was armed with six .50-caliber machine guns and could carry two 100-lb bombs.

Almost twice a year but never for long, the winds and wave action cease and the ocean and lagoon become like a mirror. It is possible during these periods to be able to look from a boat on the surface and see everything on the bottom below to depths of 100 feet or more. It was during one of these calm periods that we found a North American B-25 "Mitchell" medium bomber lying upside down on the bottom. The aircraft appears very clean as little marine growth is present on the aluminum skin of the body. We found the area where the B-25 was located to be an interesting dive location as there were usually several large sharks and barracudas nearby. Many other types of fish were present also.

The B-25 was easily adaptable to many tasks and its versatility and efficiency made it probably the best medium bomber of World War II. General Jimmy Doolittle's attack on Tokyo and other Japanese cities in 1942 was made by 16 B-25B Mitchells flown from the carrier HORNET nearly 800 miles away. During the war, these aircraft were utilized with many different bomb load configurations and turret arrangements. External adaptable racks allowed several combinations of bomb loads that could be used, including one which carried a 2,000-lb torpedo to be used against Japanese shipping.

Another group of aircraft can be found nearly two-thirds of the distance between North Pass and Mellu Island. These planes are

Divers inspect F4F that has had its engine and wings removed lying in 90 feet of water near North Pass.

Divers explore the B-25 Bomber.

Author looks over propeller separated from engine of F4U Corsair that crashed off the Roi-Namur runway.

Diver looks inside cockpit of SBD "Dauntless" dive bomber where coral has taken over. Note the two coral covered propeller blades in the forward seat.

distributed over an area of 100 yards or more and make up what could be described as an underwater museum of U.S. World War II carrier aircraft. In depths varying from 30 feet just where the drop-off into the lagoon begins to a depth of over 130 feet, there are nearly a dozen F4F fighters, Douglas SBD "Dauntless" dive bombers and possibly other types of aircraft. The planes were also partially stripped and dumped where they lie today by U.S. forces using a barge or landing craft. Like the other aircraft described previously, these show no external damage. The reason for their being dumped is unknown. These aircraft act as an artificial reef where only a sandy bottom previously existed. Various types of coral grow on the wrecks and the area has many fishes which find an abundant food supply and use the planes for shelter and protection from predators. Large and sometimes very curious grey reef sharks often swim by, stopping only long enough to circle the divers once or twice before leaving the area.

The two-seat SBDs were probably the most successful of all American dive bombers. It was armed with two flexible .50-caliber machine guns in the rear cockpit and two fixed forward-firing .30-caliber machine guns. Its chief load was 500-lb bombs, but in addition, other lighter bombs could be carried under the wings. The SBDs were the primary aircraft responsible for most of the damage leading to the sinking of the four Japanese carriers (AKAGI, KAGA, SORYU, and HIRYU) and the heavy cruiser MIKUMA during the Battle of Midway.

SBD with arresting hook visible lies upside down at 130 feet on the sand bottom.

The Mellu Island Landing Craft

A landing craft, probably an LVT, has been found approximately 200 yards from Mellu Island in the direction of Roi-Namur. It lies in about 10 to 15 feet of water against the bed of heavy coral growth along the top of the reef. The craft was probably one of those lost in the landings on the islands flanking Roi-Namur prior to its invasion. The steering controls and instrument panel are still recognizable within the landing craft. The machine gun has been removed but a lot of belted ammunition remains on the floor of the craft. The framework structure remaining is heavily covered with coral; nurse sharks often are found lying amongst the wreckage utilizing the shelter it provides.

Coral encrusted landing craft lies in shallow water on the reef near Mellu Island.

The Truk Lagoon Today

PART II

TRUK

Soon after passing over the coral reef encircling the Truk Lagoon in the Continental-Air Micronesia 727, the islands within the lagoon come into view with their jungle-like growth and green volcanic peaks. The setting is very picturesque and one can only imagine what its appearance would have been like when the Imperial Japanese Navy used the lagoon as an anchorage for the Fourth and later the Combined Fleet. The major fleet units, consisting of huge battleships, aircraft carriers and cruisers, must have made an imposing sight resting at anchor just off the large islands clustered within the lagoon.

World War II has provided the Trukese with an inheritance of numerous Japanese merchantmen, warship, and aircraft wrecks lying on the floor of the lagoon. This collection of war-related wrecks is one of the largest in the world and is an attraction that now draws over 1,000 scuba divers and snorkelers a year. The number of dive operators on island has increased to four; another provides a live-aboard vessel in the lagoon. These dive operators provide the necessary scuba tanks, equipment, and facilities to provide excellent rental, guiding, and boating services for divers. Visiting divers are invited to sightsee, explore, and photograph the wrecks but must not take or remove any artifacts found. The Truk legislature has declared the lagoon a historical monument and dictated a policy that forbids the removing of any artifacts or marine life from the wrecks. There is a fine and possible jail sentence for those who disobey this policy. It was the hope of those who created this legislation to create an underwater museum for all to see and enjoy for years to come.

Visitors to Truk Lagoon land on the runway next to the base of Mt. Tonachau on the island of Moen, the capital of Truk State. The meeting of the "island hopper" planes at the smallish Truk International Airport is always a scene of activity as crowds of islanders congregate when the flights arrive. A short drive down the main road past a modern school leads you to the real center of activity, the waterfront area. Here, Moen's population of slightly over 6,000 inhabitants swells each day as boats arrive in a continual stream with workers and visitors from the outer islands in the lagoon. Much buying, selling, and trading takes place here as copra, handicraft, fish, fruits, and other foodstuffs are brought here from other islands. Just inland from the waterfront area are the majority of stores, hotels, restaurants, and warehouses. The Economic Development Office, the Public and Marine Works (Fisheries) facilities and huge gasoline storage tanks are located in this area also.

A sign just off the main road points the way to the Blue Lagoon Dive Shop. This shop, under the management of Kimiuo Aisek, has become the primary source for equipment and diving-boating services for scuba divers. Kimiuo has pioneered much of the wreck diving at Truk and is responsible for expanding facilities, providing certified divers for underwater guides, and locating many of the Japanese World War II wrecks in the lagoon. He labored for the Japanese, loading and unloading merchantmen and warships, and observed some of the ships being sunk during the war as a young man of 17. Kimiuo is undoubtedly the most knowledgeable source for information on the wrecks of Truk.

Heading south along the coast of Moen Island, one passes a number of post-war American-built concrete structures and restored Japanese houses. Along the low-lands near the beaches, many small plywood houses dot the landscape with over-water outhouses nearby. The foliage and vegetation is prolific with coconut, banana, and even ivory nut trees distributed throughout the area. Mangroves grow along much of the water's edge. Breadfruit trees and taro patches, which supply most of the locally grown staples in the Trukese diet, are abundant.

Many reminders of the days of Japanese control remain including an old bullet-riddled lighthouse, numerous caves (some with guns still inside), and the Xavier High School which was once a Japanese

MAP OF THE TRUK LAGOON AND KUOP ATOLL

Coral runway on Moen Island in the Truk Lagoon (Truk Atoll, Eastern Caroline Islands), 1973.

Sunsets in the Truk Lagoon

communications center. The remains of several bunkers and a seaplane ramp can also be found near the site of the Continental Hotel located near the southern tip of Moen. Nearby Dublon Island, once a well built-up naval base with fleet headquarters and support facilities, supported a large Japanese community where trade stores, restaurants, and geisha houses once existed prior to the war. Today, the jungle-like growth has swallowed up much of their ruins. The remains of the hospital can still be found along with fuel and water storage tanks, and an occasional wooden post with Japanese inscriptions written on it. Many caves and tunnels are rumored to exist in the high cliffs and mountain sides on Dublon still filled with supplies, war materials, and ammunition; others reportedly contain hidden coastal defense and anti-aircraft gun installations.

There is little trouble in finding a guide for a tour of Eten Island; the local landowners are quite willing to oblige tourists for a few dollars. Trails lead from the pier on the northern end of the island towards the lone hill across what had once been the fighter airstrip and apron. Portions of the airstrip surfacing material still remain, but again the jungle is taking over everywhere. Located here is the ruins of a three-story Japanese air headquarters and communication center made of reinforced concrete with heavy steel doors and windows. Four other large concrete blockhouse structures can be found nearby including one which still contains steel mounts for a huge generator. The walls of these structures now are decorated with Trukese graffiti. A short but steep walk up to the top of Mt. Uinku leads to a large dual-purpose naval gun positioned to defend the islands from attack by air or by sea. Here, built into the protective stone walls, are entrances for a network of tunnels leading to the various defense installations and serving as protection from air attacks. The hilltop offers a fantastic view of most of the islands within the lagoon.

A trip to Param Island is rewarding. After disembarking from your boat on the northwest end of the island, one can walk a short way up the beach to a graveyard of Japanese World War II aircraft wrecks. The tangled wreckage of various types of fighters and bombers which had been damaged or destroyed by strafing and bombing attacks on the Param airfield are strewn 200 yards or more along the edge of the island.

A visitor should take time to sightsee and explore other islands within the lagoon. Most contain beautiful beaches and small villages and communities where islanders lead a simple life and derive much pleasure from taking it easy.

The Japanese have had a marked influence over the Trukese people beginning with their occupation of the islands following World War I. A great deal of Trukese-Japanese intermarriage occurred and it is highly evident in the facial characteristics of the people; many of the family names are Japanese in origin. The introduction of rice to the Trukese has made it the primary staple in their diet supplanting breadfruit and taro.

American influence on the life styles of the Trukese is noticeably apparent as more of the islanders have taken jobs to make money for buying items such as boats, motors, cars, and imported food products which line the shelves of the local stores. More young Trukese are having the opportunity to be educated in American colleges and are returning with new values and ideas.

The feelings of the Trukese concerning their future are upbeat. After uniting with Yap, Kosrae, and Pohnpei into the Federated States of Micronesia and entering into a new compact of free association with the United States, the people of Truk are working towards establishing their own destiny through self-government.

Since tourism has drastically increased in recent years, more and more visitors are seeing what Truk is all about. You don't have to be a diver or a World War II historian to enjoy what Truk has to offer. Just meeting the people is worthwhile and once a person has experienced the incredible beauty of the islands and observed the sunsets across the lagoon, Truk can become a part of you and definitely a place you'll want to return to.

Pieces and sections of Japanese aircraft destroyed on the Param airfield and periphery have been dumped along the beach.

Mysterious Truk

During the amphibious assaults and neutralization strikes against important advanced bases in the Gilberts and Marshalls, the U.S. forces were rapidly built up to mount a major offensive against Japanese strategic positions and essential supply lines in continuing to advance westward through the central Pacific towards the Japanese homeland. Truk was high on the list of priority targets because of its strategic importance in the Japanese outer defense system. It served as a vital staging point for air and sea communications between Japan and the Bismark Archipelago, the Solomons, and New Guinea. Units of the Fourth and the Combined Fleet had sailed from Truk to attack Allied forces in the battles of the Eastern Solomons, Santa Cruz Islands, and Guadalcanal. Air and sea power from Truk were also a definite threat against any projected U.S. operations against Saipan and the Marianas to the north.

Americans tended to over-emphasize the strength of this major Japanese naval base. Because Truk had been sealed off from outsiders for nearly a quarter of a century and with the uncertainty as to its geography and the extent of development of its defenses, it was held in awe and was thought of as a mysterious and formidable fortress. It became a gnawing mental hazard to the carrier aircraft pilots who felt it would be suicide to fly over it with its heavily fortified volcanic islands and hidden guns, thousands of planes, and ships of the Combined Fleet including the "super battleships" YAMATO and MUSASHI. With the buildup in the minds of the naval planners and media, it is not surprising that descriptions would be conferred on Truk as "the impregnable bastion of the Pacific," "Japan's Pearl Harbor," and "Japan's Mid-Pacific Gibraltar."

Plans were formulated for strikes against the Truk Atoll on February 16 and 17, 1944, to be coordinated with an amphibious assault on Eniwetok and the encirclement of Rabaul. The code name for this first strike on Truk was called "Operation HAILSTONE." A formidable high-speed fleet with tremendous striking power was assembled and sailed from our new bases in the Marshalls in one of the most secret operations that the Navy had ever attempted. The destination and intentions of the assembled forces were kept a secret until the fleet was steaming well on its way. When the news of the objective and the hoped-for surface battle against the Japanese Combined Fleet was spread, everyone involved was enveloped with feelings of excitement and anxiety; never before had the Navy gambled for such high stakes.

Truk first came under Japan's control shortly after the start of World War I in 1914 when it was taken from Germany. Situated near the geographical center of Micronesia, Truk was the capital of the Carolines under both German and Japanese rule. During the Versailles Conference in 1922, Japan argued that they were now her possessions. Japan was compelled to hold the islands under a mandate by the League of Nations. She was required to adhere to restrictions concerning the islands and was instructed not to fortify them. The Japanese made no attempt to fortify Truk for some time even after she withdrew from the League of Nations, but did begin developing a large navy which would eventually utilize Truk as its most important advanced naval base.

With its natural geographical characteristics, Truk was potentially one of the greatest naval bases in the Pacific. The lagoon is encircled by an outer coral reef approximately 140 miles in circumference and has approximately 245 islets. There are five navigable passes into the 40-mile diameter lagoon where there are volcanic islands with peaks up to 1,500 feet high. The maximum depth is 300 feet inside the lagoon and even with the hazardous coral heads, it provided a natural anchorage that could accommodate the entire Japanese fleet. There was little the Japanese could do to add to the natural defenses that the atoll provided. Naval gunfire from outside the reef couldn't effectively reach either the islands or the fleet anchorage within the lagoon. Ships mounting a surface attack would have to enter through passes which were protected by strongly defended islands flanking the passes on the outer reef and it was impossible to cross the reef in assault boats. Without charts of the lagoon, navigation would be extremely hazardous. The nearest entrance pass to the most important islands of Moen, Dublon, and Eten was Northeast Pass which was heavily mined. The high stone cliffs on the islands served as natural fortifications.

Truk Naval Operations

The naval base at Truk was very important to the Japanese as it functioned as the main fleet anchorage in the Central Pacific. Occupying a central and strategic position in the Carolines and situated midway between Saipan and Rabaul, Truk served as an advance base in support of most Japanese naval operations. It became the naval and defense headquarters of the Carolines area. Because of a limited budget, Japan's policy was to put available funds into the large mobile fleet itself instead of developing Truk into a first class naval base and adding the necessary defensive installations that would be needed to protect it. After July 1942, the Combined Fleet or "Rengo Kantai," consisting of ships of the First, Second, and Third Fleets, along with the Sixth Submarine Fleet, operated extensively out of Truk. The Combined Fleet was originally under the command of Admiral Isoroku Yamamoto whose flagship was the battleship MUSASHI. The Combined Fleet normally operated between Truk and Rabaul and would return to Japan for drydocking, overhaul, and personnel replacement. In Truk, the fleet replenished and rested at anchor. When Admiral Yamamoto was killed, Admiral Mineichi Koga took command of the Combined Fleet, retaining MUSASHI as flagship. Fleet units consisted of approximately 4 battleships, 4 aircraft carriers, 12 cruisers, and many destroyers. The primary anchorage for Combined Fleet units at Truk was west and southwest of Moen; it was known as Uola Road. Vice Admiral Takeo Takagi was the commander of the Sixth Submarine Fleet; his flagship was the submarine tender HEIAN MARU. The Sixth Submarine Fleet units conducted operations over a wide expanse of ocean from Australia to Hawaiian waters and beyond to the west coast of the United States. The Fourth Mandate Fleet was organized on 15 November 1939 as a Holding Force in the Central Pacific Fleet organization under orders of the Combined Fleet. Its primary mission was to protect the Mandated Islands area. Under command of the Fourth Fleet was the Fourth Base Force at Truk, which controlled all naval garrisons and installations in the Caroline Islands. In command was Vice Admiral Hitoshi Kobayashi who was replaced on 18 February 1944 by Vice Admiral Chuichi Hara.

Five airstrips and seaplane bases were built on major islands at Truk and work was started on clearing trees for a fighter strip on Mesagon Island, one of the outer reef islands. Aircraft flown directly from Japan often used Truk as a staging point to other bases such as Rabaul, Kwajalein (Roi Island), Ponape, Maloelap (Taroa Island), Wotje, Ocean Island, Nauru, and the Gilberts. Aircraft carriers occasionally unloaded planes to be ferried to their designated base destinations from Truk.

Mine fields in the passes and lagoon in conjunction with small beach defense mines were considered to be the main defensive weapons against invasion. All passes at Truk were heavily mined except North and South Passes which were used by the Japanese. Controlled mines were placed in North Pass. These were deployed in two rows, with six mines in each row spaced about 160 meters apart. In between the two rows were underwater detector coils designated to monitor and detect the passage of ships over them. The listening station on Tonelik Island opposite the pass utilized a continuous paper-tape recorder for each detector coil and could control detonation of the mines via underwater cables. The Japanese mined Northeast Pass which had previously been the long-time primary pass for entering and leaving the lagoon. Several rows of acoustic mines were laid in an area reaching from just outside the pass to well within the lagoon to prevent any enemy submarine or surface ships from entering. Piannu Pass to the west of the atoll was also especially heavily mined. More magnetic detection units were placed inside the entrance to South Pass which became the main route for the Japanese in and out of the atoll.

As the war progressed, more naval personnel were sent to Truk and four more Naval Guard Forces were formed and assigned to various islands. These included the 43rd, 47th, 48th, and 49th Naval Guard Forces. Five defense districts were formed where the Navy had the responsibility of surface and air defense. These districts with their naval commanders and Naval Guard Force components were formed as follows:

Defense District	Naval Commander	Guard Force
Moen (Includes Falo Island)	Capt. Yoshimitsu Imazato	47th
Dublon (Includes Eten Island)	Rear Admiral Hiroshi Kojima	41st
Uman	Rear Admiral Tomotaru Miura	49th
Fefan (Includes Param Island)	Capt. Furuya Yoshiro	48th
Western (Hq. on South Tol)	Rear Admiral Hiroshi Kozima	43rd

In early 1944, the Japanese began building up Truk's defenses in preparation for an expected invasion by U.S. forces. At this time, the navy placed anti-submarine and anti-torpedo nets around dock areas and certain anchorages. The coastal defenses and AA installations were also increased significantly. Over eighty 25mm and twenty 12cm AA gun emplacements along with many smaller caliber guns were positioned on islets on the reef around the atoll. Many rocket launchers were brought in from Japan. After being virtually cut-off from Japan, the navy began to improvise defensive weapons. Among these were the one-man torpedo (Kaiten) units on outlying islets intended for use in night-time suicide attacks against Allied shipping that might be in the lagoon during an amphibious assault. There were a total of 13 of these controlled torpedo raiding force bases planned on 12 islands. Secondly, the Japanese modified the standard 50-foot Daihatsu landing craft to carry two torpedoes and began to build torpedo-boat stations on Moen, Uman (3), Udot, and Tol (2).

MAJOR ISLAND INSTALLATIONS
Dublon Island

The naval base had been established on Dublon Island in November 1940 and originally included one headquarters building, eight barracks, five garages, and one sick bay. The Fourth Fleet headquarters was built in November 1943 and consisted of a large centralized concrete building, three other large frame construction buildings, and nine smaller ones. Facilities and installations were manned by the 41st Naval Guard Unit. The Fourth Fleet Navy Hospital was constructed on the northern peninsula. It had facilities to care for 850 patients in five wards and included 24 other buildings. Support facilities included 12 concrete water reservoirs, a ice house, a modern dental clinic, a pharmacy, a medical research lab, and three medical warehouses.

The Fourth Fleet's Naval Construction Department was responsible for building a seaplane base and facilities to replenish a fleet at anchor. At its peak, this department was composed of over 10,000 men whose function was to handle all the construction of fortifications, buildings, and engineering facilities for the Navy. The unit with the responsibility for providing supplies for the fleet was the Fourth Fleet Naval Stores Department which also served the army personnel at Truk. All supplies including provisions, fuel, aviation stores, clothing, and ammunition supplies came under its control. There were five radio installations at Truk under the control of the Fourth Communication corps; its center, which was a major link in the Japanese network, was located on Dublon and consisted of several frame buildings on concrete foundations, two concrete shelters for radio receivers and remote control transmitting positions, and two 30-meter steel antenna towers.

The Fourth Harbor Department, located on the southeast part of the Island near Dublon Town was responsible for the placing, upkeep, and repair of channel buoys, mooring buoys, anchors, chains, and other harbor facilities for all ships and craft. It was comprised of 22 wooden buildings, repair shops, warehouses, and barracks.

The main seaplane base was constructed on the south shore and was headquarters for the original Truk-based naval air organization, the 902nd Kokutai (Naval Air Corps), when it was established in December 1941. Following the arrival of the 17th Kokutai and various other units between 1942 and 1944, these were combined with the 902nd Kokutai to form the East Carolines Kokutai in the fall of 1944. The seaplane base had three ramps leading to a "T"-shaped service apron. Seaplane types utilizing the base included Rufes, Jakes, Petes, Mavis, and Emilys. There was over 5,000 feet of waterfront and three piers; a large "hammerhead" crane was mounted on the central pier. Installations consisted of a hangar, a control tower, barracks, and radio transmitter buildings. The aviation repair and supply installation associated with the seaplane base was known as the 104th Naval Air Arsenal. The function of the 104th Naval Air Arsenal was roughly equivalent to that of a combined assembly and repair department and an aviation supply activity. Facilities were developed for the air supply and repair department and were constructed adjacent to the seaplane base. These facilities included various shops for structural repair, propeller repair, engine repair, instrument repair, welding, carpenter service, forging, electrical repair, oxygen generating and refilling, smelting, explosives storage, three aircraft spare parts buildings, a power plant, and five barracks. At one time, it was reported to be capable of overhauling 15 aircraft engines per month. This organization was originally a branch of the Southeast Area Naval Air Arsenal which was headquartered in Rabaul until March 1944.

The South Seas Development Company (known as Nanyo Kohatsu Kabushiki Kaisha or "Nanko") had developed the dock facilities along the southwestern tip of Dublon. It consisted of a fish cannery operation and a supply storage area for the sustenance of the civilian inhabitants of Truk. After it was taken over by the Japanese Navy, it was renamed the Fourth Naval Dockyards and was utilized as the main receiving and storage areas for the military forces. Many warehouses were built along with a large refrigeration plant near the concrete piers. The area also included a headquarters building, a two-story barracks, and a large concrete fish canning facility. The Fourth Naval Dockyard had only limited capability to handle repair work on shallow draft vessels like destroyers, submarines, sub-chasers, picket boats, or harbor craft. Larger ships with major damage had to be sent to dockyards in Japan. It was kept busy providing repair work that could be augmented by repair ships and tenders in the anchorage for ships that had been damaged by U.S. submarines. This base was operated by over 1,000 men in the electrical, machine, casting, carpentry, forging, finishing, and torpedo ordnance repair shops. With the majority of effort being directed to repairs of ships anchored in the lagoon, there was heavy use made of tugs, barges, cranes, and lighters. There was a floating drydock capable of docking ships up to 2,500 tons and a 30-ton self-propelled floating crane used with the ship repair operations. In addition, there were two sawmills and large stores of lumber and building materials were stockpiled nearby. Narrow gauge railway tracks led to many of the installations and a 300-ton marine railway was under construction. The Japanese never intended to construct the necessary piers, drydocks, repair shops and installations, and storage areas needed for a large modern fleet. The major problem that confronted the Japanese was the construction costs and effort needed to blast and dredge access channels to piers were considered prohibitive.

The Truk Transportation Department was charged with loading and unloading ships and the storage and distribution of supplies. Its activities covered the area from the Nanko area docks to the Transport jetty and beyond to the South or Kohatsu jetty. With no docking facilities for large ships, fuel supplies, equipment, and ship's stores had to be lightered between ship and shore by barges and sampans. There were approximately 50 sampans, ten 15-ton tugs, one 600-ton tug, three 800-ton tugs, three water lighters, three fuel barges of 500-ton capacity or less, and 17 small harbor craft used for this purpose. Land-based equipment included 40 trucks, 50–60 two-wheel carts, and a stiff-leg derrick.

North of the repair base along the western shore, the Japanese built the 85th Submarine Base. Work had begun on this base in May 1942 and it was fully equipped to service the supplies, munitions, and minor repairs needed for a sizable submarine force. Facilities included machine shops, barracks, warehouses, a torpedo supply dump, torpedo warhead and fuze storage, an oxygen generating plant and two torpedo adjusting shops (one for compressed air and another for electric torpedoes). Torpedoes were transported by narrow gauge rail cars from cave storage to the submarine base pier and there loaded aboard lighters. There also was a rest camp with additional housing facilities for four submarine crews in-between war patrols.

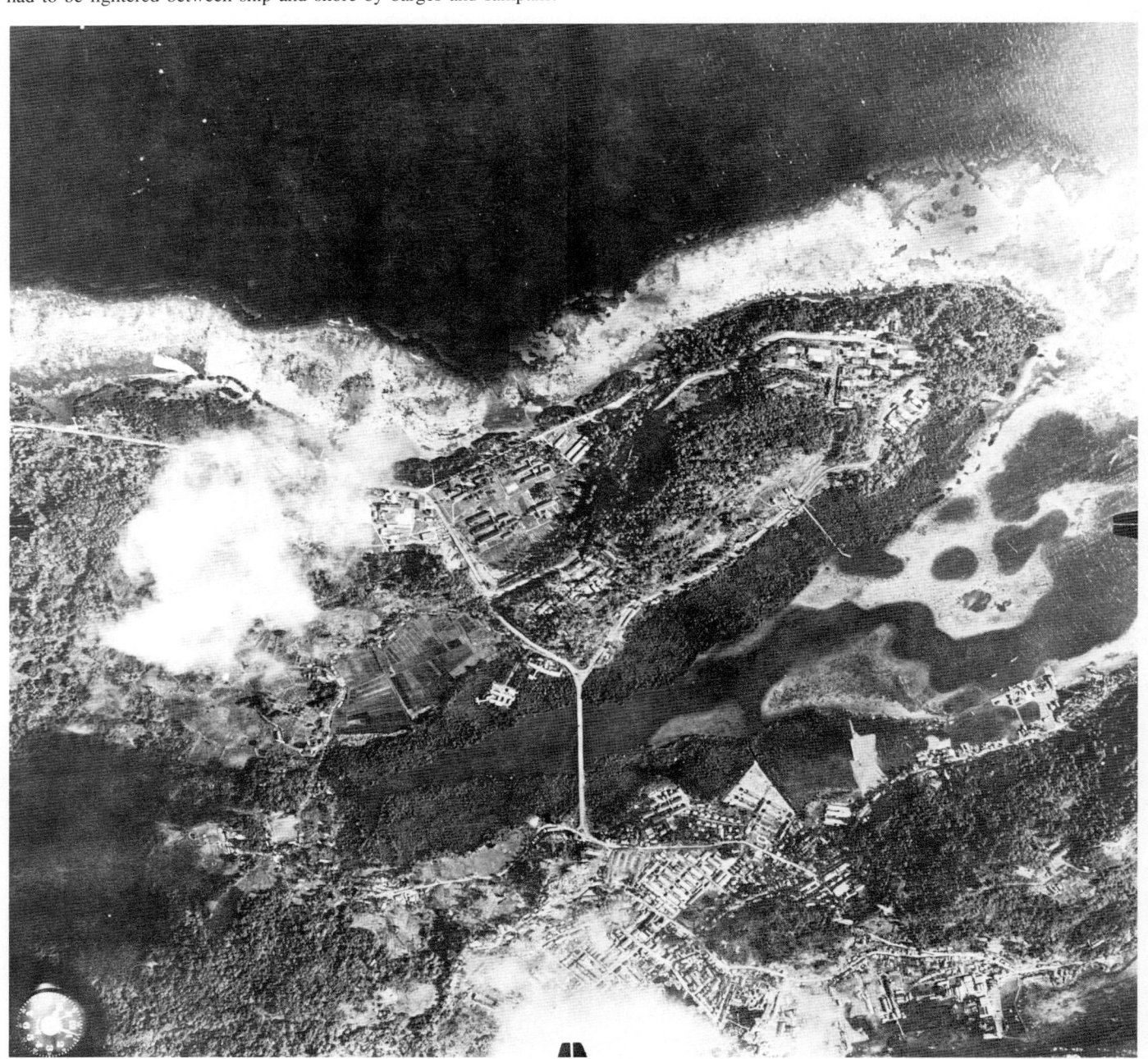

–Naval Operational Archives Photo

A causeway connects Dublon Town (lower center) to the northern peninsula where both the Fourth Fleet and Army headquarters were built (center of photo). The Naval hospital and facilities can be seen near the tip of the northeastern peninsula.

–National Archives Photo
The Moen No. 2 combination seaplane base and fighter strip can be seen in this photo of the south shore of Moen Island.

Moen Island

Two airfields were built on Moen Island to provide protection to the Truk Naval Base. The first, Moen No. 1, was constructed on the northwestern end of the island and is the same site of the landing strip being used today. It had a 300-foot by 3,750-foot runway for use by several types of fighters, reconnaissance, and bomber aircraft; nearly 80 support buildings were maintained. The construction of this airfield was begun in November 1941 and essentially completed in December 1942. Associated with the runway were networks of taxiways with dispersal lanes and other facilities. There was a parking apron at the northwest side approximately 140 feet wide by 1,900 feet long. The dispersal facilities included a 40-foot wide taxiway extending in a loop 1,200 feet south of the southwest end of the runway, 10 bomber revetments along the taxiway, two near the hangar and three at the northeast end of the runway. These revetments were 85 feet square. Just to the east of Moen No. 1 along the shoreline, the Japanese constructed extensive underground storage facilities for ammunition and gasoline. There were also several revetted buildings, garages and shops, a power plant, a large barracks and storage area, and several gun positions.

The second airfield, Moen No. 2, was a seaplane base that had been started in November 1941 and finished in April 1943. Located on the southern end of the island, it had a primary concrete ramp and apron 200 feet wide by 1,500 feet long and a secondary ramp 240 feet by 400 feet long. Facilities built in conjunction with the base included hangars, a torpedo storage installation, a radio shack, munitions storehouses, gasoline storage, a boat and seaplane basin, barracks buildings, and medium AA positions. Construction had begun on a projected fighter strip with a coral surfaced runway parallel to and about 225 feet north of the seaplane base service apron. The runway was about 175 feet wide and 3,450 feet long and constructed on fill. Two coral strips, 190 feet wide, extended across the sites of the former seaplane hangars and connected the seaplane service apron with the new runway.

Eten Island with its airstrip and installations on February 16, 1944.
–National Archives Photo

Eten Island

The airfield on Eten Island was the best constructed one in the atoll and served as Truk's principal fighter base. It was the only airfield equipped with runway lights for night operations. The runway was 270 feet wide by 3,440 feet long with a finished surface of asphaltic concrete; construction had begun on the field in August 1941 and it was completed late in 1943. A loop taxiway was built which led from the northeast end of the runway encircling Mt. Uinku and connecting the asphalt-paved repair apron at the south with the north end of the strip. Support installations included fuel and munitions storage, aircraft hangars and repair shops, a heavy concrete power house, a concrete air headquarters building, and a two-story reinforced concrete administration and radio communications building with a control tower. Japanese reports indicated 1,200 personnel and nearly 217 planes had been based at the airfield. There were 40 fighter revetments and 7 two-sided bomber revetments dispersed along the hillside adjacent to the airstrip and just off the taxi loop. These were all built in locations to utilize the protection of the hillside. Maintenance and minor plane and engine repairs were performed in the two steel hangars, on the service aprons, and while planes were parked in their revetments. Skilled mechanics from the 104th Air Arsenal on Dublon were brought in for major repair work or if possible, the planes were sent to Dublon for repair.

Eten served as headquarters for the 26th Koku Sentai (Air Flotilla) which came in from Rabaul in December 1943 and moved to Peleliu in March 1944. Some aircraft from the 22nd Koku Sentai under the command of Rear Admiral Sumikawa which had been transferred from Tinian in February 1944 and then deactivated in November 1944 were also assigned to Eten. Aircraft from other air organizations including the disbanded 21st and 25th Koku Sentais were also stationed at Eten and other airfields at Truk.

Fefan Island

The island of Fefan was used mainly as a supply center for the storage of food, ammunition, and small arms by the Fourth Naval Stores Department. A contingent of nearly 500 men from the Fourth Naval Construction Department were engaged in building roads, piers, gun emplacements, caves, and general construction. These projects were being directed by the Fourth Civil Engineering Department and included a group of about 1,169 civilian personnel. Naval Guard Unit forces stationed on the island included the 41st and 48th.

Uman Island

The Fourth Naval Communications Corps was responsible for the operation and maintenance of the radio transmitting station and radar station on Uman Island. The Fourth Civil Engineering Department and Naval Construction Departments were engaged in road building, digging caves and trenches, and general construction. Three torpedo boat stations were planned for the island but only one was completed. The one station, built to handle the modified Daihatsu landing crafts, was constructed among the mangroves along the edge of the island protected by rock revetments. Aside from the six frame buildings associated with the radio-radar station plus an army and a navy hospital, there were few other installations. There were over 600 men of the 49th Naval Guard Unit stationed on the island.

Param Island

The airfield and supporting AA defense positions manned by the

48th Naval Guard Force were the only naval installations of any importance on Param Island. The 335-foot-wide by 3,900-foot-long field located on the southern coast of the island was primarily a bomber base; construction was started in June 1943 and was eventually completed in April 1944. Fifty planes were based at this airfield. There were little or no servicing facilities for aircraft on the island and only small barracks were built due to the lack of time and materials. Other installations associated with the airfield included five taxiways leading from the runway to dispersal areas with 15 revetments, a small control tower, two warehouses and machine shops with adjoining storage and tool sheds, construction equipment and material storehouses, and an aggregate plant.

Ulalu Island

The most important military installation on the island was an R.D.F. station manned by the Fourth Communications Unit that was used for homing aircraft. A contingent of the Fourth Civil Engineering and Naval Construction departments engaged in road building and general construction were the only other groups on the Island.

Udot Island

Udot Island was manned by members of the 43rd and 48th Naval Guard Forces (approximately 200 men). Storehouses and barracks were the only installations of importance on the island. There were also contingents of the Fourth Civil Engineering and Naval Construction Units engaged in building roads and general construction.

Tol Island

The Japanese Navy had assigned nearly 6,200 men to Tol Island with the majority being civilians working for the Fourth Naval Construction Unit, the Transportation Unit and the Civil Engineering Department. In addition, nearly 1,000 men were assigned to the 41st and 43rd Naval Guard Forces. Defensive installations included two CD gun emplacements, a three-gun DP battery, a three-mortar emplacement sited to cover Piannu Pass to the west, two Kaiten one-man torpedo raiding force sites, two torpedo boat stations, an observation tower, and two searchlight positions.

FORTIFICATIONS–REEF ISLANDS

Along the encircling barrier reef of the Truk Atoll, there are almost 50 islets; these are small and widely separated with those having the greatest land area concentrated along the southeastern perimeter. The Japanese built coastal fortifications on nine of these islands to guard the outer approaches to the center of the lagoon.

Tonelik Island

Because of its strategic location on the east side of North Pass, Tonelik Island was a logical choice for a position from which to defend the northern approaches to Truk. The island is very small and heavily wooded. Installations built were directly associated with the defensive role of the island and included : two shielded 15cm (5.9-inch) coastal defense guns in the open with partially revetted emplacements, two ready magazines, two observation towers, a barracks with an annex, a revetted generator building, and a sound locator listening post-mine control station.

Northeast Island

Lying along the barrier reef about four and one-half miles north of Northeast Pass, Northeast Island was fortified along with Eli Kanibu which is a like distance south of the pass to guard this important approach to the atoll. The island is relatively large and heavily wooded. A gun emplacement was constructed with two 12cm (4.7-inch) coastal defense guns in the open. Support buildings and revetments, etc. were under construction.

Mor Island

This heavily wooded island is located in a very important defensive position alongside the entrance to Northeast Pass. Fortifications included two shielded 5.9-inch coastal defense guns with a command post containing fire control equipment, three 3-inch dual purpose gun emplacements, and an observation post of heavy concrete construction.

Eli Kanibu

Eli Kanibu is located in the midst of the barrier reef about four miles south of Northeast Pass. Coastal defense installations consisted of two 3-inch DP guns with ready magazines of concrete construction. Most of the island was under construction and clearing operations. Substantial masonry revetments had been built possibly to protect future buildings.

Salat Island

The location of Salat Island at the southeast corner of the atoll made it a strategic position for the defense of the several passes in the vicinity. Installations included two 12cm (4.7-inch) pedestal-mounted coastal defense guns, small ready magazines, and a one-story barracks and mess hall made of frame construction. The guns had no shields; the emplacements were revetted on the ocean side only.

Faleu Island

Strategically located near the center of South Pass, the main shipping channel for Japanese ships entering or leaving Truk, Faleu Island was the control center for the underwater detection system deployed in this entrance to the lagoon. The island is very small with sparse vegetation. Emplacements and construction on the island included the following: two shielded 15cm (5.9-inch) coastal defense guns in open revetted emplacements, a command post, a concrete ready ammunition magazine, barracks, a searchlight tower, a heavily revetted generator building, a shrine, an underground water reservoir, a latrine, a water distillation plant, bathhouses, mess halls and kitchens, and an observation tower.

–*Naval Operational Archives Photo*
Tiny Faleu Island exhibits a high concentration of installations and support buildings.

Otta Island

This island is located just east of Otta Pass. It was fortified with two 8cm (3-inch) dual purpose guns. Support installations included a sound locater, a searchlight, barracks, and a generator building.

Ollan Island

This island is located in a strategic position for the protection of the southwest entrances into the lagoon. The Japanese had placed two shielded 15cm (5.9-inch) coastal defense guns in the open with partially revetted emplacements.

Yawata Shima

Yawata Shima covers the approaches to the northwest entrances to the atoll. The island is small with sparse vegetation. The installations on the island were exposed from any angle of approach. Two shielded 15cm (5.9-inch) coastal defense guns had been set in open emplacements protected by a parapet on the shore side only. Support installations included two small concrete ready ammunition magazines, two small storehouses, a barracks with annex, a fire control tower, and a revetted generator building.

Truk Army Operations

The Army's 52nd Division was mobilized at Kanazawa, Japan for duty in the Eastern Caroline Islands in September 1943. An advance party of 300 officers and men of this division under the command of Lt. General Mugikura arrived in Truk in November 1943; the first major echelon of troops arrived in January 1944. There were no barracks for army use. As such, it was necessary to quarter the troops in civilian schools and houses, in a few Navy buildings, and in tent camps.

The 52nd Division was placed under the operational command of the Combined Fleet with the Eastern Army, headquartered in Japan, maintaining administrative command. At Truk, the Army and the Navy exercised joint command; coordination was obtained by cooperation and major decisions affecting both services were made in joint conference. The primary mission for the Army was purely defensive and its role would only begin when enemy troops actually attempted an invasion of the islands. When and if land actions began, the joint command structure would cease and Lt. General Mugikura would become the Supreme Commander. There were never any Army offensive operations launched or planned from Truk. In preparation for repelling amphibious landing assaults against the islands, army troops began constructing air raid shelters and beach defenses with pillboxes and mine fields. The plan of defense included the accepted temporary withdrawal and countercharge tactics but the primary plan was to fight from caves and trenches. As landing craft approached to within 1,000 to 2,000 meters of any island, Army artillery would open fire. Nearly 4,000 anti-boat mines were placed to protect the best landing beaches. When landing craft approached these reefs, normally 200 to 300 meters from shore, Japanese units were to open up with a heavy cross fire from well dug-in positions with mortars, machine guns, anti-boat mines, and small arms. Barbed wire was used to establish machine-gun firing lanes and to protect gun emplacements. Army troops were to dig in along the beaches and could fall back to preconstructed secondary positions if necessary. Machine guns, light mobile artillery pieces, and hand drawn anti-tank guns could be shifted between primary and alternate positions. The Army constructed interconnecting tunnels between most gun positions, and tank trenches and barriers were built.

In mid-February 1944, a second large echelon staged from Ujina, Japan to Truk in Convoy 3206. Two troop transports were sunk in submarine actions and a third was lost to U.S. carrier planes before arriving late in the day on 17 February. The few supplies arriving with this convoy were the last received for the Army from Japan as supply lines became almost completely severed. The Army was dependent on the Navy for supplying them with materials, including all types of supplies, ammunition, and clothing. More troops arrived in March and April followed by two detachments of troops from Mortlock Island, and a battalion from Enderby which completed the additions to the Truk garrison for the remainder of the war. The units that arrived were deployed as follows:

Date	Organization	No. Of Men	Location
4 Jan 44	52nd Division Headquarters	298	Dublon
4 Jan 44	Signal Unit	241	Dublon
4 Jan 44	69th Infantry Regiment	2,694	Dublon, Uman
4 Jan 44	Field Hospital	649	Moen, Dublon, Uman, Fefan, Tol
17 Feb 44	Transportation Unit	105	Dublon
17 Feb 44	Ordnance Service Unit	59	Dublon
17 Feb 44	Tank Unit	103	Tol
17 Feb 44	150th Infantry Regiment	2,136	Moen
17 Feb 44	Intendance Service Unit	117	Moen, Fefan, Dublon, Tol
11 Mar 44	Overseas Transport Unit	1,132	Dublon
24 Mar 44 16 April 44	51st Ind. Mixed Brigade †	4,788	Udot, Tol Fefan, Dublon
16 April 44	9th Ind. Eng. Regiment	483	Dublon
13 Sept 44 19 Jan 45	11th Ind. Mixed Regiment	1,366	Fefan, Dublon
20 Jan 45	31st Army Headquarters ††	128	Dublon
	Total	14,299	

The Army commanders of the defense districts were assigned as follows:

Defense District	Commanding Officer
Moen (includes Falo)	Col. Keizo Hayashida
Dublon (includes Eten)	Col. Taneichi Shibano
Uman	Maj. Kyuichi Kondo
Fefan	Maj. Hideaki Mori
Param	Maj. Eiji Shibata
Western (Hq. on S. Tol)	Maj. Gen. Kanenobu Ijuin
S. Tol	Maj. Jisaku Yoshida
N. Tol	Maj. Shigeki Mori
W. Tol	Maj. Jofuku Sakamoto
Udot	Capt. Kaneori Fukutome

† The 51st Independent Mixed Brigade was formed from units of the 2nd Detachment that arrived on 24 March 1944 and the 8th Detachment which arrived on 16 April 1944.

†† Lt. General Mugikura was appointed commander of the 31st Army at this time.

With the continuing air bombardments against the islands from Allied forward bases plus a devastating 2nd fast carrier raid, the Army decided to make everything bomb proof. Troops worked day and night to place all heavy machine guns and other weapons in caves with interconnecting tunnels between gun positions. Up to five alternate emplacements were constructed for each gun. The troops began living in or near the caves and tunnels which were also their battle stations. The scarcity of food made it necessary for almost all troops to dedicate much of the time to growing crops.

Australian Reconnaissance and Bombing Attacks (January 1942)

In January 1942, intelligence information gathered by the Central War Room in Melbourne, Australia pointed towards an upcoming Japanese thrust south against the advanced Australian bases in New Britain and New Ireland in the Bismark Archipelago. The Japanese long-range bombers and invasion forces were expected to come from the Caroline Islands and particularly from Truk which was 650 miles due north of Rabaul.

It became imperative to know when the Japanese would attack if any possible attempt at thwarting the enemy invasion could be mounted. Plans were formulated to make an armed photographic reconnaissance flight over Truk where heavy concentrations of shipping and aircraft would give a clear warning that an attack by the Japanese was imminent. The reconnaissance flight was scheduled for January 9th. Two Hudson Mark IV aircraft (just arrived from America) were selected for the flight. Flight crews were assembled from the Royal Australian Air Force (R.A.A.F.) Squadron No 6. This photo-reconnaissance mission was considered to be of the utmost importance and secret briefings of the crews were undertaken for four days by the Deputy Chief of the Air Staff (Commander Long), the R.A.A.F. Director of Intelligence (Wing Commander Packer), and the R.A.A.F. Staff Operations Officer (Squadron Leader Nicoll). Emphasis was made on the potential dangers getting to and from their objective plus the probability that the Japanese would detect the planes with radar and attempt to intercept them with Zeros. The two new Hudson aircraft, nicknamed "Tit Willow" and "Green's Yum Yum," were each fitted with two 20-inch cameras (one in the normal camera well near the door and one in the nose) and two extra 105-gallon fuel tanks in the cabin. On 3 January, the Hudsons were flown to Townsville (northeastern Australia). From Townsville on the morning of January 4th, the planes were directed to Rabaul. While enroute over the Trobriand Islands, warning was received that Rabaul was under air attack and the planes were diverted to Lae on the northeast coast of New Guinea. The following day another attempt to fly to Rabaul was cancelled due to the airfield being closed in by a rain squall and the planes were then diverted to Namatanai, New Ireland. The weather lifted and the Hudsons were able to land in Rabaul on January 6th; however, one of the planes ("Green's Yum Yum") developed engine problems and was forced to withdraw from the operation. The danger to the remaining Hudson due to further enemy air raids forced the crew to fly to Kavieng the same day where the aircraft was camouflaged to prevent discovery and possible destruction. This precaution was justified as the following day a Japanese flying-boat from a formation that had raided Rabaul flew over Kavieng at 5,000 feet on a reconnaissance flight. The Hudson was not detected. The final go-ahead for the mission was given on the night of January 8th and the heavily-laden Hudson took off at 0544 h the following day. The Hudson, piloted by Squadron Leader Yeowart, arrived over Truk four and one-half hours later where after emerging from a heavy rain squall, the crew found themselves over the main island...."Toll" (Dublon Island-author).

In the anchorage at "Toll Harbour," the crew spotted "12 warships that were either light cruisers or destroyers, one large warship thought to be an aircraft carrier, three merchant ships, and one hospital ship." Several float planes were circling low over the harbor and eight four-engined flying boats were moored just off the seaplanes base. The crew got the Allies' first look at the Eten Island airfield which was described as "an airfield that had been built on a small island in the harbour by excavating the centre from a hill and using the earth to build up the reef and either end to form runway." Twenty-seven bombers were counted parked wing-tip to wing-tip on the runway. The photographic run over the anchorage at 13,000 feet was half completed before the Hudson was spotted and taken under AA fire. Despite reports of aircraft taking off to intercept them, Yeowart made a second run over Eten Island before having to engage the first of the enemy fighters. Yeowart dove into a heavy rain squall and after leveling off at 500 feet altitude, he lost the enemy fighters.

After spending 25 minutes over the target to complete the photo objectives that had been assigned to the original two aircraft, the Hudson returned to Kavieng. From Kavieng, the Hudson was directed to Rabaul which had been under increasing numbers of enemy raids. The airfield was lit up with green, red, and white lights which had been placed to mark the bomb craters and safe portions of the runway. Little time was spent at Rabaul due to expected Japanese air raids and the plane was flown to Townsville where the exposed film was rushed to be developed and studied.

The information confirming the concentration of enemy forces at Truk reinforced the intelligence which pointed towards a major attack coming against Rabaul. Enemy air raids since 4 January by aircraft that were likely some of the bombers from Truk seen by Yeowart on Eten had also signaled the upcoming thrust by the Japanese.

From the interpretation of the photos taken and interrogation of the Hudson's crew, a target map was prepared for operations against the Truk Naval Base. The Central War Room ordered a night attack by six Catalinas and crews were selected from Squadrons Nos. 11 and 20. On January 12th, three of the Catalinas flew to Kavieng and three to Lorengau (small town on the northeast coast of the Admiralty Islands) for refueling before all six set out for Truk. Luck was on the side of the Japanese as weather conditions encountered by the planes was extremely bad. The last 300 miles had half-mile visibility and intermittent fierce thunderstorms. These conditions continued over the target area and all the Catalinas were forced to return without attacking the Truk base.

The failure of the Catalinas to destroy or damage the enemy forces at Truk meant a serious loss of precious time as indications were that Rabaul was almost certainly the next objective of the Japanese southern thrust. At the time, the Catalinas were the only combat aircraft the R.A.A.F. possessed that were capable of reaching Truk with a reasonable bomb-load. However, the Australian Chiefs of Staff learned that American Flying Fortresses were being staged through Australia to Java and made an urgent request for these heavy bombers to be diverted for "even one strike" on the concentrated Japanese forces at Truk. The request was denied. The fortresses were manned by skeleton crews only and even after taking into consideration the results of the reconnaissance report and intelligence the Australians had accumulated, the American view was that the Japanese's next objective was still Suva (Fiji). Furthermore, Suva would be reinforced only after the Americans had reinforced Samoa. The American commander, General Brereton, made it very clear to the Australians that his concentration on aid for General MacArthur's forces in the Philippines would take precedent over any request for aid in defense of Australian territory.

The Central War Room had no other choice but to send another group of Catalinas to attempt to attack the enemy forces at Truk. Six planes, again from Squadrons Nos. 11 and 20 were chosen for the operation. One of the pilots chosen was Lt. G.H. Hutchinson who had been lent to the R.A.A.F. by the U.S. Navy's No. 10 Patrol Wing after it had been forced south from the Philippines. On January 15th, three planes were again sent to Lorengau and the other three to Kavieng for refueling before the final round trip to Truk. While taking off from Kavieng, one Catalina crashed with loss of plane and crew and Hutchinson landed at the crash site in a vain attempt to rescue the crew. The remaining Catalina was the only one of the original three from Kavieng to reach Truk, arriving about one hour later than the three from Lorengau. This Catalina, piloted by Squadron Leader E.V. Beaumont, would be the only plane to see the base through a break in the thick overcast. Two runs were made over the target and 16 bombs were dropped; the weather closed in almost immediately and prevented the crew from seeing the results of their bomb drops.

Without the long-range heavy bombers needed to strike the concentrated enemy forces at Truk or sufficient aircraft to repel the Japanese amphibious task force when it came, the Australian defenders were virtually powerless. On January 24th, they were only able to put up token resistance against the amphibious forces which landed at Rabaul under the Japanese Fourth Fleet which were covered and supported by carrier striking forces. The small Australian garrison was quickly overwhelmed.

In short order, the Japanese made landings along the coasts of New Britain, New Ireland, Papua New Guinea, and the northern Solomon Island group effectively giving them naval and air control of the entire Bismark Archipelago. Rabaul was transformed into a powerful military base by the Japanese becoming the headquarters for the 25th Koku Sentai (Air Flotilla); Rabaul's Simpson Harbor became a fleet anchorage utilized by the Combined Fleet.

The Photographic Overflight

On the night of 3 February 1944, two U.S. Marine PB4Y photo-reconnaissance planes took off with navy photographers aboard from a newly completed airstrip on Stirling Island in the Solomons. Their mission was to make a 2,000-mile round trip to photograph the fleet base at Truk in preparation for the upcoming carrier raids and for the still planned invasion. The PB4Ys, flying at 20,000 feet, arrived undetected over the target on the morning of 4 February. Photography was limited because of the many clouds covering the atoll, but the cameras were able to photograph both Dublon Island and Eten Island with its airstrip. Caught off guard with no fighter planes airborne, the Japanese scrambled two or three Zekes and Rufe seaplane fighters in pursuit while a battleship fired on one of the PB4Ys. The Japanese failed to intercept, and after having been able to spend 20 to 30 minutes over their target, the two photographic planes returned to the Solomons to have their pictures analyzed.

The report of an enemy reconnaissance plane (the Japanese had spotted only one of the PB4Ys) seen over the atoll was enough. Admiral Koga, knowing that the Gilberts were lost and the Marshalls had just been invaded, decided that his Combined Fleet was vulnerable to attack by U.S. forces. For months, American submarines had been sinking many of the heavily loaded cargo ships bound for Truk with much needed supplies. Previous reports of a huge armada of American warships in the Marshalls coupled with that of the Truk overflight must be interpreted as an indication that an attack on Truk would be forthcoming. It was time to assemble the Combined Fleet and withdraw away from American air power and towards a source of available supplies.

Some major fleet units had departed Truk prior to the photographic overflight. Vice Admiral Takeo Kurita had already rushed the 2nd Fleet to Palau after the fall of Kwajalein. U.S. Submarine PERMIT had spotted battleships NAGATO and FUSO along with several destroyers leaving Truk about 1000 h on 1 February sailing towards Palau. The battleship YAMATO along with other battleships and cruisers had then left for Palau on 3 February. Following the reconnaissance flight of 4 February, Admiral Koga in his flagship MUSASHI withdrew from Truk with four carriers, escorts, and many of the merchantmen never to return. Admiral Sumikawa, the commander of the 22nd Air Flotilla, left with Koga to return to Japan to plead with the higher headquarters for assistance to strengthen his defenses. The MUSASHI returned via Palau with part of the fleet to Yokosuka, Japan, while the rest of the fleet remained at Palau or headed for Singapore. A U.S. submarine spotted two MOGAMI class heavy cruisers leaving the atoll as late as 10 February. Many merchantmen and auxiliaries were forced to remain at Truk because of a shortage of fuel and water and because of strong winds which had delayed their unloading.

The results of the photographic overflight were incomplete because of the clouds over Truk. Only one airstrip on Eten and the seaplane base at Dublon were visible. There were 85 planes on Eten, 30 at the Dublon seaplane base service apron, and 26 more at the adjacent aviation repair and supply installations. Photo interpreters observed 43 planes on the two Japanese aircraft carriers in the lagoon. The planes were dispersed on their decks in such a way as to indicate they were probably being shipped out to the combat zone from Japan. In briefings on board the U.S. carriers, the intelligence officers would tell their flyers, "Here, right here, there may be an airfield." The flyers would look and an "X" would mark the spot, right on a nice white cloud. There was something in those pictures though that was a big thing, an item that made everyone sit up and pay attention. It was a big group of ships. There were nearly 60 ships, half of them combatant ships, showing through holes in the clouds. The opportunity that Admiral Nimitz had been waiting for had arrived. The Navy now had a golden opportunity to return a blow at a major portion the the Japanese fleet right in its own Pearl Harbor.

TRUK LAGOON
SUMMARY OF SHIPS AT ANCHOR – FEBRUARY 4, 1944

TYPE	NW DUBLON I.	SE DUBLON I.
BB	1	–
CV	–	2
CA	4	–
CL	2	1
DD	6	3
SS	2	–
AS	1	–
AD	1	–
AP	1	3
AO	2	2
AK	6	17

Marine reconnaissance photograph taken during overflight revealed Dublon Island to the left, Eten Island with its airstrip in center, and Fefan Island to the right. Numerous merchantmen and warships are anchored around the islands.

–National Archives Photo

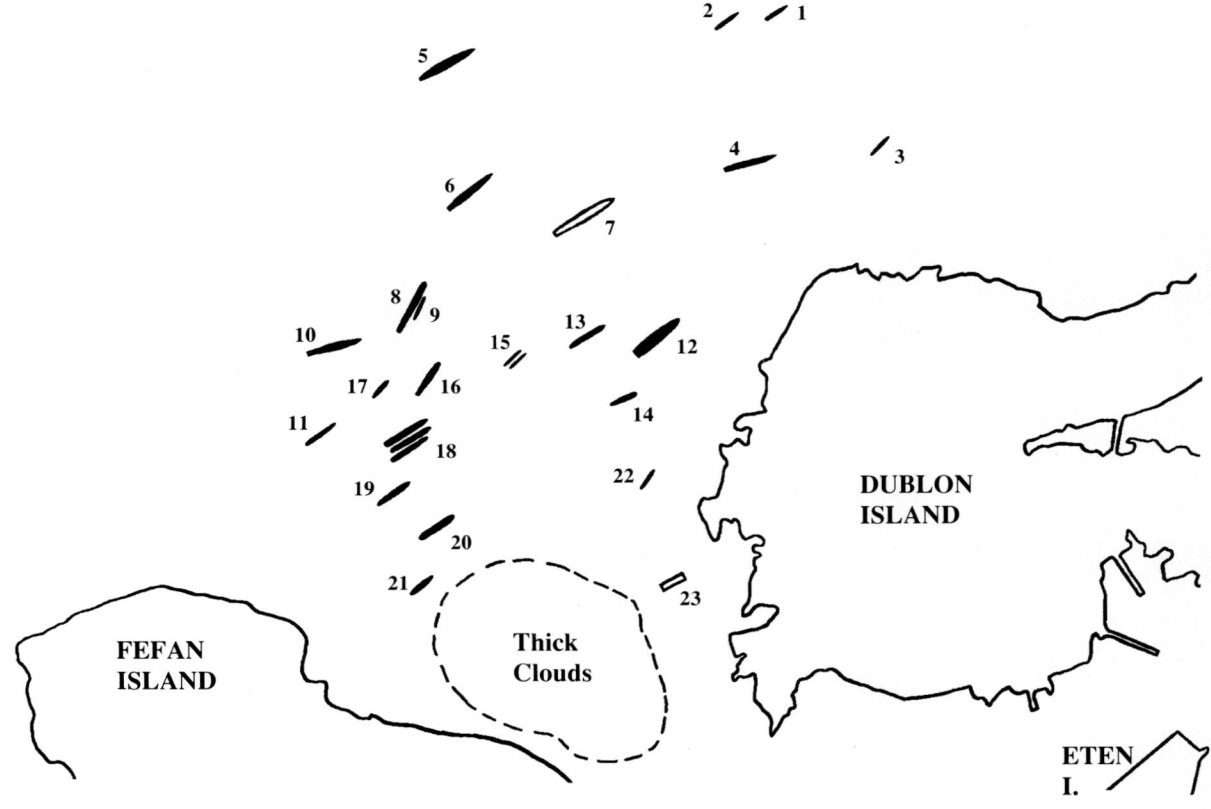

**SHIP DISPOSITION 4 FEBRUARY 1944
COMBINED FLEET ANCHORAGE**
Compiled from mosaic of reconnaissance photos
taken during Photographic Overflight

PHOTOGRAPHIC INTELLIGENCE SUMMARY
( ) – Author's Comments

1. DD 400' x 35'
2. DD 400' x 35'
3. DD 355' x 35'
4. CA – Probably ATAGO Class (Heavy Cruisers MAYA, CHOKAI, TAKAO, or ATAGO herself)
5. CA ATAGO Class (Same comment as above)
6. CA NACHI Class (MYOKO, HAGURO, ASHIGARA, or NACHI)
7. BB YAMATO (Sister ship MUSASHI)
8. AO TONAN MARU NO. 3
9. DD TERATSUKI Class (AKIZUKI, HATSUTZUKI, or WAKATSUKI?)
10. AO HUZIZAN MARU (AKA FUJISAN MARU)
11. AP-AK 380' x 55' (KENSHO MARU?)
12. AP – HEIAN MARU (Actually a Sub-tender or AS)
13. CL KATORI Class (KATORI herself)
14. AS 350' x 50' (Too short for any known Sub-tender!)
15. 2 SS 250' x 20' (Submarines)
16. AP 480' x 60'
17. DD 355' x 35'
18. CL 535' x 55' (AGANO?)
    AD 510' x 60' (AR AKASHI – Repair Ship)
    AP 525' x 60'
19. AK 460' x 65' (KIYOSUMI MARU)
20. AO 475' x 65' (HOYO MARU)
21. AK 285' x 40' (Target Ship HAKACHI?)
22. PG 250' x 35' (Surveying Ship SOYA?)
23. Floating Drydock

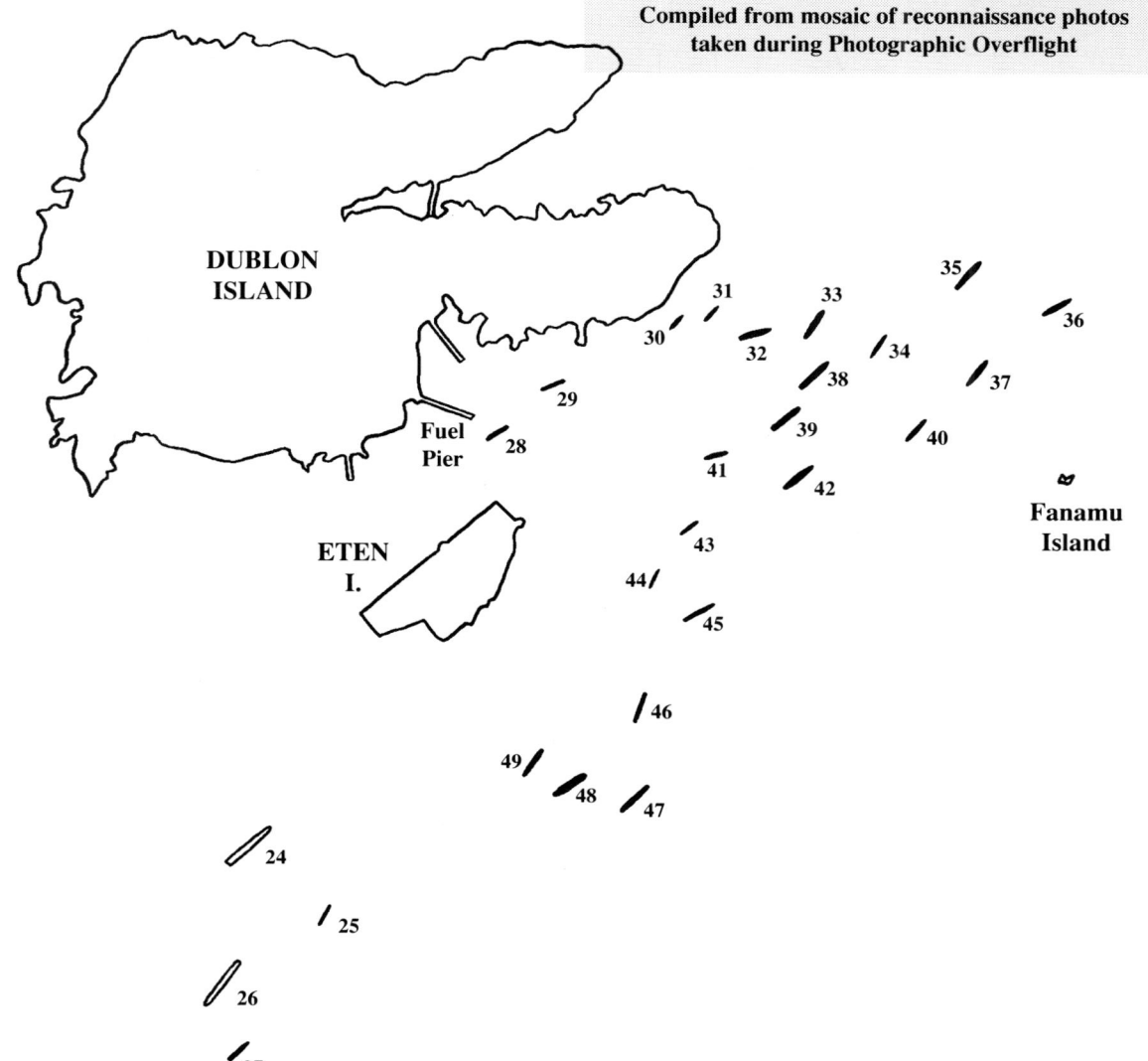

SHIP DISPOSITION 4 FEBRUARY 1944
FOURTH FLEET ANCHORAGE
Compiled from mosaic of reconnaissance photos taken during Photographic Overflight

PHOTOGRAPHIC INTELLIGENCE SUMMARY
( ) – Author's Comments

24. CV 645' x 80' (CHIYODA ?)
25. DD FUBUKI (Other DD in FUBUKI Class?)
26. CV 680' x 80' (ZUIHO, RYUHO, HIYO, or JUNYO?)
27. DD ASASHIO (ASAGUMO, YAMAGUMO or MICHISHIO?)
28. AK 420' x 55'
29. AK 350' x 50'
30. YO 200' x 35' (Patrol Vessel?)
31. DD MUTSUKI Class (FUMITSUKI?)
32. AP-AK 370' x 60'
33. AP-AK 360' x 50' (MOMOKAWA MARU?)
34. AK 360' x 50'
35. AO HOYO MARU (Aft-engine AK or AP?)
36. AO KAIZYO MARU (AKA KAIJO MARU)
37. AP-AK 326' x 45' (NAGANO MARU?)
38. CL SENDAI (NAKA)
39. NAGARA MARU Class (MKKFKM NOTO or NOSHIRO MARU)
40. AK 440' x 35'
41. AH 267' x 50' (RYUKO MARU?)
42. TAISYO MARU 440' x 55' (SEIKO MARU)
43. AK 295' x 50'
44. CM 355' x 47' (Minesweeper HAGOROMO?)
45. AK-AP TOSAN MARU (8,666 tons, KMKFKMK)
46. AK-AP 450' x 65' (HOKI MARU?)
47. AP NITTA MARU (NITTA M. converted to CVE CHUYO ATT)
48. AO 545' x 70'
49. AP 535' x 70'

The Fast Carrier Strikes on Truk (February 16–17, 1944)

Operation FLINTLOCK was still on the planning table at Pearl Harbor when Vice Admiral Raymond A. Spruance began developing tentative plans for the first carrier strikes on Truk. This new operation, designated as HAILSTONE, was originally slated for April 15, 1944. Following the success of Operation FLINTLOCK in steamrolling over the Marshalls and with the amazingly small American losses, the dates for attacking Truk were revised to February 16–17. Now the U.S. would tackle the strongest of the enemy's Pacific outposts.

The fleet sent by Admiral Nimitz to serve as the Truk striking force was designated Task Force 50 and was placed under the command of Admiral Spruance. In anticipation of the eagerly awaited surface battle with the Japanese fleet, Admiral Spruance quickly stripped down the enormous force which had gathered for the Kwajalein landings to a workable, high-speed fleet with tremendous striking power. The Japanese might get word of the operation and vanish, but there was the chance Admiral Koga would stand and fight. To that end, Spruance gathered a group of the newest and fastest battleships with cruisers and destroyers for support. Admiral Mitscher would be in charge of the carrier forces, Task Force 58. A slightly reduced version of the previous TF 58 was formed. Some large carriers, including the SARATOGA, were left to finish up at Eniwetok; slower escort carriers (CVE's) were left behind at Kwajalein to further consolidate the hard-won positions. The resulting carrier task units could send up over 500 combat aircraft. The final composition of forces were as follows:

Force Flagship (TG 50.2) Captain Carl F. Holden
Battleship: NEW JERSEY

Carrier Force (TF 58) Rear Admiral Mitscher
Group 1 (TG 58.1) Rear Admiral J.W. Reeves, Jr.
Carriers: ENTERPRISE, YORKTOWN
Light Carrier: BELLEAU WOOD
Light Cruisers: BILOXI, MOBILE, OAKLAND, SANTA FE
Destroyers: C.K. BRONSON, CAPERTON, COTTEN, COGSWELL, DORTCH, GATLING, HEALY, INGERSOL, KNAPP

Group 2 (TG 58.2) Rear Adm. A.E. Montgomery
Carriers: ESSEX, INTREPID
Light Carrier: CABOT
Heavy Cruisers: BALTIMORE, SAN DIEGO, WICHITA, SAN FRANCISCO
Destroyers: HICKOX, STEMBEL, THE SULLIVANS, LEWIS HANCOCK, STEPHEN POTTER, HUNT, STACK

Group 3 (TG 58.3) Rear Admiral F.C. Sherman
Light Carriers: BUNKER HILL, COWPENS, MONTEREY
Battleships: ALABAMA, IOWA, MASSACHUSETTS, NEW JERSEY (when not operating as an independent flagship), NORTH CAROLINA, SOUTH DAKOTA
Heavy Cruisers: MINNEAPOLIS, NEW ORLEANS
Destroyers: BELL, BRADFORD, BROWN, BURNS, CHARETTE, CONNOR, IZARD, LANG, LOWELL, STERETT, WILSON

Separate battle plans were developed for the case of a surface engagement between major fleet units and for the case where Japanese fleet units had fled, leaving all the action to the aviators. Admiral Spruance would assume tactical command in case of a surface engagement between fleet units; Mitscher would call the shots if the battle was strictly a carrier operation. Battle plans for a surface action called for the less heavily armored carriers to stand off out of gun range, protecting their own battleships and attacking the enemy's by air while the opposing heavy units slugged it out with their main batteries, the cruisers and destroyers deployed on their flanks.

It seemed impossible for a striking force the size of Task Force 50 to approach Truk undetected. Japanese aircraft on Ponape and possibly Kusaie covered the eastward approaches, and it was assumed that the fleet's carriers and planes would have to fight their way through land-based air opposition. With all the fleet units at a high state of alertness, the task groups proceeded on 16 February to position 08°17'N, 153°10'E approximately 94 miles east-northeast of Dublon Island without detection. The three carrier task groups formed a special cruising disposition in a north-south line of bearing; TG 58.1 to the north, TG 58.3 in the center, and TG 58.2 to the south. Flight operations were scheduled for two days on Dog-Minus-One-Day and Dog-Day, 16 and 17 February 1944 respectively, against Japanese shipping and aircraft (primary targets) and fleet servicing and aircraft installations (secondary targets). Planes were also assigned tertiary objectives of flying photographic and reconnaissance missions over the assigned target areas.

The flight organizations aboard the three carrier task groups were assigned as follows:

Carrier Air Group Organization

TG 58.1
    U.S.S. ENTERPRISE (CV-6)   Air Group 10
    U.S.S. YORKTOWN (CV-10)   Air Group 5
    U.S.S. BELLEAU WOOD (CVL-24)   Air Group 24
TG 58.2
    U.S.S. ESSEX (CV-9)   Air Group 9
    U.S.S. INTREPID (CV-11)   Air Group 6
    U.S.S. CABOT (CVL-28)   Air Group 31
TG 58.3
    U.S.S. BUNKER HILL (CVL-17)   Air Group 17
    U.S.S. COWPENS (CVL-25)   Air Group 25
    U.S.S. MONTEREY (CVL-26)   Air Group 30

The fighter squadron aboard the BUNKER HILL was VF-18; the dive bomber and torpedo squadrons were designated VB-17 and VT-17 respectively. The torpedo squadron planes from the various groups carried bombs during most of the strikes at Truk and bombs were carried by fighters in some instances. The dive bombers aboard the carriers were exclusively SBDs except for those aboard the BUNKER HILL which had the only squadron of SB2C Helldivers.

<u>DOG-DAY-MINUS-ONE Fighter Sweep</u>
The main objective of this pre-dawn strike was to destroy Japanese air opposition and to establish air supremacy over the islands. The five carriers participating and number of planes launched from each were: BUNKER HILL (23), ENTERPRISE (12), ESSEX (11), INTREPID (12) and YORKTOWN (12). This dawn fighter attack against Truk caught the Japanese air defenses unprepared. The Japanese had been on alert two days previous to the attack when radio voice transmissions from U.S. aircraft had been intercepted and a Betty on a routine search flight disappeared. Further search flights reported nothing and the

Japanese rationalized that the voice transmissions had originated from somewhere between Kwajalein and Eniwetok. The Japanese relaxed their alert status and for some undetermined reason decided that the forthcoming attack would not occur until the 21st of February.

The fighters began launching from their respective carriers at 0440 h and proceeded to the designated general rendezvous areas as follows:

TG 58.1 – 15 miles north of North Pass
TG 58.2 – 15 miles northeast of Northeast Pass
TG 58.3 – 15 miles east of Northeast Pass

Approaching from the north, the F6Fs completed the 46 minute flight and made a circular run encompassing nearly the whole lagoon before encountering enemy fighters. In the light of early dawn, one of the greatest all-fighter-plane battles of history began.

ENTERPRISE planes were assigned to cover the lowest altitude layer during the fighter sweep where the heaviest Japanese air opposition was expected. They initially tangled with Zekes, Tojos, Rufes, and Hamps from the Moen and Param airfields; planes from Eten Island were slow in getting launched. There were dogfights everywhere pitting fighter against fighter in a melee of smoke and flame and hurtling aircraft. The VF-10 pilots claimed 17 planes shot down and 5 damaged. Two of the planes shot down were Tojos that had just taken off from Eten when encountered and both burst into flames and crashed. The fighters were faced with the dual task of dueling the Japanese airborne planes and flying strafing attacks against the planes on the ground on the Eten and Param airstrips. They managed to strafe the Eten airfield repeatedly where planes were reported to be lined up wing tip to wing tip on the apron. Five VF strafed the field setting 3 Bettys, 9 Zekes, 4 Tojos, and 5 other fighter-type aircraft on fire. The fires among the fully-gassed aircraft turned into an inferno. Enemy AA fire shot down one F6F while on a strafing run; the pilot was lost. On the Param airfield, a Zeke was shot down just after it had taken off.

The VF-5 planes from YORKTOWN had a field day. Joining the ENTERPRISE fighters covering low altitudes, the VF-5 pilots engaged the Japanese in a fierce series of dogfights. Two pilots shot down three enemy fighters each; two others got two each. The Group Commander, who was supposed to be taking pictures and running the show, had to take time off to shoot down a Zeke which attacked him. The pilot of one Zeke, damaged and on fire, tried to make a forced landing. He tried to set the plane down on its wheels but instead one of his wings hit the ground first and then his craft was propelled down the field in flames, spinning end over end through a row of parked torpedo planes. Three of the torpedo planes caught fire adding to the pyre. The pilot who had damaged the Zeke later complained that his cartwheeling quarry came to rest just short of hitting a big four-engine plane at the end of the row of parked aircraft. Eight of the F6Fs strafed the Dublon Island seaplane base while their comrades were engaged in dogfights. Three Mavis and two Emilys on the seaplane ramp were set afire.

Pilots from ESSEX's VF-9 took the largest toll of Truk's airborne defenders. During the fighter sweep, 21 Japanese aircraft were shot down. Among the aircraft claimed destroyed that were identified were 5 Zekes, 4 Rufes, 4 Kates, and 5 Petes. Another Zeke was listed as probably destroyed. Approximately 50 Japanese planes were counted in the air. The pilots reported that the enemy fighters were using clouds for protection as Truk that morning was about half covered with fleecy cumulus. The Zeke pilots would utilize the terrific speed and attack advantage from a high altitude dive, but once that was lost, they would veer off and hide in the clouds. It appeared that with the initial advantage gone, the Japanese didn't know what to do. One pilot, Hamilton McWhorter (nicknamed "One-Slug" because his first burst of fire always scored), remarked that "they fought as though they were in a daze". The added ground target responsibility for VF-9 was the Param airfield and the Moen seaplane base, Moen No. 2. In multiple strafing attacks on aircraft identified as Kates and Bettys parked at Param airfield, 15 aircraft were reported destroyed. At Moen No. 2, about 25 planes were parked on the ramp or moored in the shallow water just off shore. Twelve of these float planes were destroyed in strafing attacks. One F6F was lost.

Planes from INTREPID arrived over target at approximately 0600 h and began making strafing attacks on the Moen bomber strip (Moen No. 1). The F6Fs were jumped by a group of enemy fighters but were able to maneuver out of harms way and counter-attack. The total number of Japanese aircraft shot down in aerial combat totaled 11; the F6Fs escaped the dogfights unscathed. Nearly 40 strafing runs were made on the Moen airfields, resulting in the destruction by fire of 15 Bettys, 8 Zekes, and one unidentified plane for a total of 24 destroyed on the ground. The Executive Officer of VF-6, Lt. G.C. Bullard, had finished 12 strafing runs up and down the Moen No. 1 strip and was retiring to the rendezvous point when he spotted a KATORI class CL heading north in the lagoon between Northeast and North Passes. While leading his division in a low altitude strafing attack on the CL, he was shot down by AA fire. He was seen to make a water landing west of North Pass, just outside the reef. Other planes shortly thereafter spotted 3 DDs a few miles away apparently waiting to rendezvous with an "ATAGO class CA" approaching from east of North Pass. One of the pilots, Lt. (jg) Odenbrett, followed Bullard's crippled F6F down and dropped a life raft, meanwhile coming under heavy AA fire from the CA. He strafed the CA in return before leaving the locality, setting fire to the VOS (observation seaplane) on the ship's catapult. Although no Japanese CA or heavy cruiser was at Truk during the attacks, it is probable that the "CA" was actually the CL KATORI which was known to be in the vicinity. The KATORI was outfitted with a catapult for launching seaplanes. The downed aviator was seen twice later in the day on Alanenkobwe Island, five miles west of North Pass. He had spelled out his name with rocks piled up on the beach and was waving when seen the second time. Before a rescue attempt could be organized, Japanese from a gun battery detachment guarding North Pass reached him and took him prisoner. He was later transferred to Japan.

The F6Fs from BUNKER HILL (VF-18) were assigned to cover the high altitude window between 20–25,000 feet. Over the target area, the fighters encountered a total of 15 Zekes and one Hamp. The single Hamp was shot down. One Zeke, part of a flight of six encountered was listed as a probable as it was burning and falling towards the sea when last seen. During retirement, the pilots observed several hits by bombers on shipping in the lagoon as the first of the shipping strikes arrived at their target areas.

On the ships of TF 50, word slowly trickled back to the admirals about the situation over Truk; a great fighter battle was in progress but the Japanese Fleet warships the marine flyers had spotted 12 days before had departed. Once again the Imperial Fleet declined battle and let another Japanese stronghold go by default. The hoped-for great surface battle would not materialize. There were however, a significant number of merchantmen or "marus" left in the lagoon plus a few cruisers and destroyers. It was going to be mostly Mitscher's show as destroying the shipping within the lagoon where American ships could not approach was a job for dive bombers and torpedo planes.

The scheduled air strikes were a mix of dive bomber (VB) and torpedo planes (VT) flying under cover of protecting fighters (VF). They would follow the pre-dawn fighter sweep at approximately hourly intervals throughout the day. Installations and shipping were already under attack before the F6Fs participating in the initial pre-dawn sweep had landed back on their carriers. At the start, the VB and VT planes were loaded with AP and SAP bombs because of the expected encounters with Japanese combatant vessels. The GP bombs best suited for merchantmen would be substituted later.

Enemy shipping was designated the primary objective for the combined plane strikes in the following order of priority:

a. Combatant carriers
b. Battleships
c. Cruisers
d. Submarines
e. Oilers
f. Other auxiliaries
g. Destroyers

Secondary targets were aircraft installations and fleet servicing facilities.

Targets for the three task groups were pre-assigned but could be shifted to accommodate changing battle conditions such as in the case where primary targets were destroyed or it became necessary for other reasons to shift to secondary targets. Excessive duplication of attacks against the same targets was to be avoided whenever possible.

DOG-MINUS-ONE-DAY Group Strike No. 1

The initial group strikes were launched between 0500–0526 h and recovered by 0815 h. The times have been adjusted from the aircraft action reports to reflect Truk local time and to be consistent with times used throughout this book. During all the group strikes, the Task Group maneuvered as a unit for launching and landing aircraft except in the case of single plane launching and recoveries. The carrier BELLEAU WOOD did not launch any air strikes on Truk shipping or installations. Carriers CABOT and MONTEREY did not participate in this group strike.

ENTERPRISE Strike 1AE

The first strike launched from ENTERPRISE was composed of 8VF, 10VB, and 7VT. The strike force joined up with those of YORKTOWN and then proceeded to a point 10 miles northeast of the reef, heading for Moen Island at an altitude of 10,000 feet with YORKTOWN planes at 12,000 feet above them. The TBFs, loaded with six 100-lb fragmentation clusters and six 100-lb incendiaries each, were tasked with the destruction of aircraft and air installations at Eten Island. When the TBFs arrived just short of the reef, the planes dived in their approaches heading between Moen and Dublon Islands towards the west. The formation then spread out, circled toward Eten and then began making dives from 8,000 feet over the target area from the east and northeast. Japanese planes on the ground were difficult to spot because of the low cloud cover and high speed dives as the planes bombed the airfield. Many fires were started throughout the target area, many from the parked planes. Photographs taken after the bombing run showed over 100 planes on the Eten airfield. The TBFs encountered no enemy planes during the strike. All planes returned with numerous small caliber holes through wing and tail surfaces from the intense AA fire but suffered no casualties.

The primary mission of the SBDs was to destroy shipping in the north Dublon anchorage. Arriving over the anchorage at 0620 h, a total of nearly 15 ships of various types were spotted in the target area northeast of Dublon Island with an equal number in the Eten Anchorage to the south. The AKITSUSHIMA, described as a MIZUHO class CVS, was the initial target selected. This choice target was attacked by the first section of 4VB scoring two 1,000-lb GP bomb hits, one just forward of the bridge and the other at the extreme end of the stern. The second section of two planes picked a large AO in an adjacent berth to the CVS but their drops were wide. The third section of four planes attacked a "FURATAKA class CA" one more berth to the eastward and scored two near misses 20 feet off the stern that were believed to have caused some damage. The pilots reported a second CA in the northern part of the anchorage east of Moen with intense AA being thrown up by each. The SBDs encountered a Dave floatplane which was believed to be spotting for the CAs below. Several DDs and another CA were noted to be heading for North Pass. (No Japanese heavy cruisers were present at Truk; the reported CAs were actually light cruisers or possibly destroyers-author).

The F6Fs performed escort duty and attacked targets of opportunity. Enemy planes encountered included 12 Zekes, 4 Rufes, and 1 Val. The Japanese planes were engaged and 5 Zekes, 2 Rufes, and the Val were shot down; the U.S. planes suffered no casualties. Strafing runs on both the east and west sides of Eten were made and five enemy fighter-type aircraft were set on fire. In other action, 5VF strafed a gunboat heading south just inside Northeast Pass. Multiple hits were reported but the gunboat did not catch fire or stop. A CL heading towards the Northeast Pass was also strafed but no damage was observed and the cruiser's course and speed did not alter.

YORKTOWN Strike 1AY

YORKTOWN launched a strike group consisting of 8VF, 15VB, and 9VT. The primary objective at launch for the TBFs was to destroy aircraft carriers and lightly armored vessels by glide bombing. Each plane was loaded with four 500-lb GP bombs. The planes split up; six planes joined together in one group and three others joined the ENTERPRISE VT planes. Many ships were seen anchored between Dublon and Uman, west of Eten Island. None of the expected large combatant ships were present; the ships were identified as mostly AOs and AKs. Two TBFs attacked a "CL or DD" north of Uman underway heading to the east. Seven very near misses, within 25 feet or less, covered the ship with water and must have caused some severe damage. Another plane scored a near miss on an AO or AK at anchor near the southwest shore of Dublon Island. Four bombs were dropped in salvo against an AK off the western shore of Fefan Island missing by 100 feet. The buildings and wharf to the southwest of the Moen No. 1 airstrip on Moen Island were hit by four bombs from another VT plane. One hit in front of a large building just southeast of the pier. Several medium bombers were spotted parked on the field by one pilot who hit two of the enemy planes and dropped its other two 500-lb bombs on the runway. Two AKs were spotted underway, one just north of Eten heading west and the other north of Fanamu Island heading east. All bombs dropped on the two missed. Two near misses off the port of of another AK lying between Dublon and Fefan Island were reported .

The SBDs concentrated on enemy shipping in the anchorage

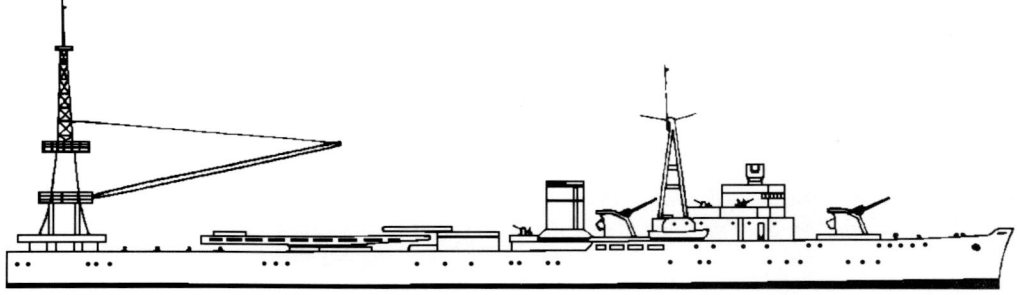

The seaplane tender/carrier AKITSUSHIMA.

northeast of Fefan and southwest of Dublon. Ships anchored in this area were vessels under repair from U.S. submarine attacks and included HOYO, KIYOSUMI, and KENSHO MARUs. The repair ship AKASHI was there also while the HEIAN MARU and an unidentified ship were at anchor closer to Dublon Island. The TONAN MARU NO. 3 was laid up further to the north. Many of the ships were reported to be just starting to get underway when attacked. The planes made dives on the target ships from the east to northwest beginning at 0620 h releasing 1,000-lb GP bombs between 1,000 and 2,500 feet. Five SBDs dropped bombs on a 4–6,000-ton AK but scored no hits. A second AK attacked by three planes was hit on the port bow and the starboard end of the stern. Another bomb was a near miss 25 feet off the bow which rocked the ship. A medium AK (2–4,000 tons) was probably damaged by two near misses, one on either side amidships. The last ship attacked was a medium AK (also 2–4,000 tons); it was hit once on the starboard bow. The planes encountered 3 Zekes west of Dublon but did not engage them. The pilots reported AA fire principally from the ships attacked but there was considerably more coming from Fefan, Ulalu, and Param Islands.

The F6F escorts encountered 6 Zekes and destroyed five of the enemy planes. Two strafing runs were made on a CL in the Eten Anchorage which silenced the ship's light AA fire. An AK underway inside the lagoon was left smoking after it was strafed.

ESSEX Strike 2A

The primary targets for ESSEX planes (10VF, 9VT, and 16VB) on Strike 2A was shipping east of Dublon and those south and east of Eten Island. The secondary targets were installations on Dublon.

The positions of ships within the lagoon attacked by ESSEX planes were roughly plotted by compilers/analysts of the aircraft action reports which included interviews of all pilots and crew-members. The descriptions of ships attacked by the dive bombers and torpedo planes are numbered to allow the reader to correlate the vessel's position in the re-produced drawing titled "ESSEX SHIPPING TARGET SUMMARY" included later in this section.

The following are descriptions of ships attacked by VB and VT planes during the strike:

1. CL – 6,000 tons. Anchored 500 yards southeast of Eten Island. VB scored hit (one 1,000-lb bomb) on stern. Explosion resulted in smoke over ship. Ship damaged. (This could have been the NAKA. She was anchored in the lagoon initially and shortly after the attacks began, left and ran for the open sea-author).
2. AK – 10,000 tons. Anchored 500 yards bearing 145 degrees from Eten Island. VB scored 1 direct hit (one 1,000-lb bomb) on stern. After smoke cleared, the stern was seen to be missing. Ship damaged.
3. AK – 10,000 tons. Anchored 3 miles from Eten Island bearing 060 degrees from Eten Island. VB scored 2 hits (two 1,000-lb bombs), 1 amidships and the other just aft of the bridge. Two large explosions were seen and the ship was burning when the planes retired. Ship damaged. (The location and the damage described point to this being the REIYO MARU-author).
4. AK – 8–10,000 tons. Anchored just southwest of Eten Island. VB scored 1 hit (one 1,000-lb bomb) on bow section. Black smoke enveloped the ship. Ship damaged.
5. CL – 6,000 tons. KATORI class. Anchored 1 1/2 miles east of northeast point of Dublon. Ship was painted two tones of green. VT scored 2 hits (two 500-lb bombs) on stern. The ship was smoking when last seen. Ship damaged. (The ship described here could have been the KATORI herself, seen before she weighed anchor and headed towards North Pass. Its more likely that the vessel was actually a DD and was mis-identified-author).
6. AO – 10,000 tons, 450 feet long. Anchored 3/4 mile bearing 150 degrees from southern tip of Eten Island. VT scored 1 hit (one 500-lb bomb) slightly aft of amidships. The ship was painted grey. Ship damaged. (Its probable that this was the SEIKO MARU, an aft-engine freighter-author).
7. AO – 4–10,000 tons. Anchored 2 miles east of Dublon Town. Ship received 1 hit by VT (one 500-lb bomb) on bow. Ship was left burning. The color of its deck was red. Ship damaged.
8. AK – 8–10,000 tons. Anchored directly east of the north point of Dublon, approximately 2 miles. VT scored 3 hits (three 500-lb bombs) across the stern; ship was left smoking. Ship damaged. (The damage incurred and location suggest it is the NIPPO MARU-author).
9. AK – 6,000 tons, 350 feet long. Anchored in the middle of Eten Anchorage. Ship received 2–4 hits by VT in salvo (two 500-lb bombs) amidships. A large explosion was observed and ship was left smoking. It was not camouflaged. Ship damaged. (This was probably the NAGANO MARU-author).

INTREPID Strike 2A

At 0520 h, INTREPID launched 13VF (including the Air Group Commander), 9VT (each loaded with six fragmentation clusters and six incendiary bombs), and 12VB (each loaded with 1,000 SAP bombs). The VT planes dropped their bombs on the seaplane ramp on Dublon and two ships near the island. Parked aircraft on the ramp were hit and several buildings were set on fire. South of Dublon, hits were observed on the port beam and starboard quarter of the CVS AKITSUSHIMA which blew out the ship's sides and started a fierce fire aboard. One hit was scored on an AK (estimated 8–10,000 tons) also south of Dublon causing a large fire and white smoke. Also, four bombs missed the KATORI underway near Northeast Pass. The Executive Officer of VB-6, Lt. J.P. Phillips, failed to return from the strike. The F6Fs flying cover for the air strike shot down one Oscar and one Val.

BUNKER HILL Strike 3A

The opportunity had come again for BUNKER HILL to put its group of SB2C Helldivers to the test. These planes had been troublesome as their hydraulic systems had been a source of endless problems for the air group mechanics and they had the reputation of being "plumber's nightmares." Also, the SB2Cs too often lost power on take-off. The first strike group consisted of 17 SB2Cs, 8 TBFs, and 4 F6Fs which took off between 0515 and 0527 h. Attacking SB2Cs approached the anchorage west of Dublon from the west and began their dives over Param Island through heavy cloud cover. The low clouds hampered observations but shipping targets were visible west of Moen and Dublon Islands. Eleven VB concentrated on the largest ship which was positively identified as a CVE, possibly the ZUHIO. The ship was observed to be just getting underway and making a slow turn towards the south. No aircraft were present on the flight deck. The SB2Cs dropped 12 bombs (three 1,000-lb GPs, four 1,600-lb APs, and five 1,000-lb SAPs); eleven pilots in VB-17 and several from VT-17 observed 2–3 direct hits, one in the center of the flight deck. Assessment of the total damage to the CVE was difficult due to the low cloud cover. The CVE was noted to be firing at the attacking planes with light but ineffective AA. However, cruisers noted east of Moen were throwing up effective fire of various types. Shore batteries were not firing particularly heavy or intense AA, but were probably responsible for hitting one SB2C as it turned east at low altitude between Dublon and Moen Islands. It was seen crashing into the water.

One SB2C dropped a 1,600-lb AP bomb on a 4,000-ton AO at anchor west-northwest of Dublon causing a large explosion and fire. It appears likely that this ship was the 1,891-ton TAIKICHI MARU. An AK (no size given) at anchor one mile northwest of Dublon was attacked by 2 SB2Cs which dropped two 1,000- and one 1,600-ton AP bombs; all bombs missed. This was probably the HEIAN MARU. The SB2Cs were not through. A cruiser, described as a CA or CL, was attacked by two planes while on a northerly course southeast of Moen Island. This was either the KATORI or NAKA. The two bombs dropped missed their target.

The VB pilots noted that bombing attacks by air groups from TG 58.1 and TG 58.2 had proceeded VB-17's attack. Other observations of shipping and ship movements were listed as follows:

- All major ships which got underway made for the North Pass. Twenty or more AKs and AOs were at anchor east of Eten Island, two on fire.
- One or two DDs, some AKs, and an AH (HIKAWA MARU NO. 2-author) were approaching North Pass.
- A large ship was seen to explode immediately east of Uman Island (RIO DE JANEIRO MARU-author).
- A large AO (actually the cargo ship HANAKAWA MARU-author) was seen at anchor east of Tol Island.

When the 8 TBFs from VT-17 approached Northeast Pass at approximately 0645 h, the KATORI was sighted five miles north of Moen proceeding towards North Pass at high speed with two DDs, the NOWAKE and MAIKAZE, following some distance to the rear. The KATORI was designated as the target for the TBFs. All eight planes broke off and made a glide bombing attack on the ship, dropping three 1,600- and sixteen 500-lb GP bombs. The strong crosswind and violent zig-zag evasive tactics of the CL prevented direct hits from being scored; only two near misses off the stern were reported and no damage was observed.

COWPENS VF and VT Strike

COWPENS launched 8VF and 9VT. One division of F6Fs covered the nine planes of VT-25 which attacked the Moen No 1 airstrip. They encountered no airborne enemy planes. Visibility was poor over the Moen field since the light from the rising sun was obscured by the 1,000-foot hill rising steeply to the side of the strip. Six of the TBFs were loaded with incendiaries and fragmentation clusters (6 each) and the other three with six 100-lb GP and six 100-lb incendiary bombs. Fires along the landward side of the south end of the runway started immediately following the first bomb drops; Betty Bombers parked on the apron were burning. The VT pilots continued making careful runs dropping bombs in the runway areas and many more fires resulted. The Japanese had stretched camouflaged netting from the runway to the hillside. Pilots reported fires starting where bombs were seen crashing through the netting. One pilot dropped his bombs on the southeast turn where he spotted about 10 Vals and Kates parked; all were painted a dark blue. Near the north end of the runway, about 12 vehicles were seen parked inboard from the runway. The entire runway was covered by smoke following the bombing runs. The second VF division covered BUNKER HILL's VB-17 planes which dive bombed Eten Island in a northeasterly direction, observing many hits and resulting fires. Two Zekes were encountered and one possible kill was scored.

–Naval Operational Archives Photo

The Dublon seaplane base and adjoining 104th Naval Air Arsenal are on fire from attacks by U.S. planes at 0830 h on the first day of the carrier strikes. An Emily and a Mavis flying-boat are recognizable amongst the many fighter seaplanes on the apron and ramps.

–National Archives Photo

Photo taken by INTREPID plane shows Moen No. 1 airfield with bomb hits on runway and among parked planes (February 16, 1944, 0830 h).

DOG-MINUS-ONE-DAY Group Strike No. 2

This second wave of strikes was launched by the carriers between 0658 and 0720 h and recovered by 1023 h. Again, planes from CABOT and MONTEREY were not scheduled.

ENTERPRISE Strike 1BE

Planes launched from ENTERPRISE included 10VF, 12VB, and 7VT in conjunction with CAP and ASP aircraft. The TBFs were assigned to attack combatant ships in the following order of priority: BB or CVs, CAs, and CLs. When warships were reported north of the atoll, the TBFs separated from the SBDs and concentrated on the combatant ships trying to escape. At 0900 h, the VT planes were vectored over to a group of "two cruisers believed to be NATORI class CLs" about 35 miles northwest of North Pass. All seven TBFs concentrated on one of the CLs, dropping six 1,000-lb GP and twenty-eight 250-lb GP bombs. One 1,000-lb bomb hit aft of the No. 2 stack, and a 250-lb bomb hit on the bow. Two more misses off the starboard bow probably caused further damage. The CL was left badly smoking and damaged. It appears that the vessel attacked was the KATORI and the other ship identified also as a CL was actually a destroyer. The crews observed a "CA" that had not yet been attacked about 25 miles northwest of Piaanu Pass on a course of 260 degrees, speed 25 knots. This was the light cruiser NAKA attempting to make a high speed escape from the atoll. Another group of ships including "one large AK, one CA, and two DDs" were spotted about 10 miles northwest of North Pass that were being strafed by VF from ENTERPRISE and YORKTOWN. At this point it appears that there were at least three destroyers in separate groups north and northwest of North Pass. Two of the DDs were members of the 4th Destroyer Division, the KAGERO class ships MAIKAZE and NOWAKE. Others present outside the lagoon could have been the SHIRATSUYU class DDs HARUSAME and SHIGURE from the 27th Destroyer Division, 2nd Destroyer Squadron or the AKIKAZE (MINEKAZE class) and MATSUKAZE (KAMIKAZE class). The large AK reported was actually the XCL AKAGI MARU.

The ENTERPRISE SBDs continued their attacks against shipping north and east of Dublon Island. After entering the lagoon from the northeast, 11 planes picked out a "large AO" scoring 2 hits on both sides of the stern. Large explosions resulted which blew out the sides and caused the ship to settle immediately. This ship is believed to be the aft-engine cargo ship, the SEIKO MARU. It was common for aft-engine vessels to be incorrectly identified as tankers. The AKITSUSHIMA, reported to be painted a light grey, was again attacked by a single SBD which scored a hit just aft of amidships. An explosion erupted aboard the vessel causing a large fire aboard. The SBDs had seen a Val over Northeast pass as they had previously approached the atoll and 2 Haps as they were beginning their dives but they had not chosen to attack the U.S. planes. As one plane was completing its pull-out, it was jumped by 4 Zekes and 1 Rufe. One Zeke was hit and was seen plunging into the sea and another was damaged in the fracas that followed. Two planes had been observed during the drops to be taking off from the Eten Island airstrip. There had been moderately heavy but not effective AA fire over the target area; the heaviest was from shore installations and the majority of the light AA was from ships in the anchorage. As the VB planes retired to the northwest, three DDs and a CL were seen proceeding west outside the lagoon.

While escorting the VB and VT planes, the F6Fs encountered six Zekes, shooting down three and damaging the other three. A lone twin-engine Sally heavy bomber was also destroyed. A "TERATSUKI class DD" was strafed north of North Pass. The DD behaved as though unaffected and no return AA fire was observed.

YORKTOWN Strike 1BY

This second strike group from YORKTOWN was comprised of 8VT, 13VB and 12VF. The TBFs launched were loaded with four 500-lb bombs each and were tasked with the mission of destroying the cruisers and DDs north of the atoll. The planes found the KATORI and a ship again described as a "NATORI class CL with 2 or 3 stacks" about 20 miles northwest (290 degrees) from North Pass about 0855 h. This second ship was actually the 2,490-ton KAGERO class DD, the MAIKAZE. Both ships were maneuvering violently and throwing up AA fire. One 3-plane section attacked the DD dropping 12 bombs in trains of four scoring three hits amidships and four near misses, two off each beam. One bomb hit destroyed one of the stacks. A large burst of flame and smoke rising to 500 feet followed the hits. The DD slowed down and trailed black smoke. It was returning fire only from the forward turret. The KATORI was attacked next by a 4-plane section which dropped 16 bombs in trains of four scoring only two near misses, one off the port quarter and one off the port beam.

The SBD crews noted two separate groups of warships located north and northwest of North Pass. Five planes picked out a "new-type DD" in the group 16 miles to the north of the pass. No hits were obtained. The KATORI, in the second group to the northwest, was the next target. A single 1,000-lb bomb hit on the stack was scored along with two near misses within 20 feet. This caused fire and black smoke aboard the CL but did not appear to make it reduce speed. The last target was the SENDAI class CL, the NAKA, now west of Piannu Pass. A 4-plane section missed with all four bombs dropped.

The F6F escorts encountered a Nick 10 miles north of North Pass; it was destroyed by a 4-plane division. Another 4-plane division made strafing runs on a CL at 0815 h 10 miles north of North Pass with no observed results.

ESSEX Strike 2B

The 12VB and 9VT planes launched were assigned shipping targets south and west of Dublon. Enemy aircraft made a stalwart attempt to intercept the attacking planes. The 14 escorting F6Fs engaged the enemy fighters in a series of dogfights and shot down 11 Zekes and 3 Hamps. The TBFs also engaged attacking Zekes, shooting down one and claiming a second probable.

Shipping targets were aplenty. Eight of the F6Fs strafed ships following the VB dive bombing attacks. Results of the strafing by the fighters were not observed. The descriptions of the ships attacked by VB and VT planes below are again numbered to correspond with ship's locations shown in the "ESSEX SHIPPING TARGET SUMMARY."

10. CL – 6,000-tons. Anchored 3/4 mile from Southwest tip of Dublon bearing 270 degrees. (Location corresponds to that of repair ship AKASHI whose configuration and size could easily be mistaken for a CL-author). Ship received one hit by VB (one 1,000-lb bomb) on bow. A large explosion resulted but no fire was seen. Ship damaged.
11. AK – 7,000 tons. Anchored 3/4 of a mile from southwest tip of Dublon bearing 270 degrees alongside CL (target no. 10 above). VB hit ship (one 1,000-lb bomb) amidships and it was observed to be on fire when pilot departed. Ship damaged. (Photographs show this ship to be same size and configuration as KENSHO MARU-author).
12. AK – 5,000 tons. Anchored 1 mile from Dublon bearing 260 degrees. (Possibly KIYOSUMI MARU but relative size reported should be larger than the KENSHO MARU-author). VB hit stern (one 1,000-lb bomb) and explosion was observed. Ship damaged.
13. AE – 10–14,000 tons. Ship was anchored approximately 2 miles east of the eastern point of Dublon. VT scored 1–4 hits (500-lb bombs) on the stern(?). It was seen to explode with terrific force and as a result sank. No other planes were seen to attack between time of hit and explosion. This was the AIKOKU MARU which looked very much like an ocean liner with large superstructure amidships and one large single stack-author).
14. AK – 8–10,000 tons. Anchored as second ship from east side of Eten Anchorage. 2 hits were obtained by VT (two 500-lb bombs) on the stern about the aft hold and the ship was left burning. Ship damaged. (Description corresponds to that of HOKUYO MARU-author).
15. AK – 6–10,000 tons, 500 feet long. Anchored one mile east of the northern tip of Eten Island (Corresponds to known location of the SAN FRANCISCO MARU-author). VT scored one and possibly 2–3 hits (500-lb bombs) amidships. It was last seen smoking. Ship damaged.
16. AK– 10,000 tons. Anchored 2 miles bearing 135 degrees from Dublon. VT scored 2 bomb hits on the port side; ship was left sinking. (Location and damage points indicate this ship is the HOKI MARU-author).
17. AK – 8,000 tons, 450 feet long. Anchored 2 miles southwest of Eten Island. VT obtained 2 hits (two 500-lb bombs), one on port side and the other on the port quarter. This ship was observed by turret gunner to list to starboard. Ship damaged. (Ship was most likely the UNKAI MARU NO. 6-author).

INTREPID Strike 2B

This strike, consisting of 12 SBDs loaded with single 1,000-lb SAP bombs and 8 TBFs loaded with a mix of single 2,000-lb GP or four 500-lb GP bombs each, was launched at 0715 h along with 12 F6F escort planes. The SBDs were instructed by the Strike Commander to drop on the Dublon Island seaplane ramp. Three pilots "didn't get the word" and dropped their bombs on a large AK south of Eten Island, scoring one hit at 0900 h. The other SBDs demolished a large building and scored hits amongst the buildings and planes on the eastern part of the ramp. At least four float planes were reported destroyed and several others damaged.

Three TBFs attacked shipping between Eten and Dublon Islands at 0825 h. An AK was hit by two 500-lb bombs. One of the pilots of these TBFs, Lt. J.E. Bridges, was last seen diving on another ship and was destroyed with his crew members by a devastating explosion that rocked the ship. This vessel, described by pilots as "obviously an AE," was the auxiliary cruiser AIKOKU MARU. The other TBFs dropped their bombs on the Eten airstrip, two hitting installations on the west end of Eten with 2,000-lb bombs and one with 500-lb bombs. A TBF went down but the pilot and crew were later recovered by the U.S.S.

BRADFORD. One F6F shot down two Zekes.

BUNKER HILL Strike 3B

The primary objective of the strike was shipping targets east of Dublon if present, or major targets trying to leave the area. Following launch at 0720 h, the 16 SB2Cs and 9 TBFs escorted by 4 F6Fs approached the atoll from the east and when about five miles east of North Pass, the KATORI was spotted accompanied by a DD, either NOWAKE or MAIKAZE, just outside the pass. A large merchant vessel just inside the lagoon began putting up some heavy AA fire as the planes approached. The cruiser and the merchant vessel, described later as a 550-foot tanker of about 13,000 tons, were selected as targets. It is likely either the FUJISAN or SHINKOKU MARUs steamed through the northern part of the lagoon and returned later. A good possibility also exists that the ship was actually the XCL AKAGI MARU and she was mis-identified. This would account for the heavy AA reported. The squadron of SB2Cs broke up for the attack about one mile northeast of North Pass and began their dives over the two target ships from north to south releasing their bombs at between 1,500 to 2,000 feet. Many of the planes strafed in their dives and after pullout, continued strafing nearby reef installations, ships and small craft. Two SB2Cs hit the KATORI 1–2 times amidships with 1,000-lb bombs. The TBFs attacked next dropping three 1,600-lb AP and twenty-one 500-lb GP bombs in a glide bombing attack from the southwest. It is believed that the planes hit the bow of the CL with one 1,600-lb and one 500-lb bomb. One near miss amidships and two near the stern were reported but there is no evidence that they damaged the ship. The cruiser slowed down and was reported to be heavily damaged and on fire from the explosions aboard when the planes departed.

The previously reported AO was attacked by 13 SB2Cs as it was proceeding through North Pass to sea. Only one hit was reported; a 1,000-lb SAP bomb caused a large explosion heavily damaging the ship. The SB2C crews reported AA fire coming from the CL, the nearby DD and a small amount of 3-inch AA coming from the reef islands east of North Pass. One Zeke and one unidentified aircraft were spotted north of the lagoon but no interception was attempted. Observation of ship disposition in the anchorages was difficult because the attack took place at the extreme north end of the atoll. A second DD and a torpedo boat were seen in the northern part of the lagoon. MAIKAZE and NOWAKE were generally close to the vicinity of the KATORI; however, DDs HARUSAME and SHIGURE were seen outside of the reef north of North Pass also. Many ships were seen in the anchorage east of Eten Island and two were on fire. A large number of ships were also seen in the anchorage just west of Dublon Island. There were large fires coming from Eten Island and from the bomber strip on the northwest side of Moen Island.

U.S.S. BUNKER HILL AIR INTELLIGENCE REPORT SORTIES NOS. 41, 42

Photographs taken during the first two strikes by specially designated photo-reconnaissance planes from BUNKER HILL were interpreted following the air raids. The results are listed here to give an accurate description of damage and of the disposition of Japanese ships and aircraft early the morning of February 16.

DUBLON ISLAND

Damage Assessment:

Three fuel fires are observed at the seaplane base on the south shore of the island. Two other fires are also seen in the nearly area. Due to smoke covering the base, no plane count or damage assessment was possible in this area.

New Installations Observed:

Three possible heavy AA positions are located on the ridge just north of the southern seaplane base. Three possible heavy AA positions are seen on the hill on the southeast point of Dublon Island.

ETEN ISLAND

Damage Assessment:

Approximately 24 planes are seen burning on the apron and the edges of the runway. Smoke is coming from the A and R shop area.

Plane Count:

Approximately 40 fighters, 6 dive bombers, and 1MB (medium or Mitsubishi bomber?) were located on the runway and apron.

MOEN ISLAND

Damage Assessment:

Approximately 13 planes are seen burning on the bomber strip (Moen No. 1). A large fire is burning on the east side of the airfield.

A large fire, probably from a larger building, is burning at the seaplane base (Moen No. 2) on the southern tip of the island.

Plane Count:

No plane count can be made on the bomber strip. Four possible planes are seen on the apron at the seaplane base on the southern tip of the island.

Shipping:

South of Eten Island.

2 AKs, 520 and 440 feet in length.

Between Dublon Island and Eten Island.

3 AOs measuring approximately 480, 300, and 240 feet in length. (Photos show these to be the FUJISAN MARU and two smaller aft-engine cargo ships similar in configuration to that of the GOSEI MARU-author).

1 unidentified ship measuring 260 feet.

1 inter-island craft measuring 140 feet.

8 small craft measuring 120 feet each.

5 small craft measuring 60 feet each.

Numerous barges and small boats.

East of Dublon Island and Eten Island.

1 possible DD which is approximately 300 feet long.

12 AKs measuring approximately 400, 400, 350, 325, 300, 300, 275, 250, 225, and 225 feet. One of the 300-foot AKs is smoking very much. A large area of burning oil is seen on the water in this area.

Southwest of Moen Island.

1 AK measuring approximately 300-feet long.

Off Northwest Corner of Dublon Island.

1 DD measuring approximately 300 feet in length (FUMITSUKI-author).

5 AKs measuring 325, 260, 250, 240, and 200 feet in length. In addition to the above mentioned ships, 1 AK can be seen sinking.

2 small craft of 60 feet each.

COWPENS VF Strike

Sixteen F6Fs from COWPENS escorted the BUNKER HILL strike force. One division covering the SB2C's attack on the CL and AO observed a single Oscar some distance away, flying east over North Pass, and a moment later 2 Zekes or Oscars were spotted flying from the direction of North Pass towards Moen. The intentions of the Japanese aircraft were not apparent as they did not attempt to attack the U.S. planes. Both the cruiser and the tanker were strafed by several of the F6Fs. No visible effect was noted.

DOG-MINUS-ONE-DAY Group Strike No. 3

The third task group strike was launched from the carriers between 0903 and 0942 h and recovered by 1229 h. The planes launched from MONTEREY provided CAP over the Task Force only.

–National Archives Photo

Panoramic view of the islands early on 16 February 1944 shows large group of ships clustered in the Combined Fleet repair anchorage between Dublon and Fefan Islands (right center) and the Fourth Fleet Anchorage (left rear). Heavy smoke is coming from the Moen No. 2 seaplane/fighter base (foreground center). The TONAN MARU NO. 3 is on fire and emitting white smoke to the right center of the picture. The ship immediately behind and slightly to the right is the repair ship AKASHI with the KENSHO MARU to its left. Behind the AKASHI are the KIYOSUMI and HOYO MARUs. Directly to the left of the TONAN MARU NO. 3 is the hospital ship HIKAWA MARU NO. 2 and further to the left are two more ships, the HEIAN MARU (largest) and an unidentified AK.

ENTERPRISE Strike 1CE

The composition of planes launched at this time from ENTERPRISE included 11 VF, 10 VB and 8 VT. Loaded with 1,000-lb bombs, the SBDs were assigned to attack and destroy the warships outside North Pass. At the rendezvous point off North Pass, a Zeke, a Rufe, and a Hamp were encountered; it appeared that they were looking to intercept any U.S. plane stragglers. The first group of warships found was composed of two DDs, a large AK, and a CA (actually a CL, the KATORI-author). The "large AK" was the XCL AKAGI MARU, which like KATORI was observed dead in the water and burning as a result of an earlier attack. The SBDs concentrated on a "FUBUKI class DD," dropping 10 bombs. No hits were attained, only two very near misses (20 feet). These caused the DD to stop. Further strafing attacks started a fire on the stern. Its likely that this DD was the SHIGURE which was actually a SHIRATSUYU class DD, an improved version derived from the FUBUKI class DDs. The SHIGURE was later reported to have its No. 2 and 3 guns damaged, the No. 2 boiler unserviceable, and its depth charge storeroom submerged. The DD suffered 36 casualties in the attacks on Truk before escaping to Palau. The sister ship of the SHIGURE, the HARUSAME, was likely damaged at this time also, although it was able to keep maneuvering at high speed and continue returning AA fire.

The TBF planes were to search out and destroy any SS, AO, or AKs within the atoll. After encountering 2 Zekes over Northeast Pass that fled when the U.S. planes approached, the planes continued on until a group of ships northwest of Dublon and west of Moen were seen and picked as their initial targets. These ships were at the center of the anchorage and consisted of a DD underway heading south, one AK and an AO about 150 feet apart heading north, and another AK about 500 yards to the west of the AK and AO on a south heading. The TBFs made their glide bombing drops southwest to northeast across the group of ships. The TBF attacking the DD missed with all four 500-lb bombs. The single AK was attacked by a 3-plane division; two hits were claimed out of 12 bombs dropped but damage was not determined.

–Naval Operational Archives Photo
Both the airfield on Eten and the seaplane base on Dublon have been hit in the first strikes on 16 February 1944. Shipping is concentrated in the Eten Anchorage and off the south shore of Dublon Island.

Twelve bombs were also dropped on the AK and AO by another 3-plane division but no hits were scored. The next target was a 10,000-ton AK steaming west at 12–15 knots from the Dublon-Moen channel. Two bombs were dropped and two didn't release. The bombs straddled the AK, the first hitting short and the second was long and very close aboard. This second bomb was scored as a near miss; the turret gunner believed that the bomb hit the edge of the ship and exploded alongside. The AK was seen to reverse its course and begin heading east following the attack. It proceeded into the channel between Moen and Dublon where it sought protection from the AA emplacement positions on the ends of the two islands. One TBF spotted a Jake float plane taxiing on the seaplane ramp on Moen No. 2. It was strafed but did not burn. Another AK, reported to be smaller than the 10,000-ton AK described previously, was spotted on the southwest side of the Moen anchorage heading in a west direction. It was the target of the last TBF with bombs remaining. The plane dove on the ship from the west-southwest direction scoring a hit forward in the vicinity of the bridge causing smoke and flames aboard.

The VF escorts encountered onlt two Hamps and since enemy fighters were scarce, they strafed a large AK in the Dublon anchorage which returned fire at its attackers. A CL and a DD outside the lagoon about four miles off North Pass were also strafed.

YORKTOWN Strike 1CY

Planes participating in this strike (12VB, 8VT, and 12VF) were assigned to attack the warships escaping northwest of North Pass. The TBFs located the KATORI in a cruising formation being led by a "large AP"; two DDs were flanking the CL. This formation was comprised of the AKAGI MARU leading the KATORI and followed by the NOWAKE and MAIKAZE. At approximately 1023 h, the KATORI was hit by two 500-lb bombs on the stern which made it stop dead in the water; a big yellow explosion occurred aboard about three minutes later. The MAIKAZE, described as a "new type DD," took a single direct hit and nine near misses. The hit was on the bow or forward of the turret which did not fire again. The DD was left smoking and dead in the water. The NOWAKE was slowed down by two near misses off the port bow. The AKAGI MARU was hit once amidships; a large explosion and fire resulted. The action reports mention that the XCL had 5-inch guns mounted on platforms on both the bow and stern. The SBDs attacked the same formation of warships with the accompanying AKAGI MARU. Damage assessment reports listed one 1,000-lb bomb hit on the stern and three near misses on the KATORI. The five planes attacking the AKAGI MARU got no hits but all scored near misses. Two near misses were also reported on both accompanying destroyers. The escorting F6Fs found no enemy planes aloft. Two strafing runs were made on the KATORI with unobserved results. Six strafing runs were made on the DDs, silencing the small AA on one. Another DD located two miles north of North Pass was reported; this was probably HARUSAME or SHIGURE. This DD had apparently been severely damaged and out of control temporarily; its bridge had been heavily shot up.

ESSEX Strike 2C

ESSEX launched 14VF, 3VT, and 16VB to attack the group of warships northwest of North Pass. The first target was MAIKAZE which had been bombed and thoroughly strafed by YORKTOWN planes and was seeping oil on the water. A single explosion was observed amidships. VB planes scored only near misses on the DD.

–Naval Operational Archives Photo
Ships anchored to the west of the submarine base (upper center of photo) along the west shore of Dublon Island from right to left include the camouflage painted HEIAN MARU, an unidentified AK, the all-white painted hospital ship HIKAWA MARU NO. 2, and the damaged and smoking TONAN MARU NO. 3. Many small craft are off shore of the Fourth Naval Dockyards or "Nanko" area in the lower center of photo.

The second target was the KATORI. The CL was circling at about 10 knots bearing 330 degrees, about 15 miles from North Pass. Bomb attacks by two VT planes left the CL dead in the water from three hits amidships and on the stern. The last ship attacked was the AKAGI MARU circling with KATORI. VT planes scored three 500-lb bomb hits on the stern. The ship was settling fast by the stern and smoking. It had disappeared when the next strike arrived.

INTREPID Strike 2C

This strike, consisting of 12 F6Fs (including the Air Group Commander), 12 SBDs (each with one 1,000-lb SAP bomb), and 8 TBFs (5 carrying Mark 13 torpedoes and 3 carrying four 500-lb bombs each) was launched at 0930 H. The VB division at 1035 h unsuccessfully attacked a DD described as an "old-type with two stacks and one gun mount forward and a turtle back" (indicated to them as a CL target) about five miles northwest of North Pass. Pilots reported that the oil slick the DD was trailing indicated it had just come out of the lagoon through North Pass, had engaged in some high speed maneuvers, and was just completing a full circle when attacked. This was the AKIKAZE, built in 1920–21. The eight TBFs were directed to the same target at 1040 h. A single 500-lb bomb hit aft of the two stacks; all other bombs and five torpedoes missed. As the planes were retiring, an Oscar shot down one of the TBFs. The Oscar was attacked and was last seen hightailing it with his engine smoking.

Six VB pilots at 1045 h attacked a "new-type DD," probably HARUSAME or SHIGURE, in the lagoon north of Udot Island heading in the general direction of North Pass. No hits were made, although one extremely close miss was observed to starboard and confirmed by photographs. The Air Group Commander and his wingman failed to return from the flight.

CABOT VT Strike

Three TBFs were launched and joined ESSEX VTs for attacks on escaping warships north of the atoll. The KATORI and the AKAGI MARU were found 15 miles northwest of North Pass, both just completing a circling maneuver to the right with the CL in the lead. The CABOT planes, loaded with 500-lb bombs, joined 3 TBFs from ESSEX and made a coordinated attack on the KATORI. All bombs appeared to miss the target.

The crews reported seeing ESSEX VTs attacking the "large AP" (AKAGI MARU). Four bombs were dropped in a rapid salvo on the ship. The first was a near miss to starboard; the second and the third exploded on the stern while the fourth was a near miss to port. A huge explosion resulted from the bomb hits. The AKAGI MARU began settling by the stern and was sinking rapidly with her decks awash when the planes retired. Both ships returned heavy but inaccurate AA fire.

BUNKER HILL Strike 3C

Assigned an objective of "major targets in Truk," the 12VB, 6VT, and 12VF responded to reports that warships had been spotted west of Truk. Searching to the south of the atoll, the planes found a "3 or 4 stack SENDAI or TENRYU class cruiser" about 25 to 30 miles southwest of North Pass underway at 25 knots on a 040 degree course. This was indeed the SENDAI class CL NAKA which had been caught at anchor earlier but now had slipped out of the lagoon and was steaming at high speed for safety. After circling to look for other enemy ships, the VB and VT planes turned back and dove from 13,000 feet on a now-turning CL at 1055 h. As the planes commenced a coordinated attack, the CL started a clockwise tight circle at high speed. The SB2Cs dropped their 1,000-lb bombs from 1,500 to 1,000 feet from northwest to southeast; no hits were made. The TBFs dove so that just prior to turning in on the target, they were in line astern and circling the ship's circular path on the opposite course. Each plane turned in at the point from which it could launch an attack on the bow area of the cruiser. Torpedo drops were made at a speed of 200 knots at an altitude of 300 feet between 800-1,000 yards from the target. The TBFs scored one and possible two torpedo hits on the CL resulting in three large internal explosions; the magazines were probably hit. One pilot continued strafing the CL 3 to 4 minutes after the others had retired. He reported that the vessel had lost way and the No. 1 turret was awash when he finally departed.

The VB pilots and crews made the following observations regarding ship dispositions in the atoll following their bombing runs:

- 10 to 12 AKs were seen east of Eten. Three were on fire.
- Three medium AKs were anchored west of Tsis.
- A large AO was anchored east of Tol. (This was the freighter HANAKAWA MARU-author).
- A TERATSUKI DD was beached southwest of Kuop Atoll. It was firing AA and appeared little damaged. (The ship was actually the old MINEKAZE class DD TACHIKAZE- author).
- Several AKs were anchored on each side of Uman Island.

The VF narrative described the NAKA as being found 25 miles southwest of Piannu Pass. It was observed to have 4 stacks. Four of the F6Fs strafed the CL from stem to stern with 1,800 rounds of .50 caliber from altitudes of 5,000 to 500 feet. The planes dove from the windward side, pulling out very low and retiring through the smoke rising from the CL in order to throw off the Japanese AA gunners. Damage from the strafing could not be assessed. The F6Fs encountered a Kate as the formation approached the Task Force. The Kate, which had been flying directly towards the F6Fs, turned and fled just above the wavetops. In a coordinated attack by two F6Fs, the tracers of one were seen to enter the cockpit and starboard wingroot of the Kate. It burst into flames and hit the water.

COWPENS VT and VF Strike

COWPENS launched 8VF and 9VT to combine with planes from BUNKER HILL for escort duties and to bomb shipping in and near Truk. The TBFs joined up with the BUNKER HILL formation and were approaching the atoll from the south close to Otta Pass when the Target Observer vectored them to the west. The NAKA had been spotted making a high speed escape 25 miles to the southwest headed on a course of 120 degrees. COWPENS VT identified the ship as a Japanese CL of the JINTSU class; the CL began firing while the planes were still 10 miles distant. The TBFs, loaded with 2,000-lb GP bombs (5 planes) and 1,000-lb AP bombs (4 planes), attacked the CL straight on. Dives were made at 300 knots from 11,000 feet and were released at 3,000 feet with pullout at 2,500 feet. The CL began radical maneuvers. Four bombs hit within 100 feet of the ship; no damage appeared to result. BUNKER HILL VB were orbiting waiting for COWPENS VT to conclude their attack. They then attacked with the same ineffectual results. BUNKER HILL VTs then initiated the well-coordinated torpedo attack described previously. COWPENS plane crews observed one torpedo hit just aft of the bridge structure which blew a ball of orange flame 300 feet into the air. A second torpedo was seen to miss the bow by a few feet. The CL slowed down and appeared to be barely underway with a large oil slick trailing astern. AA fire, consisting of mostly 25mm and 5-inch DP guns forward, slowed momentarily with the torpedo hit but was renewed again vigorously moments later.

One division of VF-25 acted as close support and the other as intermediate cover during the attack on the NAKA. The DD TACHIKAZE, aground on the reef at Kuop Atoll, was observed to be putting up accurate medium strength AA.

<u>DOG-MINUS-ONE-DAY Group Strike No. 4</u>

This series of strikes were launched between 1059 and 1122 h and recovered by 1444 h. COWPENS provided CAP only during this period; CABOT and MONTEREY did not participate.

ENTERPRISE Strike 1DE

The primary mission for the 11VB and 4VT was to destroy warships attempting to escape to the west of Truk Lagoon. The four TBFs spotted the CL KATORI and DDs NOWAKE and MAIKAZE steaming in zig-zag patterns at about 1220 h. All planes concentrated on the KATORI, dropping sixteen 500-lb bombs from 3500 feet altitude. Two hits were made, one on the bow and the second along the port side of the CL. The TBFs encountered a single Val northeast of the lagoon but did not engage.

All 11 SBDs concentrated on the KATORI, dropping eleven 1,000-lb bombs. A near miss off the port bow tossed the CL out of the water. Following two more near misses on the starboard side in quick succession, the ship was seen to be laying dead in the water and had not gotten underway as the planes retired. A Japanese DD was seen rescuing survivors from the water to the northwest from an unidentified sinking ship. These were crewmembers of the AKAGI MARU.

Four of the 7 F6Fs strafed a "small AP" about 25 miles northwest of Truk. The vessel returned light AA at the fighters. Many hits were observed but the ship didn't burn. Finding the air free of enemy interceptors, the F6Fs left the formation of VB and VT planes and made multiple strafing runs on both the Param and Moen No. 1 airfields. Some heavy but inaccurate AA fire was noted at Param Island where the planes burned two Bettys and one Zeke on the ground. One Betty was strafed and burned at the Moen field.

YORKTOWN Strike 1DY

The 8 TBFs launched as part of the strike group from YORKTOWN had an objective of performing a low-level bombing "masthead attack" on shipping targets in the lagoon. Ships attacked were spread over several anchorages and their identification and exact location is difficult to correlate in many cases. Assessment of ultimate target damage and sinking results were not observed due to the nature of the high-speed, low-level attacks on shipping during this strike. Two VT planes dropped a total of five 500-lb bombs from 200 feet altitude on two AKs, one east of Eten and the other to the west of the island. Two of the bombs missed, the three others were not seen. An AK anchored west of Fefan took a hit on the stern; the effects of the bomb were not observed. A submarine was spotted underway between Uman and Eten Islands. It had just submerged when one TBF dropped a single bomb from 800 feet with a 4–5 second delay fusing. The bomb exploded directly above or below the sub which had submerged 2 or 3 seconds before while the TBF was beginning its dive. It was believed that the effect of the 4–5 second delay fusing was similar to that of a depth bomb. A big explosion erupted from the hit and a large oil slick was seen where the sub had last been. Further observations were impossible as the TBF came under attack by Japanese fighters. This sub was undoubtedly one of the two submarines listed by the Japanese as having received minor damage from aircraft attacks on 16 February, the I–10 and the RO–42. A 300-foot AK anchored south of Eten was hit by two bombs dropped from 400 feet. One hit on the deck aft and one hit into the side on the starboard quarter. The ship was set on fire with flame and smoke coming from the aft end. Two hits were scored on the fantail of a 5,000-ton AK underway between Fefan and Eten Islands. The hits caused a big explosion but further effects were not observed. An AK (2,500 tons estimated) anchored southwest of Uman Island was the recipient of two hits into the port side aft of its beam. These hits caused an explosion aboard but again, further effects of the hits were not observed. Another AK, estimated at 2,500-tons and 300 feet long, was attacked while anchored southwest of Eten Island. One 500-lb bomb hit into the port side and exited at the starboard side throwing splinters and then exploding. The ship was set afire. The aircraft action reports note that the ship had 5-inch guns mounted on both the bow and stern and was firing rapidly at the attacking planes. To the south of the atoll, an AK anchored 100 feet off the north shore of Funamu Island was damaged by a near miss off the starboard beam. It was last seen settling by the stern. Two AKs, the first located north of Onna Island and the second west of the island were attacked by 2 TBFs. A bomb carried away the mast of one ship while two misses off the starboard beam of the other started the AK smoking amidships.

The technique to be used for these glide bombing dives was to start at a considerable altitude with the TBFs building up speeds to 360 knots before leveling off at 1,000 feet and then dropping bombs two at a time from altitudes between 100 and 300 feet. The bombs would travel almost horizontally into the sides of the ships in most cases and with the 4–5 second delay fuses would either explode inside the ship or drop down its side and explode beneath it, causing severe underwater damage. Near misses would also cause underwater damage. The TBFs were supposed to make a second run on a different target with the plane's remaining bombs, but because of attacks by enemy fighters, only 2 TBFs were able to complete their last bombing runs. The results were good despite the interference from the Japanese planes; out of 22 bombs dropped, 9 different ships received 10 hits. The VT planes encountered five Japanese fighters (3 Tonys, 1 Zeke or Hamp, and 1 Tojo) and were able to destroy one of the Tonys. In addition to the primary shipping targets attacked, one plane dropped two bombs on two small buildings at Quoi Island. Both buildings were destroyed. Another TBF also strafed a sampan east of Onna Island.

The SBDs in the strike group (13 planes) found several shipping targets available but in separate portions of the lagoon anchorages. Several sections broke off from the group to attack shipping targets of opportunity. The direction of dives were varied in most attacks. The first target AK was estimated to be 15,000 tons at anchor east of Uman. A 3-plane section obtained three hits, leaving the ship in a sinking condition. This was the ex-passenger liner, the RIO DE JANEIRO MARU. The second target reported was an 8,000-ton AK; it was attacked by 2 SBDs that scored near misses off the starboard side. The third AK (estimated at 8,000 tons) was hit on the port bow and along the starboard side amidships. Another bomb hit just 10 feet off the stern. There was a large explosion amidships. This ship was the TAIHO MARU and it was blown in two. An AK (estimated at 6–8,000 tons) was jarred with two near misses, one only 5 feet off the stern. No further results were observed. One SBD missed a small trawler and another made a 20-foot near miss with a bomb off the bow of a 5,000-ton AK. The location was not given for either.

Japanese fighters were active during the strike and the 16 VF escorts encountered 20 Zekes over the atoll, mostly around the 6,000-foot altitude level. Ten Zekes were shot down and another two were probable kills. One Zeke crashed on the hangar apron at the Eten airstrip and hit 3 Kates on the ground which exploded and burned. Three strafing runs were then made on other parked aircraft on the same apron. The F6Fs also made four strafing runs on two AKs whose locations were not given.

ESSEX Strike 2D

Planes launched from ESSEX (10VF, 8VT, and 12VB) were also vectored to the location of the warships northwest of North Pass. The F6Fs destroyed one Rufe while heading towards the target. The KATORI was the target of the fighters; 11 F6Fs made one strafing run on the ship which was estimated at this time to be 15 miles northwest of North Pass. The damage was undetermined. The VB dropped their bombs on a DD but scored only near misses. The KATORI was the designated target for the torpedo loaded TBFs. One torpedo hit the CL amidships on the port side from about 40 degrees off the port bow.

INTREPID Strike 2D

The primary objective of this strike was also to destroy the combatant ships trying to escape to the north of the atoll. The strike was composed of 16 F6Fs, 11 SBDs (loaded with one 1,000-lb SAP bomb each), and 7 TBFs carrying Mark 13 torpedoes. The KATORI, described as being located 10 to 15 miles bearing 320 degrees from North Pass, was the object of the initial attacks. At 1310 h, one SBD hit the CL amidships. The ship appeared to be heavily damaged and rocked hard by the bomb. Two torpedo hits by the TBFs at 1315 h, one just aft of amidships on the port side and the second on the starboard bow stopped the CL dead in the water. The ship was left for the U.S. battleship striking force, now seen approaching about 15 miles away.

At 1310 to 1315 h, the SBDs scored a hit on the bow of "another CL, possibly KUMA class," located slightly northeast of the KATORI. The identification was wrong; the ship described was the destroyer MAIKAZE-author. The NOWAKE was observed making radical evasive turns about 5 miles north of the cruiser.

BUNKER HILL Strike 3D

Twelve SB2Cs loaded with 1,000-lb bombs and 10 TBFs with torpedo loads were launched to attack shipping inside the lagoon. The VB and VT planes were escorted by 12 F6Fs. Upon arriving over Northeast Pass, the planes turned north and skirted the lagoon looking for shipping targets. Crews noted considerable shipping activity in the anchorage west of Dublon and north of Fefan as they continued around towards the southern part of the lagoon. After assessing the situation, ships at the southern end of the anchorage between Fefan and Uman Islands were selected as targets.

Four VT and 5VB planes picked a large AK, the AMAGISAN MARU, anchored off the southwest shore of Uman as the initial target. The ship, described as 10,000 tons and 500 feet long, was hit first by a VB plane with a 1,000-lb GP bomb and immediately thereafter by 1–3 torpedoes from the VT planes. The first torpedo hit apparently set a large quantity of fuel oil on fire. Two subsequent explosions indicated more torpedo hits. The vessel was reported sinking as the planes retired. The BUNKER HILL photo-reconnaissance plane (Sortie No. 43) overflew the AMAGISAN MARU 10–15 minutes following the attack and reported it burning fiercely and sinking by the bow. The ship had gone under by the next strike.

The SANKISAN MARU, described as a 450-foot long, 8,000-ton AK, was the next victim of the VB planes as it was anchored west of Uman. Four planes dropped five 1,000-lb bombs getting one hit forward. Two SB2Cs dropped their bombs on the "4,000-ton, 360-foot long AK" (YUBAE MARU-author) off the northwest side of Uman. The planes dropped two bombs; one hit amidships which started a blazing fire with heavy smoke. The ship was heavily damaged.

The photo-recon plane, carrying one 1,000-lb SAP bomb, dove on an AO described as 13,000 tons and 550 feet long located off the

Several vessels are on fire east of Eten and Dublon Islands in photo taken by plane from carrier INTREPID on 16 February 1944. Note layer of smoke remaining on the water in left center of photo where AIKOKU MARU has blown up and sunk.

–Naval Operational Archives Photo

southwest point of TOL Island. The bomb missed the ship. (This vessel was consistently being identified incorrectly. It was actually the 4,739-ton freighter HANAKAWA MARU-author.)

Four TBFs launched torpedoes against the YUBAE MARU (estimated 450 feet, 8,000 tons) just off the southeastern tip of Fefan Island. Pilots and crews confirmed one and possibly two hits on the target; one torpedo took an erratic course. Photos taken showed the ship sinking with the decks awash. The ship was reported gone by VT pilots on the subsequent strike (3F) and was believed sunk.

One torpedo was launched against a DD (unidentified class) underway just east of Tsis Island. The destroyer was making about 20 knots and turned hard-to-port as the torpedo was launched causing it to pass about 20 feet astern of the ship.

A single TBF launched a torpedo at the already-damaged HOKI MARU reported underway at five knots two miles southeast of Eten. The pilot and crew reported a hit which was confirmed by his wingman and crew. The ship, estimated at 10,000 tons and 550 feet long, was heavily damaged. On Strike 3F, the ship was reported burning fiercely.

VF-18 escort planes had a busy time during the strike. Four F6Fs strafed a small AK near the tiny islet southeast of Eten firing 960 rounds of .50 caliber from 3,000 to 500 feet. The vessel was left burning. Two F6Fs strafed a large AK south of Fefan expending 400 rounds of ammunition. The ship had previously been hit by a bomb. This target was probably one of the same ships attacked earlier by VB planes, either the YUBAE or SANKISAN MARUs. Three PT boats southwest of Tarik Island were targets of six of the F6Fs. After expending 2,800 rounds of ammunition, one of the PTs was left dead in the water and the other two were left burning. Enemy aircraft encountered by the F6Fs included three olive drab colored Zekes and a Val west of Dublon, one Nell over the central lagoon area, one Mavis west of Moen, and one Zeke (blue colored) south of Eten.

BUNKER HILL VB reported the status of shipping dispositions in their action report narrative. No warships were observed inside the lagoon. In addition to the ships attacked by VB, the following ships were seen:

- 1 AK smoking east of Uman Island.
- 1 AK east of Dublon on fire.
- 2 AKs east of Eten, one sunk by the stern with only the bow showing above water, and the other on fire.
- 1 ship, apparently an AP, was hit by a torpedo between Eten and Fefan Islands. The torpedo caused a large explosion and fire sending black smoke up to 4,000 or 5,000 feet.
- 1 AK was seen smoking west of Dublon.
- 3 AKs off the northeast shore of Uman were undamaged.
- Many other ships were seen in the anchorage west of Dublon and north or Fefan Islands.

COWPENS VF Strike

COWPENS launched 8 F6Fs to provide CAP over the TG 50.9 battleship attack force between 1122 and 1553 h. Four of the planes encountered enemy ships northwest of North Pass about 70 miles from the task group. The pilots witnessed the destruction of a "DD and 2 CLs" (actually one CL....the KATORI, the DD MAIKAZE, and escort vessel SHONAN MARU NO. 15-author). They strafed a DD and managed to come under fire by friendly AA. A single Val was encountered 10 miles northwest of North Pass and was destroyed.

DOG-MINUS-ONE-DAY Group Strike No. 5

The fifth coordinated group strike of the first day was launched between 1237 and 1330 h and recovered by the carriers by 1625 h. CABOT and MONTEREY did not launch their planes.

ENTERPRISE Strike 1EE

The composition of planes making up this strike group launched from ENTERPRISE included 10VB, 8VT, and 13VF. The SBDs were assigned shipping targets in the west Dublon anchorage. The planes encountered 4 Zekes as they were assembling at the rendezvous point near North Pass; the enemy fighters were apparently hanging around the area looking for stragglers or crippled U.S. strike aircraft. The VB group split into 5-plane divisions and attacked a 12,000-ton AO and a 10,000-ton AK anchored not far away from the oiler. This was the HOYO and KIYOSUMI MARUs respectively. The first division of SBDs dropped 1,000-lb bombs from 1,500 feet, hitting the HOYO MARU near the centerline of the ship just forward of the stern and leaving the tanker on fire. The second division got two direct hits out of the five bombs dropped on the KIYOSUMI MARU. The former XCL was hit just aft of amidships and on the starboard side of the stern; the ship immediately took on a list and began burning. Anti-aircraft fire over the anchorage was intense. The planes reported seeing several Zekes in the distance. An AO in the anchorage was seen hit amidships by an SBD of another air group causing a huge explosion and apparent disintegration of the vessel. This was likely the TAIKICHI MARU. A hospital ship (the HIKAWA MARU NO. 2-author) was reported underway in the anchorage.

The mission assigned to the TBFs was to destroy merchant shipping in and out of the lagoon. The planes picked shipping at the Eten Anchorage as targets. The first was a large AK taken under attack at 1430 h. Six planes dropped twenty-four 500-lb bombs....all missed. One of the remaining TBFs attacked an unidentified ship to the north heading towards North Pass. All four bombs were again misses. The final TBF attempted to bomb an AK in the Eten Anchorage on a first run but its bombs wouldn't release. The plane then proceeded to attack a DD five miles inside the reef heading towards North Pass. Two certain and another probable hit was made on the destroyer, leaving it dead in the water enveloped in smoke and flames. It is believed that this was either the AKIKAZE, HARUSAME or SHIGURE. All three destroyers suffered significant damage in the air raids.

The 13 F6F escorts spotted only one enemy aircraft, a Tony, but did not engage. Several ships in the anchorages were strafed including the following:

- 1 AO to the west of Moen Island heading south. (SHINKOKU OR FUJISAN MARU-author).
- 1 DD in the Eten Anchorage.
- 1 DD afire and beached on Uman Island.
- 1 AP afire in the Dublon anchorage. (HEIAN MARU-author).
- 1 AO in the Dublon anchorage which was set on fire by strafing. (This was either the HOYO MARU which was attacked at about the same time by ENTERPRISE VB planes or the TONAN MARU NO. 3 which had been on fire for some time-author).

Two planes strafed Param airfield hitting 3 Hamps on the ground. One was seen to explode and two others burned. The Eten airfield was also strafed with undetermined results.

YORKTOWN Strike 1EY

Planes launched to carry out this strike against enemy shipping included 13VB, 12VF, and 6VT. The TBF's mission was to destroy enemy shipping in the lagoon by glide bombing; each plane was loaded with four 500-lb bombs with .025 second delay fuses. The attacks began about 1405 h. A 3-plane section picked out the YAMAGIRI MARU described as a large (500- to 600-foot) AK near the north shore of Fefan Island. The planes strafed the ship in the beginning of their dives and then scored a single hit amidships with near misses off the starboard quarter and beam. A single TBF attacked two AKs near the south shore of Fefan; the 4 bombs missed by 200 feet. An AK on the east side of the lagoon (likely between Fefan and Dublon Islands-author) was the target of another TBF which had his bombs release prematurely. The plane did manage to strafe the ship in his dive. A 300-foot long AK, anchored west of Eten was hit by 3 of 4 bombs dropped amidships to the stern setting the whole aft half of the ship on fire. Following their bombing runs, the TBFs continued to seek out shipping and shore targets to strafe. Two planes spotted 35- and 75-foot yachts in the southern part of the lagoon. Hits were confirmed on both boats. One TBF strafed a "new-type DD" west of Moen, hitting amidships. The DD was reported to have two turrets forward returning AA fire. One 3-planes section concentrated on buildings on some of the smaller islands of Eo, Lemoil, Fanuella, and Falo Islands. The planes reported heavy AA fire from shore installations on both Dublon and Fefan Islands. Several Bettys were observed taxiing on Param Island.

The SBDs attacked shipping targets primarily in the anchorage west of Dublon and north of Fefan Island also. The first ship attacked by two planes was an AK estimated at 10,000 tons anchored northwest of Fefan Island. This was the same vessel attacked by the TBFs, the YAMAGIRI MARU. The SBDs scored one 1,000-lb bomb along the aft starboard quarter and a near miss just off the stern. The next target, also located northwest of Fefan Island, was an AK estimated between 4–6,000 tons. Two SBDs scored one hit just forward of amidships and a near miss (20 feet) off the port bow. The AO SHINKOKU MARU, also anchored northwest of Fefan Island, was hit by a single bomb amidships. An 8,000-ton AK lying north of Fefan Island, possibly the KIYOSUMI MARU, was hit on the stern. One SBD spotted two barges tethered together and managed to hit one of them almost dead center. Single planes also hit a 5,000-ton vessel located northwest of Fefan on the bow and another 5,000-ton AK took a near miss off the stern between Fefan and Dublon Islands. This second vessel was likely the KENSHO MARU. The last ship attacked was located in the Eten Anchorage; this 6–8,000-ton AK was the target of 3 SBDs which got one hit on the stern and misses off each beam.

The F6F escorts split into two divisions, one 4-plane division covered the VT planes and 8 covered the VB planes. A total of 4 Zekes and 1 Hamp were encountered with 2 Zekes and the Hamp being shot down. Seven strafing runs were made on the hangar apron on Eten Island where 3 Zekes on the ground were set on fire. Several ships in the lagoon were strafed, including 2 AKs, an AO, and a DE which was seen to explode amidships as a result.

ESSEX Strike 2E

ESSEX launched 11VF, 5VT, and 14VB beginning at 1330 h for strikes against land and shipping targets. The Param airfield was bombed by both VB and VT planes. The SBDs dropped 13 bombs on the runway and destroyed at least 5 planes. Loaded with fragmentation cluster bombs, the TBFs attacked planes parked on the ground alongside the runways; numerous fires resulted.

The F6Fs searched out shipping targets south of the atoll before joining the VT and VB planes attacking the Param airfield. All 11 F6Fs strafed the DD TACHIKAZE that was grounded on the west side of Kuop Atoll. These strafing attacks were believed to have caused considerable damage. The same fighters strafed a picket boat and a small AK in the vicinity of the DD. The picket boat blew up and sank; damage to the small AK was undetermined. The F6Fs then continued on towards Param Island where they made multiple strafing runs on the airfield. It was believed that all enemy planes present were damaged.

INTREPID Strike 2E

Another group of "four or five enemy ships, including some cruisers" were reported to the west of the atoll. Twelve SBDs were launched carrying 1,000-lb SAP bombs; all VB were directed to the west where they found a convoy at approximately 1415 h consisting of one large AK (10–12,000 tons), one medium AK (4–6,000 tons) and one AO (5,000 tons) escorted by a single DD or escort. These ships were part of Convoy No. 3206 consisting of the 5,734-ton TATSUHA MARU, the 2,764-ton RYUKO MARU, the 2,700-ton ZUKAI MARU, and the minesweeper-escort HAGOROMO MARU respectively. The convoy was moving slowly at about five knots on a course of 280 degrees.

Pilots and crews reported a direct hit amidships on the TATSUHA MARU at 1515 h which caused the ship to sink in 5 minutes. A single hit on the "AO" (ZUKAI MARU) caused an explosion and heavy black smoke; the ship was left dead in the water. The SBDs were able to only sustain a near miss on the remaining AK, the RYUKO MARU. No damage was observed. As the planes were retiring, they observed a second DD, believed to be the DD FUJINAMI or possible the minelayer-escort ship NATSUSHIMA, also on course 20 degrees, speed 25 knots, about 15 miles to the east of the first group of ships.

The 12 F6Fs carried out an independent action from the VB planes. The fighters strafed the grounded TACHIKAZE on the southwest shore of Kuop Atoll which returned intense heavy AA. A second DD, located 20 to 25 miles west northwest of North Pass steaming at eight knots on a 325 degree course was also strafed. The pilots observed a small AK (300 tons) explode at 1615 h from a bomb hit. The vessel was reported at a location of 10 miles, 225 degrees from Eten Island.

BUNKER HILL Strike 3E

Beginning at 1324 h, 15VB, 6VT, and 12VF were launched from the carrier to attack shipping in the lagoon. The VB planes were loaded with 1,000-lb bombs (two planes with 2 each, 13 with 1 each) and the VT planes with MK 13 torpedoes. Upon arriving over the target area at 12,000 feet, the attack group undertook a search of the southern part of the lagoon for targets. The TBFs concentrated on four AKs found anchored along the shore from south to southeast of Eten Island. The westernmost AK was described as approximately 4,000 tons and 350 feet long (undamaged), the next ship was about 10,000 tons and 500 feet long (undamaged), the third ship was sinking, and the easternmost ship was about 7,500 tons and 450 feet long (undamaged). The first AK could have been a number of ships; the remaining ships are believed to be the 6,938-ton FUJIKAWA MARU, the 5,385-ton SEIKO MARU, and the 4,216-ton HOKUYO MARU respectively. The formation attacked from the south in two-plane sections with each section assigned one of the undamaged ships. The first two planes launched torpedoes against the 4,000-ton ship which was anchored just west of the south point of Eten. One torpedo hit a reef (coral head) and exploded about 100 yards short of the target. The second torpedo appeared to be running true but no explosion resulted; it may have been a dud. The next target, the FUJIKAWA MARU, was anchored just south of the south tip of Eten Island. Three pilots and crews reported a single torpedo hit (exact location on the target not reported) causing a fire to break out on the ship. The second torpedo was not observed after it was launched. One torpedo was seen to hit the HOKUYO MARU which was anchored just southeast of Eten. The second torpedo missed the ship and exploded on the beach. When the planes retired, the HOKUYO MARU was on fire.

Eight of the SB2Cs attacked an AO (400 feet, 5,500 tons) northwest of Fefan Island, dropping a total of seven 1,000-lb bombs. One bomb failed to release. A single hit amidships caused an explosion and big fire aboard. The ship was reported as being heavily damaged. Its believed now that this might possibly have been the 1,891-ton TAIKICHI MARU with an aft-engine configuration. The second target was the FUJIKAWA MARU (estimated 440 feet, 7,500 tons) located "between Eten and Uman Islands." The ship was hit just aft of amidships starting a large fire with black smoke. Two bombs were dropped by an SB2C on a third ship, the UNKAI MARU NO. 6 (estimated 400 feet, 5,800 tons) located northeast of Uman and apparently undamaged

–National Archives Photo

Photo taken by YORKTOWN plane shows undamaged AK and heavily smoking HEIAN MARU just offshore of the submarine base on Dublon Island. To the right and behind is the TONAN MARU NO. 3 with smoke trailing from its aft section. Closer to Fefan Island on the other sides of the torpedo nets from the HEIAN MARU, the hull of the capsized HOYO MARU can be seen; the destroyer FUMITSUKI lies just to the south.

prior to the attack. The vessel was hit by one and possibly both bombs on the aft section. Following pullout from the dive, the ship was observed burning. It was reported as being heavily damaged. The last AK attacked was the RIO DE JANEIRO MARU (estimated 450 feet, 6,500 tons) found east of Uman Island. Four SB2Cs dropped a total of 5 bombs scoring 1–2 hits and starting a fire aboard the vessel. The ship had previously been damaged by other air groups. It was left in a heavily damaged condition.

The SB2Cs encountered 2 Zekes over the atoll as they were starting their dive bombing attacks. The Japanese pilots did not challenge the formation and dispersed immediately. The pilots and crews reported the following ship disposition observations:

- 13 AKs were seen in the area adjacent to Eten and Uman Islands.
- 8 to 10 ships were seen west of Dublon. Four were "burning nicely."
- A hospital ship (the HIKAWA MARU NO. 2-author) was northwest of Fefan Island.
- 2 to 3 DDs were maneuvering in the northern part of the lagoon.
- The DD still grounded on Kuop Atoll was firing at attacking aircraft. (TACHIKAZE-author).

The 12 escorting F6Fs from VF-18 did not encounter any enemy aircraft. Four of the planes strafed a small inter-island cargo vessel moored just south of the islet north of Moen Island (probably Falo Island-author) on retirement. The planes expended approximately 500 rounds of .50 caliber ammunition against the vessel; it was smoking and on fire as they pulled out. The F6Fs saw one VB plane hit directly by AA fire as it dove on its target at the southern tip of Moen. They witnessed several hits by bombers on enemy ships and estimated that about 8 ships were on fire.

U.S.S. BUNKER HILL AIR INTELLIGENCE REPORT
SORTIES NOS. 43,44

A specially designated photo-reconnaissance plane was launched to gather intelligence data during BUNKER HILL strikes 3D and 3E. Post-mission analysis provides some pertinent information regarding ship disposition.

Shipping:
   Near Tol Island.
      1 AK measuring 250 feet in length.
      1 small inter-island craft approximately 100 feet in length.
   Between Fefan Island and Uman Island.
      Approximately 10 AKs are observed in this area. One of the large AKs is burning and sinking.
   East of Uman Island.
      3 large AKs are seen, of which one is burning. An unidentified installation is observed on hill of Uman Island.
      1 unidentified naval vessel (possibly a mine-layer) appears to be damaged. Its position is not determined.
The following are noted in photos without location reference:
      2 DDs taking violent evasive actions.
      2 AKs definitely sinking and 2 AKs badly damaged.

COWPENS VT Strike
Nine TBFs from VT-25 were launched to bomb shipping in or near Truk at 1321 h. The primary target was the CL NAKA which had been attacked by BUNKER HILL VT earlier in the afternoon. The planes approached the atoll at 1,000 feet near Northeast Pass and then the formation circled the atoll along the west rim and headed south along the west side. The CL was found about five miles from the previous torpedo attack site which was marked by an oil slick two miles in diameter. The ship was making a slow speed (3–6 knots) approach to the southern lagoon entrance at Otta Pass. The Japanese had a small patrol craft alongside and a second small boat five miles out in case the NAKA's crew had to abandon ship. The patrol craft steered away from the CL as the TBFs circled in preparation to attack.

With no air opposition and a large target that was incapable of high speed maneuvering, the VT pilots took their time setting up their attacks. As a result, most of the bombs dropped on or very close to the target. One TBF dropped a 1,000-lb bomb which glanced off the hull on the starboard side near the stern and exploded in the water close inboard. Some small structural damage resulted as debris flew up into the air. A 2,000-lb bomb landed squarely on the stern just forward of the catapult resulting in a large explosion which hurled smoke and fire high into the air. This was immediately followed by another 1,000-lb bomb hit just aft of the third stack. The guns of the CL ceased firing for several minutes and the ship came to a dead stop following these last two hits. The entire aft section of the ship was engulfed in fire and smoke. The CL opened fire again but it now did not seem very accurate. The fires began growing in intensity during the next five minutes and the crew could be seen making preparations to abandon ship; shortly thereafter, they were either getting on rafts or jumping into the water. The TBFs remained in the area for another 15 minutes making strafing runs on the rafts and the two small craft which seemed determined to rescue the survivors. The larger of the two rescue vessels returned fire from at least four machine guns aboard. All planes finally retired with the NAKA still afloat; the pilots and crews reported the CL mortally wounded and sinking.

COWPENS VF, originally slated to provide escort of VT to the target, were diverted to furnish CAP for the U.S. BB strike force operating north of Truk. The F6Fs encountered 2 Jakes about 30 miles west of Truk. The slow enemy planes were easy targets; both were destroyed. Approximately three hours later, planes returning from the CAP mission passed close to the site of the attacks against the NAKA and reported no trace of any ship in the area. As the planes withdrew, several aircraft of the formation flew close enough to Kuop Atoll to draw intense AA fire from the DD TACHIKAZE. Pilots correctly identified the vessel as an "old DD of the MINEKAZE class."

<u>DOG-MINUS-ONE-DAY Group Strike NO. 6</u>
These strikes were the last of the first day and were primarily directed against various Japanese airfields to prevent planes from taking off for night raids and to deny use of the runways by any replacement/reinforcement aircraft brought in overnight from nearby island bases. Launches were begun at 1510 h and recovery was completed aboard the carriers by 1809 h.

ENTERPRISE Strike 1FE
The mission for this last strike of the first day was to destroy aircraft and air installations at Moen Island. The strike force launched from ENTERPRISE included 4VT, 12VF, and 10VB. The TBFs arrived at Moen No. 1 field at 1600 h where enemy fighters were spotted over the field at 14,000 feet. As the high cover VF engaged the Japanese interceptors, the TBFs dropped a total of forty-eight 100-lb GP bombs from 2,000 feet altitude on the field. Several very large fires were started and the pilots reported that the entire bomber field suffered severe damage. The Japanese defenders put up intense barrage-type AA fire but this was not effective against the dive and glide bombing attacks.

The SBDs were each loaded with one 500-lb GP and two 250-lb

GP bombs with instantaneous fusing. A total of 18–20 olive green colored Betty bombers parked along the taxi strip and in revetments were the main targets. Nine hits were made on revetments housing the twin-engine Bettys. In addition, one bomb hit caused a large explosion which destroyed several small buildings at the east end of the strip. It was believed that a total of 16 bombers were blown up or set on fire. The Japanese were thought to be preparing these Bettys for a large scale night operation against the U.S. Task Force. The bombers appeared to be fully gassed up as many were seen to explode into balls of flame and smoke when hit. The Japanese crews must have been aboard the planes as some of the Bettys were reported to be firing at the attacking SBDs. The American crews reported only light AA fire from the area of the revetments. While returning to the carrier, a submarine was spotted under attack by an OS2U and VF planes. Its location was reported as being a distance of 30 miles, bearing 222 degrees from ENTERPRISE. This may have been the second attack which damaged a Japanese submarine, either the RO–42 or the I–10.

Five of the 12VF launched carried 1,000-lb GP bombs with long delay fuses. The flight spotted a Hamp and a Rufe over Northeast Pass; the Hamp was destroyed and the Rufe damaged. Upon arrival over the Moen No. 1 airstrip, 4 Zekes were encountered which pressed a determined attack against the F6Fs. In the following fight, 2 Zekes were shot down and the others were driven away. Two F6Fs were damaged such that they were forced to make water landings outside the reef where the pilots were ultimately picked up by friendly DDs. The 1,000-lb bombs dropped by the five fighter-bombers all hit on the Moen runway. One bomb hit almost dead center in the runway, 2 more about 400 feet from the south end, and 2 about 1,800 feet from the north end. The bombs with the long-delay fuses going off throughout the evening and night would be effective in preventing the Japanese from making repairs to the runway for attacks the following day. Two divisions of the F6Fs strafed enemy fighters parked on the ground and set 11 on fire. They observed 13 Bettys burning as a result of attacks by the bombers. Two pilots strafed an AK in the Dublon anchorage with undetermined results.

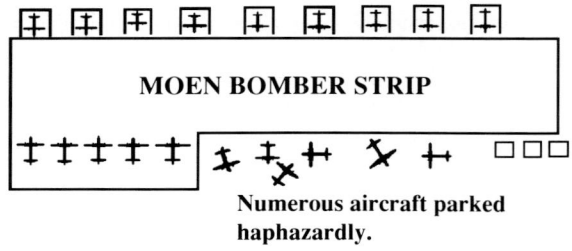

Numerous aircraft parked haphazardly.

Disposition of bombers recreated from sketch in ENTERPRISE action report.

YORKTOWN Strike 1FY

The purpose of this strike was to prevent the Japanese from using Param airfield for nighttime attacks against the Task Force. The plan was for the YORKTOWN planes (4VT and 12VB) to drop a combination of short-and long-delay fused bombs on parked planes/flight service facilities and runways respectively. Sixteen F6Fs were launched to escort the VB and VT planes.

Three TBF planes loaded with four 500-lb bombs each (instantaneous fusing) dove from east to west and dropped 12 bombs on the runway, four along the middle, four along the south side, and four diagonally. Many of the 12 or more medium bombers that had been parked along the south side and the 24 or more dispersed along the north side of the strip must have been damaged. The debris and smoke from the effects of the bomb blasts made detailed observations impossible. Three very large planes were seen off the west end of the runway prior to the attack. Two other medium bombers had been seen burning before the TBFs started their glide bombing runs. The fourth TBF attacked eleven 50-foot-long barges or landing craft full of men (approximately 50 in each) putting off from Fefan Island. It appeared that the barges were getting underway and heading towards the hospital ship, HIKAWA MARU NO. 2, to escape. Many men aboard the barges had rifles and shot at the plane during its dive, hitting the TBFs engine with 7.7mm bullets in three places. The TBF dropped its four bombs in a salvo which exploded in the midst of the barges, blowing debris high in the air and swamping all of them. It was estimated that at least 150 personnel must have been killed.

Eight of the SBDs made drops on the Japanese medium bombers parked along the sides of the field. It was believed that eight enemy planes were destroyed. Single hits were scored on other targets attacked included an A and R shop near the runway, a warehouse on the northwest tip of the island, and a revetted building near the runway

The F6Fs made four strafing runs on the Param airfield where one Nick and one Zeke were set on fire. Eight more planes were thoroughly strafed but would not burn. Four strafing runs were also made on several more targets including the Moen No. 1 airstrip, the hangar apron at Eten, a DE in the lagoon, an AK in the lagoon, and buildings on Tonelik Island opposite North Pass..

ESSEX Strike 2F

ESSEX launched Strike 2F, consisting of 8VF, 7VT, and 13VB, beginning at 1516 h again for the main purpose of destroying aircraft and installations at Param Field. The torpedo and dive bombers were loaded with 100-, 250-, and 500-lb GP bombs. There appeared to be approximately 20 planes parked along the apron and runway areas; this was the same count as taken during the earlier air strikes against the field. Many of the aircraft were observed burning as the planes retired. All the target areas on both sides of the runway were well saturated by bombs leaving many of the installations on fire also. The escorting F6Fs made repeated strafing attacks on planes previously attacked making sure that they could not be put to use in any way by the Japanese.

Two vessels were encountered and strafed by the F6Fs. The first was a DE-type vessel (estimated 1,000 tons) spotted three miles south of Udot Island. It was set afire amidships and was burning when the planes departed. The second ship was an "impressive looking yacht at anchor" on the lagoon side of Quoi Island. This craft was severely damaged but did not burn.

INTREPID Strike 2F

INTREPID's final strike of the day, consisting of 11 F6Fs (including the Air Observer), 8 TBFs (7 with two 500-lb GP bombs, one with a 2,000-lb GP bomb and all bombs with instantaneous fusing), and 11 SBDs each with 1,000-lb bombs, was launched at 1515 h. The SBDs were assigned the Moen No. 1 bomber strip. The runway was hit at about 1650 h by 10 bombs and an adjoining revetment by the 11th, destroying a Zeke.

The TBFs concentrated primarily on the Eten airstrip and nearby installations. The runway was hit by four 500-lb bombs and the 2,000-lb bomb while the revetment and hangar area was hit by two more of the 500-lb bombs. One TBF pilot picked out a small AK, possibly the 3,829-ton MOMOKAWA MARU, just south of Dublon and northeast of Eten as his target; one hit with a 500-lb bomb caused an explosion and smoke. At 1615 h, two other TBF pilots placed three 500-lb bombs near the stern of a 7–10,000-ton AK located east of Fefan Island causing explosions and smoke. This ship may have been the KENSHO or KIYOSUMI MARU.

While escorting the VB and VT planes, the F6Fs shot down one Zeke and burned one Betty on the ground. At 1515 h, a CAP was launched; the 7 F6Fs made no contact with enemy planes.

BUNKER HILL Strike 3F

Ten SB2Cs loaded with 1–2 bombs (250-, 500-, 1,000-lb GPs), 8 TBFs loaded with four 500-lb GP bombs each, and 8 F6Fs (six of which were loaded with bombs), were readied and launched at 1520 h. The primary objective was to damage the Eten airfield and render it temporarily unserviceable. The combined attack formation approached the island from the southwest. The target area was partially obscured by low clouds and smoke. The service apron, airstrip, AA batteries, buildings, hangars, and planes were hit with good results. Large explosions marked hits in designated target areas. The attacking aircraft were constantly under fire from accurate small and medium-heavy AA from Dublon and Eten. Many planes strafed following their dives on the airfield; a ship anchored just southwest of the southern tip (prong) of Dublon was in perfect target position for the planes and was raked from stem to stern with .50 caliber bullets.

The SB2C pilots and crews made the following observations regarding ship dispositions east of Eten Island:

- The bow of a combatant ship was just showing above water. (Probable AK with bow gun-author).
- A medium AK was almost awash.
- Another AK with its stern down was burning forward.
- One large AK or AP near southeast Dublon was apparently undamaged.

BUNKER HILL launched four planes from VF-18 for a CAP over the BB strike force. Four Vals were encountered at about 1645 h about 30 miles northwest of Truk....all were shot down.

COWPENS VF Strike

Five F6Fs of VF-25 were launched at 1517 h to join with BUNKER HILL planes to provide escort and to bomb the Eten airfield. Three of the F6Fs were loaded with single 1,000-lb GP bombs (all five had their normal complement of 2,400 rounds of .50 caliber ammunition). Two of the bombs were equipped with 2 hour delay fuses; the third had a 6 hour delay fuse. Two bombs were reported as probable hits on the Eten airstrip while the third was seen to splash in the water 100 feet short of the southwest end of the runway.

DOG-MINUS-ONE DAY Summary

As a result of the first day of attacks, the Japanese had a total of 56 planes shot down (including 51 fighters), 72 planes destroyed on the ground, and nearly 225 aircraft damaged. Less than 100 planes escaped damage. The heavily bombed airfields were now useless and not one enemy plane would rise into the sky the following day.

The Task Force maintained a high state of alertness as night fell because retaliatory action was expected. Attacks by Japanese aircraft based at Truk, the Marianas, or Ponape plus submarines were a strong possibility. The Japanese bogies appeared as expected on the radar screens of the Task Force ships. A series of 7 air raids, consisting of 1 to 3 planes each, approached the Task Force over a several hour period. A single night fighter, VF(N) was launched by YORKTOWN but interception was not made. A single bogie, identified later as either a Kate torpedo bomber or Betty, effected a successful low-altitude run against the Task Force and struck the INTREPID with a torpedo. The hit was scored near the stern post aft of the four propellers just as the carrier was making a 90-degree turn with 15 degrees of rudder at 25 knots. The rudder was jammed and the crosshead and rams of the steering gear were wrecked; 11 men were killed. A 30-foot hole resulted through which enough seawater came in to cause the flattop to settle 10 feet at the stern. The damage incurred would put the ship out of operation for several months. It was noted that in previous torpedo plane attacks during the Gilbert and Kwajalein Island raids in December 1943, the Japanese night snoopers dropped flare lights, float lights, and parachute flares to aid their attack groups. This time, except for one reported flare, no lights were used in their attacks. It now appeared that the attack planes as well as the snoopers were equipped with radar.

DOG-DAY Night Operations

While the torpedoing of INTREPID was a damaging blow, the Navy's return punch was much heavier. Permission was obtained to proceed with a pre-dawn strike of ENTERPRISE planes against Japanese shipping in the lagoon anchorages.

ENTERPRISE Night Raid

Torpedo Squadron 10 (VT-10) on ENTERPRISE had a special surprise worked out for the remaining Japanese ships. Having undergone long and intensive training in which the squadron simulated minimum altitude "masthead" night attacks against friendly ships, they were ready to initiate the first carrier aircraft night attack against enemy shipping. It was felt that in a night attack, they could get closer to the enemy ships without detection and attack without fighter cover. Twelve of VT-10's planes were launched in the pre-dawn towards Truk (nearly 100 miles away) at 0207 h on the 17th of February. A large and a medium-sized ship were spotted by radar and visual contact 10 miles southeast of Truk but they were not attacked. Shipping targets outside the lagoon had been placed off limits for this strike because of the possibility that friendly ships might be damaged. The TBFs approached the atoll to an initial point five miles east of Northeast Pass and then split into three divisions; two divisions totaling seven planes were assigned to make northwest to southeast runs over the anchorage area west of Moen and Dublon Islands and the last division of five planes was to make northeast to southwest runs over shipping east of Moen and Eten anchorages. The planes in the divisions broke off at one minute intervals to approach their assigned target areas at altitudes under 1,000 feet. Search and homing were to be accomplished by radar while the bomb release point was to be determined by the pilot assisted by radar. Each of the TBFs carried four 500-lb bombs with 4–5 second delay fuses; no more than two bombs were to be dropped on any single run.

Just as the 5-plane group arrived over the northeastern Dublon-Eten anchorage at 0340 h, the bright floodlights of the anchored hospital ship HIKAWA MARU NO. 2 came on illuminating big red crosses painted on its hull; the Japanese were alerted. Warning rockets and flares were fired aloft and flashes from AA fire on the ground were seen with tracers and shells exploding overhead. The Japanese were confused as to their attackers' whereabouts and were firing wildly in all directions. At 0405 h, a large searchlight on Moen Island began searching out the attacking planes. The searchlight was extinguished in a great explosion caused by a 12-hour delay bomb from the day before. No more searchlights were activated. Ships anchored close to shore of the islands presented some detection problems but several blacked-out ships in a row were found in the anchorage west of Dublon. With the bright moon-lit night, the crews began depending on visual contact supported by radar. The torpedo bombers took turns making bombing runs on the line of merchantmen, dropping two 500-lb bombs each time attempting to "skip-bomb" them into the sides of the ships while trying to avoid the AA fire which was getting more accurate as enemy gunners spotted the aircraft's exhaust flames. The greatest volume of AA fire came from ships in the anchorages. To prevent giving their positions away, the ships would not fire until the planes had retired after dropping their bombs or were within 400 yards or less from the ships making their attacking runs. The other TBFs found their targets in the Moen-Eten anchorage only after searching for 30 minutes for suitable targets. Two ships hit there burned for some time, silhouetting nearby ships and making them easy targets. Some TBFs made runs against targets only to find out at the last instant they were attacking a coral islet. One TBF was downed and seven planes flew back to the carrier with bullet holes in them. The 40-minute night attack had been very successful. Out of the 48 bombs dropped at an average altitude of release of 250 feet, 13 direct bomb hits had been observed and in

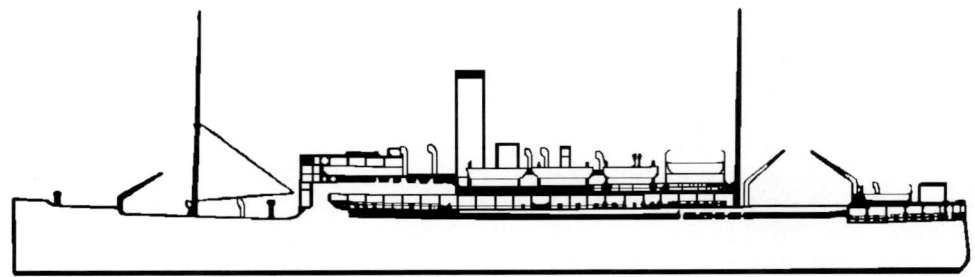

The hospital ship HIKAWA MARU NO. 2. The ship was built in 1927 as a Dutch liner and named OP TEN NOORT but was captured by the Japanese DD AMATSUKAZE on March 1, 1942. She was requisitioned as a hospital ship and named TENNO MARU; in April 1943, the ship was renamed HIKAWA MARU NO. 2.

addition, there were seven probable hits and near misses not confirmed because of the darkness. The tally of enemy shipping stood at eight merchantmen sunk and five more damaged, one of them possibly a destroyer.

The TBF pilots and crew's estimates of ships damaged and sunk from the night raid was as follows:

Ships Sunk.	Ships Damaged.
1 large AO	3 medium sized AKs
4 large AKs	2 small AKs
2 medium sized AKs	
1 medium sized AO	

The size estimates were based on the length of the ship observed. Ships were designated small if they were 300 feet or less; medium if 400 feet long; and large if 500 feet long.

DOG-DAY Fighter Sweep

Pre-dawn fighter sweeps were launched from ENTERPRISE (12VF), YORKTOWN (12VF), ESSEX (10VF), and BUNKER HILL (23VF). The primary mission of the VF sweep was to destroy any remaining Japanese air opposition and planes on the airfields. ENTERPRISE VF made strafing attacks against the Moen, Eten, and Param Islands airfields and followed that with strafing runs on AKs remaining in the target area. The pilots described the ships strafed:

- 1 burning AK in the lagoon.
- AK going east from Dublon. VB got a direct hit on this vessel.
- AA ship just north of Fefan Island.
- AP in Dublon anchorage. Ship smoked following attack.
- AK in Otta Pass.
- PC on southwest side of Kuop Atoll.
- AK southwest of Kuop Atoll. Ship was set afire from stem to stern.
- Beached DD on Kuop Atoll.
- Tug off North Pass. Vessel would not burn.

Planes from YORKTOWN made strafing runs against the Eten fighter strip, the Moen No. 1 airfield, and selected targets of opportunity without encountering any Japanese aircraft over the target area. Ten strafing runs were made on the hangar apron at Eten where 2 Zekes were set on fire and a large fire was started. At the Moen No. 1 airfield, 9 Kates, 4 Bettys, and 1 Zeke were destroyed; another Zeke was left smoking. Other targets strafed included the following:
- AA position Tarik Island.
- DD in lagoon.
- Tug in lagoon.

- AK underway in lagoon.
- AK dead in the water, returning fire.
- Pill box on Eot Island.
- Picket boat outside lagoon returning fire. Guns were silenced after attack.
- DD underway in lagoon returning fire.
- DD beached off south Koup Atoll returning fire.
- Minesweeper underway outside lagoon. Vessel set on fire and left dead in the water.

Despite being fired at by medium to heavy AA over Moen and Dublon Islands, all planes returned to the carrier.

ESSEX VF strafed the Moen No. 1 bomber strip; no new aircraft were seen (no planes from other island bases had flown in during the night) and none of the aircraft strafed on the field caught fire from the attacks. The 10 F6Fs then made continuous strafing attacks from north to south on shipping in the anchorage south and west of Dublon. Specific damage to individual targets was not observed. One F6F was hit over the target area by AA fire and had to make a forced landing inside the southern part of the lagoon. The pilot (Lt. George M. Blair) got out of his sinking plane to find his life raft riddled by bullets leaving him only his Mae West for flotation support. He was spotted by a Japanese DD which began to lob 5-inch shells toward him. His squadron mates radioed his position and despite being very low on gas, they hastily formed a strafing circle and began firing at the DD three quarters of a mile west of the pilot in an attempt to repel the on-coming vessel. The DD backed off but in a few minutes started back towards the downed pilot. The DD was again beaten off. This process was repeated several times and one by one, the F6Fs were running out of gas and having to return to the carrier until all were gone. By then fortunately, the DD had given up and departed the scene. Rescue operations were organized and an OS2U seaplane was escorted by 2 F6Fs to the scene and the pilot was rescued.

Twenty-three F6Fs from VF-18 were launched from BUNKER HILL at 0450 h to participate in the VF sweep over the target area. No enemy planes were encountered and aside from heavy AA fire over Dublon, the operation was uneventful.

DOG-DAY Group Strike No. 1

Planes were launched from the participating carriers between 0455 and 0530 h to begin the first Task Group strikes of the second day.

ENTERPRISE Strike 1AE

The first strike, consisting of 12VB and 8VF, was launched immediately following the launch of the VF sweep. The SBDs concentrated on shipping remaining in the Dublon anchorage area. Two ships, both underway, were spotted and attacked. The first was the 9,524-ton tanker FUJISAN MARU on a 090 degree course between Moen and Dublon Islands; the second was a medium AK east of Dublon. The first 3-plane division dove on the AO from 9,000 feet and dropped their 1,000-lb GP bombs at 1,500 feet scoring a direct hit on the stern and two very near misses on either side of the hit. These caused an explosion aboard and a fire broke out in the engine room. The ship stopped dead in the water and began drifting; it was down by the stern and sinking when the planes retired. The second ship was a medium sized AK (estimated at 5,000 tons) that received a single hit just aft of amidships causing heavy damage to the vessel. The identity of this ship is uncertain, but it is believed to be the MATSUTAN MARU. The crews reported that these two targets were the only ones remaining in the anchorage.

The flight strafed several small personnel boats which were proceeding toward the Moen No. 2 seaplane base on the south shore of that island. A small "40–44 class" PC was spotted coming out of North Pass as the planes were retiring. It returned fire at the strafing planes until it caught fire, exploded and sank. Pilots reported observing an AH, the HIKAWA MARU NO. 2, proceeding through the northern part of the lagoon towards North Pass. One of the SBDs was lost in an undetermined location probably due to the heavy AA fire which was more intense than the previous day.

YORKTOWN Strike 1AY

The first strike of the second day from YORKTOWN was launched at 0500 h consisting of 7VT, 8VF, and 15VB. The joint objective was to destroy facilities and planes on Eten and the Moen seaplane base (Moen No. 2) and to attack any remaining shipping in the target area. Individual TBF planes, loaded with four 500-lb bombs each, picked the targets as listed below:

- AK underway west of Small Island. 2 near misses.
- AK west of Eten Island. One 50-foot miss out of 4 bombs dropped.
- 2 AKs west of Eten Island. 4 bombs dropped, the closest miss was 100 feet.
- Hangar area southwest of the fighter strip, Eten Island. 2 bomb hits in the area.
- Wharf and buildings on the southwest end of Moen Island. 1–4 hits among the buildings.
- Installations on Merit Island. 2 buildings hit.
- Moen Island installations. Bombs wouldn't release.

Pilots reported two Japanese fighters over the atoll. The TBFs did not engage them. One of the TBFs was forced down due to AA fire and the pilot and crew were rescued by the lifeguard submarine SEARAVEN on station northwest of Truk.

The SBDs made strafing and bombing attacks against Eten airstrip installations destroying a large hangar at the southwest corner with two 1,000-lb bombs. Several parked aircraft were strafed. The Moen seaplane base was also strafed and bombed. Enemy aircraft destroyed on the ground included 4 Bettys, 6 Kates, and 3 Zekes (or Hamps) which were set on fire. Three more Kates were blown into pieces without burning. The HEIAN MARU, by now almost a burned out hulk, was damaged further by two 1,000-lb bombs aft and two close misses off the stern by 4 SBDs. One plane attacked a small harbor vessel but missed. A 6–8,000-ton AK, one of a pair of ships located between Fefan and Uman Islands, was rocked by three near misses (two forward of the bow and one just off the stern.). West of Dublon, the previously damaged TONAN MARU NO. 3 was hit again by one bomb amidships. The final target was a 10–12,000-ton AK near Eten Island which was attacked by five planes dropping their bombs from 2,500 to 1,500 feet altitude. The planes scored 2–3 near misses.

The F6F escorts found no enemy aircraft to occupy their attention and left the VB and VT planes to make strafing run attacks on the Eten fighter strip and the bomber strip on Param Island where a Nick was strafed but did not burn. More strafing runs were made on the fuel tanks east of the Dublon seaplane base. The only ships attacked were two small craft in the lagoon which were thoroughly shot up after eight strafing runs.

ESSEX Strike 2A

Strike 2A was launched at 0523 h consisting of 8VF, 6VT, and 10VB. Shipping in the anchorages east of Dublon-Eten was the objective of the strike force. The VF escorts had a routine mission; no enemy aircraft were spotted and no guns were fired. The bombers found shipping targets. The ships attacked and their descriptions are again numbered to allow correlation with the "ESSEX SHIPPING TARGET SUMMARY" which shows the location of shipping attacked in the lagoon target areas.

18. AK – 10,000 tons. Anchored 700 yards east of Dublon Town. Ship received 2 hits by VB (two 1,000-lb bombs), 1 amidships and the other on stern or port bow (conflicting observations). The ship was seen to explode and sink. It had possibly been damaged by previous strikes. (The close proximity to Dublon Town points to this being the MOMOKAWA MARU. It is believed that the ship did not sink at this time as reported, but stayed afloat until attacked by BUNKER HILL SB2Cs and sunk approximately 1 to 1 1/2 hours later on Strike 3B-author).

19. AK – 10,000 tons. Ship was underway at 2–4 knots bearing 060 degrees distance 1,000 yards from the east end of Eten Island. VT hit ship with 6 bombs (500-lb). Ship burned furiously, listing to port and sinking by the stern. (It is possible the ship was trying to get underway and dragging its anchor. The damage described and location given suggests this was the SAN FRANCISCO MARU which was attacked by ESSEX VT the previous day on Strike 2B-author).

20. AK – 10,000 tons. Anchored bearing 085 degrees from Dublon seaplane base. VT scored 2 hits (two 500-lb bombs), 1 amidships and 1 on stern. Ship was left burning. (This was the NAGANO MARU which had been attacked the previous day also by ESSEX VT planes on Strike 2A-author).

BUNKER HILL Strike 3A

The striking force consisted of 13VB, 8VT, and 4VF. The SB2Cs circled the lagoon from North Pass around to Piaanu Pass and then Kuop Atoll before crossing the rim of the lagoon and diving on selected shipping targets in the vicinity of Uman Island. The attack runs were mostly from southwest to northeast with pull-outs and final rendezvous east of Northeast Pass. Five SB2Cs attacked an AK (estimated 350 feet long, 4,000 tons) at anchor about a half mile west of Uman Island. The ship described would have been the SANKISAN MARU which had been attacked by BUNKER HILL planes the previous day (Strike 3D) or possibly the unidentified ship known as the "GUN HIGH" wreck today. One plane scored a direct hit amidships with a 1,000-lb GP bomb causing heavy damage. A second group of five planes damaged an AK (estimated 360 feet long, 4,000 tons) at anchor immediately northeast of Uman with one or two 500-lb bombs. This was either the GOSEI MARU or most likely the UNKAI MARU NO. 6. One pilot, while diving on a ship, lost sight of his target because of an interfering cloud and ended up dropping his 1,000-lb bomb on the apron of the Eten airstrip. A medium AK, probably KENSHO MARU, spotted east of Fefan Island was attacked by a single pilot who dropped a 1,000-lb bomb. The results were not observed. VB pilots and crews made the following observations over the lagoon in their aircraft action reports:

- The 10,000-ton AK heavily damaged the day before west of Uman Island had sunk. (AMAGISAN MARU-author).

- An AK was observed going under the water, decks awash, east of Moen Island. (Actually a tanker, the FUJISAN MARU-author).
- Two AKs east of Eten Island were smoking. (HOKUYO and MATSUTAN MARUs-author).
- An AH was heading out to sea through North Pass. Some pilots reported AA from this ship. (This was the HIKAWA MARU NO. 2-author).
- A DD underway was approaching Otta Pass. (Possibly the OITE-author).
- Heavy AA was coming from Dublon and Moen Islands.

The TBFs had been skirting the atoll with the dive bombers but broke off at Piaanu Pass and turned into the lagoon south of Tol Island. The first target was the HANAKAWA MARU (still being identified as a large 550-foot long, 12,000-ton oiler) spotted the previous day at the southeastern tip of Tol. It was hit by two torpedoes. The ship appeared to disintegrate in a huge explosion leaving a fuel fire on the water with black smoke rising high above. The TBFs circled Tol and proceeded east finding a second large AO (450 feet long, 8,000 tons) anchored east of Eot Island. This was the 10,020-ton oiler SHINKOKU MARU. One section attacked the ship from the south but the two torpedoes dropped missed. The remaining 4 TBFs executed a wide S-turn and attacked the same ship again with no hits. The lagoon may have been too shallow near the launching point to allow true runs by the torpedoes. The planes strafed one small craft while retiring east over the southern part of the lagoon. One TBF was lost. The pilot and two crewmembers were missing in action. The following ship disposition observations were made:

- 1 tender or repair ship was sighted heading towards South Pass. (AR AKASHI-author).
- 3 large AKs were at anchor between Uman and Fefan Islands. (SANKISAN MARU, "GUN HIGH" ship and unknown ship-author).
- 2 large AKs were at anchor east of Uman. One AK appeared to be down by the stern. (GOSEI MARU and previously damaged UNKAI MARU NO. 6-author).
- 1 AK was burning near Onna Island.

The 4 F6Fs escorting the bombers strafed two PT boats southeast of Tol Island expending 1,100 rounds of .50 caliber ammunition. One of the PTs was left dead in the water. The pilots reported a DD entering North Pass. This was likely the OITE returning to Truk with the survivors of the CL AGANO.

MONTEREY Strike 3A

MONTEREY launched 7VT loaded with torpedoes and 7VF to join with the BUNKER HILL Strike 3A attack group. The number of VT planes participating was reduced by two immediately after launch as one plane made a water landing due to an oil leak (pilot lost, crew picked up) and a second had a "hot" run by its torpedo in the bomb-bay and left the formation.

While flying along the outside of the reef, the AH HIKAWA MARU NO. 2 was sighted dead in the water just inside the North Pass. Further down the western edge, a 5- or 6-inch gun emplacement was spotted on Falalu or Lemoil Island. The planes turned north and began descent when they reached a position south of Tol Island. Two planes in the section then joined with two from BUNKER HILL in an attack against the HANAKAWA MARU lying off the southeastern shore of Tol described previously. A small AK was anchored to the north of the HANAKAWA MARU and following the drops on that ship, the planes strafed this vessel. Damage to this second vessel was not assessed.

The last pilot in the flight column saw that the HANAKAWA MARU was hit a death blow by the planes proceeding him and diverted his attention to another small AK lying at anchor off the western shore of Fala Beguets Island. The torpedo was dropped from 200 feet about 800 to 1,000 yards out; it ran true up to about 300 feet short of the AK where it porpoised, went to its port by about 30 degrees, and then missed the ship by 15–20 feet aft of the stern. The torpedo then hit the shore and appeared to explode weakly, sending up a column of water no more than four or five feet high.

The 5VT planes proceeded east across the southern lagoon where they spotted a PG or PC underway about half way between South Pass and Uman Island. The planes proceeded to strafe the ship. The vessel immediately went into a tight turn and began firing back at the TBFs with ineffective medium and light AA. Hits on the bow caused an explosion and white smoke which quickly subsided. The ship did not slow down and its maneuverability appeared unaffected.

The VF escorts were stationed in sections to the side and above the VB and VT planes. Since no Japanese planes were encountered, part of the VF made strafing runs on assigned targets in coordination with the VB and VT attacks while the remaining VF maintained high cover.

DOG-DAY Group Strike No. 2

The second group of DOG-DAY strikes from the carriers was launched between 0645 and 0720 h and recovered by 0957 h.

ENTERPRISE Strike 1BE

ENTERPRISE's second strike group of the second day consisted of 8VF, 7VT, and 8VB. The SBDs were instructed to destroy any remaining shipping and concentrated their efforts on ships in the Dublon anchorage. The first was a 600-foot AK that appeared to be the only undamaged ship in the anchorage (this was the YAMAGIRI MARU-author). Five planes dropped their 1,000-lb bombs from 1,500 feet scoring only one near miss off the starboard bow which caused some structural damage as debris was seen to fly into the air. The second AK attacked was already smoking from previous damage. A 3-plane division chose it as a target and scored one direct hit. The flight reported seeing a total of five burning AKs in the lagoon. Anti-aircraft fire was still intense over the target area with the majority of it coming from Dublon and Param Islands. Three large seaplanes (Emilys or Mavis) were seen on the Moen No. 2 seaplane base.

The targets designated for the TBFs were ships remaining in and around the atoll. The flight approached Kuop Atoll directly where the grounded DD, the TACHIKAZE, became the primary target. The destroyer began firing while the planes were still more than 10 miles out. Although the ship was stuck with its bow well onto the reef, it appeared otherwise undamaged. Seven TBFs scored three hits out of the twenty-four 500-lb bombs dropped. One plane dropped two bombs from 2,000 feet on its first pass getting a near miss 10 feet off the bow which blew in the DD's starboard bow plates. On its second pass, two bombs were dropped from 230 feet. The first hit 15 feet from the starboard side at the aft deck house, damaging the superstructure and the plane itself. The severely damaged SBD barely made it back to the ENTERPRISE. The second bomb hit along the port side of the No. 1 stack. The TACHIKAZE, with a large section of the hull blown away, slid off the reef and sank with heavy loss of life. A small AK (estimated at 5–600 tons) was spotted underway two miles south of the TACHIKAZE on a course to the southwest. Three bombs dropped missed but the vessel was stopped dead in the water and began burning fiercely as a result of the strafing attacks which followed.

YORKTOWN Strike 1BY

YORKTOWN's second and final strike group of the day consisted of 8VB, 2VT, and 6VF including a "Command Group" of 4 F6Fs which included the Air Group Commander acting in a Target Observer role. The SBDs broke off into 2-plane sections to attack ships still remaining in the anchorage area. The first AK target (no size or

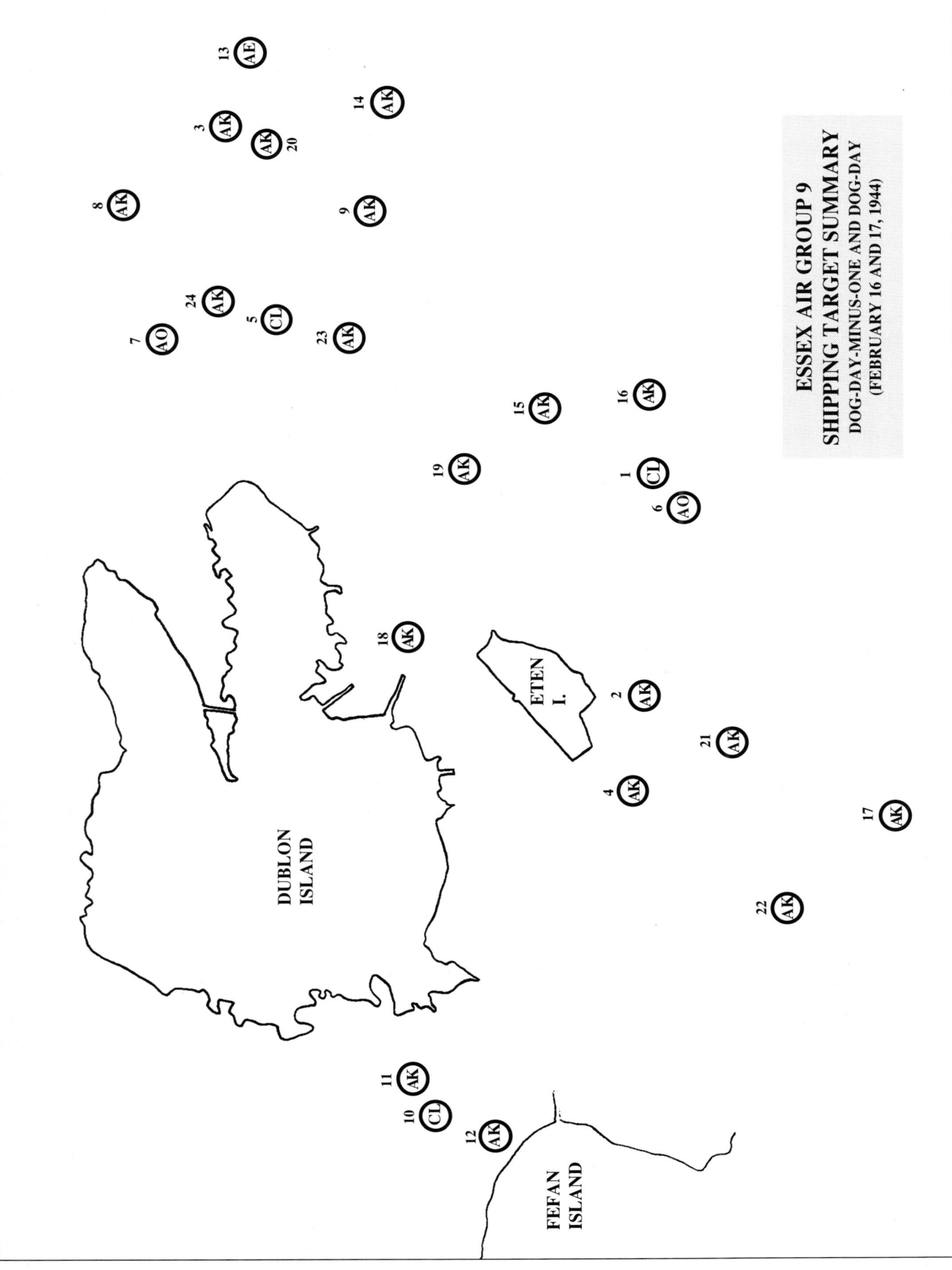

location of targets were given in the aircraft action reports) had two near misses off its port side. Bombs dropped on a second AK missed by over 100 feet off the bow. The third AK bombed was hit on the port bow. The results were not reported. One plane dropped its bomb amongst aircraft on the apron at Eten Island. The last plane had to jettison its bomb after the pilot was wounded by AA fire over the target. The SBD later made a successful crash landing on the deck of the carrier.

YORKTOWN could only launch two TBFs for this strike. Damage from enemy planes, AA fire, and operational failures had taken their toll. One plane performed a photo mission; the results of the other TBF's mission were not reported.

ESSEX Strike 2B

The final strike group from ESSEX on DOG-DAY was launched at 0715 h. The group was comprised of 9VF, 4VT, and 10VB.

Two F6Fs made strafing runs on the Eten airstrip destroying five single engine planes on the southeast corner. All the planes hit burned. The remaining 7 F6Fs followed the VB and VT planes in their diving runs strafing ships east and southeast of Dublon Island.

The VB and VT planes concentrated on ships in the vicinity of Dublon and Eten anchorages. The individual descriptions of these ships are numbered to correspond with ship locations shown in the "ESSEX SHIPPING TARGET SUMMARY".

21. AK – 10,000 tons. Ship was anchored 1,000 yards bearing 180 degrees from Eten Island (FUJIKAWA MARU-author). VB scored a hit by one 1,000-lb bomb on port quarter, leaving ship smoking. Three other bombs landed within 25 feet probably doing further damage. Ship damaged.

22. AK – 10,000 tons. Anchored two miles bearing 220 degrees from Eten Island. VB scored 2 direct hits on the bow (two 1,000-lb bombs) and 3 other bombs bracketed the ship. Explosions lifted the bow out of the water. (This was the same ship, the UNKAI MARU NO. 6, that ESSEX VT planes had attacked the day before on Strike 2B-author). Ship damaged.

23. AK – 10,000 tons. Anchored 1 mile from Dublon bearing 110 degrees. VT scored 2 hits (two 500-lb bombs), 1 on port quarter and the other 80 feet from the stern. By the time the planes retired, she was smoking and had sunk until only a small portion of the bow was visible. (Ship may have been the SAN FRANCISCO MARU which had been attacked earlier in the day by ESSEX planes on Strike 2A-author).

24. AK – 6,000 tons. Appeared not to have been damaged previously but bow was resting on reef, 1 1/2 miles east of Dublon. VT scored 2 hits (two 500-lb bombs) amidships. (It is believed that this was the 1,999-ton MATSUTAN MARU-author). The ship was burning and settling by the stern.

BUNKER HILL Strike 3B

The objective of this strike, consisting of 10VB, 9VT, and 4VF, was to destroy any remaining shipping in or around Truk. The bombers approached the atoll from the east after climbing to 10,000 feet, circled south of the atoll, and broke off to the right in dives upwind on targets. The SB2Cs were loaded with 1,000-lb GP bombs (5 planes) and two 500-lb bombs (5 planes). The dives were steep, from 10,000 feet, with releases from 2,000 feet to as low as 600 feet. Several pilots strafed in their dives and later made more strafing attacks against junks and yard craft as they retired.

The first ship attacked by the SB2Cs was the MOMOKAWA MARU (estimated 450 feet long, 8,000 tons) located 1/4 mile off the southeast tip of Dublon Island. The ship was level in the water when attacked but had previously been damaged by other air groups. Two SB2Cs selected the ship as their target and dropped 1,000-lb bombs scoring a single hit amidships. A huge explosion and fire resulted. The ship started going down immediately, leaving only the bow sticking up above the water.

The second target was the HOKUYO MARU (estimated 400 feet long, 6,000 tons) located southeast of the southeast tip of Dublon. Attacked by three planes, the ship was hit amidships by two 1,000-lb bombs causing a tremendous explosion and fire. When the smoke cleared away, the ship had disappeared. The vessel appeared level in the water prior to the attack but it had been heavily damaged previously by other air groups.

One SB2C dropped two 500-lb bombs on a large AO (actually the aft-engine freighter SEIKO MARU) lying south of Eten. The bombs missed the target.

The last target of the SB2Cs was the YAMAGIRI MARU anchored west of Fefan Island. Four planes dropped one 1,000-lb GP and six 500-lb GP bombs on the ship (estimated 550 feet long, 13,000 tons). It was hit by the 1,000-lb bomb and one 500-lb bomb. After pullout from the dives, the pilots and crews observed a large explosion aboard the ship followed by a large fire and black smoke rising up to 4–5,000 feet. The ship was assessed as heavily damaged since the fire and explosion must have certainly gutted the vessel.

The F6Fs approached the atoll at 12,000 feet where they immediately spotted a "rust-colored, old-type design DD", the OITE, steaming through North Pass into the lagoon. The call was sent for bombing planes to attack. The four F6Fs then made strafing runs which raked the bridge and set a small fire aft of the stacks. The DD took evasive action as soon as the fighters began their dives, starting an S-turn and ending in a full circle. Gun positions began firing 20mm AA at the attacking planes mainly from locations near and abaft of the stacks. A division of F6Fs from another air group joined the VF-18 planes as they finished a second series of strafing runs on the DD. Shortly afterward, the VT-17 torpedo planes arrived and the first division, consisting of five planes, launched a coordinated torpedo attack against the destroyer while it was being occupied by the strafing attacks from the fighters. One of the torpedoes caught the OITE amidships as it completed its full circle; the ship was blown in half causing it to sink in little over a minute. No survivors were seen in the water.

The second division of TBFs dove on the anchorage west of Dublon where about 10 AKs were concentrated; several of the ships were on fire. The initial target was the HEIAN MARU, described as a large AK (estimated 500 feet long, 10,000 tons), located just west of Dublon; 2 TBFs attacked with torpedoes causing 1–2 large explosions aboard the ship. The final results of their attack was not observed. The second target was an AK anchored to the west of the HEIAN MARU; it was most likely the already damaged TONAN MARU NO. 3 or the KENSHO MARU. Two TBFs attacked the ship simultaneously. One torpedo was observed hitting the ship. She was reported to be heavily damaged. Gun positions along the northeast and southeast shore of Fefan and the west shore of Dublon were putting up intense AA fire against the attacking planes.

MONTEREY Strike 3B

MONTEREY launched 14VF to join up with BUNKER HILL's strike group (3B). One F6F joined with VF-18 planes in strafing attacks on the northern part of the lagoon and the others strafed several AKs in the anchorage west of Dublon. One pilot dropped his partially-full belly tank on a medium AK; the tank hit amidships causing a large fire.

<u>DOG-DAY Group Strike No. 3</u>

These strikes were the final ones of the second day. Planes were launched from three carriers (ENTERPRISE, BUNKER HILL, and MONTEREY) between 0845 and 0930 h and recovered by 1139 h.

ENTERPRISE Strike 1CE

Twenty-four planes (10VB, 2VT, and 12VF) were launched with the primary objective of destroying specific land installations on Dublon Island. The SBDs arrived over the target at 1005 h after approaching Truk from the southeast. Some planes began bombing runs on the fuel tanks south of Dublon Town. Three hits were made on two of the large fuel tanks starting fires which sent up columns of black smoke. An ammo dump adjacent to the fuel tanks was hit setting off a series of explosions. A second suspected magazine storage area was also hit, but no large explosions resulted. A large AK located close offshore between Dublon Town and the anchorage was underway and firing at the attacking planes. A 3-plane section made runs on the ship, dropping their 1,000-lb bombs from 1,500 feet. Two close misses within 20 feet of the ship resulted causing the ship to stop dead in the water. The planes were drawing intense AA fire from installations in Dublon Town and along the southeast shore. The SBDs noted several Bettys on the apron at the Eten Island airfield.

The TBF's mission was to destroy oil storage and harbor facilities near the Dublon Town area. The two planes concentrated on the large fuel tanks scoring six direct hits on two of them. The crews reported five ships burning in the Eten anchorage, with one being half submerged.

BUNKER HILL Strike 3C

The 29 planes launched (10VB, 7VT, and 12VF) had just arrived over the target area when a message was received calling off the strike and recalling the aircraft. All bomb loads were jettisoned. The photo-reconnaissance plane (Sortie 46) took one long range photo showing a huge fuel fire burning in the fuel depot and on the south shore of Dublon Island. Three ships on fire were shown; their locations were west of Uman, northeast of Uman, and northeast of Dublon Island.

MONTEREY Strike 3C

MONTEREY launched 6VT and 8VF in a combined strike force with planes from BUNKER HILL. The target area was approached from the southeast with the planes crossing the rim of the reef between Salat and Alanilimi Islands. A group of four AKs off the northeastern shore of Uman Island was spotted and the planes dove to attack. The GOSEI MARU, which was the nearest AK, was picked as the target. The largest ship of the four, the UNKAI MARU NO. 6, had already been attacked by another air group and was on fire and emitting heavy smoke. The first 2 TBFs had erratic runs from their torpedoes. One torpedo passed forward of the bow and went "jig-jagging up the harbor." The second pair of attacking TBFs had more success. The GOSEI MARU was hit by one or both torpedoes below the forward superstructure. Fires started aboard the ship and she began sinking rapidly. The vessel was described as rusty and unkept looking. It was riding high in the water leading to speculation that its holds were probably empty.

The last 2 TBFs attacked the FUJIKAWA MARU which was already damaged and down by the stern. The first torpedo porpoised, ran past the bow of the target, and followed an erratic course up the lagoon until it hit near the runway of the southwestern end of Eten Island. The torpedo did not explode when it hit. The pilot and crew watched the second torpedo start to run true and then it appeared to stop and sink as its wake disappeared. Under fire by this time from AA guns on Eten, the planes retired to the east to join the formation. The ship suddenly was enveloped in flame with a huge explosion. It was assumed the torpedo continued its run and struck the ship.

The VF-30 planes strafed two DDs, several AKs (medium and small) and two barges. The results of the attacks was not observed.

U.S.S. BUNKER HILL AIR INTELLIGENCE REPORT SORTIES NOS. 45, 46

Photo-reconnaissance missions continued during the second day of the raids. The interpretation results listed below in entirety add to the overall picture of the damage obtained against Japanese installations, aircraft, and shipping.

ETEN ISLAND

Damage Assessment:

Twelve bomb craters are seen on the runway and two bomb craters are observed on the apron. Two large fuel fires are observed. Four planes are burning, two on the apron and two on the runway.

Plane Count:

Two Betty bombers are seen on the runway. They appear to be operational. Approximately 15 fighters are located on the apron. Due to smoke, their condition cannot be determined.

DUBLON ISLAND

Damage Assessment:

A huge fuel fire can be seen on Dublon Island. Six or seven large fuel storage tanks are located in the area where this large fire is burning.

Plane Count:

Approximately 20 fighters and two Emilys are seen on the apron at the southern seaplane base. Due to haze, determination of the plane's serviceability is not possible.

MOEN ISLAND

Damage Assessment:

Two large hangars were destroyed at the seaplane base on the southern tip of the island.

Plane Count:

Three float fighter planes are on the apron at the seaplane base. The bomber strip was not covered by these photographs.

SHIPPING

West of Dublon Island.

One possible DD in the floating dry dock. It measures 240 feet in length.

Seven AKs measuring 210, 180, 170, 160, 150, 150, and 150 feet. Two of these can be seen burning.

One unidentified craft measuring 200 x 160 feet.

Two small craft measuring 100 feet each.

Southeast of Dublon Island.

Three large AKs, one of which is burning, and one large AO are observed. Their lengths cannot be determined. (The AO is the aft-engine freighter SEIKO MARU-author).

South of Eten.

One large AK, one medium AO, and one small AK are observed here.

South of Tol Island.

One large AP can be seen exploding and burning. This ship definitely sunk (HANAKAWA MARU-author).

East of Tol Island.

One large AO is observed in this area. (SHINKOKU MARU-author).

One large ship is seen underway going towards South Pass. (This was the AR AKASHI-author). Location of this ship was obtained from the photographer.

A DD, probably MUTSUKI class, was sunk inside the lagoon near North Pass. (This was the KAMIKAZE class DD OITE-author).

Carrier Strike Summary

The two-day carrier raids of February 16–17 cost the Japanese dearly. The main airfield on Moen Island, Moen No. 1, was first attacked on 16 February when the U.S. fighters made strafing attacks on the parked planes. The first of the F6Fs arrived simultaneously with the sounding of the alarm. The attack destroyed over 50 planes on the ground out of a total of nearly 150. About half of the planes were shipboard types left by a carrier which had departed Truk about a week before. Planes torched by strafing attacks included Bettys, Zekes,

Kates, Judys, new model Jills, Irvings, and Dinahs. Damage to installations at the airfield were relatively light but included two hangars destroyed. The entire Moen No. 2 seaplane base complement of 14 aircraft, 6 Jakes and 8 Petes, were set afire by strafing and the field control tower was completely destroyed. One hangar was totally destroyed and the other received 80% damage. Following this attack, the Japanese made no attempt to rehabilitate the field as a seaplane base; they did continue work on the adjoining 1,000-meter airstrip in the hope of using it as a fighter strip and emergency field.

On Dublon Island, the Truk fuel supply base was hit hard and 60% of the tank installations and 90%, or 16,000 tons, of Truk's entire fuel supply were wiped out. This raid finished Truk completely as a fueling station. At the Dublon seaplane base, sufficient warning of the attack was received to allow between 9–12 of the 27 planes to take off. Aircraft present at the time included 7 Rufes, 10 Jakes, 8 Petes, and 2 Mavis. Aside from the planes destroyed on the ground, destruction of facilities reduced the field operating value to 30% of its original capacity. The control tower was destroyed by a direct hit by incendiary bombs and was never rebuilt. The usefulness of the air supply and repair department of the 104th Naval Air Arsenal was reduced by 80% when the structural, propeller, engine, and instrument repair shops plus two supply buildings were completely destroyed. The ship repair base area was not attacked during the raids of 16–17 February but it did force the Japanese to move the ship repair facility underground; within three months, they had constructed a well-camouflaged underground shop. The submarine base also suffered little damage, but like the case of the ship repair base, the Japanese immediately began construction of an underground station for adjusting torpedoes. The Fourth Communications Corps center, the Fourth Fleet Headquarters, and the naval base were little damaged.

Nearly 200 aircraft were congregated on the Eten airfield at the time of the raids. The majority of these planes had been off-loaded from two auxiliary aircraft carriers which had arrived almost four weeks earlier. Their captains had been concerned that any delay at Truk would be dangerous and discharged these planes haphazardly and had hurriedly departed. There were 124 aircraft of various types being staged at Eten that belonged to the Rabaul command; they were authorized for use in defending Truk should it be attacked. These aircraft and many of the others were awaiting ferry pilots to fly them to their final destination or transfer to the air arsenal on Dublon Island to be readied for service. The lack of ferry pilots and insufficient space on the airfield prevented having the planes properly dispersed in case of attack; many of the aircraft were parked nose to tail outside revetments. Despite the island having approximately 10 minutes warning of an impending attack, only between 10 and 20 aircraft were able to take off. Because of a blunder or oversight by higher headquarters, the 26th Air Flotilla had not been made subject to orders from the Truk command. One the morning of February 16, the commander of the 26th Air Flotilla was the only officer at Truk with the authority to order the planes into the air. He was not at the field with his planes and because of communication difficulties could not get word to them to take off. Very few of the planes would have been able to take off anyway since his airplanes were on Eten and most of his pilots were on Dublon. The poor dispersal of aircraft made it possible for flames to spread from one aircraft to the other as the airfield came under strafing and bombing attacks. Losses totaled 110 out of the total aircraft originally on the ground. Damage to the airstrip itself was only minor and it was repaired in two days. However, the taxi loop was so heavily pockmarked by bomb craters that its repair was never attempted. Water seepage caused by the small difference between the field elevation and the sea at high tide would have hampered all repair efforts.

Rear Admiral Sumikawa estimated there to be 30 Kates and 10 Irvings present on Param airfield when the raids commenced. The field had nearly 30 minutes warning of the attack and reports of the number of aircraft able to take off to engage the attackers vary between 6 and 22 planes. A total of 17 aircraft were destroyed on the ground in strafing and bombing attacks. Also destroyed were one mess hall and 3 trucks. The Param strip was out of commission for 20 days due to the numerous bomb craters.

Fefan Island was not a main target during the raids. However, extensive supplies of ammunition and other stores were wiped out. Immediately following the 2-day raid, the Japanese began moving ammunition from open topped dumps to tunnels and caves or transferred much to other islands.

Attacks were made on the Ulalu Island RDF station. The first attack was a strafing wave followed by dive bombers; three RDF units were wiped out and several warehouses burned.

The total numbers of Japanese planes destroyed or damaged was between 250 and 275. American air losses were light in comparison; 12VF, 7VT, and 6VB were lost, which resulted in a total of 29 pilots and crewmen lost and missing. Japanese shipping losses totaled 45 ships sunk at over 220,000 tons with another 27 vessels damaged. The following list is a breakdown and description of Japanese ships sunk or damaged during the air attacks:

OPERATION HAILSTONE
JAPANESE SHIPS SUNK OR DAMAGED
February 16–17, 1944

MAJOR COMBATANT VESSELS
SUNK

Name	Type	Description
KATORI	CL(T)	Training Type Light Cruiser
NAKA	CL	SENDAI Class Light Cruiser
FUMITSUKI	DD	MUTSUKI Class Destroyer
MAIKAZE	DD	KAGERO Class Destroyer
OITE	DD	KAMIKAZE Class Destroyer
TACHIKAZE	DD	MINEKAZE Class Destroyer

DAMAGED

AKIKAZE	DD	MINEKAZE Class Destroyer
HARUSAME	DD	SHIRATSUYU Class Destroyer
MATSUKAZE	DD	KAMIKAZE Class Destroyer
NOWAKE	DD	KAGERO Class Destroyer
SHIGURE	DD	SHIRATSUYU Class Destroyer
I-10	SS	A(1) Type Submarine
RO-42	SS	KAICHU(6) Type Submarine

MINOR COMBATANT VESSELS
SUNK

CH 24	SCS	No. 13 Class Sub-Chaser
CH 29	SCS	No. 28 Class Sub-Chaser
GYORAITEI NO. 10	PT	T 51 Motor Torpedo Boat
SHONAN MARU NO. 15	SCS	Converted Sub-Chaser
AKAGI MARU	XCL	Armed Merchant Cruiser

DAMAGED

CHA 20	CHA	No. 1 Class Aux. Sub-Chaser
HAGOROMO MARU	XAM	Special Minesweeper/Escort

SPECIAL AUXILIARY VESSELS
SUNK

HEIAN MARU	XAS	Converted Submarine Tender
FUJISAN MARU	AO	Fuel Oil Tanker
HOYO MARU	AO	Fuel Oil Tanker
SHINKOKU MARU	AO	Fuel Oil Tanker
TONAN MARU NO. 3	AO	Fuel Oil Tanker

DAMAGED

AKASHI	AR	Fleet Repair Ship
AKITSUSHIMA	CVS	Seaplane Tender
HAKACHI	???	Target/Escort Ship
SOYA	AGS	Survey Vessel

MERCHANTMEN

SUNK

AIKOKU MARU	AK	Passenger-Cargo Ship
AMAGISAN MARU	AK	Passenger-Cargo Ship
FUJIKAWA MARU	AK	Passenger-Cargo Ship
GOSEI MARU	AK	Cargo Ship
HAKUSHUN MARU	AK	Passenger-Cargo Ship
HANAKAWA MARU	AK	Passenger-Cargo Ship
HOKI MARU	AK	Passenger-Cargo Ship
HOKUYO MARU	AK	Passenger-Cargo Ship
KENSHO MARU	AK	Passenger-Cargo Ship
KIYOSUMI MARU	AK	Passenger-Cargo Ship
MATSUTAN MARU	AK	Passenger-Cargo Ship
MOMOKAWA MARU	AK	Passenger-Cargo Ship
NAGANO MARU	AK	Passenger-Cargo Ship
NIPPO MARU	AK	Passenger-Cargo Ship
REIYO MARU	AK	Passenger-Cargo Ship
RIO DE JANEIRO MARU	AK	Passenger-Cargo Ship
SAN FRANCISCO MARU	AK	Passenger-Cargo Ship
SANKISAN MARU	AK	Cargo Ship
SEIKO MARU	AK	Passenger-Cargo Ship
TAIHO MARU	AK	Cargo Ship
TAIKICHI MARU	AK	Cargo Ship
TATSUHA MARU	AK	Passenger-Cargo Ship
UNKAI MARU NO. 6	AK	Cargo Ship
YAMAGIRI MARU	AK	Passenger-Cargo Ship
YUBAE MARU	AK	Cargo Ship
ZUKAI MARU	AK	Cargo Ship

DAMAGED

13 Marus

SUMMARY – SHIPS SUNK	NUMBER	TONNAGE
Major Combatant Vessels	6	18,092
Minor Combatant Vessels	3	8,691
Special Auxiliary Vessels	10	59,058
Merchantmen	26	134,242
TOTALS	45	220,082 Tons

SUMMARY – SHIPS DAMAGED	NUMBER
Major Combatant Vessels	7
Minor Combatant Vessels	2
Special Auxiliary Vessels	4
Merchantmen	13
TOTAL	26

Strikes over the two-day period accomplished two objectives: the neutralization of the Japanese base at Truk and the destruction of numerous warships and merchant vessels without the loss of any of the U.S. surface units. Further air attacks were ordered to deny use of the naval base and to prevent the Japanese from repairing the airfields and flying in replacement aircraft which could hinder the advance of U.S. forces. The next target for Pacific forces to occupy would be the southern Marianas.

Initial B–24 Attacks on Truk

The next phase of the neutralization of Truk was the utilization of land-based B-24s from Kwajalein and Bougainville (Empress Augusta Bay). These attacks were begun on 14 March with nighttime attacks on the atoll by the 30th Bombardment Group of the 7th Air Force flying round trip (1910 miles) from Kwajalein. The Fourth Communications Corps center on Dublon was hit, destroying two buildings. Eten Island was the target of 500- and 1,000-lb GP bombs which destroyed 7 planes, damaged 19, and damaged one hangar. On 28 March, eight more planes were destroyed and another eight damaged. In the first daylight attack by heavy bombers on March 29, twenty-four 13th Air Force B-24s flew from Bougainville (1,170-mile round trip) and dropped sixty-six 500- and two hundred 100-lb bombs from 17,900 to 19,700 feet meeting heavy AA fire from land installations and three destroyers. Right after the bombs had been dropped, between 75 to 90 Zekes, Tonys, and Tojos closed in on the unescorted bombers. For 45 minutes, the bombers kept up a running fight with the Japanese planes for 100 miles. Fifteen bombers were hit; one B-24 received a 20mm shell hit between the No. 3 engine and fuselage. Gasoline gushed through the shell hole. The Japanese were also using air-to-air bombing techniques to oppose bomber formations and one Zeke dropped a phosphorous bomb near the damaged B-24 causing its escaping gasoline to catch fire. As the B-24 began falling, 5 Zekes followed it down, strafing the plane continuously until she hit the water. The fuselage sank immediately. This was one of only two planes lost; the other B-24 crashed upon landing. The casualty count was 20 killed and 10 wounded. The B-24 gunners claimed to have destroyed 31 Japanese aircraft confirmrd, 12 probable kills, and 10 more damaged. The main target had been Eten Island. Photo-interpreter reports revealed that the B-24s had scored 200 direct hits, with the majority placed on runways, aprons, shops, and hangars. Forty-nine aircraft were claimed destroyed on the ground.

On March 31, twenty-two 13th Air Force B-24s from Bouganville were intercepted by nearly 50 enemy fighters that harassed the heavy bombers for nearly 40 minutes. American gunners dropped 39 of the enemy planes but 4 B-24s were lost. These late March attacks were responsible for heavy damage to 10 barracks and an uncompleted hangar on the Moen No. 1 airfield. Eighty percent destruction to the barracks of the Fourth Construction Department headquarters and 40% damage to of the Fourth Fleet headquarters on Dublon Island were also attained. An ammunition dump on Fefan was destroyed by a direct hit; this was the only bomb to hit the island.

In a series of attacks with the combined efforts of the 7th and 13th Air Forces through April 7, 130 enemy aircraft were claimed to have been destroyed in the air and on the ground. These losses, plus those incurred to airfields and ground installations were effective in holding down the Japanese at Truk and preventing any retaliatory attacks on U.S. forces in the Mandated Islands.

Truk Revisited — Fast Carrier Strikes of April 29–30, 1944

The Central Pacific advance by U.S. forces continued following the initial air strikes against Truk on 16–17 February 1944. Plans were formulated to support the seizure of the Marianas and to advance towards the New Guinea-Philippine Islands axis of attack. The seizure of Eniwetok was carried out between 17–22 February and Task Force 58 followed that with a one day strike on February 23rd on Saipan, Tinian, and Guam in order to soften up the Japanese defenders prior to the scheduled landings. Enemy forces at Palau were a threat to landing operations and Task Force 58 attacks were scheduled on 30–31 March; in addition, the less important bases of Yap, Ulithi, and Woleai were struck also. With the nearly complete destruction of Japanese air strength and the belief that the mountainous islands within the atoll were very difficult to take by direct amphibious assault, the decision was made by the Joint Chiefs in Washington to bypass Truk. Landings would not be attempted. The push by U.S. forces in the Pacific would be better served by leaving the flattened naval base to wither on the vine. The northern New Guinea area targeted for capture was Hollandia. The depot and air-base complex there (five airfields) served as a rear support area for the majority of New Guinea's Japanese Army defenders. Mitscher took three task groups to batter the Hollandia area including positions to the west at Wadke, Sawar, and Sarmi, and strikes were made over a 3-day period ending on April 24 in support of the invasion by U.S. troops at Humbolt and Tanah Merah Bays. Following these raids, Admiral Nimitz decided to take another swipe at Truk along with Ponape and Satawan in the Western Carolines. This action was planned in the hope that it would keep Admiral Koga and his Combined Fleet off balance and would prevent Japanese air support during the upcoming Marianas campaign. The carrier air attack on Truk would directly support the U.S. force's capture and occupation of Eniwetok Atoll and Green Island (Green Island is located 100 plus miles north of Buka, Bougainville) by preventing the Japanese from sending aircraft reinforcements.

The second Task Force 58 strike against Truk was scheduled for 29–30 April. The objectives of these raids were to destroy enemy shore installations, stores, fuel, ammunition, and ships with emphasis being placed on destruction of shore installations and aircraft. The Task Force 58 carriers and air groups assembled for these raids were as follows:

Carrier Force (TF 58) Vice Admiral Mitscher

Task Unit 58.1.1 (Rear Admiral J.J. Clark)
U.S.S. HORNET (CV-12)	Air Group 2
U.S.S. BELLEAU WOOD (CVL-24)	Air Group 24
U.S.S. COWPENS (CVL-25)	Air Group 25
U.S.S. BATAAN (CVL-29)	Air Group 50

Task Unit 58.2.1 (Rear Adm. A.E. Montgomery)
U.S.S. YORKTOWN (CV-10)	Air Group 5
U.S.S. BUNKER HILL (CVL-17)	Air Group 8
U.S.S. MONTEREY (CVL-26)	Air Group 30
U.S.S. CABOT (CVL-28)	Air Group 31

Task Unit 58.3.1 (Rear Admiral J.W. Reeves, Jr.)
U.S.S. ENTERPRISE (CV-6)	Air Group 10
U.S.S. LEXINGTON (CV-16)	Air Group 16
U.S.S. PRINCETON (CVL-23)	Air Group 23
U.S.S. LANGLEY (CVL-27)	Air Group 32

The decision to hit Truk again proved a good one, for the atoll had been reinforced. Despite the almost daily bombing runs by the land-based B-24s, planes from Rabaul and elsewhere had been flown in during March, and numbers were again considerable and had to be reckoned with. Task force 58's second air raid was not going to be a surprise visit to the Japanese at Truk. They had to be tipped off and on alert because of the frequent visits by long-range bombing and reconnaissance planes. Ever since the Task Force had left Hollandia and headed north, prowling Betty Bombers had been following and undoubtedly sending position reports to the command at Truk.

<u>The Fighter Sweep</u>

The launch of the VF sweep from the carriers was delayed for up to one hour due to the task groups being in a series of rain squalls. The F6Fs encountered a thick layer of stratus clouds from 5,500 to 7,500 feet upon arrival over the target. The Japanese were alerted and ready; a total of 57 planes rose from the Truk airfields in retaliation including five on patrol. Moen No. 1, Eten, and Param fields contributed 20, 29, and 8 planes respectively. The Japanese planes engaged the F6Fs over the islands employing to good advantage a layer of clouds for concealment and surprise attacks. YORKTOWN launched 16VF. These fighters shot down five Zekes and one Tony over the target area. One Betty and two single-engine planes were strafed and burned on Eten Island. The F6Fs also strafed a small cargo vessel between Dublon and Fefan Islands and set it afire. CABOT's planes shot down 17 enemy planes and LEXINGTON's 20 more but both fighter squadrons lost four planes and three pilots each. LEXINGTON's planes engaged the enemy fighters in low altitude dog fights beneath the cloud layer. The 8VF launched by LANGLEY engaged the enemy above the cloud layer and equalled LEXINGTON's success by destroying 20 Japanese fighters. HORNET's pilots complained that the Japanese airborne fighters were so heavily outnumbered that few of HORNET's pilots got a chance to shoot at enemy planes and none of the destroyed enemy planes were claimed by them.

<u>Task Group Strikes</u>

The main strategy of the composite striking groups was to have the F6Fs strafe the airfields initially and bombers following make them targets of day-long overlapping strikes. Scheduled ASP and CAP patrols would meanwhile cover the Task Force.

HORNET Strike Operations

The first strike from HORNET was launched immediately following the completion of the launching of the VF sweep. The objective was the airfield and installations on Param Island. Intense, heavy, and medium AA fire was encountered over Param coming from the central ridge north of the airfield, running roughly east to west. Fire from batteries on this ridge and additional light and medium fire from guns and automatic weapons on and around the field made low strafing and bombing runs dangerous. As a result, the attacks were carried out at a somewhat higher altitude than had been anticipated. Pilots reported 20 to 25 enemy planes parked in the dispersal areas adjacent to the runways and reported several bomb hits and many strafing runs on this area. It was estimated that at least five enemy planes were damaged by this strike.

Succeeding strikes attacked Fefan Island, Param (again), and the small island of Faleu, situated on the atoll reef at its southern extremity. This little island was seen to contain several coast defense guns and various buildings. It was heavily bombed and photographs later indicated that the installations were almost completely destroyed. Objectives on Fefan which were strafed and bombed included barracks, Government offices, a power plant, and AA positions. Renewed strikes on Param added to the damage to grounded planes and raised the total of those believed severely damaged to 20 aircraft. In addition, the attacking planes concentrated on a jetty on the south shore, a pier on the northwest corner of the island, and a group of buildings also in the northwest corner of the island. The buildings were razed by fires and the pier and jetty heavily damaged.

Attacks on shipping during the day were almost negligible as the only vessels sighted were small harbor or coastal craft, mostly anchored between Dublon and Fefan Islands. One of these vessels anchored just off the northeast point of Fefan was strafed and reported left on fire.

Only one plane was lost, a TBF presumably shot down by AA fire. The pilot was able to make a water landing inside the lagoon to the south. The crew swam to the reef, inflated their rubber boat after crossing, and rowed to seaward. All were rescued by a lifeguard submarine. For the day, HORNET's Air Group 2 participated in six strikes and the VF sweep while launching 90VF, 73VB, and 39VT.

On 30 April, the VF sweep and first strike again were directed at Param Island. Visibility was not good and AA fire was still intense. Most of the bombs were dropped on the heavy AA gun positions. For succeeding strikes, the target area was shifted to Dublon Island and Strike 2B effected considerable damage to the fuel tank area, to buildings at the rear of the seaplane ramps, to a building in the Nanko dock area, and to Dublon Town. Considerable damage had been done to Dublon Town prior to this strike, but is was believed that hits were obtained on several good targets. On the following strike, visibility had deteriorated and heavy cloud cover was encountered over Dublon Island. This necessitated a change of target areas to Moen Island for most of the planes where gun positions and a small fuel dump were bombed. One plane found a hole in the overcast and bombed some buildings on the northwestern side of Dublon. Two two-engine dive bomber-type aircraft were seen on the edge of the Dublon seaplane base and were strafed; the air strip was observed to be no longer operational. The VB flight diverted to the small island of Boquet on the east side of the reef and obtained hits on the buildings seen on the island. Succeeding strikes for the day were called off. A total of 93 sorties had been flown.

BELLEAU WOOD Strike Operations

BELLEAU WOOD launched six scheduled strikes against installations on the islands of Param, Uman, and Fefan on April 29. Some of the F6Fs of VF-24 were utilized as bombers along with the TBFs of VT-24. At Param Island, buildings were set on fire and the F6Fs strafed heavy AA batteries and three aircraft in revetments. One Judy was shot down along with a Zeke which had been previously damaged by fighters from another air group. "Five small craft and a tanker" were strafed near Uman Island. One small craft was split in two and sunk. Land targets on Uman included an already-silenced heavy AA emplacement, piers, and buildings. The F6Fs also strafed installations on Tsis Island in the lagoon and Faleu on the reef. Buildings on Tarik Island were bombed and strafed. Following an unscheduled afternoon strike on the Satawan airfield in the Nomoi Islands, a VF strike group returned to Uman Island where 3 F6Fs dropped 1,000-lb bombs on buildings at the southern end and a series of strafing runs were made on installations on small islands including Salat, Otta, and Ollan to the southeast. Some small craft were strafed around Uman and buildings on several of the small islands were set on fire including some at Mesegon Island on the reef. On April 30, BELLEAU WOOD's planes were launched for scheduled CAP and ASP patrols only; no strikes were made against targets at Truk.

BATAAN Srike Operations

Planes from BATAAN provided CAP/ASP only on the first day of the raids, April 29. On 30 April, the BATAAN launched one VF sweep and due to cancellation of flights in the late afternoon, only three of the six scheduled strikes were made. The VF sweep and the first strike concentrated on the airfield and AA guns on Param Island.

Installations on Dublon, Moen, and Eten were hit by the second and third strikes. All targets were strafed and 13 tons of bombs dropped. Returning pilots reported a thorough strafing job of AA positions and 3 Nells parked on Moen No. 1 airfield, plus bomb hits on the airstrip on Eten and Param Islands. Buildings on Dublon were also hit. One TBF was hit by AA at 3,500 feet over Param but was able to complete the attack before heading south with his plane trailing smoke, followed by protecting fighters. A successful water landing was made 5 miles south of the reef. The 3-man crew then climbed into a rubber raft and 40 minutes later were rescued by a submarine (U.S.S. TANG) on duty south of Truk. BATAAN's Air Group 50 flew a total of 48 sorties.

YORKTOWN Strike Operations

YORKTOWN launched its first composite strike group (14VF, 15VB, and 9VT) at 0721 h, about 23 minutes before sunrise. At 0755 h, a large group of enemy planes were picked up closing the Task Group from the northeast (the direction of Truk) flying at 5,000 feet. YORKTOWN's strike group was ordered not to intercept as BUNKER HILL had dispatched its CAP to make interception. The CAP was unable to intercept because of poor visibility and the enemy planes proceeded towards the Task Group. Three Jill torpedo planes were spotted at 0815 h, closing the formation at high speed low on the water. The screen and YORKTOWN opened fire on the lead plane which was able to drop a torpedo directed at the SAN FRANCISCO just before the plane crashed in flames. The other 2 planes had by then spotted YORKTOWN and were making runs on the carrier. They flew at an estimated 220 knots directly into a concentrated stream of fire from the YORKTOWN; neither plane was able to release its torpedo before they were downed. The YORKTOWN flight continued on to attack Eten Island. The SBDs were each armed with one 500-lb SAP and two 250-lb GP bombs. The TBFs were loaded with a combination of 100-lb GP bombs, 140-lb incendiary clusters, 130-lb fragmentation clusters, and a 350-lb DB bomb. The F6Fs strafed and burned four single-engine planes and damaged a Betty and another single-engine plane. The bombers scored many hits among aircraft parked on the hangar apron and revetments. Ground targets bombed on Eten included the hangar and adjacent buildings, the radio station, the runway, apron, and revetments. The radio station on Uman Island was also destroyed.

Five more strikes were sent by YORKTOWN over the target during the first day, each composed of from 12–13 VB and 6–8 VT with fighter cover. The F6Fs on the last four strikes carried 500-lb GP or 1,000-lb SAP bombs. The VB planes carried either one 1,000- or a 500- and two 250-lb bombs, partly GP and partly SAP. The VT carried 500- or 2,000-lb GP bombs except for the first strike when 100-lb GP, fragmentation clusters, and incendiaries were loaded. A total of 224 sorties over the target for the day were completed; this was a record high for the YORKTOWN. The Air Group 5 planes were directed the first day primarily at Eten Island. Virtually all of the 65 aircraft present on the airstrip were either destroyed or rendered non-operational through strafing and fragmentation-incendiary bombing during the VF sweep and first strike. These included aircraft parked on the hangar apron and in revetments. Buildings reported destroyed included the 2 large hangars, 2 large nose hangars, 2 ready fuel depots, 10 aircraft repair shops, and a large barracks. Other installations damaged were the radio station, the four concrete buildings behind the hangars, a 5-inch gun battery on the hill with a small building nearby, and numerous revetments. The airstrip runway was pitted with 37 bomb craters, and 15 more craters were spread across the service apron in front of the hangars. On Dublon, six buildings were destroyed and four damaged in the Nanko area and undetermined damage was done to the large radio station. Two buildings in the barracks area at the Naval Base and two revetted structures southeast of the Nanko area were damaged also. At Uman Island, the radio station was hit and large fires were started by bombing and strafing Onna and Fananan Islands.

Air operations on the 30th were concentrated at the Nanko area on Dublon Island. The radio station and fish cannery plant were believed to have been badly damaged as well as many barracks and other buildings in this closely built up area. The two revetted structures along the shore east of Nanko were again hit and damaged. A fuel oil tank and buildings in the northwest section of Dublon Town were damaged. Further damage was inflicted on Eten Island installations as the southeast hangars and service apron were heavily attacked as well as the four concrete buildings still standing. The large building at the summit of the hill was hit twice. The large radio station on Moen Island was hit by eight 500-lb bombs and 11 more bombs were dropped on the Moen No. 1 airfield runway and apron, destroying at least one twin-engine aircraft. The small islands of Ozen, Notter, and Onna were also attacked. YORKTOWN fighters shot down two single-engine torpedo planes (Kates or Jills) over the target areas. They were the only two Japanese aircraft observed over Truk on the 30th.

MONTEREY Strike Operations

MONTEREY's Air Group 30 flew 52 sorties over the target on April 29th in addition to flying CAP and ASP. Two F6Fs were lost during the day; both pilots were rescued by U.S. destroyers. The planes concentrated on Eten and Moen Islands and destroyed 13 planes on the ground, three building concentrations, one heavy AA position, and damaged many other buildings and small craft in the harbors. Following the report of a submarine contact by destroyer MACDONNOUGH, a TBF from MONTEREY joined with the destroyer STEPHEN POTTER and several combined "hunter-killer" attacks were made with the DDs dropping depth charges. A large oil slick appeared on the surface along with deck planking, a Japanese book wrapped in tissue paper, and other personal gear. One of the Emperor's under sea raiders was considered to be a probable kill. This was confirmed later to be the submarine I 174.

On April 30, 25 sorties were made over Truk with the planes carrying 100- and 500-lb bombs in addition to 16 CAP and 8 ASP. Targets destroyed included a hangar on Eten Island and a radio station on Moen. Buildings and installations on several other various islands were damaged. MONTEREY planes also strafed several gun positions. The afternoon strikes were cancelled due to poor weather over the target.

CABOT Strike Operations

CABOT planes made five composite strikes, six VF-only strikes, and three VF photo missions during the two days of attacks. In several of the strikes, CABOT planes accompanied those of YORKTOWN. The F6Fs of VF-31 were utilized for both escort duty and for bombing; many of the fighters were fitted for carrying 1,000-lb bombs. On Eten Island, the administrative building complex, the hangars, gun emplacements, and revetments were bombed and strafed. The Nanko section, in particular the barracks area, along with other targets were hit on Dublon. Also targeted were the RDF station on Uman, the power station on Moen, and installations on Fanamu, Eli Kanibu, and Salat Islands. The VF photo-reconnaissance planes concentrated on getting vertical photographs of Eten Island.

Three F6Fs from CABOT encountered a 1,000-ton AK and a 60-foot sampan at a location 215 degrees, 30 miles, outside the lagoon from Moen Island while being vectored out to intercept attacking planes. Strafing attacks enveloped the ship in flames. It appeared to be loaded with ammunition, as many small explosions were seen in the holds of the vessel. The 60-foot sampan stood by during the attacks on the AK, and since no enemy planes were sighted, two strafing runs were made on it. The sampan was set afire. Other shipping targets included a barge found near Fanamu Island which was set on fire after a strafing attack and a "2,000-ton AO" at Uman Island was sunk. A small AK was spotted anchored at the north end of Fefan Island. It was hit by a single bomb on the bow. Several small boats were strafed at Moen Island.

ENTERPRISE Strike Operations

On the first day of the air strikes, assigned targets for ENTERPRISE were primarily located on Moen Island. Ground targets bombed and strafed included the airstrip, aircraft, and installations at the Moen No. 1 airfield, the Moen No. 2 seaplane base, and the radio station. In addition, installations on Tol, Yawata Shima, Falo, Ollan, and Ulalu (including the RDF station), were bombed and strafed. Three medium VB-type planes were destroyed on the ground at Moen No. 1. In air battles, 6 enemy planes (5 Zekes and 1 Tony) were shot down and one Val was listed as probable. One F6F was lost. A total of 172 sorties were flown including photo flights and target CAP.

On April 30, planes bombed and strafed the seaplane base and adjacent installations on Moen Island, installations on Tol and Fefan Islands, and the naval base, seaplane base, Nanko area, and Dublon Town on Dublon Island. Buildings and gun positions on the islands of Ollan, Param, and Eten were subjected to strafing attacks. ENTERPRISE aircraft flew a total of 116 sorties over the target, losing 2 VT planes. Of the three aircraft lost through the entire action over two days, all personnel were rescued by seaplanes or submarines.

LEXINGTON Strike Operations

Following launch of the VF sweep on April 29th, bogies appeared on the LEXINGTON's radar screens and after a CAP from LANGLEY was unable to make contact with the enemy planes due to poor visibility and squalls in the area, two Japanese dive bombers passed over the outer screen flying low and fast attempting to execute a masthead bombing attack. One plane, identified as a Judy, was shot down but the other was able to drop a bomb which missed astern of the carrier. This second plane escaped. The other planes of this group unsuccessfully attacked Task Group 58.2 which was 15 miles away from LEXINGTON's Task Group 58.3. LEXINGTON launched its first strike group following the enemy plane attack and subsequently four more strikes throughout the first day for a total of 202 sorties. Air Group 16 targets assigned on the 29th were the airfield, seaplane base, barracks area, supply area, and radio center on Moen Island. Eighteen Japanese planes were shot down, five planes destroyed on the ground, two fuel dumps and one ammunition dump blown up, several barges sunk, numerous buildings destroyed, and unknown damage inflicted on supplies in the area at Moen. Several buildings were destroyed on attacks on Ulalu Island. Three F6Fs were shot down in aerial engagements.

An initial flight of 12VF was launched on April 30 as a fighter sweep and this was followed by four strikes during the day. A total of 132 sorties were flown over the target with only one plane lost in combat. The pilot and crew of the downed SBD were picked up by a rescue vessel. Targets assigned on this second day of the strikes were the naval base, supply area, fuel depot, and naval headquarters on Dublon Island following an initial strike on Moen. Three enemy planes were burned on the ground, two fuel dumps burned, 15 large buildings destroyed and additional unknown damage inflicted in the assigned areas. Shipping targets found on the 30th included a "130-foot patrol boat" set afire in a position north of Falo and east of Falas Islands and an armed escort vessel claimed sunk 700 yards northeast of Fefan Island.

PRINCETON Strike Operations

PRINCETON launched six strikes totaling 24VF nd 17VT plus 6 CAP and 6 ASP on 29 April. Targets assigned to Air Group 23 on this first day of attacks were all on Moen Island. Initial attacks concentrated on the seaplane base (Moen No. 2) where two float planes on the ramp and several support buildings were destroyed. The VF escorts shot down a Tojo, and turret gunners of two TBFs downed a Tony that dove on them from out of the clouds. On the south side of the Moen No. 1 airfield, both VF and VT planes bombed and strafed barracks, buildings and a jetty. Two F6Fs also strafed Faleu Island on the south rim of the

–Naval Operational Archives Photo
Vertical photo taken by LEXINGTON plane at 0930 h on 29 April shows the heavily damaged landing strip, taxiways, dispersal lanes, and parking apron of the Moen No. 1 airfield complex.

lagoon. Target observers assigned objectives a second time on Moen No. 1 and further bombing and strafing runs were made against revetments at the southwest end of the runway and also the buildings south of the runway.

On 30 April, PRINCETON planes formed parts of the second and fourth strikes against Truk of four strikes made by Task Group 58.3 during the day. In addition, three ASP and four CAP were flown. Shortly before the first strike, the target assignment was changed from Moen to Dublon Island. The first strike, which included 3VT and 6VF, dropped 500-lb bombs on Dublon Town and the Nanko dock areas and a heavy AA position east of Dublon Town. The planes encountered intense AA of light, medium, and heavy calibers. During the final strike, the 8VF and 3VT found heavy overcast over the target and planes diving through it bombed the first suitable targets on either Dublon or Moen Islands. Buildings were hit in Dublon Town and on the northeast tip of Moen. The dispersal areas and runway of Moen No. 1 were bombed and strafed. Planes from PRINCETON, like those of BATAAN and ENTERPRISE, claimed no shipping damage because they either concentrated their attacks on land targets or were assigned CAP or ASP over the Task Force.

LANGLEY Strike Operations

Aircraft from LANGLEY were scheduled for launching strikes throughout the 29th against Moen Island primarily while maintaining CAP and ASP over the Task Group disposition which maintained a distance of about 90 miles from Truk. Ground installations damaged or destroyed included the following:

Moen Island
Barracks and buildings on the west coast of Moen
(north of the reservoir) destroyed.

–Naval Operational Archives Photo

Moen No. 1 airfield following attack at 1530 h on 29 April 1944. The airstrip exhibits numerous bomb craters and dark wavy lines. Revetments and some support buildings are visible while several fighter and bomber aircraft are parked on the apron and dispersal areas; some of the planes appear to still be operational.

Repair shops on the eastern side of Moen No. 1 airfield damaged by bombing and strafing.
Barracks in the prison area damaged and destroyed.
Gas drums and loose stores at the base of cliff east of Moen No. 2 field damaged or destroyed (fires resulted from bombing).
Moen No. 1 runway damaged by bombing.
Coastal defense position on east peninsula damaged by strafing..
AA positions around both airfields damaged by bombing and strafing.
AA positions on the sides and shoulders of Mt. Toladian damaged by bombing and strafing.

Dublon Island

Repair shops and buildings on the west and northwest apron of the seaplane base were strafed.

Tol Island

Buildings along the east coast near Lamoseu Bay damaged by bombs and strafing.
Buildings along the west coast along the northern part of Lemotol Bay damaged by bombs and strafing.

Yawata Shima

Buildings and gun positions bombed and strafed.

Eten Island

AA positions at ends of the airstrip damaged by strafing.

On the Moen No. 1 airfield, LANGLEY VF and VB planes destroyed 2 and damaged 7 Japanese planes on the ground which appeared operational. The two squadrons combined to further damage 18 more planes that had probably already been damaged. F6Fs dropping fragmentation bombs or strafing possibly damaged 10 more planes which were on the Lagoon edge of the west runway parking apron.

Several shipping targets were encountered during the strikes including a 130-foot patrol vessel which sunk after being set afire by strafing north of Falo and east of Falas Islands (this vessel had just previously been set on fire by LEXINGTON planes). A 140-foot sub-chaser was spotted towing an empty barge toward Kuop Atoll; this vessel was probably sunk after being thoroughly strafed and set on fire (pilots of subsequent strikes were unable to find the vessel and barge). Other craft damaged by strafing included an "FTD" (forward target director?) southeast of Uman Island, a 150-foot patrol or AA vessel left dead in the water northeast of Falas Island, one 40- and one 90-foot yardcraft to the southeast of the Dublon seaplane base, and two

–Naval Operational Archives
Photo taken at 1500 h on 29 April shows details of installatiions at submarine base (left rear) and Fourth Naval Dockyards (right). Note floating drydock with floating crane nearby.

camouflaged fishing boats on the west side of Tol's southwest peninsula.

U.S.S. BATAAN
PHOTOGRAPHIC INTERPRETATION REPORT NO. 4
TRUK ISLANDS — APRIL 30, 1944

BATAAN flew seven photographic sorties over the target on 30 April. The results of these missions was a photographic interpretation report that provides some interesting observations on the status of installations and shipping following this second important carrier strike on Truk. The report is presented here almost in its entirety.

SUMMARY:
Runways on Eten, Moen, and Param Islands are unserviceable.
A total of 40 planes are possibly serviceable, and 44 are definitely destroyed or badly damaged.
AA defenses at Moen and Param Islands are much stronger than was previously reported, especially with regard to light and medium caliber weapons.
There are approximately 150 barges at Dublon Island.

DUBLON ISLAND as of 1300 h
(Coverage is discontinuous of the shore from the Nanko area to Dublon Town.)
3 Jakes and 6 Rufes are on the service apron at the seaplane base. Two planes of each type are possibly serviceable.
Approximately 150 barges are observed at Dublon. The majority are located near the Nanko area.
One of the two remaining large tanks in the tank farm area has a large hole in the side and may be assumed to be empty.
Coverage is not complete enough to make an assessment of building damage.

MOEN ISLAND as of 1430 h
(Coverage incomplete, but generally good of south and east coasts.)
Airfield.
Aircraft: (NB haze permits only major damage to aircraft to be observed.)
A total of 36 planes, 7 twin-engined and 29 single-engined, are on the ground. Nine planes including 4 twin-engined are definitely damaged or destroyed.
All others are possibly operational.
Dispersal:
Planes are widely dispersed throughout the revetment area and along the northwest edge of the runway. The majority of the planes are not in revetments although empty revetments are available.
Runway:
The runway appears inoperational.
A dark material, possibly oil, has been spread in wavy lines over the entire length of the runway. This may be an attempt to make it less easily visible.
Defenses:
6 new medium AA and 21, possibly 23, new light AA guns are located in this area.
Two heavy AA previously reported are not observed.
The defenses are listed as follows:
   5 - medium AA on the northwest spur of the hill opposite the center of the runway.
   1 - medium AA 200 yards east of the northwest end of the runway.
   12 - light AA at the southwest end of the runway. Five of these were previously reported.
   2 - light AA in the revetment area 300 yards east of the southwest end of the runway.

8 - light AA on the spur of the hill opposite the center of the runway.
5 - possibly 7, light AA at the northeast end of the runway. Three of these were previously reported.
2 - light AA on the crest of the hill overlooking the airfield.

Damage:
Approximately 40 buildings are destroyed in the barracks area south of the airfield.
The hangar at the airfield is burned.
Smoke is rising from three places in the revetment area and there is a large fire about 1,000 feet south of the airfield.

Shipping:
10 barges and boats are adjacent to the pier in the barracks area.

Seaplane Base. (Coverage is of eastern end only.)
Aircraft:
None observed.

Runway:
Only east end visible. It is serviceable.

Defenses:
There are 3 camouflaged CD or DP positions at the top of the bank 400 yards northeast of the east end of the runway.
2 medium AA are located at the east end of the runway. One was previously reported.

Storage:
Tunnels are dug in at the bank at the inland edge of the road.

East Peninsula.
Defenses:
The four CD guns at the end of the eastern peninsula are confirmed. They are camouflaged with nets and foliage.
3 medium AA are located immediately west of the CD battery.
4 light AA are located roughly 100 yards west of CD battery, one at each corner of the Shinto shrine.
11 gun emplacements are added to the 3 previously reported heavy AA on the top of the table-topped mountain in the east central portion of the island. These are probably occupied by medium caliber guns.
4 light AA surround the radio station.

Damage:
2 buildings are destroyed and the roof of the radio building is pierced by a bomb.

Shrine:
There is a large Shinto shrine located roughly 100 yards west of the CD battery.

PARAM ISLAND as of 1055 h.
(Coverage includes only the western 2/3 of the runway and the southwestern tip of the island.)
Aircraft:
6 planes are observed in the area. Three including a Kate, a Tony, and an unidentified single-engined plane, are possibly serviceable.

Runway:
There are a minimum of 9 hits in the runway. It is possibly serviceable for fighters.

Defenses:
Defenses not previously reported consist of the following:
1 - medium AA 200 feet west of the pier on the south side of the runway.
4 - medium AA located on the extreme southwest tip of the island.
1 - heavy AA 150 feet north of the southwest end of the runway.

Stores:
Narrow pile of loose stores, possibly empty fuel drums, are located along the south edge of the runway.

Shipping:
Five 50-foot barges, a 40- and a 30-foot boat are tied to the pier.

ETEN ISLAND as of 1300 h.
(Coverage includes west end of runway and dispersal area and northwest corner of the island.)
33 planes plus piles of plane wreckage are observed. 6 of the planes; 5 single-engined and a probable Dinah; are possibly serviceable.
Many more planes to have burned here than at Moen and Param Islands.
There is a minimum of 10 hits on the runway. It is unserviceable.

OLLAN ISLAND.
(Coverage consists of about 1 and 1/2 mile distant oblique photographs)
A clearing on the southwestern edge of the island contains probably 1 and possibly 2 CD gun emplacements.

Carrier Strike Summary

During the fast carrier strikes of April 29–30, planes from the three Carrier Task Units made 2,200 sorties and dropped 785 tons of bombs on shore installations and whatever shipping they could find in the anchorages and around the atoll. By late April, large vessels had all but abandoned Truk as a port of call, and one medium freighter and a badly damaged WAKATAKE class escort vessel were the only ships of any size in the harbors. Final Task Force 58 assessments of shipping destroyed listed only one small freighter, two sub-chasers and a single 150-foot vessel as definitely sunk even though a number of small craft were claimed (and photographed) as sunk or damaged including two small diesel tugs, several gasoline launches, assorted luggers, yard craft, and sampans totaling nearly 20 craft. Japanese sources confirmed these estimates to be approximately correct listing only three small ships as sunk at Truk, the HINO MARU NO. 2, MINSEI MARU, and SPECIAL SUB-CHASER NO. 38. SAPPORO MARU was listed as damaged.

The Japanese mounted a strong attack against the Task Force on April 29th. The attacking force was believed to have consisted of between 20–45 fighters protecting 6 to 8 of the new type Jill torpedo bombers. These attacks were successfully repelled. Japanese sources listed 104 aircraft dispersed at four island airfields at the time of the raid as follows: Moen No. 1, 6 Bettys and 20 Zekes; Eten, 10 Irvings and 35 Zekes; Param, 12 Judys and 13 Kates; Dublon, 8 observation and reconnaissance planes. Their estimates totaled 59 aircraft destroyed in the air (including the 5 Kates on Patrol) plus 34 more on the ground for a total of 93. American photo-interpretation estimates were quite different. These estimates listed 167 Japanese aircraft present with 60 destroyed on the ground. In addition, American pilots claimed 63 planes destroyed in the air for a total of 123. Of the planes shot down,

46 were claimed to be Tonys and Zekes and the others were Kates. Many others were partially damaged in the strafing attacks. Only 11 planes in almost impregnable revetments remained serviceable. The anti-aircraft fire was the heaviest and most accurate faced to date by the American planes and it was responsible for the downing of 20 planes. Six other aircraft were lost in combat and 9 more were operational losses. Twenty-eight of the 46 airmen downed in the water around the atoll were rescued by either rescue submarines or float planes.

The air raids of April 29–30 caused more damage to ground installations and buildings than any other attacks including the initial strikes on February 16–17. Many installations that had previously gone undamaged were hit for the first time. These raids increased the damage on Moen Island to an estimated 75% of its installations. There had been 30 Zekes and 6 Betty bombers dispersed on the Moen No. 1 airfield. The 20 Zekes were scrambled with a 30-minute warning to intercept the first wave of attacking American aircraft leaving the 6 Bettys which were strafed and burned. Almost all the usable installations remaining on Moen No. 2 were finished off including the barracks, power plant, and storehouses which were completely destroyed.

Damage following the raids on Dublon were estimated to be 40% of the installations. Nearly 50% damage was effected to the Fourth Fleet Headquarters with huge losses in records and office equipment along with having its communications capability interrupted. About 20% damage to the naval base was accomplished. Repairs were not attempted and after another heavy bomber raid in mid-July when 60% more was damaged, the naval base personnel were driven into the hills where they constructed shacks from salvaged material. The remaining 10,000-ton fuel tank and two smaller tanks were badly damaged. At the seaplane base, the hangar and 12 barracks buildings were totally destroyed. The raid completely neutralized the value of the remaining buildings except the power plant and the oxygen generating plant at the supply and repair department. The 200-ton fuel barge was destroyed leaving only a 50-ton barge to complete all re-fueling tasks for both surface craft and submarines. The ship repair facility had not been hit during the raids of 16–17 February, but the Japanese had moved the installation and within three months the shop was relocated to a well-camouflaged underground location. Despite these efforts, the facility was hit during the raids of April 29–30 causing damage of approximately 25%. A single direct hit on the machine shop destroyed 30% of the equipment and knocked out the repair base for a month. Like the ship repair facility, the submarine base had not been hit on 16–17 February and the Japanese had immediately begun construction of an underground station for adjusting torpedoes. This base was first hit in the April 29–30 raid and losses of 40% to buildings and 25% to torpedoes were suffered.

Attacks against Eten Island virtually nullified the airstrip for further operations. Damage to all installations was estimated at 80% following the raids. After 11 fighters were destroyed on the ground and all barracks, 2 hangars, and 50 aircraft engines were destroyed, the airstrip was abandoned. Damage to installations on Fefan Island rose to 20% following the raids. Two open-type provisions warehouses and another provisions warehouse were destroyed. Damage was also inflicted to a torpedo dump and an air raid shelter. The raids dealt a crushing blow to facilities on Param Island where damage to all installations was now at 15%. Six planes were destroyed on the ground in strafing attacks and aircraft engines and spare parts, 15,000 liters of gasoline, and four tons of provisions were rendered useless. The runway and taxiway were pitted further by bombs causing damage which was enhanced by the difficulty to make runway repairs on the island. Up to 80% of all installations on Ulalu were estimated to be destroyed following these raids on the island including all barracks and warehouses remaining. The island of Uman itself had not been attacked in the previous raids. The raids of 29–30 April hit the radio station and left one transmitter building burned, one transmitter building demolished, and a transmitter destroyed. This resulted in the elimination of transmitting facilities as the radio station was not repairable and was never replaced.

Further B-24 Attacks and B-29 Experimental Raids

The land-based B-24 attacks on Truk continued through October 1944, dropping more than 4,000 tons of bombs on Japanese installations. The effect of these bombings and the carrier raids of April 29–30 reduced the amount of serviceable aircraft to less than a dozen planes. The Japanese had fair success using Irving night fighters equipped with manually operated searchlights against the B-24s during nighttime raids. Air-to-air bombing techniques used during daytime attacks and AA guns accounted for the downing of B-24s also.

Beginning in October 1944, flights of between one and 30 B-29 bombers flew experimental bombing runs over Truk to prepare them for combat missions over the Japanese home islands. The crews on these flights would experience a moderated overwater flight and would be exposed to light Japanese defenses. These flights would also serve to keep the Truk Atoll neutralized so the 7th Air Force B-24s (which had been engaged in that task) could move from Kwajalein to Guam. In the 10-month period that followed until the end of the war, 32 missions were flown and 1,727 tons of bombs were dropped. The inferior forces of planes remaining at Truk with only 6 or 7 planes flyable at one time were ineffective in trying to defend against the B-29s flying at their conventional bombing altitudes of 25,000 feet.. The Japanese fighters couldn't climb to the necessary altitudes quickly enough to attack the B-29s and eventually were ordered to take off and disperse until the B-29s were gone. None of the B-29s were downed over the atoll.

The British Carrier Attack
(June 14–15, 1945)

In June 1945, a British carrier task force made attacks on Truk. The operation was code-named "INMATE" and was carried out by Task Group III.2 consisting of the following fleet units:

Task Unit One:	Carrier IMPLACABLE (Flagship)
Task Unit Two:	Cruiser SWIFTSURE
	Escort Carrier RULER
	Destroyer TERMAGANT
Task Unit Five:	Cruisers NEWFOUNDLAND, HMCS UGANDA, HMNZS ACHILLES
Task Unit Fifteen:	Destroyers TROUBRIDGE, TEASER, TERPSICHORE, TENACIOUS

The first strike aircraft, consisting of Avengers, Fireflies with rockets, and Seafire fighter-bombers, was launched at dawn from a position 85 miles southwest of Truk on the 14th of June. One Avenger had to ditch during the raid and one Seafire was shot down over Moen. The first British night strikes in the Pacific were launched from IMPLACABLE on the night of June 14–15 using Avengers that utilized flares to place their bombs. Further air attacks continued on the 15th in addition to bombardment of shore installations by cruisers and destroyers. These attacks caused little damage and in actuality served only as a training exercise to give battle experience to new units of the British Fleet.

The Japanese Surrender

The Japanese at Truk were informed via a message dropped by a plane on 28 August 1945 that they would be given the opportunity to surrender and to expect the arrival of American military representatives. The destroyer U.S.S. STACK and destroyer-escort U.S.S. OSMUS arrived on 30 August with General L.D. Hermle, USMC and 12 officers who met with Rear Admiral Sumikawa, Chief of Staff to the 4th Fleet, and five ranking Japanese officers. The Japanese were informed of the requirements preliminary to surrender and given a copy of the "Articles of Surrender" which were to be signed at a later date.

On 2 September, Japanese surrender party boats came alongside the cruiser U.S.S. PORTLAND with a delegation comprised of Lt. General Shunzaburo Mugikura (CinC of 31st Japanese Imperial Army), Colonel Waichi Tajima (Chief of Staff to Magikura), Lieutenant Kenzo Yoshida (Aide to Magikura), Vice Admiral Chuichi Hara (Truk 4th Fleet Commander, Japanese Imperial Navy), Rear Admiral Aritaka Aihara (Head of the Japanese South Seas Government, Eastern Branch), Rear Admiral Michio Sumikawa (Chief of Staff to Hara), and Lt. Ryo Kichi Morioka (Aide to Hara). Vice Admiral George D. Murray, USN, Commander Marianas, accepted the surrender of all Japanese held islands under the Truk Headquarters on behalf of Fleet Admiral Chester W. Nimitz, CinC United States Pacific Fleet.

Task Group 50.9 Battle Report

ENEMY SHIPS ENCOUNTERED:
  KATORI (CL)
  MAIKAZE (DD)
  NOWAKE (DD)
  SHONAN MARU NO. 15 (Converted Sub-Chaser)
  CH 24 (Sub-Chaser)

In accordance with orders from Commander Task Force 50 in NEW JERSEY, the battleships IOWA and NEW JERSEY, cruisers NEW ORLEANS and MINNEAPOLIS, and destroyers BRADFORD, IZARD, CHARETTE, and BURNS left the formation at 0950 h to perform an offensive sweep starting north and sweeping counterclockwise around the Truk Atoll. The group's objective was to intercept and destroy any Japanese ships trying to escape the on-going air attacks. It was felt that any ships encountered would have already been worked over by the various air groups and would be in damaged condition. For this reason, the TG 50.9 ships were referred to as the "cripple hunters." Planes from TG 58.3 (COWPENS) were directed to furnish CAP for the group.

The TG 50.9 ships encountered a group of enemy ships about 15 to 20 miles northwest of North Pass. The closest ship was a "1,000-ton merchantman," actually the 355-ton converted submarine chaser SHONAN MARU NO. 15. Twelve miles beyond was a badly damaged CL (the 5,890-ton KATORI) and a "large modern destroyer possibly of the FUBUKI class" (the 2,490-ton KAGERO Class DD MAIKAZE). A second DD, identified at the time as a cruiser, was fleeing on a course directly away from the U.S. warships; this was the NOWAKE, a sister ship to the MAIKAZE..

The screening destroyers took SHONAN MARU NO. 15 under fire at 1310 h followed by NEW ORLEANS three minutes later. NEW JERSEY then began firing salvoes of 5-inch shells into the now-burning sub-chaser at a range of about 1,000 yards. The ship then disintegrated in a violent explosion raining debris 1,000 yards in all directions. The nature of the explosion led observers to believe that she was loaded with gasoline. It was not observed whether SHONAN MARU NO. 15 returned fire, but it did appear that the crew stayed with the vessel until the end. The IOWA and NEW ORLEANS passed close to the area where the vessel had sunk shortly afterwards and spotted about six survivors. Most of the survivors were wounded; it appeared that they had been blown overboard.

The order meanwhile had been given to MINNEAPOLIS and NEW ORLEANS to "close and sink enemy cruiser." Both ships began firing salvoes at a range of 19,000 yards. Initially, MINNEAPOLIS was missing long and NEW ORLEANS short. Even though the KATORI was heavily hit and most of her guns out of action, the cruiser returned fire with AA guns and the large 5.5-inch after gun.

–National Archives Photo

Converted Sub-Chaser SHONAN MARU NO. 15 is on fire and smoking moments before exploding violently.

–National Archives Photo
Light cruiser KATORI on fire and listing after being worked over by U.S. carrier aircraft. Note torpedo wake approaching rear of ship from behind. The KATORI stayed afloat until U.S. naval units arrived and finished off the crippled ship.

About this time, torpedoes fired by KATORI were seen to surface short of NEW ORLEANS and run very close astern to IOWA. This development prompted heavy fire against the Japanese CL and several hits were observed. She was ablaze then both fore and aft. The cruiser was still returning fire but not effectively even though four shells landed within 50 yards of MINNEAPOLIS; the remainder of the shells fell short. Finally, after being under fire from MINNEAPOLIS and NEW ORLEANS for 13 minutes, the KATORI turned over on her port side, capsized, and sank at 1337 h. Large gaping holes could be seen in her bottom and only then did the crew abandon ship. There were three boatloads of survivors, approximately 150 men. These were strafed by two planes of the CAP.

Heavy fire was now being directed at the nearby destroyer, the MAIKAZE. The crippled DD suddenly turned at bay. As her bow came around, several alert air patrols circling overhead noticed splashes just off the destroyer's beam. The pilots spotted the telltale thin, white, bubbly wakes of the torpedoes and radioed the Task Group immediately: "Torpedoes approaching you." Gunners aboard the IOWA spotted the torpedoes and began firing from a 40mm battery which helped mark their positions. The IOWA escaped from what would otherwise been at least one sure torpedo hit by going to emergency flank speed and hard left rudder. One torpedo passed 125 yards ahead and the other 15 yards astern. The battleships then opened up with their 5-inch guns against the destroyer which by now had taken a terrific amount of punishment and was ablaze from stem to stern. Finally MAIKAZE broke in two and sank stern first. Fuel kept on burning and emitting heavy black smoke from the surface where she went under. No survivors from the MAIKAZE were seen.

While the U.S. warships were concentrating on the KATORI and the MAIKAZE, the NOWAKE was making her escape at high speed to the west. The battleships straddled the DD at long range with their 16-inch main batteries but did not stop her.

Following the destruction of the MAIKAZE, KATORI and SHONAN MARU NO. 15, the IOWA-NEW JERSEY battleship Task Group continued its anti-shipping sweep around Truk until another target described as an enemy trawler was spotted by a lookout. The ship was sighted at 20,000 yards bearing 254 degrees from the Task Group, and the destroyer U.S.S. BURNS was detached from the screen of Task Group 50.9 to investigate and destroy the Japanese vessel. After identifying the vessel as a small patrol craft or sub-chaser, BURNS opened fire with her 5-inch guns. A close-range duel began as the vessel returned BURNS fire with her forward 3-inch gun scoring misses both short and over the DD. Within minutes, BURNS began scoring direct hits on her target, starting a fire which apparently was quickly extinguished. The DD then closed the range between the two vessels and opened fire with her 40mm guns. The target soon became shrouded by smoke and spray. After a short cease-fire to observe the sub-chaser, BURNS again opened up with her 40mm guns. Sixteen minutes after BURNS had begun to fire, the target vessel sunk by the stern in position 07°24'N, 150°30'30"E. BURNS had expended 265 rounds of 5-inch and 500 rounds of 40mm ammunition against the sub-chaser. Between 50 and 75 Japanese survivors were spotted in the water; BURNS rescued six of them. The others refused to be taken aboard. Three depth charges (depth setting 50 feet) were then dropped on the men who had refused rescue. The identity of the ship, the 438-ton SUB-CHASER NO. 24 (CH-24), was learned from the interrogation of the prisoners that had been rescued from the water. Information furnished by them established that CH-24, which was assigned to SubChasDiv-23, had sortied from Truk early on the 15th to rendezvous with a five-ship convoy from Japan about 150 miles north of Truk. After the convoy did not show, CH 24 had set on a course back to Truk. The sub-chaser made contact with four merchantmen and a small escort on the morning of the 16th, which proved to be the missing convoy (one ship had been sunk by enemy aircraft the day before). CH 24 and the convoy proceeded towards Truk until mid-afternoon when a Japanese DD approached their group and informed them that Truk was under heavy air attack. The sub-chaser had been ordered to continue along toward Truk while the merchantmen turned westward to escape.

TECHNICAL SUMMARIES:

KATORI
Type: KATORI Class Light Cruiser
Displacement: 5,890 tons
Dimensions: 425.75/52.25/18.83 feet
Machinery: 2-shaft geared turbines, 3 Kampon boilers, 8,000 SHP.
Speed: 18 knots
Radius: Unknown
Complement: Unknown
Armament: Four 5.5-inch dual mounted deck guns, two 5-inch DP guns, four 25mm AA guns; four 21-inch torpedo tubes; 1 catapult and floatplane.
Built: 1939 by Mitsubishi, Yokohama
Remarks: 6th Fleet Flagship

MAIKAZE/NOWAKE
Type: KAGERO Class Destroyers
Displacement: 2,490 tons
Dimensions: 381.33/35.42/12.33 feet
Machinery: 2-shaft geared turbines, 3 Kampon boilers, 52,000 SHP.
Speed: 35 knots
Radius: 5,000 miles at 18 knots.
Complement: 240
Armament: Six 5-inch DP (dual-mounted) guns, four 25mm AA guns, two 13mm guns; 8 torpedo tubes (2 sets, 4 abreast); 16 depth charges.
Built: MAIKAZE – 1941 by Fujinagata Zosensho, Osaka
NOWAKE – 1940 by Maizuru Dock Yards
Remarks: Assigned to the 3rd Fleet's Carrier Striking Force. Primary duty was to engage enemy carrier groups and battleships.

SHONAN MARU NO. 15
Type: Submarine Chaser (Converted 1941), ex-Whaler
Configuration Sequence: M–F–M
Gross Tonnage: 355 tons
Dimensions: 134.5/35.42/12.33 feet
Machinery: Unknown
Radius: Unknown
Complement: Unknown
Built: 1939 by Osaka Iron Works, Osaka
Owner: Nippon Suisan K.K.

CH 24
Type: No. 13 Class Submarine Chaser
Displacement: 438 tons
Dimensions: 167.33/22/9 feet
Machinery: 2-shaft geared diesels, 1,700 BHP.
Speed: 16 knots
Radius: Unknown
Complement: Unknown
Armament: One 3-inch high-angle deck gun forward of the bridge, two 13mm (dual-mounted) AA guns; 136 depth charges.
Built: 1941. A total of 15 vessels of this class were constructed. It is not known at which shipyards individual vessels were built. The following is a list of shipyards and number of vessels of this class built in each:

Tsurumi	(4)
Mitsui	(2)
Hitachi, Sakurajima	(3)
Ishikawajima	(2)
Yokohama	(2)
Harima, Aioi	(2)

Remarks: Developed from the CH 1 and CH 4 classes but more compact and with distinctive clipper bow. Small tripod mast, 1 rudder, 2 depth charge throwers.

Convoy No. 3206

ULTRA intercepts of Japanese naval traffic reported that Convoy No. 3206, including the AKs GYOTEN, SHINKYO, RYUKO, ZUKAI, and TATSUHA MARUs, the DD FUJINAMI, the escort vessel AMAKUSA, PC 31, SCS 24, and the special minesweeper HAGOROMO MARU, were scheduled to arrive at Truk on 17 February. One section of this convoy, believed to have included GYOTEN MARU, SHINKYO MARU, FUJINAMI, AMAKUSA, PC 31, and SCS 24, was intercepted by the submarine U.S.S. TANG; the GYOTEN MARU was sunk by a torpedo in this action. The second section of the convoy, including HAGOROMO, TATSUHA, ZUKAI, and RYUKO MARUs, was discovered on 16 February by 12 SBDs from INTREPID (Strike 2E) at 1415 h about 90 miles west of Truk steaming on course 280 degrees at five knots. Pilots described the convoy as consisting of one 5,000-ton AO, one 6,000-ton AK, and one 10–12,000-ton AK in column in that order, escorted by a patrol boat or small tug. The "10–12,000-ton AK," described as having a single, squat stack amidships, little superstructure, and well decks piled up with crates such that they seemed to be as high as her bridge, was attacked by 4VBs who scored one direct hit with a 1,000 SAP bomb near the stack. The target AK belched bright red flame and then exploded violently, sinking within five minutes after the hit. The AK described was the 5,764-ton TATSUHA MARU, the largest vessel in the convoy. A decoded dispatch later reported that the TATSUHA MARU was bombed and sunk by aircraft about 75 miles west of Truk at 1423 h on 16 February at approximately 7°48'N, 150°27'E. At 1810 h, PC 31 reported that she had rescued 300 persons from TATSUHA MARU and at 2230 h, FUJINAMI reported that 800 personnel aboard TATSUHA MARU had been rescued while 500 more were still missing.

The reported "5,000-ton AO" with a catwalk and stack aft clearly visible, was attacked by 6VBs that dropped six 1,000-lb SAP bombs scoring three direct hits which caused an explosion and then heavy smoke. The ship was left dead in the water. This vessel actually was the new 2,700-ton engines-aft cargo ship ZUKAI MARU. Japanese message traffic on 18 February reported the losses of ZUKAI MARU in addition to GYOTEN and TATSUHA MARUs.

The ship reported to be a "6,000-ton AK" which was also attacked by INTREPID VBs was described as having a single stack, well decks, spar masts, and gun platforms on both the bow and stern. Four VBs attacked this vessel dropping two 1,000-lb SAP bombs which scored one close miss that covered her forecastle with sea water. The ship was last seen to be continuing forward while making a slow turn to starboard. The identity of this vessel was confirmed in message traffic as being the 2,764-ton RYUKO MARU; she also was reported to have picked up some survivors of the TATSUHA MARU. The following day, the FUJINAMI reported that the RYUKO MARU was on fire and that if she did not enter harbor and unload immediately, there was danger that the ammunition aboard her would explode. The FUJINAMI estimated that the ships would arrive off the South Channel (Minami Suido) of the Truk Lagoon at 1300 h on 17 February and requested that arrangements be made to handle the RYUKO MARU's cargo at once. The Japanese were able to get the ammunition out of the ship's hold before it exploded and to get the fires aboard under control. Later ULTRA messages showed that the RYUKO MARU left Truk on 2 March accompanied by two other merchantmen and three escorts for Merevan, Woleai and that she was later sunk in the carrier strikes on Palau on March 30–31.

The "patrol boat or tug" escorting the convoy was not attacked; this was the 234-ton special minesweeper/escort HAGOROMO MARU. She survived the war and was returned to mercantile service.

Returning aircraft observed a destroyer on course 280 degrees, speed 25 knots, 15 miles east of the convoy. Instead of a destroyer, this vessel may have been the minelayer/escort NATSUSHIMA which arrived with the FUJINAMI and RYUKO MARU on 17 February. One of the VB aircraft approaching the battleship task force to make a message drop advising location of these enemy ships and results of the VB sweep was shot down by IOWA's AA weapons.

TECHNICAL SUMMARIES:

TATSUHA MARU
Other Names: TATUHA MARU (Kokutai spelling)
TATSUBANE (Alternate Japanese name)
CORBY CASTLE
VIRGILIA (Original)
Type: Passenger-Cargo
Configuration Sequence: M–K–F–M
Gross Tonnage: 5,784 tons (VIRGILIA was listed as 5,697 tons in Lloyd's Register.)
Dimensions: 423.3/56/28.7 feet
Machinery: Diesel engines made by J.G. Kincaid & Co., Ltd., Grk., single screw, 550 NHP.
Radius: 15,000 miles at 10 knots.
Complement: Unknown
Built: 1918 by Russell & Co., Port Glasgow, Scotland.
Owner: Japanese – Tatuuma Kisen K.K.
Original – Cunard Steamship Co., Ltd.
Remarks: Two decks.

ZUKAI MARU
Other Names: ZUIKAI MARU
ZUIKAKU MARU
Type: Standard Type 1C Cargo Steamer
Configuration Sequence: Unknown
Gross Tonnage: 2,700 or 2,827 tons (?)
Dimensions: 321.4 o.a./44.9/20.8 feet
Machinery: Vertical triple expansion engines, aft-engines, single screw, 1,800 iHP.
Radius: 5,800 miles at 11 knots
Complement: Unknown
Built: 1942–44
Owner: Unknown
Remarks: Listed in some sources as a converted merchant cruiser.

THE WRECKS OF THE

TRUK LAGOON

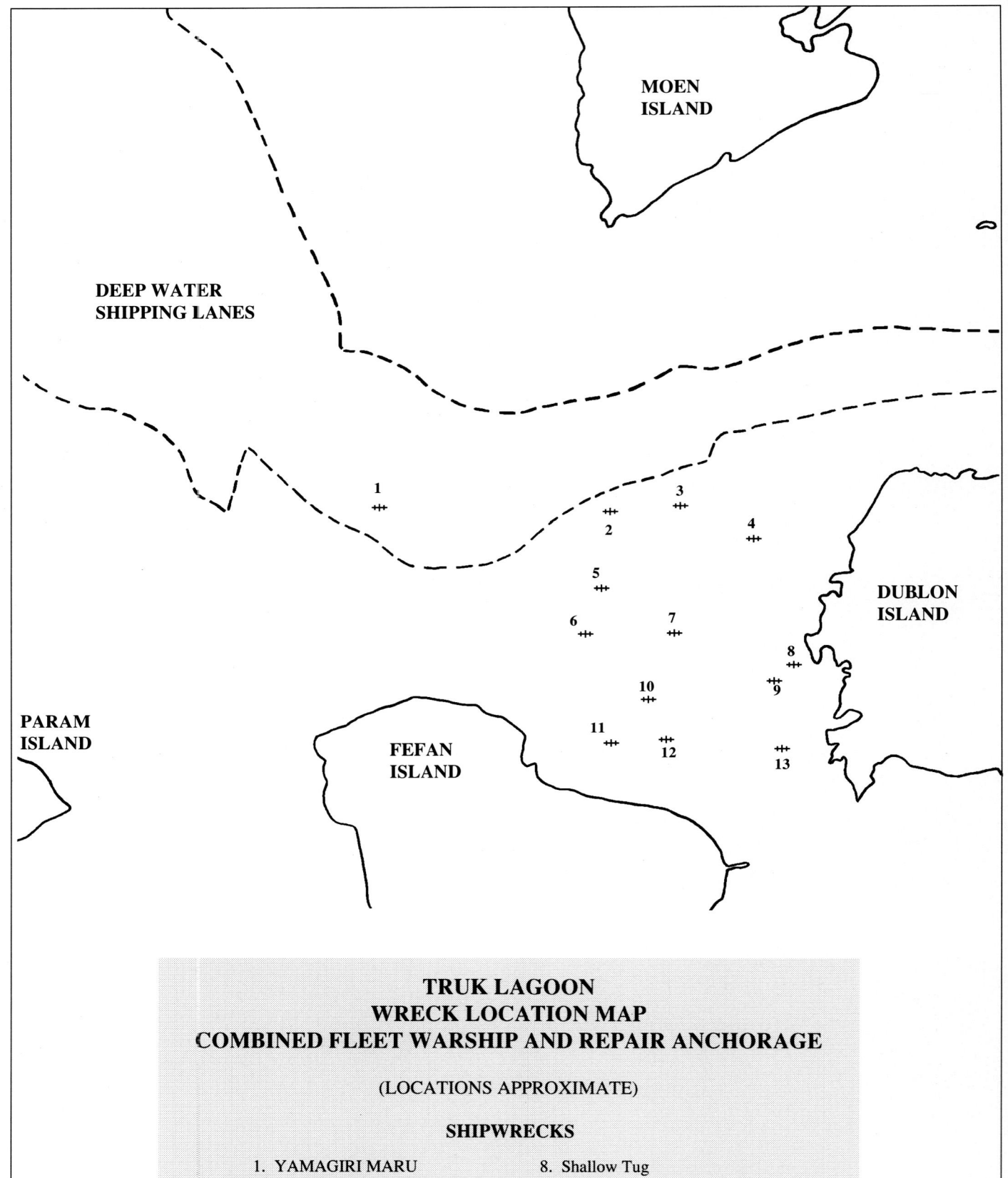

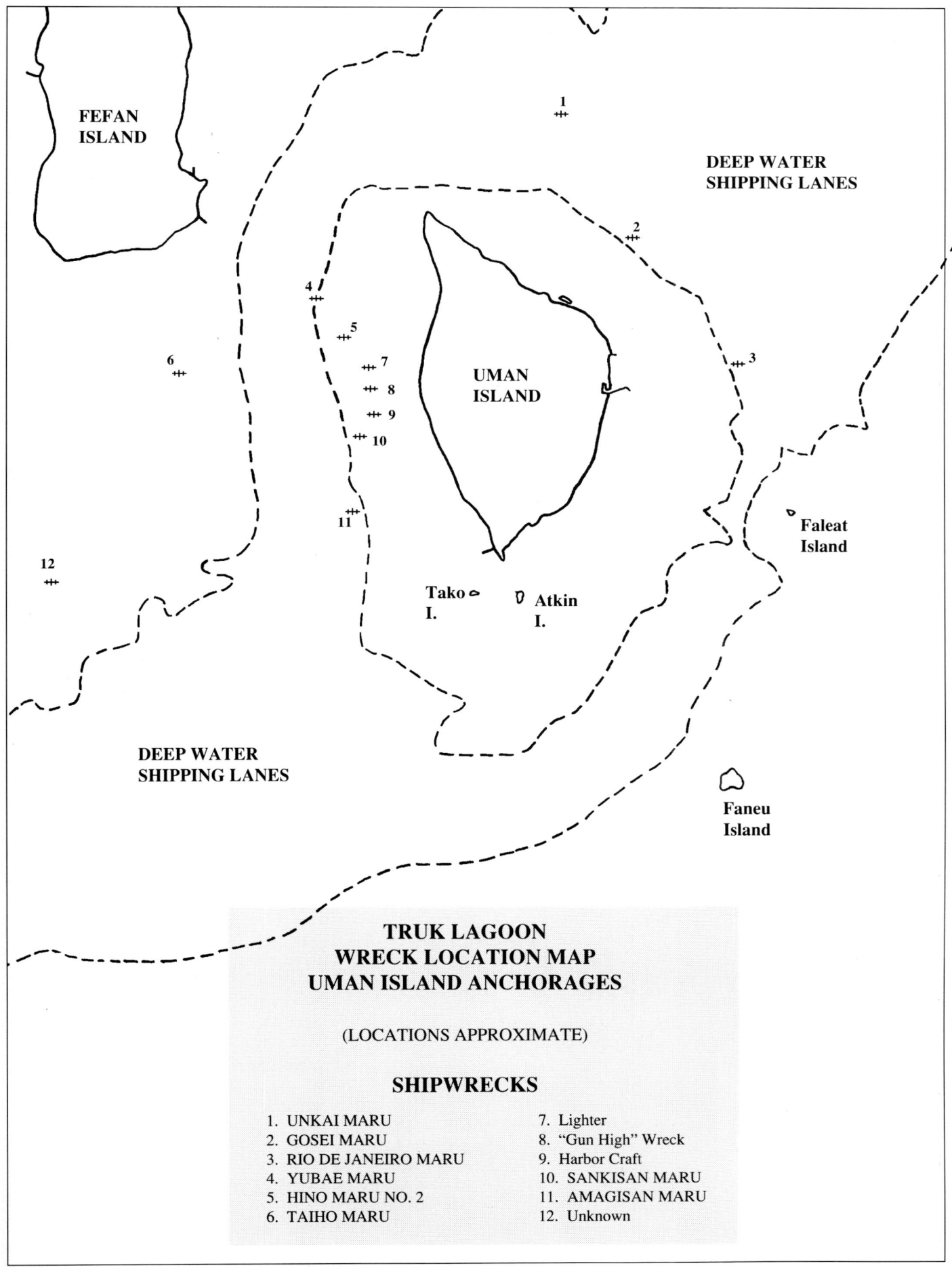

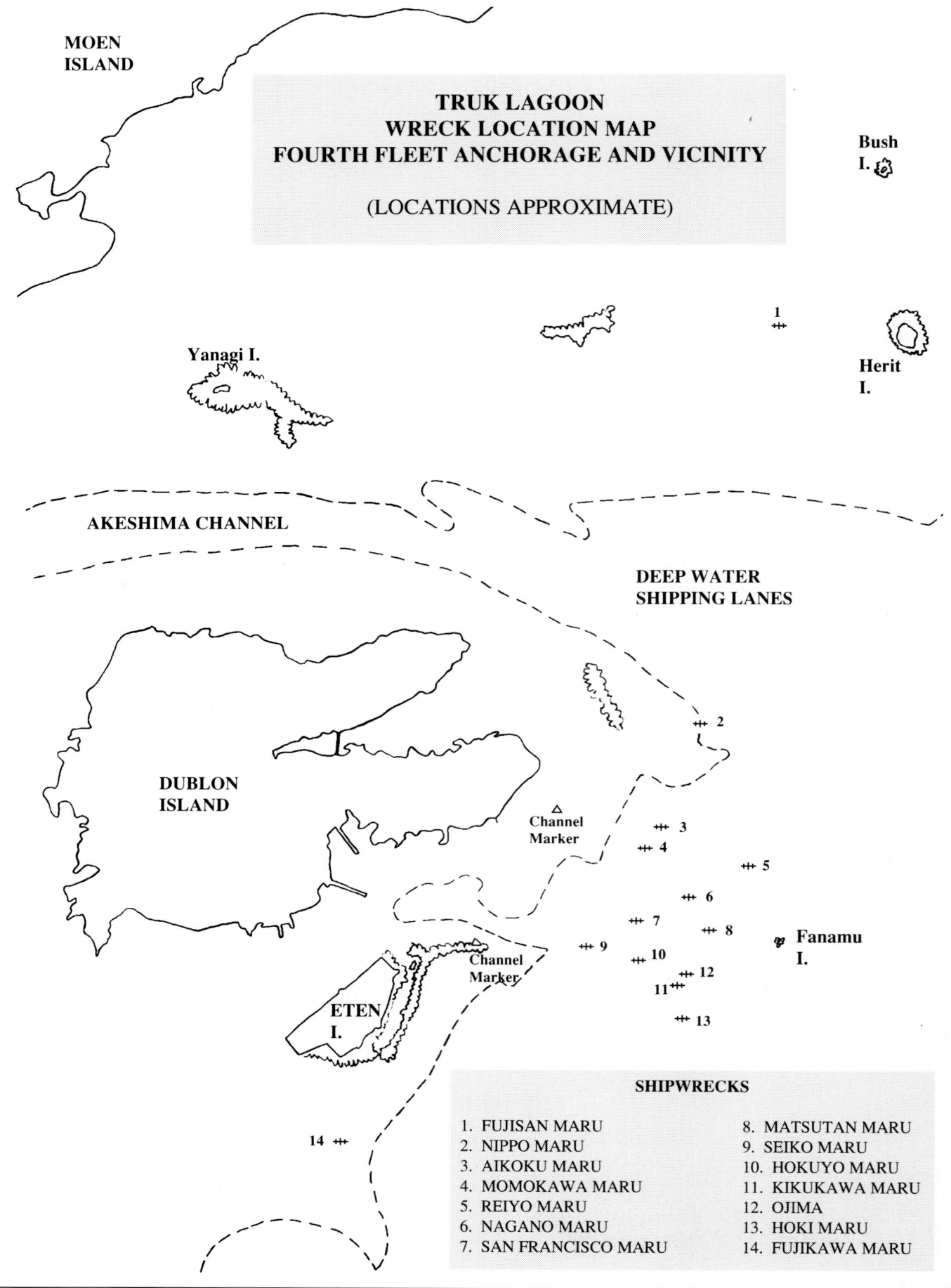

SHIPWRECKS

The AIKOKU MARU

The AIKOKU MARU was a 527-foot long twin-screw ship built in 1939 to provide world-wide passenger and cargo service for Osaka Shosen K.K. (Osaka Mercantile Steamship Co., Ltd.). The 10,437-ton vessel could accommodate 400 passengers and steam at 21 knots. Her commercial service career was cut short when she was requisitioned by the Japanese Navy. She was first designated for use as a transport and then later in August 1941, she was converted to an armed merchant cruiser (XCL). The Japanese Navy had recognized the success of the German armed merchant cruisers and accordingly took over a total of 14 merchant ships and armed them in preparation for their new role. At the outbreak of the war, the AIKOKU MARU was part of Cruiser Squadron 24 under direct command of the Combined Fleet. She was outfitted at this time with an impressive array of armament consisting of eight 5.5-inch deck guns, four torpedo tubes, and light AA guns. To enhance the ship's capability in the role of a raider, additional re-fitting was performed to allow the vessel to carry two reconnaissance float planes.

The Japanese deployed both the AIKOKU MARU and her sister ship, HOKOKU MARU, together on raiding operations. In one of the initial sorties by the two ships, they encountered the U.S. owned freighter SS VINCENT on December 12, 1941 about 600 miles northwest of Easter Island. The 6,210-ton ship had been en route from Brisbane, Australia to New York via the Panama Canal. The ship was stopped by the raiders but managed to send out a distress call. The entire 37 man crew were taken prisoner and held on HOKOKU MARU. The raiders then torpedoed the SS VINCENT and sank her. The crew members were later put ashore at Oita, Japan on February 13, 1942. Two crew members died in a Japanese prison camp; the others survived and were repatriated following the end of the war. The next known encounter was with the SS MALAMA, a 3,275-ton freighter owned by the Matson Navigation Co. of San Francisco. The MALAMA had sailed from Honolulu on 12 December 1941 in convoy with five other merchant ships escorted by two DDs, she was carrying an "ultra secret cargo" (military equipment and supplies, some of it highly classified)

—Imperial Japanese War Museum Photo
XCL AIKOKU MARU with its camouflage painting at anchor in Seletar Bay, Singapore – 7/29/42.

to Manila. The convoy was dispersed and the MALAMA sailed on alone. A small biplane with twin floats and a "Z-1" on its vertical stabilizer circled the ship several times on 21 December while she was cruising past Tubuai Island (Society Island group). The plane then disappeared without further incident. A second similar plane marked "Z-11" appeared the morning of 1 January 1942; this plane fired across the bow and signaled the MALAMA to stop. The float plane then disappeared to the northwest. The master of the MALAMA advised Radio Raratonga of the situation and then had his crew prepare for a rapid scuttling if necessary to prevent the ship and its cargo from being captured. Five hours later, the floatplane marked Z-11 returned and signaled for the crew to abandon ship. The plane emphasized the command by firing its machine guns. It was now observed to be carrying bombs under its wings. The crew then executed the scuttling procedure and disposed of all important codes and papers. Two lifeboats were then lowered and the crew abandoned ship taking along charts, sextants, and a chronometer in each boat. The plane made several threatening passes over the lifeboats and then concentrated on bombing the MALAMA. Several direct hits were scored including one observed to hit directly on hold No. 3 where a large quantity of oxygen cylinders were stored. The resulting explosions and fire dealt a death blow to the ship. The boat's sails were rigged and a course set to the north. Little progress was made as the wind died leaving the ocean in a dead calm state. Approximately three hours after the floatplane had first appeared, two ships were sighted. The AIKOKU and the HOKOKU MARUs arrived on the scene and the crew, consisting of 33 men plus 5 U.S. Air Corps Specialists, were taken prisoner and placed on the AIKOKU MARU. The ship's officers were subjected to intense questioning for several days as the original floatplane had never returned to the raider mother ships. The Japanese suspected the MALAMA of being responsible for shooting the aircraft down. The crew was off-loaded at Oita along with the crew of the SS VINCENT which had been held aboard the HOKOKU MARU. All the prisoners were put aboard the collier KOTO MARU and quartered in the coal bunker spaces while being transported to Shanghai. The crew was interned in various prison camps in China, Korea, and Japan during the next 3 years and 9 months. Two of the crew died in the coal mines at the Hakodate prison camp on Hokaido and the 2nd Engineer had to be sent to a mental hospital in Shanghai. Following the cessation of hostilities, the remaining crew members were repatriated and arrived in San Francisco on October 24, 1945 aboard the SS CAPE MEARS.

While supporting units of the 8th Submarine Squadron in the Indian Ocean in May 1942, the AIKOKU and HOKOKU MARUs captured the 7,986-ton Dutch motor tanker GENOTA and sank another vessel. During this operation, the AIKOKU MARU was acting as a supply ship (including torpedoes) and a fuel tanker for the submarines it supported. The Japanese Navy later renamed the captured ship the "OSE" and enlisted her into the naval tanker fleet on 20 July 1942. The New Zealand ship HAURAKI was seized by the two raiders on 12 July 1942 while cruising between Fremantle and Colombo. She was also enlisted into the Japanese Navy and renamed the "HOKI MARU." The HOKI MARU happened to be at Truk during the U.S. carrier raids of 16–17 February 1944 and was sunk along with the AIKOKU MARU. On 11 November 1942, the two XCLs attacked the 6,341-ton Dutch tanker ONDINA escorted by the Indian minesweeper BENGAL traveling from Fremantle to Diego Garcia. In the engagement, the BENGAL succeeded in hitting the vastly superior-armed HOKOKU MARU causing it to explode violently and sink. The AIKOKU MARU, which had meanwhile set the tanker on fire, immediately broke off the engagement and withdrew. The heavily damaged ONDINA was brought back to Fremantle.

The U.S. Submarine HALIBUT spotted the AIKOKU MARU while on patrol north of Truk on 16 July 1943. An attack was made culminating in a torpedo hit which caused medium damage including the flooding of the No. 6 hold, shaft alleys, and etc. The ship suffered 21 casualties. The AIKOKU MARU made it to Truk where temporary repairs were made; she then returned to the Empire for major repairs.

The AIKOKU MARU did not leave the Empire until January 1944. Under strict secrecy, she was part of a convoy carrying troops which were part of the 1st Amphibious Brigade which were destined for service in the Marshalls. This army amphibious organization had been detached from the Kwantung Army in Manchuria and routed to the Marshalls by way of Fusan in Korea, Saeki in the home islands, and finally Truk. The majority of the troops and civilian employees of the unit were landed on Eniwetok. Those aboard the AIKOKU MARU were partially off-loaded on Ponape; the ship then returned to Truk just prior to the U.S. carrier strikes. The AIKOKU MARU was sunk by Task Force 58 planes while anchored east of Dublon Island. She was attacked between 0815 and 0830 h on 16 February by INTREPID and ESSEX planes who hit her with 500-lb bombs and saw her explode violently and sink almost instantly.

Our group of divers made our first dive on the wreck in the month of April when there were 20- to 25-knot winds and rough water over the site of the wreck. After making several attempts to establish a firm anchor on the wreck and then having all sorts of difficulties putting on our diving equipment in the rocking boat, it was a relief when we finally dove in and got to the calm water below. We descended to the top of the smoke stack at a depth of 80 feet. There is a large amount of coral and sponge growth all around the stack and top section of the bridge. Two interesting coral-covered AA guns are mounted on the boat deck on the port and starboard sides. The bridge structure just forward of the stack has disintegrated; the foreship has been blown up completely. The superstructure and hull have been sheared away by the terrific explosion forward which was observed during the attack. It was this explosion that caught the INTREPID TBF in its blast destroying the plane and its crew.

There are three deck levels below the boatdeck. The immediate deck below can be entered from the starboard side through a large gaping hole in the superstructure. A passageway there leads directly to a large galley area where large ovens, china, sinks, bottles, and large hot water containers are located. The mess is located just forward; the remains of large tables and their frames are lying about. Exploration of the lower decks cannot be completed in a single dive because of the depths. There are large open rooms at each level with numerous heads. The partitions which separated the living quarters and staterooms have long ago deteriorated. The muck is rather deep throughout. Most of the cabin areas are well lit but a few are pitch black. There are wires hanging down from the ceiling in many places and divers must keep from being caught in them.

The wreck of the AIKOKU MARU was located and first dove on by members of Jacques Cousteau's expedition that came to Truk in 1969 to film the wrecks. Divers at that time filmed the then still unidentified wreck lying in 200-plus feet of water. Scenes from the film produced during that expedition showed the divers descending past the two AA guns on the top of the boat deck. They then penetrated deep into the wreck at 170 feet into the special living quarters built in between decks and around the first rear hold. Film footage revealed the bones of what appeared to be a hundred or more men lying in the muck on the floor of these quarters. More recent exploration into the between-decks living quarters have confirmed the location and existence of the remains of hundreds of the troops mentioned previously. The force of the shock wave from the blast which disintegrated the foreship tore through these quarters probably killing all the soldiers instantly. Bent bulkheads, doors flung from their hinges, shattered china, and remains of bunks torn from the walls are testimony of the destruction which occurred. The troops had obviously been crowded into the cramped quarters; in places the bones were lying in heaps.

The remaining two holds aft appear to not have any more living quarters built into them. The contents of these holds have not been examined because of the extreme depths. A deck gun on a platform is

–National Archives Photo

Several ships are on fire from attacks by U.S. aircraft east of Dublon Island while the large AIKOKU MARU (lower left center) has yet to be hit. Note the small craft tied to its stern. The large ship to the left of the photo smoking heavily is the REIYO MARU. The aft-engine freighter SEIKO MARU is also recognizable in the center of the group of ships to the right. One small power craft has apparently just left the AIKOKU MARU and is heading towards Dublon Island. A second small craft is underway and circling in the right foreground.

–National Archives Photo

Photo taken from INTREPID aircraft shows AIKOKU MARU exploding east of Dublon Island.

–Photo by Bill Remick
Skulls and other bones lie amongst scattered debris deep inside the AIKOKU MARU.

mounted on the top of the large deck house on the stern. The high angle at which the barrel points indicates a dual-purpose capability. It may well have been firing at planes during the attack on the ship. Photographs taken during the attack show a Daihatsu-like landing craft tied to the stern of the ship when she was attacked. The small craft is not visible on the bottom when viewed from the fantail.

In July 1984, a Japanese delegation arrived in Truk to collect the remains of the dead aboard the AIKOKU MARU. The Shinto religion embraces the worship of ancestor spirits and it is believed that the souls of the men who perished in battle live in limbo; only by recovering the remains and performing appropriate ceremonies can the souls be set free. At that time, the remains of approximately 400 men from aboard the AIKOKU MARU were recovered. The remains were cremated and the bone ash transported back to Tokyo where the ashes were spread at sea following ceremonies at the Tomb of the Unknown Soldier.

TECHNICAL SUMMARY:
Type: Transport (Re-converted October 1943)
　　　　　Armed Merchant Cruiser (Converted August 1941)
Configuration Sequence: M–K–F–K–M
Gross Tonnage: 10,437 tons
Dimensions: 498/66/29 feet
Machinery: Two diesel engines, twin-screws.
Radius: Unknown
Complement: Unknown (crew), 400 (passengers)
Built: 1939 by Tama Zosensho K.K., Okajima
Owner: Osaka Shosen Kaisha

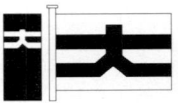

Remarks: Built as a passenger liner.
　　　　　　Three decks.
　　　　　　Eight transverse watertight bulkheads.
　　　　　　Telephonic inter-ship communications.

The AKAGI MARU

Early in the morning of February 16th, the AKAGI MARU started heading through the northern part of the lagoon following DDs NOWAKE and MAIKAZE and the CL KATORI when it was spotted by VF planes from INTREPID and COWPENS retiring from their initial fighter sweep strike. The ship was strafed by a single F6F from INTREPID at this time who reported starting a fire aboard the vessel.

–National Archives Photo
The AKAGI MARU before being converted into an armed merchant cruiser.

BUNKER HILL pilots attacking KATORI on Strike 3B just north of North Pass reported a large merchant vessel just inside the lagoon putting up heavy AA fire. The AKAGI MARU continued following the KATORI and two DDs and was attacked next by 5 TBFs from BUNKER HILL. Only close misses were observed with bombs dropped by the TBFs; one COWPENS VF fired 2,400 rounds at the ship without visible effect.

The vessel was next attacked by YORKTOWN, ESSEX, and CABOT planes in position about 15 miles northwest of North Pass between 0930 and 0945 h. YORKTOWN's Strike 1CY, consisting of 8VT, 14VB, and 12VF, discovered the KATORI at 0930 h with escorting DDs NOWAKE and MAIKAZE, and "one large freighter with 5-inch gun platforms fore and aft, maneuvering at high speed in position about 10 miles northwest of North Pass." The AKAGI MARU was leading the formation followed by KATORI which was flanked by the two DDs. YORKTOWN VBs and most VTs attacked the warships, but one TBF dropped two 500-lb bombs on the large freighter and scored one hit amidships which started a fire and a delayed explosion aboard the ship. At 0945 h, these same ships were attacked by 3VT, 15VB, and 4VF from ESSEX (Strike 2C) and 3VT from CABOT. Most planes again concentrated on the warships, but one ESSEX VT dropped four 500-lb bombs and scored three direct hits on the stern of the freighter. This left the ship smoking and settling fast by the stern. A single CABOT VT then dropped four more 500-lb bombs on the "AMAGISAN MARU class freighter" (very similar in both size and appearance to AKAGI MARU), scoring two direct hits on the after well deck, causing a violent explosion and leaving the ship with her after well deck under water and sinking fast.

ESSEX Strike 2D, arriving over the scene at 1300 h, reported the freighter was no longer visible and INTREPID planes attacking the warships after noon saw wreckage, life boats, and a large oil slick one to two miles astern of them. An intercepted Japanese report on the air strikes listed the AKAGI MARU as having been bombed at 0935 h and sunk at 1200 h about 20 miles northwest of North Pass.

Unlike the KIYOSUMI MARU and the AIKOKU MARU, the AKAGI MARU was still being utilized by the Japanese Navy as an armed merchant cruiser when sunk at Truk. After being placed under charter to the Japanese Navy and converted to an armed merchant cruiser assigned to the 5th Fleet in January 1942, she was equipped with four 6-inch deck guns and several smaller caliber AA guns.

TECHNICAL SUMMARY:

Type: Armed Merchant Cruiser (Converted January 1942)
Configuration Sequence: M–K–F–K–M
Gross Tonnage: 7,398 tons
Dimensions: 462.5/62/28 feet
Machinery: Diesel engines, single screw, 2,248 NHP.
Radius: 36,000 miles at 15 knots.
Complement: 62 (crew), 4 (passengers).
Built: 1936 by Mitsubishi Jukogyo K.K., Nagasaki.
Owner: Nippon Yusen Kaisha
Remarks: Two decks, cruiser stern, refrigerated machinery.
Reported sinking location 7°54'N, 151°25'E.

The AMAGISAN MARU

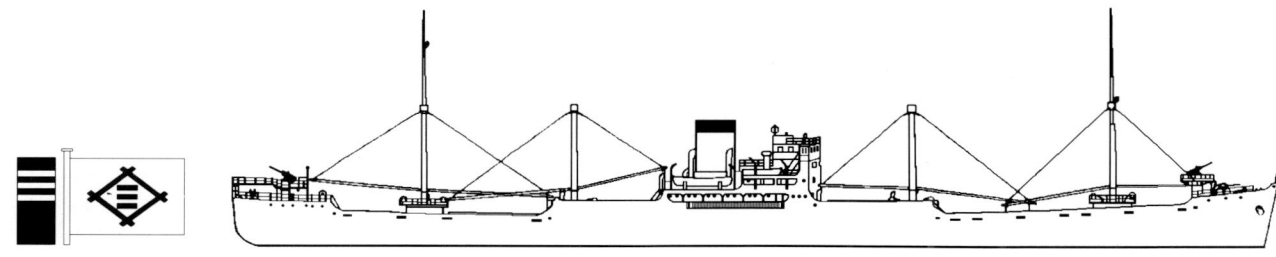

MITSUI BUSSAN KAISHA

A coded dispatch originated by ComDesDiv-27 on February 14, 1944, reported that DesDiv-27 (DDs HARUSAME and SHIGURE), OITE, FUJISAN MARU, SHINKOKU MARU, and AMAGISAN MARU had arrived at Truk. The ships in this convoy were dispatched to their assigned anchorages which for the AMAGISAN MARU was southwest of Uman Island.

BUNKER HILL planes on Strike 3D on the first morning of the air raids attacked shipping at the southern end of the anchorage between Fefan and Uman Islands. The AMAGISAN MARU, described by the aircraft action report narratives, was the largest ship in the anchorage, estimated at 10,000-tons and 500 feet long. The ship was attacked in turn by 5 SB2Cs and 4 TBFs at 1250 h. She was first hit by a 1,000-lb GP bomb and then the TBFs followed that with a solid torpedo hit just forward of amidships on the starboard side. One photo taken during the attack shows the ship being hit by a torpedo forward and about to receive another aft. A fuel oil fire started aboard and a large trail of heavy black smoke billowed up from the ship. Within 15 minutes of the attack, the ship was burning fiercely and sinking by the bow. It had gone under by the next strike.

We had a difficult time in finding the AMAGISAN MARU as the wreck was only recently discovered and our guide had only been to the site once before. The anchor we were dragging finally caught on something below and we donned our scuba gear and entered the water. After descending along the anchor line to a depth of 90 feet, we could look below us through the blue-grey haze to see that we were anchored on a coral head instead of the wreck we were searching for. I was about to abort the dive when I spotted the outline of a ship's hull off in the distance. We swam over to the wreck and found the ship lying with a 45-degree list to the port side with its forward section on a 140 foot bottom. The name of the ship, the AMAGISAN MARU, was welded in large letters on the hull at 95 feet near the bow with the corresponding kanji characters positioned above. A large black coral bush about eight feet high was growing on the hull alongside. The port anchor line disappeared from the bow off into the distance. The bow gun is mounted on a large platform and is very picturesque, especially when viewed with backlight from below.

A tanker truck has fallen from the deck and lies on the bottom opposite the forward holds; the cab and hood have collapsed. The forward mast lies against the truck. The No. 1 hold contains only a few crushed 50-gallon-sized barrels. The second hold contains aircraft wings and parts, more barrels, and wood planking. At the aft end of the hold, a large car with its cab mostly intact can be found. Its ends are

–National Archives Photo
Smoke rises from AMAGISAN MARU which has been bombed and torpedoed. Several small vessels are in the background while a second large ship is partially visible behind the end of Uman Island in the right center of the photo. Fefan Island is in the rear with Param Island behind it.

crushed and there is a large hole in the roof. There is a 10- to 12-foot long aileron (paravane) used for minesweeping hanging off the port side. The No. 3 hold just forward of the bridge exhibits a large gaping hole which resulted from a torpedo hit on the starboard side. Coral growth on the wreck at this depth was almost non-existent.

The bridge area was very open with almost everything having fallen to the bottom side. Burnt planking substantiated that the ship had been on fire before sinking. Pieces were lying all over the floor of the bridge. The helm and the ship's telegraph stood upright and a compass and a telescope were lying nearby. The ship's safe was found; it was salvaged from the ship some years later. Its contents were not publicized. Divers exploring the deck below the bridge reported that the mess was located there. China with the owner's stack markings was found along with several exquisite vases and a telephone.

Three large rings encircle the funnel representing the stack markings of the Mitsui shipping company. The aft section of the wreck lies in progressively deeper water. We explored this portion of the wreck by swimming at the 140 foot level past the rear goalpost and mast to the stern. The holds were too deep to explore. The deck near the stern has been blown apart from an apparent bomb explosion. There is a gun mounted on a platform at the stern.

TECHNICAL SUMMARY:

Type: Passenger-Cargo
Configuration Sequence: M–K–F–K–M
Gross Tonnage: 7,620 tons
Dimensions: 450/60/27.5 feet
Machinery: Diesel engine, single screw, 1,230 NHP.
Radius: 33,000 miles at 16 knots.
Complement: 48 (crew), 7 (passengers).
Built: 1933 by Mitsui Bussan Kaisha
Owner: Mitsui Bussan Kaisha
Remarks: Assigned to the 11th Air Fleet. 2 decks, cruiser stern, eight watertight bulkheads.

CH 29

ULTRA information indicated that at 0531 h on the 16th of February, SUBCHASER NO. 29 was ordered to rendezvous with a convoy known at the time to have been at a position of 8°00'N, 149°00'E. Later in the day, the vessel originated a message stating that she expected to make rendezvous at 1430 h. The CinC 4th Base Force reported in a coded message that on 19 February SUBCHASER NO. 29 and SHONAN MARU NO. 15 had sortied from Truk on February 16th to aid in escorting a convoy and that as they had not been reported since that time, it was feared that they had been sunk by U.S. air attacks on Feb. 16–17. On February 24, the CinC 8th Base Force at Rabaul requested information as to the whereabouts and status of SUBCHASER NO. 29, the TAMA MARU NO. 8 (sunk Feb. 20 in the Bismark area), and the Navy Tug NAGAURA (sunk Feb. 22 off Kavieng). On 31 March 1944, SUBCHASER NO. 29 was deleted from the Japanese Sub-Chaser List. The codebreakers received a captured copy of a coded message of April 26, 1944 which stated that Sub-Chaser Division 32, composed of SUBCHASERs NOs. 28, 29, and 30, was being disbanded because its flagship, SUBCHASER NO. 29, had been lost due to an enemy air attack on February 17. No mention of SUBCHASER NO. 29 was forthcoming in Fleet message traffic, captured documents, or prisoners since that date.

Monograph No. 116 lists the SUBCHASER NO. 29 as being sunk by enemy aircraft west of Truk on the 17th of February. No specific attack in available aircraft action reports describes a corresponding action in that location which might have resulted in the sinking of the vessel. Its possible that the small PC which was seen entering through North Pass on 17 February and sunk in strafing attacks in the northern part of the lagoon by ENTERPRISE TBFs (Strike 1AE) was actually SUBCHASER NO. 29.

TECHNICAL SUMMARY:

Type: No. 28 Class Submarine Chaser
Displacement: 420 tons.
Dimensions: 160.75/22/8.75 feet
Machinery: 2-shaft geared diesels, 1,700 BHP.
Speed: 16 knots
Radius: Unknown
Complement: Unknown
Armament: One 3-inch high-angle deck gun, two 13mm dual-mounted AA guns; 36 depth charges.
Built: 1942. A total of 34 vessels of this class were built. It is not known at which shipyards individual vessels were constructed. The following is a list of shipyards and numbers of vessels of this class built in each:

Tsurumi	(3)
Mitsui	(3)
Hitachi, Sakurajima	(3)
Ishikawajima	(2)
Hackodate Dock	(5)
Hitachi, Innoshima	(4)
Kawaminami	(4)
Niigata Iron Works	(7)
Naniwa, Osaka	(3)

The FUJIKAWA MARU

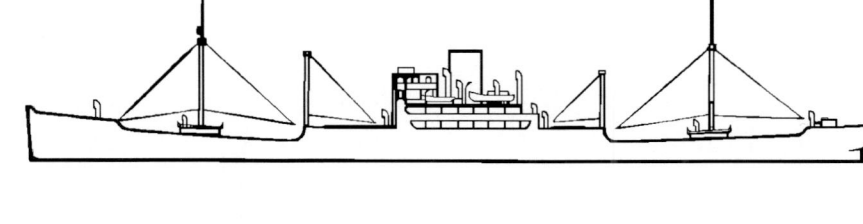

TOYO KAIUN K.K.

Built in 1938 for Toyo Kaiun Kisen Kaisha as a passenger-cargo ship, the FUJIKAWA MARU was requisitioned two years later by the Japanese Navy to be used as an armed aircraft transport or ferry. She was one of ten merchant ships to be converted for this role and prior to the outbreak of the war, was based in Indo-China as part of Air Flotilla 22 under the command of the 11th Air Fleet. In this role, she was tasked for the delivery of planes and aircraft parts to island bases. The ship suffered medium damage from a torpedo attack by a U.S. submarine on 12 September 1943 northeast of Truk. At this time, the FUJIKAWA MARU underwent major repairs and upon completion was re-rated as a transport in January 1944. It is interesting to note that even though the ship had been reclassified, she was fulfilling the role of an aircraft ferry when sunk in the February 16–17 raids on Truk.

On my initial visit to the Truk Lagoon, the first shipwreck that our group would dive on was to be the FUJIKAWA MARU. We first spotted her two masts sticking out of the water after we had taken a route through the Fefan-Dublon channel and rounded the southwest end of Dublon Island. The wreck was facing east with about 25 feet of her forward mast and about 15 feet of her rear mast rising above the calm water. I was amazed at the prolific marine growth on the mast below. Most of our group's previous wreck diving experience had been on the ships sunk at Kwajalein where little or no growth is found.

The wreck of the FUJIKAWA MARU was indeed different; below us was a submarine forest of coral, sponges, algae, and other growth we had never seen before. As we descended, I noticed schools of baitfish congregated around the mast and larger species of many types swimming in all directions around the wreck. Soft corals of the species Dendronepthya were hanging from the mast, the rigging, the loading derricks, the railings around the decks, and on structures everywhere. The different colors of the soft corals, the "zig-zag" clams (actually oysters), and the various types of sponges was something to behold. We could see that the mast we were descending alongside was situated between two cargo holds below with their hatch cover beams in place. My dive partner pointed aft where I spotted 7 or 8 large barracuda swimming over the deck with the bridge superstructure looming behind them. We swam forward to the bow with its raised gun platform and 4.7-inch deck gun which was almost unrecognizable due to the coral and sponge growth covering them. The gun had a large branching coral almost five feet in diameter growing from the center of the gun barrel. Boxes positioned behind the rear of the gun on the platform contained live ready ammunition. We decided to swim around the outside of the hull where the marine growth continued to be very thick. Various types of gorgonians, large black coral bushes, and long strands of white and black colored "whip coral" covered the hull. As we swam down below the gun towards the forecastle, I noticed a large spare anchor attached to the bulkhead near the starboard doorway leading to the compartments below. There were two entrances into the forecastle; inside, we found some partially burned gas masks, water hoses, and some very large naval artillery shell casings.

The upper level of the forward hold contained a few bottles and crushed 50-gallon-sized barrels. After swimming to the bottom level at 90 feet, we found aircraft parts including tires, propeller blades, machine guns, and wing tanks. A single torpedo body was lying on one side of the hold. A curious find was an outboard motor that someone had propped up against a wing tank. Many dangerous items were present also: small arms and belted machine gun ammunition; 4.7-inch brass shell casings; and some 1 1/2-foot-long objects with handles and insulator-type ceramic material on their ends which could be bomb detonators. It was obvious that a diver should be very careful not to touch or dislodge any of the explosive cargo that the hold contained. The No. 2 hold had very little in the upper level except for a few scattered bottles and barrels, but the lower section contained several stripped fighter plane bodies, spare wings, and several rows of large aircraft bombs protruding from the muck.

On later dives, we explored the single-level hold just forward of the mid-ship structure. After descending between steel hatch cover beams, we found a large ventilation system with a fan arrangement which evidently supplied fresh air to the engine room below decks. Passageways on both the port and starboard sides led aft underneath the mid-ship structure to the hold beyond; a series of storage rooms are built against the outer hull. The muck and debris was deep inside the rooms which appeared empty except for a few large saki bottles. The hold aft, No. 4, showed considerable damage on the starboard side; hull plates were torn and separated and it was apparent the ship had received a torpedo or skip-bomb hit.

At maindeck level in the aft end of the mid-ship structure, we entered one small room that contained hundreds of "Dai Nippon Beer" bottles. These bottles lay in piles covering the whole floor of the room. A few feet away on the port side was a passageway leading to the interior of the ship. The first room was a galley with huge ovens and a large bronze grinder mounted along one wall. Swimming down the passageway, we passed the latrine on the left with a row of urinals

–Naval Operational Archives Photo
The FUJIKAWA MARU (left center of picture) with a small craft tied to her stern appears undamaged early on the first day of attacks. The TONAN MARU NO. 3 is damaged and is emitting a column of white smoke in the background. Two other vessels are underway, one small AK off the stern of the FUJIKAWA MARU and a GOSEI MARU class AK circling to the right.

Two examples of beautifully colored soft coral – Dendronepthya species (FUJIKAWA MARU).

against the wall. The next room beyond contained green tiled bathtubs and showers. A doorway on the right led to a catwalk landing with stairs leading to the engine room below. The passageway led to a large room forward which extended from one side of the ship to the other. The floor was covered by muck and debris several inches thick. There was lots of wiring hanging from the ceiling and insulators, bottles, and many other items lying about. The next deck above can be entered from a companionway forward. This area served as crew's and officer's living quarters and personal effects such as shoes, inkwells, and uniforms can be found. Radio equipment is scattered about forward with more insulators and wiring lying about. This level, like the one below, had been gutted by fire. Mounted on a wall was a large porcelain water filter with the following inscription on its side:

No. 1
Okano's Improved Carbon Water Filter
Manufactured by Okano & Co., Ltd.
Kobe, Japan

In the wheelhouse of the bridge at the upper deck, I looked for the ship's telegraph and rudderstand with no luck. I learned later they had fallen down through the weakened flooring one or two decks below. The captain's quarters were evidently located along the port side. Single rooms containing a latrine, bathtub, and what appeared to be a small living area were found. As I swam towards the starboard side, I could see something white sticking out from the muck under a detached door. I investigate and found three different dishes, all of which had the "TK" flag symbol of the ship's owner, Toyo Kaiun K.K.

On top of the bridge are two structures covered with heavy growth; one appears to be a type of communications antenna while the other looks like a dual-barreled AA gun. In 1974, a small makeshift shrine was found on the top of the bridge. A Japanese delegation had placed it along with several smooth-surfaced rocks bearing kanji characters, a statue of sorts, and a rather fancy glass case with what appeared to be the names of the crewmembers of the ship written on it. It had been recently placed there as a tribute to those whose lives had been lost when the ship was attacked and sunk.

The FUJIKAWA MARU is so large and has so much to see that it takes several dives to begin to see everything. The stern is deeper than the bow by 15 to 20 feet. Mounted on the poop is a large gun similar to the one mounted forward. The barrel is almost 15 feet long. This deck gun and actually the whole stern area has a lot less marine growth than the forward section of the wreck. The compartment below the deck gun looked as though it had been used for ammunition storage.

The hatch cover beams on the rear holds have have been removed; its possible that the majority of the cargo in these holds had been offloaded prior to the air attacks. The upper level of the rear hold is packed with galley stores. The port and starboard sides of the hold held many cases of beer bottles with their necks sticking up out of the deep muck. Towards the rear, we found a beautiful but broken china teapot, mess kits, and some pans which had the Japanese Navy symbol, an anchor with the rising sun, on their bottoms. I reached into the muck in one place and found a collection of china dishes, saucers, and cups that were stacked in a broken crate. There were no identifying flag symbols or markings on these china pieces. The lower level of the hold at 115 feet had several unopened crates of what appeared to be more china.

The U.S. aircraft action reports make it fairly clear that the FUJIKAWA MARU was bombed by planes from several air groups on February 16th; BUNKER HILL planes (Strike 3E) claimed a torpedo hit on a ship at 1420 h whose description and location appear to coincide with that of the FUJIKAWA MARU also. Photographs show the ship still afloat the next morning. ESSEX dive bombers (Strike 3C) scored a 1,000-lb bomb hit on the port quarter and scored three close misses; the ship was on fire and smoking when they withdrew. The final attack was by two MONTEREY VT planes (Strike 3C) which reported seeing the ship already heavily damaged and down by the stern. They witnessed a huge explosion which enveloped the ship in flames possibly from one of their two torpedoes launched against the vessel.

TECHNICAL SUMMARY:

Other Name: HUZIKAWA MARU (Kokutai spelling)
Type: Transport (Re-converted January 1944)
　　　　Aircraft Ferry (Converted 1940)
　　　　Passenger-Cargo (Original)
Configuration Sequence: M–K–F–K–M
Gross Tonnage: 6,938 tons
Dimensions: 437.4/58.5/26 feet
Machinery: Diesel engines, single screw, 840 NHP.
Radius: 50,000 miles at 13 1/2 knots.
Complement: 40 (crew), 4 (passengers)
Built: 1938 by Mitsubishi Zosensho, Nagasaki
Owner: Toyo Kaiun K.K.
Remarks: Two decks.

The FUJISAN MARU

The FUJISAN MARU was built in 1931 in Harima for Lino Shoji Kisen Kaisha to be used as a commercial tanker. This 9,524-ton vessel, with a length of 512 feet and a beam of 65 feet, was equipped with a diesel engine and a single screw and was capable of 19 knots. In 1941, the ship was requisitioned from the merchantmen fleet, placed under direct charter to the Japanese Navy, and then attached to the Combined Fleet.

The Japanese formed a Northern Area Force in conjunction with their Midway operation in May-June 1942. The FUJISAN MARU was included as part of a supply group of oilers supporting this Northern Area Force which made a thrust into Alaskan waters. The main purpose of this operation, which included strikes at Dutch Harbor in the Aleutians and a planned occupation of Kiska, Adak, and Attu, was to disguise their Midway attack intentions and draw U.S. naval units in that direction. In attacks on the Japanese force on 18 June, the U.S. Army Air Force sank one of the other Japanese supply tankers accompanying the task group, the 6,800-ton NISSAN MARU.

Photographs taken early on the morning of 16 February show the FUJISAN MARU moored to the fuel pier on the south side of Dublon Island. INTREPID planes (Strike 2B) reported the tanker to be getting underway at the time of their attacks on the Dublon seaplane base and Eten Island installations. Reports by various air groups help to trace the actions taken by the vessel over the two days of attacks. It appears the ship made for North Pass where BUNKER HILL dive bombers (Strike 3B) made an attack on an oiler described as being 550 feet long, 13,000 tons. She was reported hit by a single 1,000-lb SAP bomb as she was proceeding through the pass to sea; a large explosion resulted. All air groups began attacking the warships grouped north to northwest of North Pass. The captain of the FUJISAN MARU must have decided to turn around and return to the lagoon as the ships outside were the focal point of a lot of unwanted attention. The ship may have been the oiler reported underway by ENTERPRISE planes

–National Archives Photo

The FUJISAN MARU

–Naval Operational Archives Photo

Vertical photo shows the tanker FUJISAN MARU at the fuel pier on Dublon's south shore on the morning of 16 February 1944.

China locker aboard FUJISAN MARU contains pieces of many sizes and shapes. Large serving platter at right exhibits a beautiful design.

(STRIKE 1EE) later that day to the west of Moen Island.

When ENTERPRISE dive bombers (Strike 1AE) arrived over their anchorage target area at first light on the morning of the 17th, they spotted the FUJISAN MARU underway making a dash for safety towards the east between Moen and Dublon Islands. The SBDs dropped three bombs on the tanker just after she made a turn to the north, scoring a hit on the stern and two near misses. The ship was mortally stricken, lost headway, and began foundering in the wind. Photos show the ship half under water with her bow high in the air. She sank shortly thereafter.

Some divers among the Continental Airlines-Air Micronesia pilots spotted a large oil slick on the water on an extremely calm day in 1975 and by following up with nearly a three week search, were rewarded when fathometer readings and traces of oil on the surface pinpointed the location of the wreck. When I first dove on the FUJISAN MARU, it was on a cloudy day with 4- to 5-foot waves on the water in the exposed wreck location southeast of Moen Island. I figured it was quite an accomplishment for our guide, Jercy, to even find the wreck at all because of the distance from land and the lack of landmarks for aligning our position over the site. After only two attempts to anchor on the wreck, we hooked something and our four divers descended down the anchor line. At 110 feet, we could see a dim outline of the wreck below. The anchor had snagged some superstructure on the forward part of the bridge at 140 feet. The ship was lying with her bow pointing towards the northeast end of Moen Island while listing about 45 degrees to the port side. The mast forward of the bridge had some coral growth but there was little on the rest of the wreck. It appeared that the entire bridge superstructure had been gutted by fire prior to sinking. The roof over the wheelhouse had disappeared either due to salt water deterioration or fire, leaving only exposed beams over the top section. While swimming downward toward the port side, I came upon a ship's telegraph of a type I had never seen before. A control cable running to the side was attached to the upper section of the telegraph. Others I have seen have the control cables attached through their base into the deck below. Deep into the wheelhouse at 175 feet, the ship's compass was spotted lying in the silt. One deck down, we found a china locker with three shelves stacked with various types of dishes. A single large serving platter with an intricate design in blue was lying beside the locker. There were no Lino Shoji K.K. house flag markings on any of the china. Many other objects were lying around the china locker including brass lanterns, a ship's clock, and other unidentifiable artifacts. It was obvious this wreck contained a multitude of interesting things. Excitement in exploring this wreck was contagious amongst all the divers and the 20 minutes bottom time we had allowed for the dive was over before we hardly knew it. Time and depth prevented a thorough exploration of this magnificent wreck. While ascending past the forward section of the mid-ship superstructure, I noticed a large 15- to 20-foot-diameter indentation in the hull. Undoubtedly, this was the result of a near miss with an aerial bomb.

TECHNICAL SUMMARY:

Other Name: HUZIZAN (Kokutai spelling)
Type: Naval Tanker (1941)
Configuration Sequence: M–K–M–F
Gross Tonnage: 9,524 tons
Dimensions: 490/65/28 feet
Machinery: Diesel engine built by Maschinenfabrik.,

Augsburg. Single screw, 1,857 NHP.
Radius: 16,000 miles at 15 knots.
Complement: 48
Built: 1931 by Harima Sanbashi & Engineering Co., Ltd., Harima.

Owner: Lino Shoji K.K.

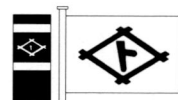

The FUMITSUKI

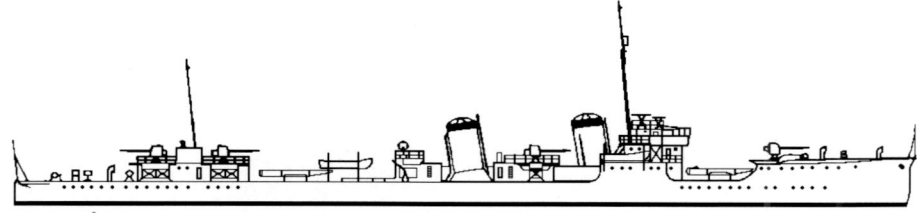

The destroyers FUMITSUKI and sister ship SATSUKI were damaged in air attacks in Stephen Strait north of Rabaul on January 4, 1944. During attacks by U.S. aircraft later in the month (Jan. 31), further damage was inflicted to the FUMITSUKI. Rabaul at this time was frequently being bombarded in air attacks and since the destroyer could not safely receive the repairs she needed, the decision was made to transfer her to Truk.

When attacking aircraft arrived at Truk on the morning of the 16th of February, the FUMITSUKI was moored several hundred yards southeast of the HOYO MARU in the anchorage reserved for ships undergoing or needing repair southwest of Dublon Island. The FUMITSUKI remained at anchor through the mid-morning unscathed while nearby higher priority ship targets were being attacked. She was undoubtedly the DD reported in the anchorage that was returning AA fire at the attackers. When the bombers singled her out around midday, she weighed anchor and with only her one usable engine, tried to evade the enemy planes. Evasive tactics were not successful; the FUMITSUKI was hit by a single bomb which stopped her dead in the water. The destroyer MATSUKAZE attempted to tow the FUMITSUKI towards shore where she could be beached and possibly salvaged. With the destroyer taking on water and listing, towing the stricken ship against the wind was impossible and rescue was abandoned. The hospital ship, HIKAWA MARU NO. 2, pulled alongside and shielded the ship from the attacking planes for some time while the FUMITSUKI drifted to the northwest with the wind and eventually dropped both anchors to inhibit further movement. The FUMITSUKI shipped water up to her upper deck and began to take on a heavy port list. An intercepted dispatch reported that at 2034 h, she was in danger of sinking in position 4,300 meters bearing 38 degrees from Udot Island. A follow-up message reported that the ship sunk at 1530 h the next day.

The discovery of the wreck site was only accomplished after a Japanese writer and diving enthusiast, Tomoyuki Yoshimura, persisted in researching Japanese war reports and interviewing survivors, including the captain of the ship, whom he located by advertising in Japanese newspapers. Using the information gathered, Yoshimura found the wreck of the FUMITSUKI in April 1987 with the help of Blue Lagoon Shop personnel. The destroyer lies upright with a 25 degree list to port on a 130-foot bottom. She lies facing south which suggests that she was probably drifting beam to the wind when she sunk.

The 4.7-inch dual purpose bow gun at approximately 115 feet depth is covered with sponge and coral growth. Ready ammunition shells in boxes are positioned to its front and rear. The windlass mounted forward has two chains extending away from it, but the port anchor chain has been severed and does not go through the hawsepipe. This is consistent with the reports of the ship drifting with its anchors dragging after having its remaining engine knocked out. Compartments that appear to have been crew's quarters are located in the forecastle. Just behind the bow gun on the foredeck is the forward 3-torpedo, 24-inch torpedo launcher mounted on a machined swivel mount. Torpedoes were transported (winched) from the aft storage compartment forward on a narrow gauge track mounted on the starboard deck. Outboard of the track is what appears to be a gun mount, probably used for one of the 13mm AA guns. Its not known if the gun had been removed or had been blown from its mount. On top of the smallish bridge at 100 feet, binoculars are attached to a swivel mount on a pedestal surrounded by a low railing. Immediately aft is a 5-6-foot rangefinder. The bridge superstructure itself is in fairly good shape. Inside, the ship's two telegraphs stand side by side with Japanese kanji characters visible on their faces. The pointers on the telegraphs are in different positions. The port telegraph has the pointer fixed at 12 o'clock, while the starboard is at 3 o'clock. There are many gauges here and voice speaker tubes which are attached to a wall leading down towards the engine room. The ship's bell was found in the bridge but has been hidden to prevent pilfering.

Only one of the stacks, the aft one, is still standing. Human remains have been found on the floor of the engine room below. Since the crewmembers were off-loaded ashore before the destroyer sank, these remains are probably those who were killed in the initial bombing and/or strafing attacks by U.S. planes. Larger AA guns, probably 25mm, have their barrels missing; the shields are intact and covered with heavy growth. The searchlight is not mounted aft of amidships where it is supposed to be; in its place are bomb-like projectiles in racks.

The aft torpedo launcher has been removed. The lifeboat davits are still in place nearby. Bent and torn superstructure in the aft section is the result of bomb damage which split the hull and ultimately caused the flooding and sinking of the destroyer. A single 4.7-inch deck gun can be found near the stern. The stern itself and the deck above are buckled; this may have resulted partly from bomb damage and also from the ship slamming against the bottom stern-first when it sank.

TECHNICAL SUMMARY:

Other Names: FUMIZUKI
HUMIDUKI (Kokutai spelling)
NO. 29 (Original)
Type: MUTSUKI Class Destroyer
Displacement: 1,913 tons (after reconstruction)
Dimensions: 320/30/9.67 feet
Machinery: 2-shaft Parsons geared turbines, 4 Kampon boilers, 38,500 SHP

Speed: 33 1/2 knots
Complement: 150
Armament: Originally - Four 4.7-inch 45-cal DP guns, two 7.7mm MGs; six 24-inch torpedo tubes (10 torpedoes); 16 mines; 18 depth charges. 1941–42 - Two 4.7-inch 50-cal DP guns, twenty 25mm AA, five 13mm AA; six 24-inch torpedo tubes; 36 depth charges.
Built: 16 February 1926 by Fujinagata Zosensho, Osaka, completed 3 July 1926. Rebuilt 1941–42 as fast transport.
Remarks: Assigned to the 22nd Destroyer Division, 3rd DD Squadron as part of the Outer South Seas Force. Its primary duty was to engage enemy task forces.

The GOSEI MARU

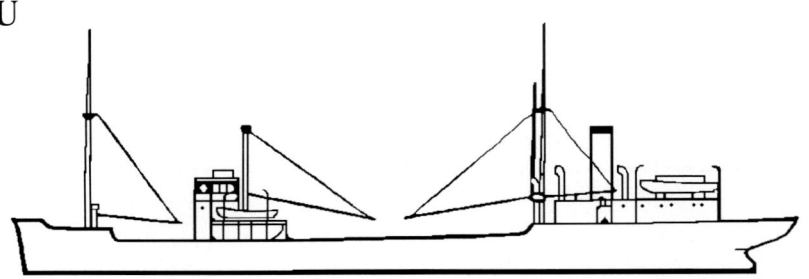

The local names given to the wreck, the "Stern High Wreck" or the "Diagonal Ship," offer a clue to the disposition of the GOSEI MARU. The ship rests on her port side facing southeast on a diagonal plane with her stern resting against the edge of a coral drop-off and her forward section sloping towards deeper water. We found the wreck on my first trip to Truk by skirting the coral drop-off about 200 yards from shore on the east side of Uman Island until we nearly struck the stern railing which lies just a couple of feet below the surface. The outline of the wreck below could easily be seen from the dive boat.

The large 4-bladed propeller lies in 30 feet of water and lends itself as an excellent subject to photograph. Over a period of many years, the amount of coral growth on the blades seemed to increase significantly every time I returned to dive on the wreck. As you swim around to the deck side past several lifeboat davits mounted on the periphery of the stern, the small crumbling smokestack, the engine room hatch covers, and the large rear mast with the derricks and rigging still in place come into view. The small stern cabins show evidence of fire and contain little except beer, saki, and fruit jar-type bottles. Open hatches with circular glass ports allow divers entry to the engine room. Large air scoops lie to the side canted at odd angles. The aft hold contains two dangerous-looking cannisters (3 feet long, 1 1/2 feet in diameter) and a few bottles. Further forward near midship, the No. 2 hold contains torpedo bodies and a few crushed 50-gallon drums. The ship had probably been supplying torpedoes to submarine tenders or to the torpedo boat station on Uman Island. A large kingpost lies aft of the remaining bridge structure and large winches for loading and unloading the holds can be seen on the deck. The ship took a torpedo hit in the forward hold and the resulting explosion from the torpedo hit destroyed most of the bridge and cabin superstructure and caused several buckles along the sides of the hull. The bow lies against the seabed in 120 feet of water.

The orientation of the wreck makes it perfect for natural light photography. With the aft section of the wreck lying in relatively shallow water, plenty of exploration time is available making the GOSEI MARU one of the more popular wrecks to dive on.

Three small, engines-aft freighters of the GOSEI MARU class were photographed at Truk during the U.S. air attacks on 16–17 February 1944, but this one off the northeast shore of Uman Island was the only one sunk; the other two showed no damage. Japanese dispatches reported the GOSEI MARU as having sunk about 0918 h on the second day of the air strikes. The GOSEI MARU was one of a group of four AKs off the eastern shore of Uman selected by MONTEREY and BUNKER HILL aircraft (Strike 3C). The attacking planes approached from the southeast after crossing the reef between Salat and Alanelimo Islands. The GOSEI MARU was the closest and was described as "rusty and unkept looking." The largest ship of the group, the UNKAI MARU NO. 6, had already been attacked and was smoking heavily. The first two planes that attacked got erratic runs with their torpedoes. One torpedo passed forward of the bow and went "jig-jagging up the harbor"; the second torpedo ran through all four ships just narrowly missing three of them. One of the second pair of VTs from MONTEREY hit the GOSEI MARU below her forward superstructure on the starboard side opposite the forward hold. The ship was observed to disintegrate and sink immediately. Pilots reported that it did not burn rapidly and was probably empty or nearly so as it rode very high in the water.

Searches for the name of the ship on the hull in both the bow and stern areas have not been successful and no owner's stack markings have been found on the smokestack. Perhaps the best confirmation of the wreck's identity is the finding of china with an "upside down peace symbol" on them in the forecastle. This symbol is unmistakably the house marking of Yamashita Kisen Kaisha. Research has shown that the Yamashita shipping Company acted as managers of the GOSEI MARU for its owners.

During 1976 and early in 1977, several reports of large explosions at the site of the wreck were reported by the residents of Uman Island. Investigations showed that the 8,000-psi high pressure flasks in the torpedo bodies were blowing up intermittently. Charges were placed around the remaining torpedo bodies and the air flasks were blown in April 1977.

TECHNICAL SUMMARY:

Type: Cargo
Configuration Sequence: M–K–M–F
Gross Tonnage: 1,931 tons
Dimensions: 272/40/17.5 feet
Machinery: Aft-engines (steam), reciprocating, single screw.
Radius: 4,000 miles at 10 knots
Complement: Unknown
Built: 1937 by Tsurumi Seitetsu Zosen K.K., Yokohama
Owner: Koun Kisen K.K.
Manager - Yamashita Kisen Kaisha
Remarks: One deck. Ship was designed as a coastal freighter and was built in quantity prior to the outbreak of war and since.

The "Gun High" Wreck

The nickname given to this wreck is indicative of the ship's small bow gun located just a couple feet below the surface. The gun and the whole foreship can be seen from the surface. This shallow wreck is often visited following the first dive of the day and is an excellent spot to snorkel while accumulating surface time. The "Gun High" is located only about 130 yards from shore on the west side of Uman Island between the wreck of the lighter and a small harbor craft.

The vessel is upright with about a 10-degree list to the starboard side and slopes downward along the drop-off towards the stern where the depth to the deck is nearly 25 feet. The ship had taken terrific punishment. The skeletal framework of her hull and superstructure are all that is left as it appears that she had taken several bomb hits and had been on fire for some time before sinking. It looks like the ship had been attacked while under way, and after being hit and probably with fires aboard, had been run aground to prevent her from sinking in deep water. The bow is facing shore in about 30 feet of water; there are no extended anchors.

The foremast positioned between the No. 1 and No. 2 holds is bent over to the starboard side with its top lying on the bottom in the sand. This is evidently due to an explosion (probably a bomb burst) next to the base of the mast. The bridge superstructure and funnel are completely destroyed. The ship's diesel engines are lying on the bottom about 20 yards away next to a large unexploded bomb (which has since been removed).

Two more interconnecting holds are located in the aft section of the wreck. There is a large split in the ribbing of the side of the hull plates on the starboard side and the hull on the port side is collapsed inward to the bottom. The rear mast is lying over the edge of the wreck to the aft starboard side. Two unexploded bombs, each nearly four feet long, are lying in the aft hold (No. 4). The stern area itself is a tangled pile of twisted metal. It is obvious that the attacking aircraft had expended a great deal of effort in disposing of this cargo ship.

Along the starboard side about 10 feet from the top of the foremast lying in the sand is the small frame of a 4-wheel railroad car of some sort. Another 20 feet away are the remains of a small wooden vessel; its engines lie in the center of its wreckage.

The wreck described has not had its identity confirmed. It has been known as the HINO MARU NO. 2 for some time but this 4-hold, 2-mast ship appears much larger than the HINO MARU's 998 tons and 200-foot length.

The GYORAITEI NO. 10

This motor torpedo boat was apparently sunk to the west of Truk by attacking carrier planes on 16 February 1944. No wreck of her type has been found by divers within the Truk Lagoon.

The Japanese motor torpedo boats (GYORAITEI in Japanese means torpedo boat) were originally developed from the design of a British-made Thornycroft-type craft captured in Canton, China in 1938. Design of the GYORAITEI NO. 10 class, the T 51 or "Type A Ro-gata," were further based on the German "schnellboot" plans. The vessels built were intended to be used as division boats. They were known for an inherent structural weakness and were considered to be the wrong length to cope with Pacific waves.

TECHNICAL SUMMARY:

Type: T 51 or Type A Ro-gata Motor Torpedo Boat
Displacement: 80 tons
Dimensions: 104.3/16.5/3.7 feet
Machinery: Vulcan geared gasoline engines, 2-shaft, 3,600 SHP.
Speed: 29 knots
Complement: 18
Armament: Two 25mm AA guns; two 18-inch torpedo launchers, 4 torpedoes; 4 depth charge throwers, 8 depth charges.
Built: 1943 by Yokohama Yacht Co., Tsurumi

The HANAKAWA MARU

KAWASAKI KISEN KAISHA

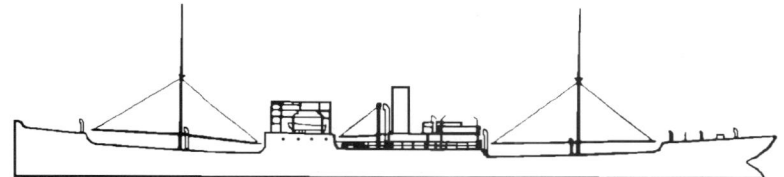

The wreck of the HANAKAWA MARU is located several hundred yards from shore near the southeast end of Tol Island. It is rarely dived on due to the 1 hour and 15 minute plus travel time to the site and the fact that diving the wreck is discouraged because it is easy for divers to get burned from the aviation gasoline or other caustic substance present. It was considered out-of-bounds for some time, although I believe this was not an official policy. There is a strong smell like stale fuel oil that serves as a strong indicator that the dive boat is over the wreck. This smell is very similar to that present at the wreck of the KEMBU MARU at Roi-Namur which had aviation gasoline aboard and posed a burn problem also to divers. Diving experience on that wreck had shown that the caustic substance was present primarily in the muck that had accumulated in the rooms and deck spaces, but sometimes just swimming over holds known to have barrels of aviation gasoline in them was sufficient to get burned. Droplets of gasoline are continuously rising from the barrels stored in the holds below and spreading across the surface above the HANAKAWA MARU.

From the dive boat, it is possible to see the masts and some faint lines of the deck and superstructure of the wreck lying upright on the lagoon floor. There had been a flying bridge built above the midship superstructure. Only a few steel frame support structures remain lying about. The wood planking on the deck and the walls had long since disappeared. The superstructure here at 50 feet is covered with heavy marine growth. A four-foot high ship's telegraph or rudder stand is mounted on the deck; it is very difficult to identify as it is covered by a thick algae or moss-type growth. Nearby, there is a large green bottle made of thick glass lying in the open. This bottle, which was estimated to be 1 1/2 feet in diameter and 2 1/2 feet high, was a type often used for storing caustic substances such as battery acid.

On the deck and sides of the hull, the coral growth is extremely prolific. There are fan corals (gorgonians), various hard and soft corals, and several long strands of "jeweler's" or "whip" corals. There are two entrances to the deck below the flying bridge. Inside, there are racks of corroded radio equipment and loose wiring hanging from the ceiling. A large fan coral was almost completely blocking one entrance doorway. This large room exhibited a particular look I had seen before; a fire had swept through the whole superstructure. The floor in the rooms at main deck level was covered by a fine layer of muck. Just inside the entrance, there was a few pieces of china, some with the flag symbol of Kawasaki Kisen Kaisha. The rest of the room appeared empty except for some objects lying along the extreme port entrance. There, lying in the shallow muck, was a large clock and four human skulls.

Exploration of the foreship leads past a large mast heading towards the bow. There is a large hole nearly 40 feet in diameter on the starboard side where a torpedo had hit opposite the No. 2 hold. This hold contained 50-gallon-sized drums which evidently held some aviation gasoline or other caustic substance that had burned some divers previously. Except for a few more drums in the upper level, the No. 1 hold appeared empty. The depth to the bottom of the holds was approximately 100 to 110 feet. The forecastle and the bow itself were covered with heavy coral growth; the anchor chain was out on the starboard side. There was no deck gun mounted.

The ship's superstructure is split; the extended cabin areas do not connect with the midship superstructure. In between is a shallow single-level hold connecting with the engine room. Above deck, just forward of the engine room hatch covers, is an unusual large kingpost with air ventilators attached to a crossbar at the top.

The upper level compartments in the cabin area served as a crew or passenger quarters. There is a room with several latrines and another with ovens and a huge metal bowl almost three feet in diameter that may have been used for laundry or possibly for cooking rice. In a room below deck level aft of the engine room, there is a large galley with china, bottles, and more human remains lying all about. No flag markings were found on the china here. The only design at all was two pale green stripes. Mounted on the stern is a strange looking short-

The short-barreled 4.7-inch anti-submarine gun on the stern is almost completely covered by marine growth.

barreled gun almost completely covered by coral growth. This gun is a short range 4.7-inch anti-submarine weapon and the first I had ever seen on a Japanese ship. In the stern compartments beneath the gun, several barrels or depth charges are lying inside the entrance; a few large artillery shells were also present. Aside from a fire extinguisher on one wall, the rooms appeared empty.

On the second morning of the initial air raids, BUNKER HILL and MONTEREY planes combined on a joint strike (3A) forming the first attack group of the day. The group arrived over Northeast Pass and the torpedo planes broke off to the north and skirted the atoll in a counter-clockwise direction circling the reef until Piannu Pass was reached. At this point, the planes turned north into the lagoon dropping altitude gradually as they approached Tol Island from the south. The large "12,000-ton oiler" that had been spotted the day before was lying 500 yards off the southeastern shore about a quarter of the way between the tip of the island and the fueling dock. The ship was described by the pilots independently as being the size of the U.S.S. LACKAWANNA or CIMARRON Class oilers. She was at anchor with her stern oriented towards Tol Island. As the planes swung north past the target ship, the VT-17 flight leader broke off a single two-plane section for the attack followed by a second section from VT-30. These planes made a sweeping S-turn which permitted them to deliver a broadside attack from the south. VT-17 narrative from action reports described the action: "The four planes flying in column dropped on the target. The first torpedo dropped hit amidships." VT-30 narrative continued: "Unfortunately it was too late to stop the next three (torpedoes) from dropping. The last one made an erratic run, hitting near the fuel dock on Tol. The other two probably hit also but were wasted on this target as there was a burst of flame, an explosion, and black smoke billowed up to four or five hundred feet almost immediately after the first torpedo hit." The explosion of the torpedo combined with the instantaneous ignition of aviation gas in the cargo holds appeared to have completely disintegrated the ship. Within three or four minutes, nothing remained where the ship had been except a fuel fire spread over the surface of the water.

The HANAKAWA MARU was the ship described as the AO or oiler by the pilots. The reason for this mis-identification is unknown as she was not an aft-engine vessel which could have misled the pilots.

The ship was reportedly engaged in off-loading army troops when caught in the air attacks. After she sank, burning debris floated ashore and started a fire in a mangrove swamp and spread to some man-made structures including a church. The priest was reportedly under arrest by the Japanese and was on Udot Island at the time.

TECHNICAL SUMMARY:

Type: Passenger-Cargo
Configuration Sequence: M–K–F–M
Gross Tonnage: 4,739 tons
Dimensions: 367.5/52/30 feet
Machinery: Diesel engines, single screw, 2,000 SHP
Radius: 14,000 miles at 10 knots.
Built: 1942 by Kawasaki Dockyard Co., Kobe
Owner: Kawasaki Kisen Kaisha

The HAKUSHUN MARU

Monograph No. 116, The Imperial Japanese Navy in World War II, is an official compilation of Japanese ships damaged or lost during operations of the Japanese Army and Navy during the period 1941–45. It lists the 7,112-ton HAKUSHUN MARU, a miscellaneous auxiliary or Type AG, as being sunk by aircraft on February 17, 1944 at Truk. Because the HAKUSHUN MARU and the HOKI MARU (ex-HAURAKI) are both listed as being 7,112 tons with twin screws, there has been some confusion between the identity of a known shipwreck located southeast of Eten Island. Photographs have now confirmed that wreck to be the HOKI MARU. The HAKUSHUN MARU could very well have been sunk elsewhere in the lagoon, and if so, may be the last large shipwreck yet to be found at Truk.

The HAKUSHUN MARU was built under the War Standardization program set up by either the Bureau of the Navy (Kansei-Hombu) or the Office of Transportation. This standardization program was characterized by the utilization of mass production techniques and the economic usage of ship-building materials. Ships completed under this program were built without domed plated and double thickness decks; the amount of ribs was reduced; the extra outer shield of the smokestack was eliminated; and the ships were constructed with a mirror or flat stern. The HAKUSHUN MARU was built under the Type 2 TA series (tanker variant of Type 2A). Specialized private shipyards involved in the building of this Type 2A (or AT) series included the following: Mitsubishi (Kobe and Hiroshima), Mitsui (Tamano), Kawaminami (Koyakijima), and Hitachi (Kanagawa). Many of the characteristics of the war standardization program ships are unknown as they were built during the war and no Lloyd's Register information is available.

TECHNICAL SUMMARY:

Type: Type 2 AT War Standardization Tanker
Configuration Sequence: M–M–F (probable)
Gross Tonnage: 7,112 tons
Dimensions: Unknown
Machinery: Unknown
Radius: Unknown
Complement: Unknown
Built: Unknown
Owner: Unknown
Remarks: Lost at a reported location of 7°22'N, 151°45'E.

The HEIAN MARU

The first morning of the air raids found the HEIAN MARU anchored just off the northwest shore of Dublon opposite the Naval Station and the submarine servicing base. Pictures taken early on the 16th show the ship, with its hull painted a dazzle camouflage design, anchored about 500 yards off shore. A medium sized AK lies off its starboard quarter about 250 yards away and the brilliant all-white painted hospital ship, HIKAWA MARU NO. 2, is anchored about 600 to 700 yards to the northwest.

YORKTOWN VB (Strike 1AY) scored hits on three ships anchored west of Dublon at approximately 0630 h; the HEIAN MARU is believed to have been hit near the bow at this time. This bombing attack started fires aboard the vessel. Two SB2Cs from BUNKER HILL (Strike 3A) attacked the ship with two 1,000- and one 1,600-lb bombs, but all three missed. Photos taken mid-day show the ship smoking very heavily with its superstructure enveloped in a fiery inferno. The unidentified AK by this time had been re-positioned closer to shore. The narratives in the aircraft action reports for ENTERPRISE VF (Strike 1EE) describe the "10,000-ton AK" (HEIAN MARU) as on fire with a "large AO" (TONAN MARU NO. 3) further to the west. On the 17th, YORKTOWN VB (Strike 1AY) again attacked the ship scoring two hits aft and a close miss. ENTERPRISE VT (Strike 1BE) dropped bombs nearly two hours later scoring a near miss off the starboard bow causing pieces of superstructure to fly into the air. Later, TBFs from BUNKER HILL (Strike 3B) apparently attacked the HEIAN MARU for the final time. As the planes approached, it was noted that the ship was on fire and smoking heavily. One to two torpedo hits caused 1–2 explosions aboard; the results of the torpedo hit(s) were not observed.

An intercepted Japanese message of 20 February stated that "The HEIAN MARU received several enemy torpedo and bombing attacks in the battle of Truk on the 16th and 17th and sank at 1403 h, February 17th in position 07°23'N, 151°51'E. Two persons were killed and 28 wounded." The time cited would translate to 1503 h Truk local time.

The HEIAN MARU was built at a cost of $15,000,000 in 1930 by Nippon Yusen Kaisha (NYK); she was the third ship built for North Pacific passenger-cargo service between Japan (Yokohama) and Seattle. The first two vessels were the sister ships HIKAWA and HIYE (HIE) MARUs. The interior decoration aboard the HEIAN MARU was designed in the "old English" style and this theme was carried out in the ship's lounge, reading room, writing room, and dining salon. Such decoration was considered a major innovation in ships at the time. On the HEIAN MARU's maiden voyage in January 1931, the ship set a new transpacific speed record for NYK ships. Seattle shippers engaged in the Oriental trade spread the word through the media that the arrival of the new ship might be regarded as a gesture of friendship from the business interests of Japan. Following the friendship theme, the ship's owners opened up the HEIAN MARU to the public, letting nearly 15,000 people tour the vessel. The crowds were so great that hundreds had to be turned away.

The wreck of the HEIAN MARU can easily be seen from the surface as a large patch of yellow-green colored water. The up-raised starboard side of the ship immediately gives the diver an idea of the

The HEIAN MARU – January 1931.

immense size of the ship. The wide side hull extends 150 feet or more off into the distant gloom of the lagoon. Oil and air bubbles can be seen leaking through portholes and small cracks in the hull. The dive boat operators usually attach an anchor near the bridge which is well forward on the ship. The depth to the side here is 40 feet. Little or no damage from bombs or torpedo hits can be seen on the hull along this starboard side. The depth along the side of the wreck gets progressively deeper towards the bow where the name of the ship is clearly outlined on the hull at a depth of 70 feet. The Romanized letters of the name are raised almost two inches off the hull and stand nearly 18 inches high. The corresponding kanji characters are placed above.

The name of the ship, HEIAN MARU, is plainly visible on the hull. The ship was named after the ancient city of Heinkyo, "The City Of Peace And Tranquility." The MARU kanzi character is directly above the E and I while the others appear above and to the right of the N extending over the "MARU" name (not shown).

Over the edge of the bow on the top of the forecastle, there is a large gun platform. It is possible the bomb hit on the bow mentioned in the aircraft action reports blew the 4.7-inch deck gun from its mounts. The port anchor chain extends from the ship leading to a huge cylindrical mooring buoy now lying on the bottom. Two chains and a thick electrical cable lead from the buoy towards shore. Large winches are mounted on the deck and several hoisting booms are attached near the huge forward mast. The two holds here are partially covered and access is difficult; they appeared empty except for a few bottles and some small cartons and cannisters.

The wooden flying bridge that had been constructed over the top of the wheelhouse is gone. The rest of the superstructure is intact and almost everything in the wheelhouse and cabins in the decks below has fallen to the port side on the bottom. A large pile of debris including remains of burnt decking and other items several feet thick is lying there. While swimming outside the hull around the bottom, we found boxes, barrels, an AA gun, and piles of tangled debris. An extensive cabin area lies behind the bridge with the huge smokestack and engine room located in its midst. The passageways on the two decks are very narrow. Lots of twisted metal is indicative of bomb damage or results of the torpedo hit(s) on the port side of the hull. A large running light with red glass is mounted along the side of the cabin area. The corridors in several places have boxes and unidentifiable equipment in them. Two periscopes are lying in one of the passageways and a stack of dishes were found in the corner of a corridor. The glass in most of the porthole covers shows melting and bubbling effects due to the fire which swept through the whole cabin area.

A thorough exploration of the wreck is difficult because of the orientation of the ship on its side and lack of easy access to the interior. Several torpedo bodies are located in a small hold aft. When I last looked them over, it was apparent that all except one had been blown apart from the high pressure air inside. Kimiuo Aisek later insisted that no set charges had been used to blow up these torpedo bodies; they had blown on their own accord. The stern section contained several compartments which may have served as crew's quarters. A large gun platform is mounted here and again, the gun itself is missing. Our curiosity got the best of us and we swam down and looked at the bottom where we could see what appeared to be the 4.7-inch deck gun lying where it fell when the ship sank and rolled over on its side against the lagoon bottom. The deck gun that had been mounted on the bow is probably lying on the bottom also. The force by which the ship struck the bottom must have been considerable to knock the guns loose. With the ship on its side, the large screws are elevated off the bottom and are very interesting to see and photograph. The starboard screw lies at a depth of 80 feet.

The HEIAN MARU had been an integral part of the 6th Submarine Fleet from its inception when it was based at Kwajalein and again after it was moved to Truk. Through most of 1943, the sub-tenders assigned to the three submarine squadrons of the 6th Fleet were the HEIAN, the HIE, and the YASUKUNI MARUs. The HIE MARU was attacked by U.S. Submarine DRUM on 17 November 1943 and sunk approximately 300 nautical miles north-northwest of New Ireland. The loss of HIE MARU and a number of submarines forced changes in the composition of the 6th Submarine Fleet. The following is the order of battle for the 6th Submarine Fleet based at Truk on 1 January 1944.

Sixth Submarine Fleet

Flagship: KATORI
Tender: YASUKUNI MARU
   12th Submarine Division   I-169, I-171, I-174, I-175, I-176
   22nd Submarine Division   I-177, I-180, I-181, I-185
   34th Submarine Division   RO-36, RO-37, RO-38, RO-39, RO-42, RO-44

1st Submarine Squadron
Flagship: I-11
Tender: HEIAN MARU
   2nd Submarine Division   I-16, I-19, I-21, I-39, I-40
   15th Submarine Division   I-32, I-35, I-36, I-38, I-41

8th Submarine Squadron   I-8, I-26, I-27, I-29, I-37
   30th Submarine Division   I-162, I-165, I-166, RO-110, RO-111, RO-112

11th Submarine Squadron   I-42, I-43, I-45, I-52, I-183,
Flagship: CHOGEI   I-184, RO-40, RO-41, RO-43,
Tender: TSUKUSHI MARU   RO-113, RO-114, RO-115

On January 31, 1944, U.S. Submarine TRIGGER found a convoy of three large ships and three escorts. In a night surface attack, TRIGGER hit and sunk NASAMI, a small minelayer-escort and fired torpedoes at the largest ship in the convoy which blew up and went down. TRIGGER then had to return to Pearl Harbor with what was deemed to be an unsuccessful patrol because of the unfired torpedoes left in her racks and tubes. Meanwhile, Japanese battle damage reports had provided U.S. codebreakers with news of the attack on the convoy. The large ship sunk northwest of Truk had been the 11,933-ton sub-tender YASUKUNI MARU. Just overhauled, she was returning to Truk loaded with the best of the Japanese Navy submarine repairmen along with spare parts and important submarine stores. Only 43 survivors from the sinking ship were picked up. The officers and crew of TRIGGER received a hero's welcome when they returned to Pearl Harbor.

The CHOGEI was built during the 1920-28 Fleet Program; she was one of the first submarine depot ships to be designed and built for the Japanese Navy. She was fitted out as a submarine flotilla flagship to operate with the fleet and control her submarine flotilla during operations as well as supporting the boats at harbor. The CHOGEI was outfitted with a reconnaissance seaplane (Alf) to support her role. There were no reports or other evidence of her being present during the air strikes at Truk. She was damaged late in the war, repaired, and served in the repatriation service before being broken up in 1946–47.

The TSUKUSHI MARU was not present at Truk during the February 16–17 air strikes. She remained a 6th Fleet sub-tender until January 1945 when she was converted and re-classified as a transport. The ship was damaged by a mine southeast of Shimonoseki in July 1945 and was captured in August 1945. The damage from the mine was repaired and she was entered into the repatriation service until 1947 when she was returned to her original owner. She was eventually sold to the Pan-Islamic Steamship Company in 1952.

TECHNICAL SUMMARY:

HEIAN MARU
Type: Submarine Tender (Converted 1941)
Configuration Sequence: M–K–K–F–K–M–K
Gross Tonnage: 11,614 tons
Dimensions: 510/66/30 feet
Machinery: Two 8-cylinder 4 stroke Burmeister & Wain diesel engines, 2 shafts, 190 NHP.
Radius: 18,700 miles at 15 knots.
Complement: 150 (crew), 285 (passengers)
Armament: Two 4.7-inch low-angle deck guns, AA guns.
Built: 1930 by Osaka Tekkosho.
Owner: Nippon Yusen Kaisha
Remarks: 3 decks, nine watertight bulkheads.

The HINO MARU NO. 2

The HINO MARU NO. 2 was listed as of March 1944, in the captured Combined Fleet Secret Standing Order No. 17 (organization of the Japanese Fleet) as a converted gunboat assigned to the 11th Air Fleet, Southeast Area Fleet. She was reported by the Japanese as having been "beached and destroyed by enemy planes at Truk on or about May 1, 1944." This vessel is believed to be one of several small freighters damaged during the raids of 29–30 April, but cannot be identified as the specific target of any one group of planes. The only ship of approximately the size that was claimed as definitely sunk was a "2,000-ton AO" reported hit by a single 500-lb bomb from CABOT planes at about 1445 h (Strike 3E) on 30 April near Uman Island. The ship was left burning with a column of smoke rising over 1,000 feet high, and later seen resting on her side on the bottom. An aft-engine cargo ship or auxiliary was often described as a tanker (AO) and this may be the reason for its being described as such by attacking aircraft. The fact that the HINO MARU NO. 2 is an engines-aft vessel cannot be confirmed; however this vessel sunk by CABOT planes appears to be a reasonable candidate.

The "Gun High" wreck is thought by many to be the HINO MARU NO. 2. However, the Gun High wreck is a 4-hold cargo ship and appears to the author to be much longer that the 200 feet length of the HINO MARU NO. 2. For this reason and with the information above, it is believed that the small vessel lying on its starboard side north of the Gun High and the Lighter wrecks in shallow water is actually the HINO MARU NO. 2. This vessel has a narrow "V"-shaped hull that is very distinctive. The small craft has some raised letters on its hull where its name has been placed but the letters are not recognizable because of the destruction and marine growth on the hull.

The vessel has a small gun mounted on a platform forward. It was almost covered with sand the last time I dove on the wreck. There is little of interest for divers. The small compartments and holds are empty and the stern area at a depth of 40 feet is almost completely demolished. There appears to be a sonar ranging device mounted on the bottom of the hull.

TECHNICAL SUMMARY:

Other Names: DAI-NI HINO MARU, DAI-FUTA HINO MARU
Type: Converted Gunboat
　　Miscellaneous Auxiliary (Converted 1943)
　　Gunboat (Converted 1942?)
　　Transport (Original)
Gross Tonnage: 998 tons
Dimensions: 200/35/17 feet
Machinery: Oil engines, single screw, 144 NHP
Built: 1935 by Mitsubishi Zosensho, Kobe
Owner: Nippon Shokuen K.K.
Remarks: Cruiser stern.

The HOKI MARU

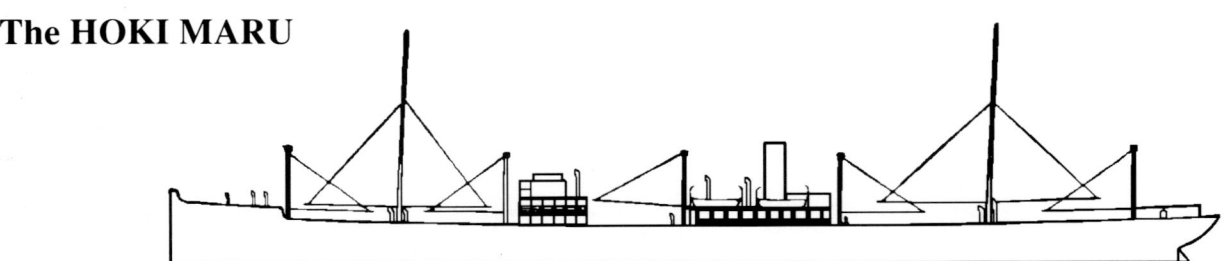

The identification of the southernmost wreck in the Eten Anchorage with large twin-screws was a mystery for a long time after it was found in 1973. In recent years, the true identity of the ship has been established as the HOKI MARU from previously classified data and photographs. Originally known as the M/V HAURAKI, the ship was seized by the armed merchant cruisers HOKOKU and AIKOKU MARUs while cruising between Fremantle, Australia and Colombo, Ceylon (now Sri Lanka) in July 1942. The ship was built in Scotland and had been owned by British and then New Zealand corporations. After capture, the ship was renamed HOKI MARU and sent to Japanese shipyards for modifications. She was assigned to the Yokosuka Naval Transportation Department and designated for use as a cargo ship serving bases in the mandated islands.

The skunk-like smell of fuel oil is very strong above the wreck and spots of gasoline are often seen spreading on the surface. At 100 feet, the stern deck area shows considerable damage from one or more bomb explosions. The air ventilators are bent over and the deck house has collapsed. There is a flag pole still standing on the end of the stern. When looking over the edge of the stern, the twin propellers can be seen resting on the bottom. Two tall kingposts are located just forward of the deck house and are unusual in that they are not joined by a cross piece. In the aft hold, a single bulldozer faces forward alongside the remains of a truck. There are other vehicles together with heavy machinery lying forward between the two levels of the hold. A second bulldozer has been reported, but it has not been confirmed by a second source. It was the presence of the bulldozer(s) that gave the wreck its local nickname, "The Bulldozer Ship."

The huge aft mast is still standing between the two after holds. The next hold forward contains gasoline or oil drums along with airplane engines. Large kingposts are located just forward of this hold. The extended mid-ship superstructure including the boatdeck, funnel, and bridge is severely damaged with little structure left recognizable. The remaining section of the wreck forward of the bridge is almost obliterated. Twisted remains of the hull and other wreckage can be seen lying about the seabed. Further forward, the bottom becomes progressively deeper; the remains of the forecastle can be seen resting in deep water at approximately 170 feet.

The wreck was placed off-limits shortly after being discovered because divers were coming into contact with some caustic substances that produced burns on the skin. The substance could have been acid which was contained in some 2-foot-high bottles present or from the aviation gasoline leaking from the barrels in the holds. Divers should avoid the bottles mentioned and any substance suspended in the water in the vicinity of the wreck.

The HOKI MARU was anchored southeast of Eten Island and on the first day of the air strikes was the target of several air groups. She was attacked first by ESSEX TBFs (Strike 2B) and was damaged by bomb hits. Photographs show her on fire amidships but not in any danger of sinking following this attack. Around mid-day, she was bombed by TBFs launched from YORKTOWN (Strike 1DY) in the "Masthead Attack" and shortly thereafter was torpedoed by BUNKER HILL planes (Strike 3D) and left on fire. When last seen as the final strike of the day was completed, the ship was totally ablaze and smoking heavily. She may also have been damaged by the YORKTOWN nighttime attack but she sank before the next strike of the second day arrived over their targets.

TECHNICAL SUMMARY:

Other Name: M/V HAURAKI (Original)
Type: Cargo
Configuration Sequence: K–M–K–K–F–K–M–K
Gross Tonnage: 7,112 tons.
Dimensions: 450/58/31.4 feet
Machinery: Diesel engines made by North British Diesel Co., Glasgow, twin screws, 3,010 HP
Radius: Unknown
Complement: Unknown (crew), 12 (passengers).
Built: 1921 by William Denny & Brothers – Dumbarton Scotland.
Owner: Japanese – Unknown
　　Previous – Union Steamship Corp. of New Zealand
　　Original – Unknown....British
Remarks: Plumb bow, counter stern.

The HOKUYO MARU

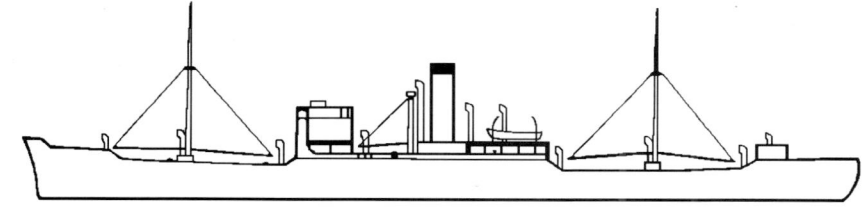

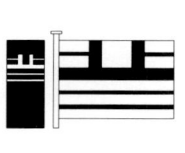

KITA NIPPON K.K.

In 1973, a shipwreck found in the Eten Anchorage southeast of the location of the SEIKO MARU was tentatively identified as the HOKUYO MARU because of her apparent size and visible stack markings indicating the Japanese owner to be Kita Nippon Kisen Kaisha. The wreck reportedly had very little marine growth because of her depth. The bridge lies at a depth of 160 feet, thereby making the bottom depth approximately 200 feet. The bridge contained two telegraphs, a ship's compass, and the helm with its wheel. Further exploration of the wreck was not attempted at that time. Because of its depth, the wreck has lured few divers since its discovery.

TBF planes from ESSEX (Strike 2B, 16 Feb.) attacked an 8–10,000-ton AK at a location that corresponds with that of the HOKUYO MARU, scoring two bomb hits near the aft hold and causing a fire to break out. She also appears to be the ship described as a 7,500-ton "previously undamaged" ship about 450 feet long attacked by BUNKER HILL TBFs on Strike 3E later in the day. Of two torpedoes launched, one hit the ship and the other exploded on the beach. The ship was on fire when the planes left the scene. The final attack which sunk the ship was made by BUNKER HILL dive-bombers in Strike 3B on 17 February. The ship was attacked by three SB2Cs which hit the vessel twice amidships with 1,000-lb bombs; the ship erupted in a huge explosion and when the smoke cleared away, the ship had sunk. The pilots noted that the target ship had been heavily damaged previously.

The ship's name, HOKUYO, translates as "North Sea." The ship was designed and built as a large capacity cargo ship for the shipping company Kita Nippon K.K. in 1936.

TECHNICAL SUMMARY:

Type: Passenger-Cargo
Configuration Sequence: M–F–M
Gross Tonnage: 4,217 tons
Dimensions: 357/49.2/24 feet
Machinery: Reciprocating with LP turbines, single screw, 350 NHP.
Radius: 6,000 miles at 13 knots.
Complement: Unknown (crew), 3 (passengers)
Built: 1936 by Uraga Dock Co., Ltd., Uraga
Owner: Kita Nippon K.K.
Remarks: Two decks, cruiser stern.

The HOYO MARU

On November 6, 1943, the HOYO MARU was torpedoed by a U.S. Submarine west of Truk. Intelligence files list the submarine as U.S.S. HADDOCK, but other sources attribute the attack to U.S.S. SCORPION. Three Japanese dispatches regarding the HOYO MARU were intercepted on 6 November:

0648 h – "The fire on the HOYO MARU has not been extinguished. She is unable to navigate and is drifting in position 08°07'N, 149°56'E. Although the YAKAZE (a DD-author) is carrying out rescue operations, she is unable to approach because the fire is out of control.
1130 h – "From commanding officer NAGARA (a CL-author), arrived at scene at 1130 h. After section of HOYO MARU burning heavily and ship down by the stern about 15 degrees. Apparently no one remaining aboard...."

The HOYO MARU – San Francisco Bay, March 21, 1941

1710 h – "From commanding officer NAGARA. Fire aboard HOYO MARU now extinguished. Because there is danger of (tow rope?) breaking, will proceed to Truk in company with KINJO MARU upon her arrival......"

The HOYO MARU was successfully towed to Truk and anchored north of Fefan and west of Dublon Island. She was identifiable from pictures taken during the photographic overflight and in photographs taken on the first day of the air attacks along with the repair ship AKASHI and other damaged vessels, apparently still under repair after the torpedo attack. The HOYO MARU was the recipient of heavy bombing attacks by ENTERPRISE VB planes (Strike 1EE) and YORKTOWN VB/VT (Strike 1EY). Photos taken shortly after showed the ship capsized and sunk with part of her keel and her single screw above water. Photos taken during the April 29–30 air attacks showed her in the same position.

When diving first opened up on the shipwrecks at Truk, there were only a few known shipwrecks and the identity of several was uncertain. The capsized tanker lying about 400 yards northeast of Fefan and west of Dublon was a wreck in that category. Someone had dubbed the shipwreck the TONAN MARU NO. 3 and she was called by that name for some time. Jim Lawson, a very knowledgeable wreck diver from Kwajalein and one of my dive buddies there, was part of a group who had made one of the very first diving trips to Truk. Jim tipped me off that certain characteristics of the wreck looked wrong for the TONAN MARU NO. 3 and we discussed and studied information on Japanese ships in the O.N.I. 208–J Japanese Merchant Ship Recognition Manual that would hopefully enable me to correctly determine the identity of the tanker. Armed with drawings, photos, and a partial list of ships thought to be lost at Truk, my group of divers arrived with one of our main objectives being to establish the correct identity of this new wreck.

Anchoring the dive boat over the wreck is very simple as the hull amidships is only 8 to 12 feet below the surface and is covered with hard coral. The up-raised hull from the surface looks more like a coral head than a sunken ship. The wreck lies on an east-west plane and the bow had to be to the east as that was the direction the wind was blowing from when most of the ships were sunk. In this case, the bow was pointing directly towards the center of Dublon Island. We descended along the side of the hull directly to the bottom at 75 feet. Small black coral bushes were growing everywhere and the hull was covered with dull-colored marine growth. The water near the bottom was clouded and murky. The top of the bridge is crushed against the seabed and when we entered a doorway, it was impossible not to kick up large clouds of muck which hampered our visibility almost completely. No clear passageway could be found leading to the interior of the bridge or cabins in the other decks. The wreck looked very dangerous to enter as many structures had collapsed and many more looked shaky. There was a recognizable catwalk aft of the bridge extending towards the stern. Large valves, wheels, and pipes are still attached to the deck, but many have fallen to the bottom. A large bare gun platform is mounted on the bow. The gun had either been jolted from its mount or since the ship had been incapacitated and under extensive repair, had been removed to strengthen land defenses. Some letters and kanji characters were located on the starboard hull but not enough were remaining to enable us to tell what the name was. A swim around the hull to the port side produced more letters but the name was not intact. The letters we did find, O-Y-O with the MARU suffix, made it plain that this was the tanker HOYO MARU. The letters of the name had been welded onto the bow and a few looked as though someone had been attempting to pry them loose.

The ship appears to have been hit by two or more bombs aft of amidships. There is considerable damage on the starboard side and hull. The damage sustained in the air raids, possibly combined with that suffered in the earlier submarine attack, broke the ship's back. The hull is split almost in two aft; a large gap appears between the plates. The stern superstructure and the engine room itself appear to have received bomb hits and had been on fire. The engine room is a veritable jungle of torn and twisted pipes, catwalks, control mechanisms, and machinery strewn about. Part of this damage was due to a torpedo hit (probably by the submarine attack described above); there is a torpedo hole on the port side at a depth of 50 feet.

The HOYO MARU was built in 1936 as a commercial oiler for the Nippon Tanker shipping company. After being requisitioned by the Japanese Navy to serve as a 4th Fleet tanker in 1941, a triad kingpost was added just aft of the funnel. The Japanese Navy sometimes added these kingposts and removed them just to confuse tanker identification by the Allies.

In April and May, 1942, the HOYO MARU was one of three oilers of a transport unit supporting the Port Moresby Invasion Group which was part of the Japanese Operation "MO." The invasion group was forced to turn back after major fleet units of the Japanese and American Navies fought the Battle of the Coral Sea.

TECHNICAL SUMMARY:

Type: Naval Tanker (1941)
Configuration Sequence: M–K–M–K–F–K
Gross Tonnage: 8,691 tons
Dimensions: 475/61/30 feet
Machinery: Diesel engines, single screw, 1,163 NHP.
Radius: 19,000 miles at 16 knots.
Complement: 50
Built: 1936 by Mitsubishi Jukogyo, Yokohama.
Owner: Nippon Tanker

The I 169

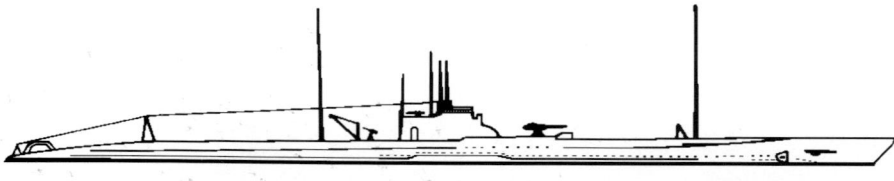

The I 169 was a large KAIDAI-type cruiser submarine and one of six of the I 168 class. The submarines of this class did little to distinguish themselves during World War II with he exception of the I 168 which sank the carrier U.S.S. YORKTOWN and the destroyer HAMMAN in the Battle of Midway. None of the ships of this class survived the war.

In December 1941, at the outbreak of hostilities between Japan and the United States, the I 169 was assigned to the 6th Submarine Fleet based at Kwajalein in the Marshall Islands. She was one of eight units assigned to Submarine Squadron 3 supported by the sub-tender TAIGEI. During the Pearl Harbor attack, the I 169 was one of 30 Japanese submarines participating; she was assigned to patrol south of Oahu. While on patrol during this operation, the I 169 fouled herself in anti-submarine nets while keeping watch on the harbor entrance. She became so firmly entangled that all attempts of steaming forward and

Diver films the stern section of the I 169 submarine.

backward and alternatively flooding and blowing the ballast tanks failed to release her. Meanwhile American destroyers and escorts could be heard on the surface above. With all hope seemingly lost and the crew about to suffocate due to the buildup of carbon dioxide inside the submarine, the officers and crew ate a "last meal" and prepared for the worst. One last desperate attempt to escape the nets using full-speed-astern released the submarine. It was brought to the surface immediately and luckily found no U.S. ships in sight. The I 169 had time to replenish its air supply before destroyers were spotted and the submarine was forced to crash dive. Perhaps this experience was a forewarning of what was to come.

The I 169 was part of the Advanced Expeditionary Force in May/June 1942 during the Japanese offensive directed at Midway. In May 1943, she was sent to the Aleutians with seven other submarines to reinforce seven RO boats already in the area. These submarines delivered 125 tons of supplies and picked up 820 men from Attu and Kiska to be transferred back to Japan. During the U.S. invasion of the Gilberts, the I 169 and eight other submarines were sent in response to the landings. When submarine operations from the Kwajalein Atoll became endangered by January 1944, the 6th Submarine Fleet and the I 169 were moved to Truk.

The submarine arrived at Truk following a patrol for replenishment of fuel and supplies under the command of Lt. Commander Shigeo Shinohara. After receiving a warning of an impending American B-24 air raid heading for Truk on 2 April 1944, the I 169, which had been loading stores aboard, proceeded to submerge about 1100 h to lay on the bottom until the raid was over. This was the standard procedure since there were no submarine pens at Truk. When the submarine failed to return to the surface, a rescue tug was sent to the site and a diver sent down to investigate what had happened. The upper valve of the storm ventilation tube in the aft part of the conning tower was open a couple of inches. The valve had either been opened by mistake or someone had forgotten to close it during submergence and the diver found the control room to be completely flooded. The diver received responses to his hammering from within four of the five hatches (excluding the control room beneath the conning tower) which indicated that the crew had been able to close the watertight doors sealing off the flooded control room. Evidently the remaining crew couldn't for some reason blow air into the ballast tanks to allow the sub to rise to the surface. Perhaps the only controls for doing this were located in the flooded control room. Truk was by no means a first-class naval base and rescue or lifesaving apparatus was severely limited, but since all indications were that there was only a small amount of flooding on the submarine, a repair ship with a 30-ton crane was dispatched to the site on the 3rd of April and work was started to hoist the bow section to the surface. At about 1530 h, the lifting cables broke, making it obvious to the rescuers the flooding inside was more extensive than originally estimated or water was still leaking into the other compartments. Tapping responses were only coming from one aft compartment at this time and holes were tapped in the hull to allow air hoses to be inserted to blow the ballast tanks but the rescuers couldn't signal those crew members still alive inside to open the air valves to the ballast tanks. Later at 2330 h, all responses from inside the submarine stopped. The remaining air inside had been used up and those who had been alive had suffocated. Nighttime B-24 raids caused the rescue work to be interrupted and when operations were able to resume, it was decided to continue to try to determine the cause of the sinking. Hardhat divers spent approximately six weeks attempting to find a way to raise the submarine and 32 bodies were recovered during this period. With the threat of impending invasion by U.S. forces in the minds of the Japanese, the 6th Fleet command bombarded the I 169 with depth charges to prevent its being compromised to the enemy.

It is interesting to note that <u>Monograph No. 116, The Imperial Japanese Navy in World War II</u>, reports that the captain survived. Since no report confirms any recovery of survivors after the submarine failed to surface, it must be assumed that the captain was not aboard when the vessel was forced to submerge to the bottom upon receiving the air raid warning.

The I 169 was found in 1971 by a group of divers that had come to film the wrecks in the lagoon. The submarine was entered at this time through the engine room hatch and the interior of the submarine with the remains of its crewmembers scattered about was filmed. The resulting movie from this diving expedition was shown in Japan causing much concern. Nearly $100,000 was raised in Japan to fund an expedition to retrieve the remains of the entombed crew of the I 169. In August 1973, the Fukuda Salvage Company from Japan brought a salvage vessel along with six professional divers to Truk. These divers, outfitted with wet suits and double tanks, joined two Micronesian and two American divers and began gathering the bones of the crewmembers by hand and then by finally using an 8-inch dredge to find remains scattered around the floor of the submarine which was covered by debris and muck. As the personal effects and remains (including 35 intact and 35 to 40 piecemeal skulls) were brought to the surface, a Shinto ceremony was performed utilizing saki as holy water to spread over the bones and water over the site of the wreck. With these remains of 70 or more men from the I 169, the total remains of nearly 100 had been found including those removed by the Japanese shortly after the submarine sank. Since the normal crew complement was 70, it is a possibility that workmen involved in loading stores onto the submarine or other support personnel had been aboard when the submarine was forced to dive during the air raid. The dredge produced many personal effects such as books, pictures, cameras, watches, shoes, clothing, gas masks, and etc. These items were left with the Trukese administrators. After completing their grim task, the Japanese divers attempted to weld the hatches shut and seal the "tomb" forever. After this was done, the human remains, along with photos of the crewmembers that relatives had brought along plus personal effects found in the submarine, were burned in a pyre again as part of a Shinto ceremony.

The water clarity northeast of Fefan Island in the area where the I 169 was lost is poor. The structure of the submarine wreck below becomes visible only after divers have descended nearly 70 feet or more. The forward section of the wreck including the bow has been heavily damaged; there are piles of jagged steel and twisted wreckage strewn all over the seabed. Several torpedo tubes are scattered amongst the rubble. Very little coral growth is present anywhere on the wreck. The conning tower is almost unrecognizable as it has been subjected to depth charge bursts which have left it blown apart and offset to the side of the submarine. The 3.9-inch deck gun, which had been mounted just forward of the conning tower, is now lying in the midst of a pile of unrecognizable wreckage at a depth of 130 feet. No sign was found of the 13mm AA gun which had been fixed on the deck aft of the control tower. The hull is intact on the aft ship although the upper wooden surface deck has deteriorated leaving only exposed beams and the inner pressure hull visible. It was interesting to see a closed hatch below the main deck level which had provided access to the crawl space between the deck and the pressure hull. Between the conning tower and the stern, there are three more hatches at deck level. Air hoses and cables rest along the sides of the hull which the would-be rescuers had used. There is a triangular antenna/flag pole mounted on the stern just a few feet behind the final hatch which leads to the engine room. The stern has been also heavily damaged from depth charges. It appears the Japanese concentrated on destroying the stern of the submarine. The shafts and propellers are bent and twisted from close explosions. The depth of the bottom near the propellers is nearly 150 feet.

The men whose lives were lost when trapped aboard the submarine when it was sunk during the war were not the last to die inside the I 169. Somehow, the hatches had been opened after the Japanese divers had attempted to weld them shut. In April 1974, a member of a group of six divers from Kwajalein drowned as he got trapped below the grating separating the upper and lower levels of the engine room. He ended up under the grating almost directly beneath the open engine room hatch where he was unable to get turned around to retreat from the narrow passage he had swum into. His attempts at getting through the grating failed and he ran out of air and drowned. His dive partner tried to get him through the grating and he ran out of air also, forcing him to make an emergency ascent to the surface. The trapped diver was finally removed and brought to the surface; resuscitation attempts proved unsuccessful and he was pronounced dead on arrival at the Truk hospital.

I hope the tragic part of the saga of the I 169 is over. The submarine really provides an excellent opportunity for divers to see and explore a wreck with an interesting history. Divers preparing to explore the wreck of the I 169 should certainly take into consideration the depth of the wreck and the dangers involved in penetrating into the interior of the submarine.

TECHNICAL SUMMARY:

Other Name: I 69 (Original)
Type: I 168 Class (Type KAIDAI 6A) Submarine
Displacement: 1,400 tons (1,785 max., 2,440 submerged).
Dimensions: 336.58/26.92/15 feet
Machinery: 2-shaft Kampon 2-stroke diesels, 2 electric motors, 9,000 BHP, 1,800 electric HP.
Speed: 23 knots (diesel), 8.2 knots (electric).
Maximum Dive Depth: 230 feet
Radius: 14,000 miles at 10 knots (surface), 65 miles at 3 knots (submerged).
Endurance Time: 45 days
Complement: 70
Armament: One 3.9-inch deck gun, one 13mm AA gun; six 21-inch torpedo tubes (4 in bow, 2 in stern) and 14 torpedoes.
Built: 1935 by Mitsubishi Zosensho, Kobe.

The KATSURAGISAN MARU

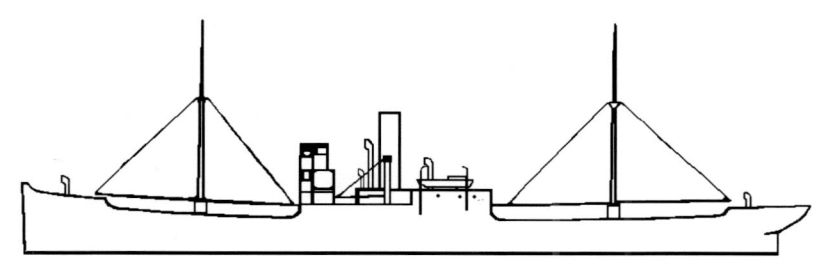

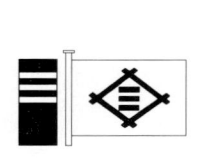

MITSUI BUSSAN KAISHA

The KATSURAGISAN MARU was one of the few vessels whose loss at Truk is attributed to means other than by U.S. forces. Her loss was learned through intercepts originating from the Commanding Officer Special Base Force No. 4 at Truk who reported that the ship was struck by a mine and sank after entering the Northeast Channel on January 7, 1944 at 0530 h. Further traffic reported to the Headquarters Grand Surface Escort Force on 8 January 1944 included the following message: "In view of the disaster to KATSURAGISAN MARU desire that all convoys bound for Truk be advised of minefield situation within the lagoon." In answer to this advisory message, the Grand Surface Escort Force sent the following message to a long list of addresses including all convoy and escort units: "Consideration of the incident of KATSURAGISAN MARU striking a mine at Truk leads to the conclusion that escort vessels are not being informed on the status of area restricted to navigation (message goes on to give lengthy direction for notifying all concerned, the location of mine fields, etc.)."

Unconfirmed rumors persist of a shipwreck having been found north of Moen Island in deep water. It is possible that the vessel did not sink immediately after being struck by a mine in the Northeast Pass; she may have limped or drifted towards Moen before sinking. The site is consistent with the reported sinking location of 7°30'N, 151°30'E.

TECHNICAL SUMMARY:

Other Names: KATSURIGISAN, KATURAGISAN (Kokutai spelling)
Type: Cargo
Configuration Sequence: M–F–M
Gross Tonnage: 2,427 tons
Dimensions: 285/42/23.2 feet
Machinery: Reciprocating, single screw, 181 NHP.
Radius: 4,800 miles at 10 knots.
Complement: 41
Built: 1925 by Mitsui Bussan Kaisha
Owner: Mitsui Bussan Kaisha
Remarks: Two decks.

The KENSHO MARU

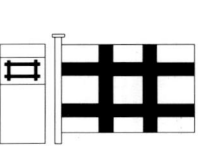
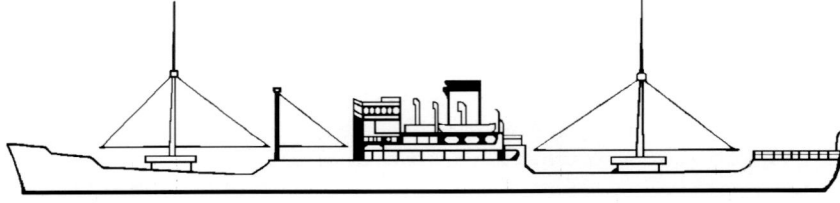

INUI KISEN K.K.

The captured diary of a Japanese on Kwajalein states that "in the fourth attack on 24 December 1943, 20 heavy bombers appeared over Kwajalein; a hit on the after part of the KENSHO MARU set the ship afire. When the KENSHO MARU was about to sink, it was run aground at a shallow place and the fire was stopped after three hours." Intercepted dispatches regarding the KENSHO MARU included one that noted that "On 3 January 1944, the KENSHO MARU departed Kwajalein for Ryotto (Truk) towing the IKUTA MARU and was scheduled the same day." A dispatch on 9 January stated that certain gear sent via the KENSHO MARU had been spoiled by a flood in the hold of the vessel. There is no indication as to what caused the flooding, nor when it occurred. Two hours later on 9 January, CinC 4th Fleet directed the No. 2 EIKO MARU (or KENSHO MARU) from Kwajalein to the Empire. Following the above dispatches, the KENSHO MARU disappeared in message traffic completely and was not heard from again until on 6 March 1944 when a fragmentary message was intercepted that was sent from Palau to Hiroshima. The HOYO, SHINKOKU, YAMAGIRI, KENSHO, HANAKAWA, FUJISAN, REIYO, and MOMOKAWA MARUs were listed but the reason could not be ascertained. At the time, with the exception of the KENSHO MARU, all of the vessels were known to have been sunk as a result of the 16–17 February carrier strikes. This was the first indication to the intelligence assessment group that the KENSHO MARU may have been sunk at Truk also.

Photographs show the KENSHO MARU at anchor where she was sunk in the anchorage north of Fefan and west of Dublon Islands right next to the repair ship AKASHI and other ships still under repair. The ships in this anchorage were first attacked by SBDs from YORKTOWN on Strike 1AY on the 16th; the KENSHO MARU may have been the AK hit on the stern by a 1,000-lb bomb at this time. ESSEX SBDs (Strike 2B) shortly thereafter reported attacking three ships west of Dublon. Two of the ships were a "6,000-ton light cruiser and a 7,000-ton AK along side," and the third was a 5,000-ton AK anchored to the southwest of the first two. Study of the photographs showing the ships described by the ESSEX VB pilots helps to clarify the observations made. The "light cruiser" is actually the 9,000-ton repair ship AKASHI. The ship close by with a possible M–K–F–M configuration appears to be the KENSHO MARU and the ship to the southwest is the KIYOSUMI MARU. The ESSEX planes scored a single 1,000-lb bomb hit amidships and left the KENSHO MARU on fire. The ship remained afloat and was attacked by ENTERPRISE, MONTEREY, and BUNKER HILL planes on the 17th. The BUNKER HILL VTs (Strike 3B, Feb. 17) reported hitting the ship with a torpedo causing heavy damage. It is interesting to note that the KENSHO MARU may well have been the "medium AK" that one F6F pilot dropped his partially-full belly tank on causing a large fire amidships. None of the aircraft reported seeing the vessel sink before they retired.

The KENSHO MARU was found in 1980 by Klaus Lindemann during a fathometer search lying upright with a 20-degree list to port facing northwest on a 130-foot bottom. The 385-foot ship is in relatively good structural shape and offers divers a good opportunity to do lots of exploring and sightseeing. A 3-inch bow gun is mounted on a platform above the forecastle. There are three boxes of ready ammunition flanking the gun. Exploration of the space within the forecastle itself has not yet been possible as the two entrance doors were firmly jammed shut. An anchor lies on the deck amidst much debris; it has probably been jarred from its stowed position against the bulkhead. The two large forward holds are empty of cargo.

The top of the bridge at 60 feet is easily accessible as most of the roof between support beams has either fallen in or has been consumed by fire prior to the ship's sinking. There is a considerable amount of soft coral growth here and of interest is a large-sized set of binoculars on a circular wheel pedestal, the ship's compass and binnacle cover, large racks of radio equipment, a strong box, and the telegraph. In the compartments one deck below, there are lots of beer and saki bottles, porcelain bowls, and some china. None of the china pieces was decorated with the flag markings of the owner, Inui Kisen K.K. These rooms can be exited through an entrance at main deck level on the lower port side at 95 feet.

Aft of the bridge, open hatches allow access to the engine room below. The cylinders, separated into 2 sets of 3 each, and the heavy machinery and catwalks make good photographic subjects. The bronze builder's plaque, covered with pinkish-red colored sponge growth, was located by the author on his initial dive on the wreck and its location described in the first edition of this book. Upon returning to Truk following the publication of the book, the builder's plaque had disappeared.

The funnel has no recognizable owner's house flag stack insignia markings. While exploring the rooms one deck below, the crew's mess was located on the starboard side. A large clock was found lying there amongst bottles, bowls, and other smaller articles in the shallow layer of muck and debris. The remaining rooms on this deck level and the one below are open and have easy access. There is a lot of area to explore.

Aft of the midship and cabin superstructure, the No. 3 hold was found to contain cargo consisting of large plumbing/sewer equipment including 20-foot-long pipe sections, big valves, sinks, and acetylene/oxygen tanks. The No. 4 hold was empty of cargo. Looking over the side of the stern, the screw shaft can be seen to be bent to the starboard approximately 10 degrees. This damage could have been sustained at Kwajalein prior to the Truk attacks.

TECHNICAL SUMMARY:

Other Name: KENSYO MARU (Kokutai spelling)
Type: Passenger-Cargo
Configuration Sequence: M–K–F–M
Gross Tonnage: 4,862 tons
Dimensions: 384.4/52.5/30.3 feet
Machinery: Diesel engines, single screw, 642 NHP.
Radius: 21,600 miles at 15 knots.
Built: 1938 by Tama Sanbashi Co., Tama
Owner: Inui Kisen K.K., Kobe
Remarks: 2 decks, cruiser stern.

The KIKUKAWA MARU

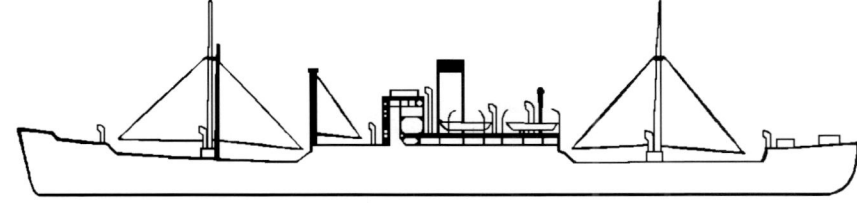

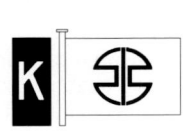

KAWASAKI KISEN KAISHA

The loss of the KIKUKAWA MARU was learned indirectly by U.S. forces. Following the invasion of Kwajalein in January 1944, a copy of the <u>Inner South Seas Area Force Secret Directive #2–43</u> issued by the Fourth Fleet Chief of Staff on October 1943 was captured. This document, which included discussions on operation, policies, and shipping conditions, contained the following note:

"On October 7, 1943, the KIKUKAWA MARU (3,833-ton AK) exploded and sank off Truk, resulting in the loss of valuable personnel. Many smaller vessels have been lost in a similar manner. These losses have been partially attributed to overloading; cargo should be stowed only after careful advance planning in the hope of minimizing the recurrence of similar disasters."

Further information came to light from the diary of an unknown Probational Officer, possibly of the 53rd Infantry Regiment, captured at Cape Gloucester, New Britain, in 1944 which supplements the above official statement.

"October 8, 1943 - (The writer) transferred to OKITSU MARU (at Truk). Last night we heard a terrific explosion. Heard this morning that it was caused by one of the transports in the harbor which caught fire and sank after the explosion. About 40 to 50 XLCs which had gone to extinguish the fire were blown to pieces. About 50 men went down with the ship."

The diary of an unidentified member of the 892nd Naval Air Group located in the Marshalls and Gilberts contained the following notes:

"August 10, 1943 - KIKUKAWA MARU arrived (at Emidj)
August 16 - I proceeded to Kanin.
October 23 - According to stories that I heard, the KIKUKAWA MARU was finally sunk after leaving Japan, and so we shall not get the fuel truck destined for us."

The KIKUKAWA MARU caught fire while anchored in the Eten Anchorage (approximately 7°22'N, 151°54'E) just east of Eten Island. The salvage vessel OJIMA was sent to assist her and while OJIMA was alongside the stricken vessel, the fire aboard the KIKUKAWA MARU reached the volatile cargo that she carried and the resulting explosion sunk both vessels.

The wreck of the KIKUKAWA MARU was found in 1976 during a fathometer search. The 354-foot ship was blown apart; only the section forward of the bridge was found resting about 100 degrees over on its starboard side at 120 feet atop an underwater hill. The name of the vessel was found on the forward hull. The forward hold contains oil or gasoline drums, a large compressor and a lot of unidentifiable machinery. The hold located where the ship blew apart contained aircraft spare parts, some of which have spilled out on the floor of the lagoon. Parts of aircraft bodies, engines, wheels, and propeller blades lie in the hold and seabed amongst a tangled collection of machinery and the remains of a truck. It appears the aftship completely disintegrated. There was little or no diving activity on the shipwreck until June 1980 when she was again found by using a fathometer. Since then, the wreck has been dove on only a few times.

TECHNICAL SUMMARY:

Type: Passenger-Cargo
Configuration Sequence: M–K–F–M
Gross Tonnage: 3,833 tons
Dimensions: 354/50/27.5 feet
Machinery: 2 direct reciprocating geared engines, single screw, 333 NHP.
Radius: 11,000 miles at 12 knots.
Complement: Unknown (crew), 10 (passengers)
Built: 1937 by Kawasaki Dockyard Co., Kobe
Owner: Kawasaki Kisen Kaisha
Remarks: 2 decks, cruiser stern.

The KIYOSUMI MARU

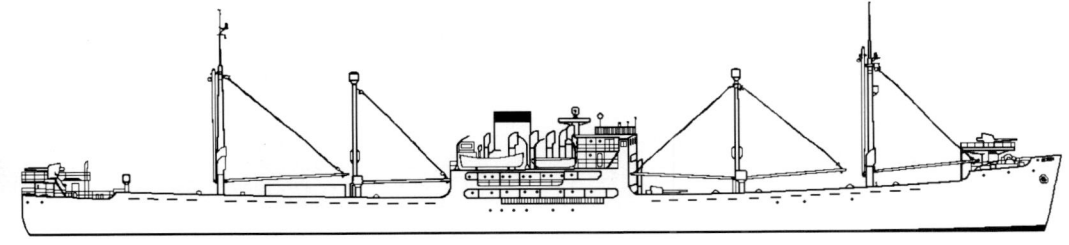

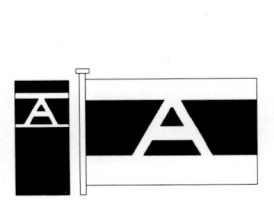

KOKUSAI KISEN K.K.

When built in 1934 for the Tokyo-based shipping company, Kokusai Kisen K.K., the KIYOSUMI MARU was to be used for passenger-cargo service. In August 1941, she was converted by the Japanese Navy into an armed merchant cruiser (XCL). Her new armament installed at this time consisted of four large deck guns (140mm or 5.5-inch low-angle type), several AA guns, and two torpedo tubes. She was placed under direct command of the Combined Fleet in Cruiser Squadron No. 24 along with the AIKOKU and HOKOKU MARUs.

The KIYOSUMI MARU participated in the Japanese offensive directed at Midway Island in May-June 1942. The Japanese were making a thrust at Midway and the Western Aleutians in the hope of drawing Admiral Nimitz into a confrontation where units of the Combined Fleet could annihilate the U.S. Pacific Fleet. The KIYOSUMI MARU was a part of the Transport Group of the Midway Occupation Force which consisted of a Transport and Seaplane Group and a Minesweeping Group. The other main Japanese forces of the Combined Expeditionary Force were organized into the Carrier Striking Force and the Main Body under command of Admiral Yamamoto. The Battle of Midway turned into a major American victory and the Japanese were forced to give up their plans to occupy Midway.

Because of the limited success of the armed merchant cruisers in raiding allied shipping, the KIYOSUMI MARU was converted back to a transport in October 1943. No information has been found indicating that the ship was successful as an armed raider.

On November 4, 1943, the KIYOSUMI MARU was bombed and damaged by planes while en route from Truk to Rabaul. She was towed by the CL ISUZU to Kavieng. The ship was set upon again by attacking aircraft during an air strike on Kavieng on the 25th of December and was set afire but damage was reported as light. On 30 December, she evidently began to proceed to Truk under her own power escorted by the DD YUKAZE and MINESWEEPER NO. 22. The U.S. Submarine BALAO was on patrol near the Bismark Archipelago 400 miles north of the Admiralty Islands on 31 January when it spotted "a very large fairly new motorship similar to KINKA MARU"; the target ship was zig-zagging and was using 90- to 130-degree changes of course. The ship was part of a convoy apparently consisting of "an escort ahead, then KINKA, and a small, smoking AK astern." BALAO attacked at 2345 h on 1 January, firing 6 torpedoes at the "KINKA" (KIYOSUMI MARU and KINKA MARU are very similar in both size and appearance). The submarine both saw and heard 3 torpedo hits between the bridge and the after goalpost. She was forced deep after her attack and at 2348 h, she heard the target's screws stop and for the next hour heard loud crackling and breaking up noises.

An intercepted message at 1605 h on 2 January reported that KIYOSUMI MARU had been torpedoed. She was disabled and dead in the water drifting westward at 1 knot speed, and that her noon position had been 04°37'N, 146°56'E. Other messages of Jan. 2–3 indicated that the CLs OYODO and NAKA, the DD TANIKAZE, and CH 29 were proceeding toward the KIYOSUMI MARU and that about 0830 h on 3 January, the OYODO was preparing to take her in tow. Later, the captain of the OYODO reported he had taken off 71 injured men from the stricken vessel and that he had departed the scene of the disaster at 1730 h. It was not confirmed by U.S. Intelligence, but apparently the OYODO succeeded in towing her back to Truk. On February 7, the KIYOSUMI MARU was incorporated into the Inner South Seas Force sometime after her arrival which indicated the Japanese considered her operational or close to being operational. A further intercepted message of February 18 stated that on 16 February while she was inside Truk Harbor, KIYOSUMI MARU was attacked by enemy planes. At 0900 h, she was set on fire by a direct bomb hit on the No. 2 hold, and at 1330 h she was hit by one bomb on either side of her bridge. A total of 43 persons were killed and nine seriously wounded. Some time afterwards, as a result of the above damage and a number of near misses, the KIYOSUMI MARU sank.

The initial bomb hit on the bow of KIYOSUMI MARU was probably accomplished by YORKTOWN SBDs on Strike 1AY. The ship was one of the "large AKs" hit southwest of Fefan described in the attack narrative. ENTERPRISE SBDs (Strike 1EE) were responsible for the bomb hits on both sides of her bridge; the target was described as a "10,000-ton AK." Planes from the YORKTOWN (Strike 1EY) made the final attacks against the ship.

Today the KIYOSUMI MARU is lying on her port side on a 120-foot bottom facing east about 600 yards from Fefan Island. A large oil slick from her fuel tanks usually extends across the water from the surface above the wreck. This is the reason for her local name, "The Oil Slick Ship." From the surface, the KIYOSUMI MARU looks similar to a yellow-green shallow coral head. Dive boats usually catch an anchor along the midship superstructure. Depth to the up-raised starboard side at this point is 40 feet. The water in this area where the

A white milky substance suspended in the water partially envelopes one of the two bicycles found in a hold of the ship.

wreck lies normally is very murky. There is little marine growth on the wreck except for the "onion peel" algae.

It should be emphasized that a thorough exploration of the 453-foot long shipwreck takes more than a single dive. There are a lot of things to see at 100 to 120-foot depths and diving on the wreck should not be limited to repetitive dives.

The bow rests at a depth of 70 feet with a bare gun platform mounted over the forecastle. The name of the ship can be found on the exposed hull nearby. A narrow entrance in the forecastle, now more wide than high due to the wreck's orientation on its side, leads to a small lantern locker above the passage nearly 25 feet forward. There are approximately a dozen beautiful lanterns still in the shelves they were originally stored in. The ship appears to have taken a skip-bomb or torpedo hit on the starboard side in the forward hold as there is a 30-foot-diameter hole in the hull with the plates blown inward. The hold is empty of cargo except for a huge lathe lying in its midst with a beautiful gorgonian growing on it. Hold No. 2 contains some large steel tanks, a few stray 50-gallon-sized drums and two bicycles which were strapped against a bulkhead. Empty gun platforms are positioned on the deck opposite each of the two forward holds. The guns had been removed when the KIYOSUMI MARU was converted back to a transport ship. The bottom of the third hold is blown apart, probably the result of the blast of a large bomb. Torpedo tubes are located alongside this hold along with a large bronze range finder approximately seven feet long lying at the 90-foot level just forward of the bridge.

Large winches and loading equipment are highly noticeable as are the tall goalposts fore and aft of the bridge. The tops of the goalposts are mushroom-shaped ventilators. The upper deck above the wheelhouse has collapsed and finding an entrance is difficult. Damage here is the result of 1,000-lb bombs. By looking through a partially blocked window, it is possible to see two ship's telegraphs. Access into lower deck compartments beneath the wheelhouse can be made from a rear entrance; china, pots, pans, and human remains lie on the floors of these rooms. Just aft of the bridge, there are two dual-barreled AA guns almost completely covered by a mossy-looking substance and coral growth. One was still in its stored position while the other had broken loose and was lying in an entrance. The huge smokestack still stands; it has a bronze chain-driven whistle attached. The large "A"-shaped stack insignia of the original owner, Kokusai Kisen K.K., can still be made out on its side. There is little of interest in the holds aft. Two more empty gun platforms can be found abreast of the No. 5 hold and another on the stern of the wreck. There is another torpedo launcher position alongside the aft hold.

TECHNICAL SUMMARY:

Other Names: KIYOZUMI, SEITO MARU (alternate reading)
Type: Transport (Re-converted October 1943)
Armed Merchant Cruiser (Converted August 1941)
Passenger-Cargo (Original)
Configuration Sequence: M–K–F–K–M
Gross Tonnage: 8,614 tons
Dimensions: 453.5/60.7/28 feet
Machinery: Mitsubishi-Sulzer diesel engine, single screw, 2,187 NHP.
Radius: 34,000 miles at 16 1/2 knots.
Complement: 50 (crew), 12 (passengers)
Built: 1934 by Kawasaki Jyuko Co., Kobe
Owner: Kokusai Kisen K.K.

The KOTOHIRA MARU

The 30-ton picket boat KOTOHIRA MARU was reported sunk on 15 April 1944, most likely the victim of a land-based bomber attack on the islands. The vessel may have been sunk in shallow water as there is a reference to the wreck having been subsequently broken up. The wreck of the KOTOHIRA MARU has never been identified by divers.

The Lighter

This slender vessel was found by the author in May 1972 while snorkeling in search of the "Gun High Wreck" on the west side of Uman Island. At that time, the location of the wreck was noted (but not carefully) and plans were made to return to it when the divers had some remaining bottom time. We did not get around to returning to the wreck again during that trip and searches on subsequent diving trips for it were unsuccessful. It was not found again until April 1978 when snorkelers again spotted it from the surface. The report of the find again made a search for it seem worthwhile and we re-located it in the following month..

The wreck lies upright on an incline facing towards Fefan Island with the deck level near the bow at 70 feet and near the stern at 60 feet. The forward compartments in the bow served as living quarters and mess area; a rack built into a wall here contains china of various types. A small flying bridge with a wheel, a brass lantern, a telegraph, and a binnacle is built just forward of captain's cabin and a separate room which houses a large generator. Some of the items found in the captain's quarters included a ceramic head rest, an ash tray, the remains of some uniforms, some amber-colored glasses, and a box of records with the labels still intact.

Just forward of the compartment containing the generator are four hatches built into a square configuration. Some stainless steel tags are attached to the top of each hatch with Japanese kanji characters etched upon them. The engine room lies towards the stern of the 130-foot-long vessel. A second large generator is fastened on the deck above. Entrance into the engine room can be made through a port side doorway. There is enough room to swim between the diesel engines and the roof above. A rack has been built into the aft starboard wall; tools of various types are mounted on it. The vessel has a small single smokestack.

The MATSUTAN MARU

Identification has not been confirmed but the wreck found close to Fanamu Island (directly east of the northern tip of Eten Island) appears to be the same size (1,999 tons) and configuration (M–F–M) as the MATSUTAN MARU. The ship lies upright alongside a reef which rises up to eventually form the small island of Fanamu. The anchors are both in the stored position; the vessel was underway when sunk and an attempt may have been made to beach the ship.

The MATSUTAN MARU was built under the Japanese War Standard Construction program which provided for the mass production of ships with basic designs. She was one of 14 ships built in the Standard Type 1D program between 1942 and 1944 by private shipyards as part of a class of 1,900-ton cargo steamers.

The wreck was found in 1980 lying on a 150- to 160-foot bottom. The forecastle can be entered through open doors at 125 feet. Aside from a few shovels, cans and cables, the forecastle space is empty. No gun is mounted on the bow above. The No. 1 hold has two trucks lying across the hatch cover beams. The frames of the trucks are intact but the external body metal has collapsed. These trucks were flatbeds with cranes mounted just behind the cab; they both had dual wheels on their rear axles. Divers have reported a third truck to be lying on the bottom off the side of the ship. The No. 2 hold interconnects with the forward hole. Here, artillery shells, oil drums, and cables are strung about in disarray. The No. 2 hold contains bags of cement, a large compressor on wheels, and an unidentified type of engine.

The mid-ship superstructure has a flying bridge and the main bridge with two decks below. The smokestack is still standing but has been damaged considerably. Two AA guns had been mounted to the boatdeck aft of the stack.

The first of the aft holds (No. 3) appeared to contain oil or gasoline drums only. The rear mast, which was situated between the two rear holds, has broken off just above its base and has fallen to the starboard side. It looks like the ship took multiple bomb hits in and alongside the No. 4 hold. The hull is buckled and separated and the deck plates on the port side are bent and twisted.

A 3-inch gun is mounted on a platform over the stern. There is a rudder control wheel mounted next to the gun platform. The wooden parts are gone but the metal rim remains. This served as an emergency steering position.

The MATSUTAN MARU is believed to be the ship attacked by ENTERPRISE SBDs on the 1st strike (1AE) on February 17th east of Dublon Island. Heavy damage was reported from a bomb hit just aft of amidships. She was also thought to be the "6,000-ton AK" shown in photographs as beached on a reef east of Dublon and hit by TBFs from ESSEX (Strike 2B) at 0820 h.

TECHNICAL SUMMARY:

Other Names: MATSUTANI MARU, SHOTAN MARU
Type: Standard Type 1D Cargo Steamer
Configuration Sequence: M–F–M
Gross Tonnage: 1,999 tons
Dimensions: 285.7/40/20.3 feet
Machinery: Vertical triple expansion engine, single screw, 1100 iHP.
Radius: 3,800 miles at 10 knots.
Complement: Unknown
Built: 1942
Owner: Unknown

The MINSEI MARU

From the many reports of small craft reported damaged or sunk during the carrier air raids of April 29–30, three candidate vessels were picked by JANAC as most-likely being the MINSEI MARU:

(1) The 130-foot "patrol boat with clean lines and grey paint" which was strafed and set afire by LEXINGTON planes at 0920 h on 30 April and later sunk by LANGLEY planes at 0925 h while underway north of Falo and east of Falas Islands ("midway between Falas and Northeast Islands").

(2) The picket boat sunk between 1000–1200 h on 30 April south of the reef east of Ollan Island by MONTEREY planes.

(3) An "armed escort vessel" claimed sunk by LEXINGTON planes at about 1200 h on 30 April at a location 700 yards northeast of Fefan Island.

TECHNICAL SUMMARY:

Type: Converted Minelayer/Escort
Gross Tonnage: 300, 378 (?) tons

The MOMOKAWA MARU

KAWASAKI KISEN KAISHA

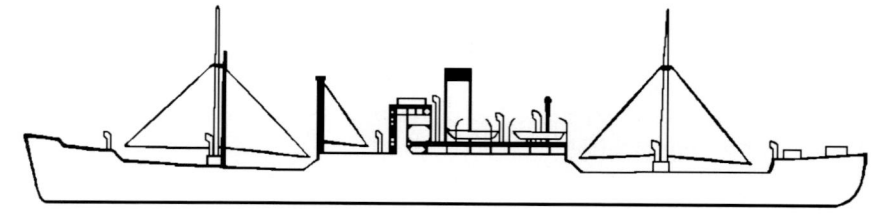

The MOMOKAWA MARU was found during a fathometer search in 1982 making the wreck one of the most recent finds in the Truk Lagoon. The wreck is located nearly 1/2 mile from the Dublon Island shore line lying on its port side in 130 feet of water. She lies slightly off-line between the positions of the SAN FRANCISCO and AIKOKU MARU wrecks. The identity of the wreck was established after the ship's bell was found lying on the bottom where it had fallen from the bridge. Later, the name of the ship was located on the forward starboard side of the hull. The ship's name, MOMOKAWA, translates as "Peach River."

ESSEX, YORKTOWN, and BUNKER HILL planes attacked several ships in the anchorage where the MOMOKAWA MARU was located on the first day of the air raids. The MOMOKAWA MARU was damaged but was not in danger of sinking following the bombing attacks. On the morning of the 17th, BUNKER HILL SB2Cs (Strike 3B) attacked a ship described as a 450-foot, 8,000-ton AK located 1/4 mile off the southeast tip of Dublon Island. The ship was reported to have been damaged previously but was level in the water when the attack began. The ship was hit by a 1,000-lb bomb amidships causing a huge fire and explosion. Only the bow was remaining above water when the planes retired.

My dive partner and I decided to begin our first dive by swimming to the bow and working our way aft. It was quickly evident that little growth existed on the wreck as the hull was very clean looking. Swimming around the front of the shipwreck, we noticed the port anchor chain extending outward. There was no bow gun or platform. Entering the No. 1 hold, we immediately started seeing aircraft parts including wing tanks, folded wings, propeller blades and a portion of a large aircraft fuselage. Truck parts were also in evidence including a truck frame with dual rear wheels and several extra tires along with other unrecognizable equipment that had spilled out of the hold and was strewn in piles against the seabed. Several large naval artillery shells were lying in a pile. The body of the aircraft we'd spotted had apparently been stowed in both the interconnecting No. 1 and No. 2 holds and as we swam into the second hold, we could see that the aircraft's fuselage had been broken apart evidently when the ship had slammed its side against the bottom of the lagoon. Anxious to try to identify the aircraft type, I swam forward and found a cockpit and nose fairing separated from the body. It had the appearance of a Douglas DC-2 or DC-3! Through later research, I found out that there were many Japanese-built DC-3s used throughout the Pacific theatre of operations; these aircraft were named Tabby by the Allies. It appears that this naval transport plane was indeed the same as we'd found in the holds of the MOMOKAWA MARU.

The ship has a kingpost aft of the second hold and a third small hold that leads to compartments built below main deck and extending aft. Most everything in the bridge has fallen to the bottom where there was a large deep layer of muck and debris. The ship's telegraph and rudderstand are still standing and a large compass was lying along a wall. In the deck level below the wheelhouse, we found several pieces of china exhibiting the house markings of Kawasaki Kisen Kaisha. Cheny, the diving guide accompanying us, beckoned to me to come over to where he'd found the ship's bell. The ship's name, MOMOKAWA MARU, was clearly visible along with its corresponding kanji characters; however, below this was the number "2601" included where you would normally expect the date the ship was built to be placed.

The smokestack shows no visible stack markings; its top is bent and may have been damaged by a bomb burst. The rear holds were empty except for some oil drums. The large mast situated between the holds is intact but the deck and hull alongside show considerable damage as the plates are torn and deformed. There was no gun mounted where you'd expect a stern gun; instead, there is an artillery piece similar to the bow gun of the SEIKO MARU mounted forward on the deck on the starboard side. Its wheels have been removed and the gun is supported on a swivel mount. There is another gun mount on the port side but the gun is missing.

TECHNICAL SUMMARY:

Other Name: MOMOGAWA MARU
Type: Passenger-Cargo
Configuration Sequence: M–K–F–M
Gross Tonnage: 3,829 tons
Dimensions: 354/50/23 feet
Machinery: Steam turbines, single screw, 333 NHP.
Radius: 10,000 miles at 13 knots.
Complement: Unknown
Built: 1941 by Kawasaki Dockyard Co., Ltd., Kobe
Owner: Kawasaki K.K.

The NAGANO MARU

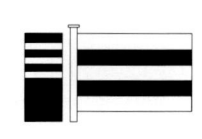
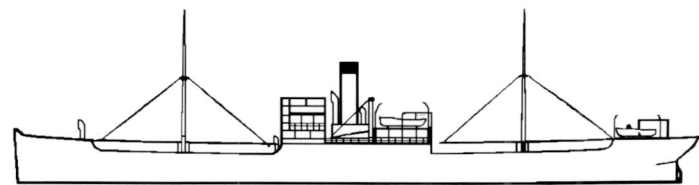

NIPPON YUSEN KAISHA

A group that had just completed their dives on the SAN FRANCISCO MARU in March 1978 spotted an oil slick nearby extending from the east on the surface of a calm sea. The only person with any remaining bottom time was the Trukese boat driver who was also a diver. After being sent down to investigate, he was able to find an upright wreck. The location of the wreck was noted and in the days following, the wreck was revisited and identified as the 3,824-ton NAGANO MARU by the name on the forward hull. China with the owner's flag insignia was also found inside the cabins in the midship superstructure.

The extreme depth (160 feet to the deck) has prevented thorough exploration of the shipwreck. Divers have reported the ship to be armed with both bow and stern deck guns and two AA guns on the boatdeck. The only damage noted was probably due to bomb bursts. The smokestack has been bent over from its base and the forward mast is knocked over.

The NAGANO MARU was the target of torpedo squadron planes from ESSEX on both days of the February 1944 air raids; other air groups may have contributed to her sinking also. On February 16th, ESSEX VTs (Strike 2A) hit a "6,000-ton, 350-foot long AK" with a salvo of two to four 500-lb bombs causing a secondary explosion and fire aboard. The ship was reported to be in the middle of the Eten Anchorage. The following day, the ship was attacked again (Strike 2A) and two more 500-lb bomb hits, one amidships and one on the stern, were scored. The fires aboard were raging when the planes retired.

TECHNICAL SUMMARY:

Type: Passenger-Cargo
Configuration Sequence: M–F–M
Gross Tonnage: 3,824 tons
Dimensions: 345/50/24 feet
Machinery: Reciprocating (oil), single screw, 842 NHP.
Radius: 11,000 miles at 10 knots.
Complement: Unknown
Built: 1917 by Mitsubishi Dockyard & Engineering Works, Nagasaki.
Owner: Nippon Yusen Kaisha
  Kinkai Yusen K.K. (previous)
Remarks: Army transport. 2 decks.

The NAKA

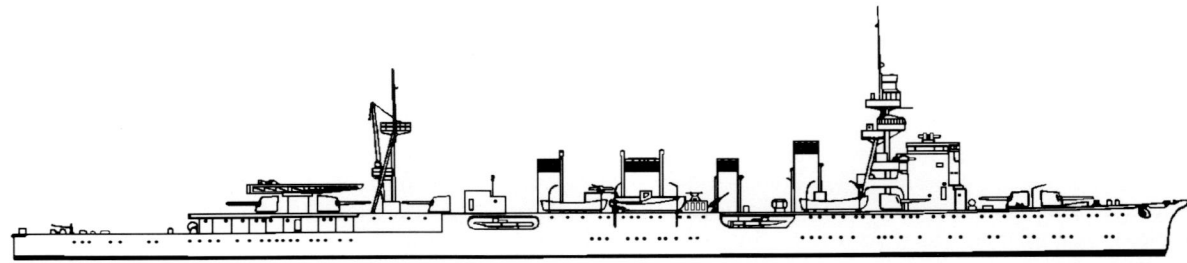

ESSEX planes on Strike 2A early in the morning of February 16th, reported two sightings and attacks on 6,000-ton CLs. One was anchored 500 yards southeast of Eten Island and the second one was 3/4 of a mile east of the northeast point of Dublon Island. This second location is approximately where a SENDAI class CL identified by photo interpreters had been anchored during the photographic overflight two weeks earlier and may have been the NAKA. It appears that the cruiser got underway shortly thereafter and was next reported making a high speed run away from the atoll to the southwest.

BUNKER HILL aircraft (Strike 3C) were vectored towards the cruiser and found her about 25 miles southwest of Piannu Pass (west end of atoll) making about 25 knots heading towards the pass. The ship was identified then as a SENDAI or TENRYU class light cruiser with 3 or 4 stacks. She was putting up only light AA fire. The ship became the target of a coordinated attack by the TBFs and SB2Cs (VT- and VB-17). As the attack began, the cruiser started a tight clockwise circle at high speed. The torpedo planes dove so that just prior to turning in on the target, they were in line astern, circling the ship's circle on the opposite course. Each plane would then turn in at the point from which it could launch an attack on the bow of the ship. The torpedoes were dropped from 300 feet at 200 knots between 800 to 1,000 yards away from the cruiser. One and possibly two torpedoes hit the ship; these produced three internal explosions which were most likely the magazines going up. All bombs dropped by VB-17 appeared to miss the ship. Several of the escorting fighters strafed the ship, diving from an altitude of 4,000 to 5,000 feet. The strafing raked the cruiser from bow to stern, but the total damage could not be accurately assessed. As BUNKER HILL's aircraft left the area, the cruiser was noted as being practically dead in the water and down by the bow with her No. 1 turret awash.

BUNKER HILL's pilots figured NAKA was finished but she was able to get underway again and was found by COWPENS' Air Group 25 planes about 1445 h. The ship was located about five miles from the BUNKER HILL attack trailing an oil slick "two miles in diameter." The cruiser was proceeding slowly at a speed estimated at between 3 to 6 knots towards the southern lagoon entrance at Otta Pass. There were two other vessels in the vicinity standing by for removing the CL's crew in case she was abandoned. One vessel was a patrol craft (PC) hovering alongside the cruiser; the other was a "small boat" about five miles away.

The COWPENS' TBFs started individual bombing and strafing runs from 11,000 feet at the CL, now practically a sitting duck. The PC was seen to immediately clear the vicinity of the NAKA as the TBFs began circling to attack. The CL began to put up heavy AA fire against the attacking aircraft. The ship took a 2,000-lb bomb hit in the stern section just forward of the catapult. The resulting explosion hurled smoke and fire several hundred feet into the air. One plane's 1,000-lb bomb glanced off the hull on the starboard side near the stern and exploded in the water. Another armor piercing 1,000-lb bomb landed just aft of the third stack turning the entire aft section of the CL into a cloud of fire and smoke. This final bomb hit caused the previously intense AA fire to cease for several minutes. The cruiser was then dead in the water and the fires aboard seemed to grow in intensity for the next few minutes. However, when the VT planes swooped in low to strafe the rafts and the two rescue vessels, the cruiser again started up AA fire. The PC was noted to be returning the strafing fire from the attacking planes from at least four machine guns.

With no fighter cover, the decision was made to head back to the carrier without waiting to confirm if the CL sunk. Upon withdrawing, the pilots observed the cruiser's crew jumping from the sides of the ship and others getting into rafts floating alongside the stricken vessel.

COWPENS' fighter pilots returning from a CAP over NEW JERSEY and IOWA approximately three hours later passed over the area and reported no traces of any ship. The NAKA had finally sunk.

TECHNICAL SUMMARY:

Type: SENDAI Class Light Cruiser
Displacement: 5,195 tons
Dimensions: 520/48.4/16.1 feet
Machinery: 4-shaft Gihon geared turbines, 12 Kampon boilers, 90,000 SHP.

Speed: 35 1/4 knots
Radius: 7,800 miles at 10 knots, 1,300 miles at 33 knots.
Complement: 450
Armament: Seven 5.5-inch 50-cal. guns, two 5-inch 50-cal. DP guns, four 25mm AA, six 13mm AA; eight 24-inch torpedo tubes (dual mounted); 80 mines; 1 aircraft.
Built: 1925 by Mitsubishi Zosensho, Yokohama
Remarks: Assigned to the 4th Fleet, 14th Cruiser Division.

The NIPPO MARU

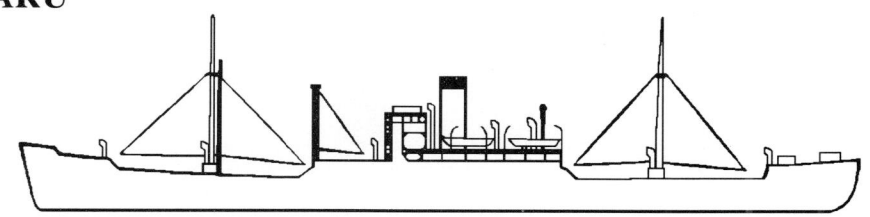

On February 10, 1944, the NIPPO MARU arrived in Truk accompanied by YUBAE MARU, KITAGAMI MARU, SUBCHASER NO. 33, TAKUNAN MARU NO. 2, and SHONAN MARU NO. 5. The ship was the early prey of ESSEX TBFs participating in the first group strike (2A) of the day in attacks against shipping east and southeast of Dublon and Eten Islands. At approximately 0815 h, the planes scored three hits with 500-lb bombs in the stern area. The bomb explosions heavily damaged the ship and started fires aboard. Her sinking was not observed but she had gone under by the time the AIKOKU MARU was sunk just to the south of her two hours later.

The wreck of the NIPPO MARU was discovered and dived upon in 1969 by the Cousteau expedition and film footage of the wreck was shown in "Lagoon of Lost Ships;" however, she was not identified at that time. The wreck lies further north than any of the cluster of ships east of Dublon. She was re-discovered in 1980 lying just off a narrow coral reef on a 140- to 160-foot bottom. The wreck faces almost due north parallel to the shore line against the side of a steep underwater hill in an upright position with a 20- to 30-degree list to the port side. Since her recent discovery, the NIPPO MARU has become one of the most popular wrecks in the lagoon due to the ship's interesting cargo of war materials and other shipboard items aboard. The wreck is very clean in terms of coral, sponge, and other growth in contrast to such popular (and shallower) wrecks as the FUJIKAWA MARU and SHINKOKU MARU which have very heavy marine growth on them.

Large winches and a small gun platform can be found on the bow. The port anchor extends outward from the ship. Like many of the Japanese ships, a spare anchor is secured against the superstructure near the forecastle entrance. There are numerous personal effects strung out in the muck on the floor of the forecastle suggesting it may have served as crew's quarters. The forward hold contains hemispherical beach-type mines, detonators, 2-foot-long artillery shells, huge bottles (known to contain caustic substances), gas masks, oil drums, and other cargo lying in disarray. Off to the side, there is a truck frame with dual rear wheels and an instrument panel (approximately 2 feet by 8 feet) with numerous intact gauges. Beneath the well deck and the forward mast, the No. 1 and No. 2 holds interconnect; stored here are two beautiful 4-foot-long bronze range finders (used to determine the range between ship's guns and attacking aircraft or other ships), assorted bottles, mess kits, gas masks, teapots, shoe soles, canned goods, and much more. The lower level of the second hold contains at least four huge square container tanks. The presence of these containers lends credence to the NIPPO MARU being listed as a converted water carrier; these containers were used to store water and the ship was able to supply water to other vessels and/or island outposts. Two of these metal containers washed up against the nearby reef shortly after the ship went down and eventually sank in shallow water.

A Japanese tank (probably a Model 97 medium tank) is resting on the port side deck opposite the forward end of the No. 2 hold. The turret gun is missing; these tanks were often transported without the gun installed. Ladders lead up from the foredeck to the main deck where there is a small access hold just forward of the mid-ship superstructure. Coal was loaded aboard the ship through this hold and stored in the spaces below. Passageways leading aft on each side of the ship lead past a series of storage rooms.

The wheelhouse has the ship's telegraph and helm standing in its midst. The wooden ship's wheel has long since deteriorated, but the metal rim hangs on its original support hub attached to the rudder stand. The compass lies on the floor of the wheelhouse nearby; the ship's bell was found here also but it has since disappeared. Towards the rear of the wheelhouse, there is a strongbox lying against the wall. This box may contain codes and ciphers that the Japanese reported as lost when the NIPPO MARU was bombed and sunk. Several pieces of china were strung about on the floor also with a ship owner's flag insignia design later found to be that of the Kobe-based shipping company Nippoh Kaiun K.K. Its possible that there was a change of ownership from Okazi Honten to Nippoh Kaiun or that the latter was managing the ship for the owner.

There are two decks of cabins/compartments below the bridge. The first deck has a large galley on the starboard side. The remaining small rooms look like they were utilized as crew's quarters; there are remains of bunks, clothing, and personal objects lying about. The compartments at the main deck level can be entered easily from the aft end where the entrance doors are wide open. The entrances lead to a large open room with passageways leading forward to cabins on the outside and entrances to catwalk landings leading to the engine room below on the inside. The outer cabins were also crew or officer's quarters. A 3-inch-high rectangular box containing bronze navigational instruments was found in these quarters.

Aft of the bridge, the stack stands upright but with its side damaged (collapsed apparently due to a bomb burst). The owner's stack markings were present but not well-defined enough to recognize because of the damage. An intriguing find was three more containers that appeared to be additional strongboxes. Two were located on the deck and another in the center of a companionway aft of the raised superstructure above the engine room. This number of strongboxes is rare on these wrecks; in the past some of these "strongboxes" have been broken into only to find ordnance of various types.

Three howitzer or anti-tank guns can be found on the deck on the starboard side adjacent to the No. 4 hold. These look like U.S.-made 37mm anti-tank guns and if so, were probably captured by the Japanese in the Philippines. These guns were thrown about and lie askew on the deck, testimony to the force of the bomb blasts which rocked the ship.

Metal case containing brass navigational instruments was found in the bridge of the NIPPO MARU.

China found in the bridge of NIPPO MARU exhibits the decorative flag symbol of the Nippoh Kaiun K. K. shipping company.

The little amount of marine growth on the rudder stand of the NIPPO MARU (left) standing within the mostly enclosed wheelhouse is in striking contrast to that found on the HANAKAWA MARU (right) which is almost unrecognizable due to the prolific growth on the exposed flying bridge.

The No. 1 hold contains many hemispherical beach-type anti-invasion mines, large acid bottle containers, stacked ammunition, and a gas mask.

The hold adjacent to the guns contains quite a collection of interesting cargo. Included are hundreds of beer and other bottles, radio communication equipment, ceramic insulators, bowls, bed frames, dishes, cans, and many more unidentified items. A machine gun is lying on the deck a few feet aft of the anti-tank guns; its mount with dual support rings is lying alongside.

The aft hold held little cargo except for several spare 5-inch gun barrels. Two more barrels were found on the starboard deck above. There was no stern gun or mount. The only fixed armament aboard the ship appears to be AA guns. One dual-barreled gun has fallen from the top of the bridge to the deck forward and a second is reported to have been dislodged from its mount and is now lying on the seabed nearby.

TECHNICAL SUMMARY:

Type: Cargo-Water Carrier (Converted)
Configuration Sequence: M–K–F–M
Gross Tonnage: 3,764 tons
Dimensions: 353.6/50/23 feet
Machinery: 2 steam turbines DR geared, single screw, 500 NHP.
Radius: 10,000 miles at 12 knots.
Built: 1936 by Kawasaki Dockyard Co., Ltd., Kobe
Owner: Okazaki Honten K.K.
Remarks: Cruiser stern. Ownership change possible as wreck is stocked with Nippoh Kaiun K.K. china. The NIPPO MARU has the same configuration as the MOMOKAWA and KIKUKAWA MARUs.

Two range finders lie in disarray in hold with bottles and other supplies.

The OITE

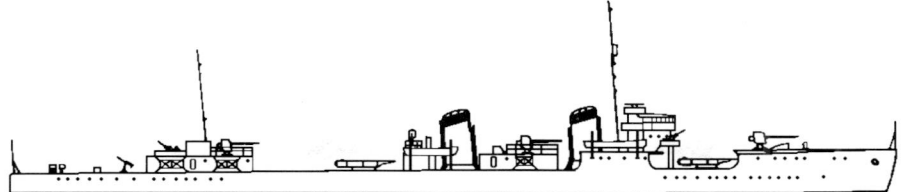

On 14 February 1944, the destroyer OITE left Truk with the light cruiser AGANO heading for Saipan and then on to the Empire. The captain of the OITE was up for promotion and was going to be leaving his command to be joining the Naval Staff at Yokosuka. The two vessels were detected about 160 miles northwest of Truk by the U.S. Submarine SKATE with Lt. Commander W.P. "Bud" Gruner, Jr. on his first patrol as captain of a submarine. The AGANO was misidentified as a heavy cruiser of the KAKO class. This was the sort of target that no submarine skipper would want to miss. The captain executed a submerged attack at sundown on the cruiser and fired four torpedoes at 2,400 yards; three or four of the torpedoes hit causing explosions and fire aboard. The AGANO had already in her service career survived numerous bombings and a previous attack where she had been damaged by U.S. Submarine SCAMP. Her luck had run out; she was mortally wounded. The OITE searched for the attacking submarine but SKATE was able to slip away undetected. The AGANO was slowly sinking and the OITE stayed with her throughout the night and the next day. Fuel was transferred aboard the OITE from the stricken CL. When it finally appeared that sinking was imminent, nearly 460 of AGANO's officers and crew including her captain were transferred aboard and the OITE headed towards Saipan. The destroyer reported the sinking of AGANO to Truk and in return was ordered to return to Truk with the survivors.

The OITE appears to have been observed initially by BUNKER HILL VF pilots during the fighter sweep early in the morning of the second day of the air raids. The DD was reported entering North Pass. The Japanese Naval commander in charge of the coastal defense gun crew at Tonelik Island bordering North Pass radioed the OITE questioning her on why she was returning to the atoll while Truk was under heavy attack. The destroyer captain radioed in reply that he was following orders. After the OITE was inside the lagoon and possibly as a result of the radio exchange between the captain and the island gun battery commander, she received another message from Truk headquarters ordering the ship to turn back and head for Saipan once again. The OITE captain replied "I'm already inside the lagoon." Nothing further was heard from Truk headquarters. By then the OITE was under strafing attacks by F6Fs from BUNKER HILL and then MONTEREY (Strikes 3B); the captain of the OITE was killed by machine gun bursts which raked the bridge and set the DD ablaze abaft of the stacks. Command of the ship was taken over by the captain of the AGANO. Five TBFs from BUNKER HILL arrived to join-in on the attacks against the hapless destroyer. In the melee that followed, the OITE was hit by a single torpedo amidships while executing a radical high speed maneuver. The destroyer was blown in half and sank immediately.

Only about 20 men survived the sinking out of the crew of the OITE and survivors from AGANO. Four of these survivors have returned to Truk in later years. Much of the preceeding commentary was derived from conversations between a gunnery captain from OITE who returned to Truk and Kimiuo Aisek. The gunnery captain had been able to swim to a small island after the OITE sank.

After the Japanese writer and researcher, Tomoyuki Yoshimura, received survivors accounts and studied all available records, he set out to find the wreck of the OITE. Together with Gradvin Aisek, Kimiuo's son, and a Trukese by the name of Lilipas from the island of

–*National Archives Photos*
Photo planes document the last moments of the Japanese DD OITE which has entered the northern part of the lagoon through North Pass. The destroyer was the target of several fighters which made multiple strafing attacks (top) against the wildly maneuvering vessel. The fighters occupied the DD's attention while torpedo planes attacked. OITE is hit by a torpedo amidships (bottom) and erupts into a tremendous explosion. The ship is blown in two; the two sections of the DD sank rapidly.

Pis who had seen droplets of oil spreading on the surface above the wreck, the OITE was found using a fathometer on March 1, 1986 after five days of searching. After a couple of tries, their dive boat's anchor snagged something solid. The divers encountered nearly 50 sharks near the surface; their numbers tapered off as they descended towards the wreck below. The divers found the anchor had snagged the bow structure near the bottom at a depth of between 200 to 220 feet. The entire foreship including the bridge is upside down. There is a space from the bottom opposite the torpedo tubes forward to swim through a vertical entrance into the ship's mess. China including teacups and several saucers have been found. The bridge is immediately aft of the forward torpedo tubes but lies jammed against the sand of the seabed. Because of this, the bridge has not been penetrated.

The stern is separated from the forward section by about 40 feet; it rests upright with the upper structure at a depth of 180 feet. The visibility over the whole wreck is very good and the wreck is relatively clean of marine growth. Human remains are scattered about everywhere in the companionways, hatches, doorways, and on the sea floor around the wreck. A large 4.7-inch gun is mounted in the center of the stern. There are also two dual-barreled AA guns mounted on the sides fore and aft of the large deck gun.

The Blue Lagoon Dive Shop has been the only diving service operators to take divers to the wreck of the OITE. Kimiuo Aisek emphasizes that the wreck is very exciting but should only be dove on by professionals with significant diving experience at the depths necessary to explore it.

TECHNICAL SUMMARY:

Other Name: NO. 11 (Original), Re-named in 1928
Type: KAMIKAZE Class Destroyer
Displacement: 1,400 tons
Dimensions: 327/30/9.6 feet
Machinery: 2-shaft Parsons geared turbines, 4 Kampon boilers, 38,500 SHP.
Speed: 37.3 knots
Radius: 3,600 miles at 14 knots.
Complement: 148
Armament: Three 4.7-inch DP deck guns, six to ten 25mm AA guns, two 7.7mm guns; 2 pairs 21-inch torpedo tubes; 4 depth charge throwers, 18 depth charges.
Built: 1924 by Uraga Dock Co., Ltd., Tokyo
Remarks: Improved version of the MINEKAZE class. Nine units of the KAMIKAZE class were built. The OITE was attached to the 4th Fleet. Its primary duty was to conduct escort operations between the Inner South Seas and Rabaul.

The OJIMA

On 7 October 1943, the OJIMA was summoned to the Eten Anchorage to assist the KIKUKAWA MARU which had a fire on board. While attempts were being made to extinguish the fire, a tremendous explosion erupted from the KIKUKAWA MARU and both vessels were sent to the bottom with heavy loss of life.

The OJIMA was blown in two. The foreship lies about 200 feet northeast of the wreck of the KIKUKAWA MARU on its starboard side at a bottom depth of 120 feet. Two holds and a mast are intact along with the bow section; beyond that is utter destruction. The tug had been anchored when it sank. Lying to the south, part of the midship superstructure and stern have been found in deeper water. Large and small pieces of both the tug and the KIKUKAWA MARU lie between the two separate sections of the tug. An intact Daihatsu landing craft lies upright amongst the wreckage. It had evidently been tied alongside the KIKUKAWA MARU prior to the explosion.

TECHNICAL SUMMARY:

Type: TATEGAMI Class Salvage Tug
Displacement: 800 tons
Dimensions: 160.7/31.2/11.3 feet
Machinery: 2 reciprocating vertical triple expansion engines, 2-shafts, 2,200 iHP.
Speed: 15 knots
Radius: Unknown
Complement: Unknown
Armament: Two 25 mm AA guns; 6 depth charges.
Built: 1940 by Maizuru Kaigun Kosho
Remarks: Equipped with three 5-ton and one 10-ton derricks, salvage pumps, compressors and workshops.

PATROL BOAT NO. 34

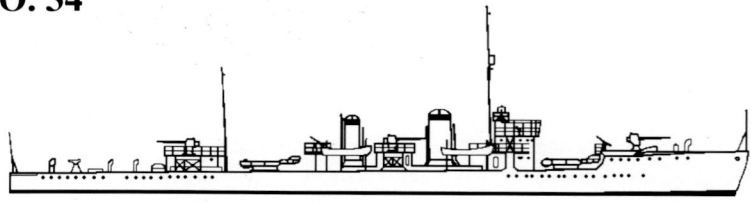

The MOMI Class destroyer SUTSUKI before being converted to a patrol boat (re-named PATROL BOAT NO. 34).

It seems likely that the "Shallow Destroyer" wreck lying 150 yards north of the anchor marker on the west side of Dublon is PATROL BOAT NO. 34. The vessel has been fitted with a makeshift bow which may have been necessary due to a collision with another ship. PATROL BOAT NO. 34 had been towed to Truk for repairs following the collision. The sloping ramp mounted on the stern is perhaps the best clue to the identity of the wrecked vessel. I believe that the ramp was fitted on the stern to carry a 46-foot Daihatsu landing craft. The only craft known to be lost at Truk with this configuration is the PATROL BOAT NO. 34.

The PATROL BOAT NO. 34 was originally named SUTSUKI when built in 1921 as a MOMI class destroyer. Her displacement was

770 tons, her length 280 feet, and her beam was 26 feet. She was fitted with 2-direct-drive turbine engines which allowed her to attain a maximum speed of 36 knots. The ships of this class mounted two pairs of 21-inch torpedo tubes, three 4.7-inch deck guns, and two 7.7mm AA guns. Four depth charge throwers were fitted on the stern; 36 depth charges could be carried. The crew complement was 110 men.

In 1939, the SUTSUKI and eight other vessels of the MOMI class were reclassified and refitted to be special patrol boats. At this time, SUTSUKI was renamed PATROL BOAT NO. 34. As part of the modifications, one boiler was removed decreasing her speed to 18 knots and ballast was added raising her displacement to 935 tons. Just prior to the war, the aft funnel and one of the torpedo tube pairs were removed and its stern was modified such that it was raked down to the waterline. She was re-designed then to carry and launch a 46-foot Daihatsu landing craft capable of holding 150 troops. At least one of her 4.7-inch deck guns was removed and the number of depth charges carried was reduced to 18. It was in this capacity that PATROL BOAT NO. 34 participated in the Japanese offensive against Midway as part of the Transport Group of the Midway Occupation Force.

In March 1943, PATROL BOAT NO. 34 was severely damaged at Kavieng (New Guinea) in a collision with the old MINEKAZE class DD YAKAZE after which she was towed to Truk for repairs. She was sunk on July 3, 1944, but the circumstances are not fully known. Some reports indicate that she was sunk by aircraft while another suggests that she might have been sunk by U.S. Submarine STURGEON.

By comparing profiles of the wreck and that of the SUTSUKI, it is obvious that if they are one and the same, a considerable section of the damaged bow and foreship was removed when the bow was replaced. The bridge was either modified at that time or destroyed later.

The wreck is located in shallow water about 400 yards from shore facing west towards Fefan Island. It lies in an upright position with a 20-degree list to port. The vessel is easily seen from the surface as the depth to the deck near the bow is 10 feet, declining to a depth of 30 feet near the stern. The replacement bow has an unusual pointed shape; this, plus the large steel reinforcements, tend to make it look very awkward. A narrow fin is mounted along both sides of the hull almost the entire length of the vessel. Two large high-speed screws held with heavy mounting brackets are lying against the bottom. Varied coral growth exists around the front of the bow with only a small amount being present on the rest of the wreck.

The remaining superstructure is in poor shape due to the bomb and fire damage aboard that it suffered before sinking. The wreck appears to be deteriorating rapidly; much of the damage may be due to its being in shallow water. The forward decks are littered with debris and much has fallen to the bottom along the port side. Investigations of the equipment and debris here have produced what appears to be torpedo launching tubes. The remains of a torpedo body lies on the edge of the deck above. Nearby, the fins and rear section of a large exploded bomb can be found also.

Narrow hatchways on the deck aft lead to rather large rooms below. A search through the debris and muck lying on the floors of these rooms has produced some lamps, gas masks, pieces of clothes, shoes, medicine bottles, and an automatic rifle in a very corroded condition. Piping, gauges, switches, and turnwheels of various sizes and shapes are mounted along the walls.

A single elliptical smokestack is mounted above the engine room forward. Behind it is a raised structure with a large bare gun platform mounted on top of it. Another 25 feet aft is a second structure and gun platform above. The torpedo tubes were evidently mounted on the deck between the two structures with the gun platforms.

TECHNICAL SUMMARY:

Other Names: SUTSUKI (Original)
                             SUSUKI (Kokutai)

Divers swim over the superstructure of the shallow wreck.

Type: Patrol Boat (ex-MOMI Class Destroyer), Converted 1939.
Displacement: 935 tons
Dimensions: 280/26/8 feet
Machinery: 2 direct-drive turbine engines, twin screws, 12,000 SHP.
Radius: 3,000 miles at 15 knots (DD configuration).

Speed: 18 knots
Complement: 110 (DD configuration)
Armament: Two 4.7-inch deck guns, six 25mm AA guns; 18 depth charges.
Built: 1921 by Ishikawajima Zosensho, Tokyo.
Remarks: Originally, 21 MOMI class units were built.

The REIYO MARU

Located during a fathometer search in 1973 and again in 1980, the REIYO MARU is one of the deepest wrecks in Truk and is only very rarely dived on. The wreck lies upright on the seabed with the depth to the deck nearly 170 feet. The bridge is reported to be heavily damaged and both masts have been toppled from their bases. A thorough exploration of the holds and superstructure has not been attempted due to the extreme depths.

A 10,000-ton freighter reported by pilots to be anchored three miles from Eten Island bearing 060 degrees from that island was attacked by dive bombers from ESSEX (Strike 2A) on the first day of the air strikes. The planes scored two 1,000-lb bomb hits, one amidships and the other just aft of the bridge. The attackers observed two large explosions which left the ship ablaze. The ESSEX planes were unable to confirm the sinking of the ship, but it appears that the REIYO MARU sank shortly after the attack described above.

TECHNICAL SUMMARY:

Type: Passenger-Cargo

Configuration Sequence: M–K–F–M
Gross Tonnage: 5,446 tons
Dimensions: 444/53.2/29.4 feet
Machinery: Reciprocating engines made by Ishikawajima Sanbashi & Eng. Co., Tokyo, single screw, 513 NHP.
Radius: 13,500 miles at 10 knots
Complement: 48 (crew), 4 (passengers)
Built: 1920 by Asano Sanbashi Co., Tsurumi
Owner: Toyo Kisen Kabushiki Kaisha, Tokyo

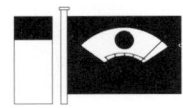

Remarks: Attached to the Yokosuka Navy Transport Department. Two decks, split superstructure.

–National Archives Photo
The REIYO MARU in Limon Bay, Cristobal (Panama Canal Zone) – 4/26/37.

The RIO DE JANEIRO MARU

The locating of the wreck of the RIO DE JANEIRO MARU was not straight-forward on my first trip to Truk. Our dive guide was Frankie Knowles who to my knowledge was the only woman ever hired by Kimiuo Aisek to lead divers to the wrecks. There were only 8 to 10 known shipwrecks that were being dove on at that time. Frankie had the boat driver position the boat to where the palm trees on the near shore lined up with the first and fourth windows of the church further inland. When they were lined up, we headed our boat on a line 180 degrees from shore until I spotted a large yellow-green object under the water. It was the "RIO." We were on the east side of Uman Island skirting the drop-off about 400 or 500 yards from shore. The waves were running between three and four feet high as this area is unprotected when the wind is from the northeast. We could see Trukese houses and people on the shore including a group fishing in the shallows near the island.

The RIO DE JANEIRO MARU is lying on her starboard side facing east along a 110-foot bottom. The dive guides typically anchor near amidships where the depth to the side of the hull is the shallowest, 35 feet. A large 6-inch deck gun is mounted above the forecastle with its nearly 15-foot-long barrel pointing downwards toward the seabed. The forecastle compartment below the gun was used for ammunition storage and probably contained a hydraulic system for transferring shells up to the gun platform. There are several places where objects have been blown outward through the hull plates and the bulkhead shows the effect of an internal explosion. This damage is from the ammunition exploding; it is believed that heat from the fires aboard the ship caused them to blow up.

A swim over the hull will lead you to the port anchor chain extending outwards towards the bottom. On the hull nearby, the name of the ship has been welded in large 18-inch Roman letters across the side of the ship with the corresponding Kanji characters above. Large degaussing wires on the hull encircled the whole exterior of the ship to prevent attracting magnetic mines. The No. 1 hold contains several large artillery shells which may have been used with the bow gun. Heaps of burnt rubble fill the hold. Large winches and other cargo handling equipment are mounted fore and aft of the forward mast. In the No. 2 hold just forward of the bridge, there are two large gun barrels with a machined wheel (movable turret?) almost 15 feet in diameter.

After entering the midship structure at main-deck level from the forward end, you enter into a large companion way. About 20 feet down the passage, there is a doorway leading into the ship where several stacks of china can be found which have been fused together with a foul-looking material that has melted against them. These had fallen down from a nearby doorway leading to the ship's galley. The bridge is empty as everything including the ship's telegraph, helm, and rudder stand have fallen to the bottom where there is now a large pile of rubble. The muck and debris here is several feet thick. The forward part of the bridge sported large rectangular windows while "D"-shaped portholes were mounted along the side walls; the heavy glass is still intact.

The funnel appears undamaged and except for the "onion peels"

The upper port side of the wreck of the RIO DE JANEIRO MARU.

–National Archives Photo
The passenger liner RIO DE JANEIRO MARU.

–Naval Operational Archives Photo
The RIO DE JANEIRO MARU lies at anchor on the east side of Eten Island on fire from the bow to amidships.

The commercial stack markings of the owner, Osaka Shosen Kaisha, are plainly outlined on the side of the funnel.

(ruffled white algae) lying all about, it is almost free of marine growth. The stack markings of the owner are easily seen.

The ship sunk as a result of bomb damage incurred on the starboard side of the hold aft of the boatdeck (hold No. 4). The hull plates are blown apart due to one or more bomb bursts. This caused the ship to take on water, list to starboard, and finally sink.

The rear holds are empty except for the ever-present beer bottles and a few 50-gallon drums. The stern section at 60 feet contains more rooms and compartments which may not only have been used as crew quarters, but also for troops and supplies. Another 6-inch deck gun is mounted on the stern. Over the edge of the hull, the shallowest of the 4-bladed twin screws can be reached at a depth of 80 feet.

The RIO DE JANEIRO MARU was built for passenger liner service in 1930. She was requisitioned by the Japanese Navy in 1940 and converted to a submarine depot ship (tender) and placed under direct command of the Japanese Combined Fleet. The "RIO," along with the CL YURA and six submarines, comprised Submarine Squadron 5 of the 1st Battle Fleet based in Hiroshima Bay up until 10 July 1942.

At that time, she was attached to the South-West Area Force and was then employed in operations in and out of Truk. On 27 July 1942, she was attacked by the submarine U.S.S. SPEARFISH about 95 miles east of Camranh, French Indochina. On 28 July, the ship reported that she had received medium damage but was able to proceed. An intercepted message on 5 August mentioned repairs to the ship at Hong Kong. Following the repair work, the ship returned to the South-West Area of operations and was active in the role of a sub-tender until September 1943 when she was returned to the Empire where she underwent conversion to her new role as a transport.

Intelligence files list the following excerpts from intercepted messages regarding the RIO DE JANEIRO MARU:

(1) Message of 17 February at 0730 h, giving preliminary results of the carrier strike against Truk, lists RIO DE JANEIRO MARU as one of the ships sunk.

(2) Message of 18 February states that at 1200 h, February 16th, while within Truk Atoll, the RIO DE JANEIRO MARU was bombed,

Bronze shipbuilder's plaque recovered from the "RIO."

caught fire, and at 0030 h (17 February) sank. (All secret documents were destroyed by fire so there was no danger of their having fallen into enemy hands).

(3) Message of 20 February mentions something (probably equipment) being lost when the RIO DE JANEIRO MARU sunk.

(4) The RIO DE JANEIRO MARU was deleted from the War Organization List as of 13 March, and detached from the jurisdiction of the Sasebo Naval District as of 31 March.

The attack at 1200 h on the first day of the air raids corresponds to the masthead attack by YORKTOWN SBDs (Strike 1DY) which reported three hits and the target ship being left in a sinking condition. She was most likely attacked by other air groups also but SB2Cs from BUNKER HILL (Strike 3E) in the afternoon scored 1–2 hits with 1,000-lb bombs and started fires aboard. The pilots reported the ship had been previously damaged and was left in a heavily damaged condition. The RIO DE JANEIRO MARU sank overnight and was not visible during the attacks on the second day.

TECHNICAL SUMMARY:

Type: Transport (Re-converted September 1943)
　　　　Submarine Tender (Converted 1940)
　　　　Passenger Ship (Original)
Configuration Sequence: M–K–K–F–M–K
Gross Tonnage: 9,626 tons
Dimensions: 461/62/26 feet
Machinery: Two 6-cylinder 2-stroke diesel engines, twin screws, 1503 NHP.
Radius: Unknown
Complement: 150 (crew), 1140 (passengers)
Built: 1930 by Mitsubishi Zosensho, Nagasaki
Owner: Osaka Shosen Kaisha
Remarks: Eight decks, refrigeration machinery, cruiser stern.

The SAN FRANCISCO MARU

–National Archives Photo

The SAN FRANCISCO MARU – 1937.

A wreck located in 1973 during a fathometer search was tentatively identified as the SAN FRANCISCO MARU; since then, divers have found the ship's bell with the name on it, thus confirming its identity.

The wreck is located upright on a 240-foot bottom between the MOMOKAWA and the HOKUYO MARUs in the Eten Anchorage. Locally nicknamed the "Million Dollar Wreck" by some people referring to the worth of the ship's completely loaded cargo of war materials, the SAN FRANCISCO MARU is considered by many divers as the most exciting wreck in the Truk Lagoon.

Exploration of this deep wreck usually begins with the foreship as it is shallower than the aftship and the diving guides are quite adept at catching their anchor on the forward mast. The mast is usually the first part of the wreck visible as its top lies at a depth of 95 feet. The outline of the wreck's superstructure becomes visible as divers descend to a depth of about 90 feet. Forward of the bridge on the foredeck opposite the No. 2 hold are two medium-type armored tanks (believed to be Model 97s) with a large truck inboard on the starboard side and a single tank of the same type resting on the port side at a depth of close to 165 feet. One tank on the starboard side is partially on top of and leaning against the other. The truck's fenders and body panels have collapsed leaving only the frame, the engine, and the tires (dual wheels in the back) intact. The single tank on the port side is positioned at an angle on the deck with its left front tread overhanging the side of the ship. An excursion off to the side of the ship on the port will confirm the existence of a steamroller which now lies on its side on the seabed. There are reports of another truck being found along the bottom on the port side further aft; its possible that it had been carried on deck with the single tank and steamroller. These vehicles have either been blown overboard by heavy bomb explosions nearby or they fell when the ship was sinking. Its quite possible the ship hit the bottom at an angle either bow or stern first followed by the remainder of the ship which slammed against the seabed. Both explanations are possible and explain the vehicles having been tossed about. Two large trucks can be seen under the hatch cover beams in the No. 2 hold. They have large cylindrical tanks mounted on their beds. Oil or gasoline drums and what appears to be aircraft bombs are stored with these two trucks.

The No. 1 hold is filled nearly to its top with rows of stacked hemispherical beach-type mines and boxes of detonators. Some of the boxes alongside the mines appear to contain extra "horns" that are inserted in the mines and which cause it to detonate on contact. The bow gun mounted on a platform was pointing to the port and appeared to be one of the 3-inch types. A large amount of sponge and coral growth covered the length of the gun.

The bridge can be entered through the top as the outer roof and wall structures have been destroyed by fire, leaving only open spaces between the support beams. There is a single ship's telegraph in place in the wheelhouse. A second telegraph, reported to be hanging over the front of the bridge by its cables, was probably mounted in the awning deck above the wheelhouse. Towards the back of the wheelhouse, there are two large compasses, some binoculars, and some of the ever-present beer bottles. Broken china and medicine bottles were spotted one deck below; not much time was allocated to searching here due to the depth and potentially dangerous hanging wires and structures. There is supposed to be a speed-measuring device in the bridge consisting of a bronze machined instrument which produced a graphic paper display from information being fed to it by a device which is trailed in the water behind the ship. Its presence could not be confirmed.

The ship suffered bomb damage amidships. The smokestack is crushed and has fallen forward. It lies overhanging the small midship access hold. Two tall air funnels are still mounted between the split superstructure amidships but their scoop-shaped tops are missing. Below, there are rows of engine hatches on each side of the raised superstructure over the engine room with most of the hatch covers open. Rooms aft of the stack one deck below served as the crew's mess; china serving platters, rice dishes, cups, and bottles are strewn about in the muck.

The first of the aft holds contains rows of stacked torpedo bodies. Some individual torpedoes are lying askew possibly because their high pressure air tanks have exploded. The rear hold is filled to its top with depth charges. The deck plating opposite the rear of the hold on both sides of the ship has been ripped apart and the hull plates split. This bomb damage must have been responsible for the sinking of the ship.

The earliest mention of the SAN FRANCISCO MARU in intercepted Japanese message traffic intelligence files was a damage report stating the ship had received minor damage from attacking aircraft at Wewak, New Guinea on 4 May 1943. Prisoner interrogations confirmed that the ship had arrived in Truk on February 5, 1944 and that she had remained there when the rest of her convoy sailed again on 12 February. Action photos taken on 16 February show the ship lying in the anchorage southeast of Dublon Island with fire and smoke rising amidships. The SAN FRANCISCO MARU is believed to have been attacked by several air groups including those from YORKTOWN (Strike 1DY, 16 Feb.), BUNKER HILL (Strike 3E, 16 Feb.), and ESSEX (Strikes 2A on 16 Feb. and 2A, 2B on 17 Feb.). It appears that the ship sank after being hit by six 500-lb bombs dropped by TBFs from ESSEX on Strike 2B on the 17th. Following this attack, she was reported to be burning furiously and sinking stern first.

TECHNICAL SUMMARY:

Other Name: SAN FURANSHISUKO (Japanese interpretation).
Type: Passenger-Cargo
Configuration Sequence: M–K–F–M
Gross Tonnage: 5,831 tons
Dimensions: 385/51/27 feet
Machinery: Reciprocating, single screw, 440 NHP.
Radius: 13,000 miles at 10 knots.
Complement: 40 (crew), 2 (passengers)
Built: 1919 by Kawasaki Dockyard Co., Ltd., Kobe
Owner: Yamashita Kisen Kaisha

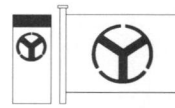

Remarks: Attached to the Yokosuka Navy Transportation Department. Two decks plus an awning deck (steel).

The SANKISAN MARU

On February 16th, four SB2Cs on Strike 3D from BUNKER HILL's VB-17 picked out shipping targets one-by-one along the western shore of Uman Island. The SANKISAN MARU was the second ship attacked in the anchorage following the AMAGISAN MARU. The ship was hit forward by a 1,000-lb bomb at this time and was strafed by the VF-18 fighter escorts. The BUNKER HILL planes returned to the same anchorage on the first strike (3A) of the 17th. The ship was the intended target again of five more SB2Cs which reported a single direct hit amidships. It is not known which air group made the bomb or torpedo hit which caused the entire stern section and midship superstructure to completely blow up. The deck and side plates of the hull are blown back to the sides to such an extent that it is probable that ordnance stored in the aft hold exploded after the ship was hit.

The nickname given to the SANKISAN MARU long before her

–National Archives Photo

Photo shows ships anchored on the west side of Uman Island. SANKISAN MARU has just taken a torpedo hit amidships on the starboard side opposite the mid-ship superstructure. A second torpedo can be seen heading through the water towards the ship; this was probably the torpedo that demolished the ship's stern. Smoke from Eten Island and ships on fire in the Eten Anchorage can be seen in the background.

identity was known was the "Uman One-mast Wreck," referring to her location only 500 yards from shore on the west side of Uman Island and its having a single foremast that stuck out above 12 feet above the water.

The bow of the ship is relatively undamaged. This area, like most of the foreship has a large amount of off-white-colored soft coral growth everywhere. The port anchor chain is stretched outward. The name of the ship is located on the hull here, but it will take a lot of scraping and cleaning to see it again.

Two heavily damaged trucks lie on the port side of the deck above the forward hold at the 50-foot level amongst scattered debris. Only the frames and tires remain. For 15-plus years, a large anemone with several resident clown fish was nestled in the top of one of the truck tires. It only recently was reported to have died. The No. 1 hold contains rifle and machine gun ammunition, grenades, and artillery shells. At one time, there were rows of depth charges stored here with a large tarp thrown over them. More munitions and boxes of 12-inch-long depth charge detonators were stacked on top of the depth charges. The No. 2 and No. 3 holds interconnect and contain two trucks on the upper levels and airplane engines, cowlings, propeller blades, and canned goods on the bottom level.

In 1974, the depth charges in the forward hold were removed and a large bomb lying on the bottom opposite the stern of the wreck were detonated. The operation was performed under the direction of Steve Aiken, the very knowledgeable and capable Public Works Demolition Engineer for the Trust Territory. The dangerous cargo needed to be removed to make the wreck safe for sport divers. A large LCU with a crane was used to lift the depth charges from the hold and they were stored temporarily on an LCM before being transferred to a specific underwater storage area. This undertaking was completed with the removal of 284 depth charges and several rounds of 4.7-inch artillery shells. These explosives were later used to blast small boat channels in the coral and to blast several coral head projections which posed a hazard for boats.

The SANKISAN MARU has an interesting history. Originally built as a 4,776-ton cargo ship in 1920 for D.D. Todd Construction Company in Tacoma Washington, she was named the RED HOOK. Between 1920 and 1942, she went through several name changes from RED HOOK to COMMERCIAL TRAVELER to NELSON TRAVELER to POINT ESTERO to finally ESTERO in 1939 before she was captured by the Japanese in 1942. At his time the Japanese renamed her the SANKISAN MARU, but she is identified also as the YAMAKISAN MARU on various Japanese inventory lists.

Much of the beautiful coral growth I had witnessed in the first few years of diving the wreck of the SANKISAN MARU had withered and died for a period lasting several years following the removal of the hazardous explosive devices aboard. This might have been due to the picric acid being released from the depth charges when they were removed. In the last few years, the marine growth has made a comeback, but the numerous trucks have deteriorated to the point where the ones on deck are almost unrecognizable and the ones in the holds have had their cabs and hoods crumble to the floor. The SANKISAN MARU has much to see and exploration is still very interesting, but she is not the beautiful wreck I remember.

TECHNICAL SUMMARY:

Other Names: YAMAKISAN MARU (Internal to Japan)
ESTERO (1939)
POINT ESTERO
NELSON TRAVELER
COMMERCIAL TRAVELER
RED HOOK (Original)
Type: Cargo
Gross Tonnage: 4,752
Dimensions: 380.3/53.1/27 feet
Machinery: Reciprocating engines, single screw, 472 NHP.
Radius: Unknown
Complement: Unknown
Built: 1920 by D.D. Todd & Construction Corp. in Tacoma, Washington.
Owner: Japanese – Yamashita Kisen K.K.
Original – Erie Basin Towing & Hoisting Co., New York.
Remarks: Two decks. Ship was captured by Japanese.

The SAPPORO MARU

The SAPPORO MARU was a 400-ton fishing trawler requisitioned from the merchant fleet by the Japanese Navy and converted to a submarine chaser. She was damaged by U.S. carrier aircraft during the fast carrier strikes on April 29–30, 1944 and reported sunk on May 4th. She went down north of Fefan Island and just southwest of the KIYOSUMI MARU; the wreck was buoyed for years following. The SAPPORO MARU is one of the few wrecks not located in recent years.

TECHNICAL SUMMARY:

Type: Sub-Chaser (Converted), ex-Fishing Trawler

Configuration Sequence: Unknown
Dimensions: 145/24/14 feet
Gross Tonnage: 400 tons
Machinery: Oil engines
Radius: Unknown
Complement: Unknown
Built: 1930 by Mitsubishi Zosen Kaisha, Ltd., Hiroshima
Owner: Nippon Suisan K.K.
Remarks: Port of Registry was Tobata. Vessel was used as a refrigerated fish carrier.

The SEIKO MARU

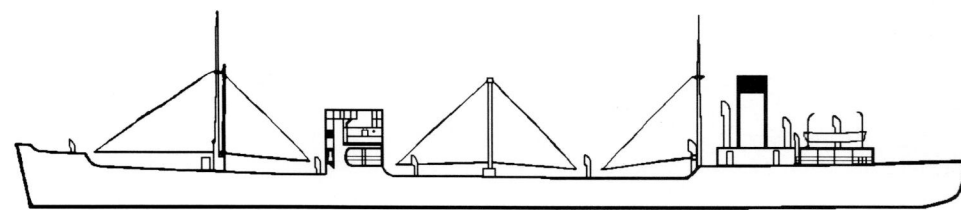

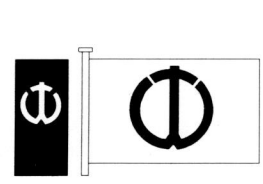

DAIREN KISEN K.K.

During the afternoon of July 31, 1943, U.S. Submarine POGY sighted a convoy consisting of a "KAMOGAWA MARU (6,641-ton) class XCVS with an XCVS of the KINUGASA MARU (8,407-ton) or KANSAI MARU (8,614-ton) class, a TAISHO MARU (4,816-ton) type freighter, and a small DD or PC escort, proceeding on course 155 degrees at nine knots." Intelligence reports later helped piece the identities of the ships in the convoy and it is now believed to have consisted of one (unidentified) XCVS, the 7,497-ton XAPV MOGAMIGAWA MARU, the 5,385-ton SEIKO MARU, and the patrol frigate FUKAI. MOGAMIGAWA MARU (436 feet long) is generally similar in appearance to both KINUGASA and KANSAI MARUs mentioned by POGY, although she has a counter stern while the other ships have cruiser sterns. The MOGAMIGAWA MARU is a sister ship to the FUJIKAWA MARU; and the SEIKO MARU is a sister ship to the TAISHO MARU. After night fell, POGY made a surface approach and then proceeded to make a periscope attack on the ships in the convoy. The following are excerpts from submarine attack reports:

"At 2302 h/31 July, in position 11°16'N, 153°34'E, POGY fired 4 torpedoes from 2,400 yards range at the largest ship in the convoy, the KINUGASA or KANSAI MARU class vessel, which was described as being about 460 feet long. The night was clear with the stars out, but with no moon, making for questionable visibility up to 14,000 yards. POGY went deep to evade the escort, but heard two hits and heard target's screws stop. While being depth charged by the escorts, POGY heard two series of sharp explosions followed by loud rumblings which lasted over ten minutes and which sounded like an earthquake. These were terminated by a loud but dull, heavy explosion as the target presumably blew up and sank.

At 0050 h, POGY rose to periscope depth and saw the escort lying about 4,000 yards astern, apparently picking up survivors. No other ships were in sight. POGY therefore went deep and cleared the area.

In response to a contact report from POGY, U.S.S. STEELHEAD, who was also in the area, changed course to intercept the convoy. Just as dawn was breaking, STEELHEAD sighted an engines-aft freighter of the TAISHO MARU class, freshly painted gray with buff goal posts and white masts, accompanied by a sub-chaser. The AK was dead in the water and smoking heavily, apparently either damaged or picking up survivors in position seven miles bearing 330 degrees from the scene of POGY's attack. At 0504 h, the freighter got under way on course 240 degrees.

At 0507 h, in position 11°20'N, 153°30'E, STEELHEAD fired four torpedoes at the AK from 1,500 yards. As STEELHEAD went deep immediately after firing, she heard two explosions timed as corresponding to hits from her second and third torpedoes. The sub-chaser then delivered a depth-charge attack, during which STEELHEAD heard her target's screws stop. At 0550 h, loud crackling and crunching noises were heard in the direction of the target. These noises terminated at 0602 h. At 0815 h, STEELHEAD surfaced and saw nothing, but she heard depth charges going off until late that afternoon, which indicated that the escort had remained in the area and that the target had sunk."

Coded message intercepts later confirmed that the MOGAMIGAWA MARU was sunk at 2310 h on 31 July in position 11°08'N, 153°16'E. A diary found at Kwajalein had the following entry for July 31, 1943: "The radio message came through that the MOGAMIGAWA MARU had been sunk off Truk by an enemy submarine. It had left Yokosuka on 24 July." The SEIKO MARU was torpedoed at 0610 h in position 11°08'N, 153°18'E; she was later reported at 1113 h to be still afloat but in grave danger of sinking. Based on the non-appearance of references to the SEIKO MARU in message traffic following the attack by STEELHEAD, the ship was assessed the status of "known sunk."

Enterprise SBDs (Strike 1BE on February 16th) were the first to attack the SEIKO MARU, hitting the ship on both sides of the stern. Following large explosions which reportedly blew out the sides, the ship was observed to settle immediately. The ship was described as a "large AO" probably due to her aft-engine configuration, standard for tankers. An AO, described as approximately 10,000 tons, 450 feet long, and painted grey in color, was bombed by ESSEX torpedo planes on Strike 2A later the same day. It was reported to be lying about 3/4 of a mile bearing 150 degrees from the southern tip of Eten Island. The ship was reported to have been hit by a 500-lb bomb aft of amidships. This is ship number 6 shown in the "ESSEX SHIPPING TARGET SUMMARY." The ship is the SEIKO MARU; again, she was mis-identified as an oiler. The observation by attacking plane pilots and crews that the ship was painted grey with white masts corresponds with those made by STEELHEAD when she torpedoed the SEIKO MARU. A VB pilot from BUNKER HILL (Strike 3B) dropped two bombs which missed on an AO "lying south of Eten" on the second day of the raids and one large AO was observed southeast of Dublon Island in photos taken by BUNKER HILL's photo-reconnaissance plane at the same time: this again appears to describe the SEIKO MARU as no actual tanker was visible in photographs taken in this area and none are known to be sunk there. The SEIKO MARU was apparently still afloat when the air operations ended mid-day on the 17th.

JANAC had to re-evaluate the status of the SEIKO MARU following the interception of two dispatches from CinC 4th Fleet at Truk on February 17–18 stating that she had been sunk during the U.S.

–Photo Courtesy of the Truk Continental Hotel
The SEIKO MARU (center of photo) is on fire and sinking stern first. Two attacking planes can be seen overhead. Large vessel to the right is the HOKUYO MARU.

air raids of February 16–17; she was also deleted from the Japanese merchant marine records in a list published by the Naval General Staff on March 13, 1944. The revised assessment was changed to "heavily damaged by STEELHEAD's attack and sunk by aircraft on February 16–17, 1944."

It is not known whether the SEIKO MARU had been restored to operating condition during the six and one-half months intervening between STEELHEAD's attack and the air strikes. No evidence is available showing she made any passages during that period. The SEIKO MARU was not positioned in the repair anchorage west of Dublon Island where the damaged ships HOYO MARU, KIYOSUMI MARU, KENSHO MARU, TONAN MARU NO. 3 YAMAGIRI MARU, and FUMITSUKI were anchored. The SEIKO MARU does seem to be anchored in the exact spot where she was sunk in photographs taken during the overflight of Truk on 4 February 1944. She is listed as ship No. 42 in the Photographic Intelligence Summary covering that overflight on page no. 83.

The SEIKO MARU was found during a fathometer search in the Eten Anchorage in 1973. She lies upright with her bow pointing south in 160 feet of water approximately 800 to 1,000 yards due east of the northern tip of Eten.

When I first dove on the wreck, it was a calm, sunny day and the top of the foremast could be seen from the surface about 30 feet down. After entering the water, we swam down past the cross-tree-type mast carefully skirting the large amount of rigging still hanging from its coral-encrusted top; the rigging is probably weakened and should be considered dangerous. We descended to the top of the bridge at 100 feet where there is a rudder stand and two ship's telegraphs mounted where there had been a flying bridge. The rudder stand was almost unrecognizable as it is covered with a multi-colored layer of marine growth making it an interesting photographic subject. An AA gun was placed here at one time but now all that remains is its mount. Wanting to explore the inner cabins below decks, we swam over to the side of the wreck and found a doorway leading to the first deck below. Inside, there are interesting items lying about everywhere in the thin layer of muck including shoes, uniforms, buttons, bottles, and a large ship's compass built into a carrying case with its needle still pointing towards the north. An open access through the floor invited exploration below and we swam down to the second deck level at 120 feet. A cabinet built into the wall contains several pieces of china of various types; the house flag symbol of the ship's owner, Dairen Kisen Kaisha, was on several of them. Small rooms to the side contained the standard latrine and bathtub. Racks of radio equipment and wiring can be found in the compartment along the starboard side along with more china lying in the muck. A blowtorch is mounted to the remains of a shelf or wall panel. This room like the deck above had been gutted by fire.

Little coral growth exists in the bridge area except for some soft coral trees growing in entrance doorways. While swimming above the main deck and forward holds toward the bow, we could see no indication of cargo below and exploration of the holds was not attempted because of the depth. At a depth of 120 feet on the bow, we found that instead of the usual deck gun and platform, the Japanese had substituted a field artillery piece. It is standing on wooden spoke wheels, one of which has collapsed. The muzzle of the gun is fitted into a slot on the bow railing. There is a lot of coral growth in this area covering most of the bow and forecastle.

On later dives, I was able to explore the aft section of the wreck. The deep hold aft of the bridge is empty of cargo. A large kingpost is positioned between this hold and the single level hold No. 4. The aft hold (No. 5) is elevated to main deck level and has its hatch cover beams in place. It appears empty also. A second huge mast is located between the aft hold and the boatdeck. The funnel still stands upright; no stack markings of the owner are visible. Two large air ventilators are positioned forward of the funnel and four more are located above the engine room and deck house. Spare propeller blades are strapped against the deck house superstructure. The raised deck plating along the port side is caved in and a jagged hole can be seen in the hull plates below. This damage is the result of the bomb or bombs which were responsible for sinking the ship.

The bell has been taken from the wreck and can be seen at the Fisheries building in downtown Moen. The name "SEIKO MARU" and date, 1940, are etched on one side while the name of the owner, "Dairen," is on the other.

TECHNICAL SUMMARY:

Type: Cargo
Configuration Sequence: M–K–M–F
Gross Tonnage: 5,385 tons
Dimensions: 392.5/53/30 feet
Machinery: Aft engines, single screw, 2 DR geared steam turbines made by Ishikawajima SB & Eng.Co., Tokyo.
Radius: 4,900 miles at 12 knots.
Complement: Unknown
Built: 1940 by Harima Zosensho K.K., Aioi
Owner: Dairen Kisen K.K.
Remarks: Employed for civilian cargo duties. One deck, suitable for heavy lift cargo.

The SHINKOKU MARU

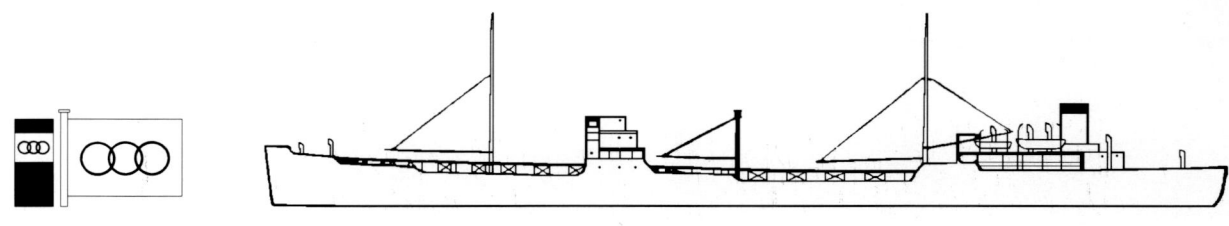

KOBE SANBASHI K.K.

Built as a commercial tanker for Kobe Sanbashi K.K. (the Kobe Pier Co., Ltd.) in 1940, the 10,020-ton SHINKOKU MARU was requisitioned by the Japanese Navy as a naval tanker in 1941 and assigned to the Combined Fleet. In May-June 1942, she was one of five oilers comprising a supply unit supporting the Carrier Striking Force (First Mobile Force) in the Japanese offensive against Midway Island in which the Japanese carriers AKAGI, KAGA, HIRYU, and SORYU were sunk in the Battle of Midway. On 17 August 1942, she was torpedoed by a U.S. submarine at a position 7°40'N, 151°05'E. She received only minor damage at that time and was repaired shortly thereafter. She was the target of another submarine, possibly PETO, on 7 July 1943 at a position 00°37'N, 148°06'E. ULTRA information provided U.S. intelligence with the following dispatches:

"From supervisor of SHINKOKU MARU. We find that fuel oil tank No. 2 (1,400 tons light oil) was flooded in the torpedo attack of the 7th."

"In order to speedily repair torpedo damage (slight damage to forward oil tank) to the SHINKOKU MARU under this command it is required that she dock within the period approximately 20–23 July at Soerabaya (eastern Java) or Singapore. Advise regarding convenience."

The ship was repaired at Singapore and was again operational after 15 August 1943.

The SHINKOKU MARU arrived at Truk prior to the carrier strikes on 14 February. It seems probable that she was one of the oilers along with the FUJISAN MARU reported by pilots to be underway on 16 February either west of Moen Island, in the northern part of the lagoon, or even the one spotted outside of North and Northeast passes. It appears that the SHINKOKU MARU was anchored northwest of Fefan Island after mid-day on the 16th and was the AO that received a bomb hit amidships by YORKTOWN SBDs (Strike 1EY). BUNKER HILL VT planes (Strike 3A) made six torpedo drops on the SHINKOKU MARU described as being anchored east of Eot Island following the attack which sunk the HANAKAWA MARU near Tol Island at about 0700 on the morning of the 17th. All torpedoes missed. TBFs from another unknown air group were responsible for sinking the ship in a torpedo attack later in the day.

The ship's masts protruded from the water after the vessel was sunk. Some time later, the top portions were blown off with explosives because of their possible hazard to shipping and the once highly visible wreck was lost and ignored for many years. She was most recently rediscovered in December 1971 during a diver search. Her identity was established shortly thereafter when the ship's bell with the name engraved on it was found.

One dive is definitely not enough to experience the wreck of the SHINKOKU MARU. The most important areas to see are the superstructure with the bridge and cabin areas below decks located forward and the aftship. These two areas are separated by 150 to 175 feet; when considering that the ship is 500 feet long, there is a lot of territory to explore even in several dives. If divers are limited to two dives or a single day on the wreck, it is best to begin the first dive with the deeper aft section. While descending to the wreck below, it is interesting to look about at the varied fish life. Many small fish make the wreck their home and this draws the larger fish such as rainbow runners, tunas, groupers, and sharks. The huge smokestack is covered with prolific marine growth; there are many colors and types of soft corals, gorgonians, and sponges. The aft cabin areas are at a depth of 100-plus feet. These were crew's quarters which are built above and to the sides of the engine room. At deck level, there are port and starboard entrances. The port entrance opens up to a large room where remains of several of the ship's crew can be found. Although the muck is rather deep here, some interesting artifacts have been found by searching underneath including a sword and scabbard. The starboard entrance leads to a large corridor with small rooms off to the sides. These were supply storage rooms and in some, small boxes and containers can be

Bronze trim wheel control in wheelhouse of SHINKOKU MARU was used for maneuvering. Wheel has since been removed from the wreck. The center hub of the ship's wheel is visible at left (top).

Polyps of a type of tube coral grows on a stalk of "whip" or "jeweler's coral" (SHINKOKU MARU).

Red soft coral – Dendronepthya species (SHINKOKU MARU).

seen half-covered with muck. Doorways aft of these cabin areas lead to a catwalk landing with the engines below. On the port side, a gaping torpedo hole can be seen; this was responsible for sinking the ship. It is possible to exit through the open skylights above. Once when my dive partner and I did this, we noticed another diver from our group beckoning to us to come to him. We swam rapidly down the the stern deck where we found a huge grouper making passes at the divers there. This great fish was nearly six feet long and probably weighed 300 pounds. He had a startling array of teeth which he showed constantly through his widely-opened mouth. He was not awed at all by the first two divers, but four seemed to be too much for him. After we tried successfully to surround him to take pictures, he decided finally that it was time to retreat.

Aft of the cabins and stack, there is a huge triad kingpost which was used in loading oil aboard the ship. It is heavily covered with growth also. A large deck gun, which is almost unrecognizable due to the marine growth on it, is mounted on the stern.

The dive guides often attach their anchor to the kingpost amidships. After entering the water from this location, the bridge of the ship forward is easy to see. The smooth lines of the superstructure are hidden behind the massive marine growth. The depth to the deck level where the lower cabin structure begins is about 80 feet. The cabins can be entered through rear entrances easily. A few feet inside is a cart with tea cups, rice dishes, saucers, and many bottles of various types and descriptions stacked up on its top. A few minutes of searching through the deep muck on my first visit to the wreck produced three large china pots still in their packing boxes, some small saki cups, and more china saucers and cups. These have almost all disappeared over the years. The forward side of the room evidently served as a pharmacy and sick bay. Scattered about the floor are medicine bottles of all shapes, sizes, and colors. An unusual find was a large stack of records. On the port side, an operating table is set up and drawers nearby contained medicines, more bottles, and syringes. Small rooms with partitions now missing contain a bathtub and urinals. It is possible to swim through the ceiling access to the deck level above. Here, a decorative lamp hangs from the ceiling, and to one side is a large generator. Once partitioned cubicles here served as officer's quarters. Small objects found protruding from the muck include many personal effects, porcelain bowls, a typewriter, and a dial telephone. Some uniforms were lying in a pile with the four-stripe insignia of a captain on them. There is another room with a bathtub and latrine. A large box in one corner of the room contained several hundred coins; these were made of what appeared to be aluminum and were later identified as Sen, valued at 1/100 of a Yen.

The next level above is the wheelhouse. The outer structure has a collection of soft tree corals of almost every imaginable color; sponges, gorgonians, and "zig-zag clams" are everywhere. Divers are almost forced to push the soft coral growth aside to enter the wheelhouse. Care should be taken to avoid the delicate, almost transparent hydroids in some places. These can cause painful stings. Inside, the helm (with only the wheel hub remaining), two ship's telegraphs, the ship's compass, and the bridge-to-engine room voice tubes are intact with beautifully colored sponge growth covering them. There was a bronze trim wheel at one time, but someone has pilfered it. The floor of the wheelhouse has only a shallow layer of muck and debris; there are interesting items visible everywhere including a clock, two lanterns with blue glass, and several light fixtures. Photography can be difficult at times due to the clustered groups of small fish known as opal sweepers. You must shoo them away from anything you want to take a picture of. A flying bridge had once been built to starboard of the main wheelhouse. The wooden structure is now gone and another single telegraph is mounted on the deck.

If time permits, it is worthwhile to swim forward traversing over hatches and catwalks past the forecastle to the bow. There is a rather small 3-inch deck gun mounted on a small platform with heavy coral growth all around. Several boxes of artillery shells lie on the platform behind the gun. A special dive over the bow alongside the encrusted hull to the seabed at 120 feet can be very interesting. At times, large grey sharks congregate in the area and it is their habit to circle almost continuously from in and out of the bluish gloom when divers are present. These heavy-body sharks make great photographic subjects.

TECHNICAL SUMMARY:

Other Name: SINKOKU (Kokutai spelling)
Type: Naval Tanker (1941)
Configuration Sequence: M–K–M–F–K
Gross Tonnage: 10,020 tons
Dimensions: 500/65/29.5 feet
Machinery: Eight cylinder, double action oil engines.
Radius: 18,500 miles at 15 knots
Complement: Unknown
Built: 1940 by Kawasaki Jyuko Co., Kobe
Owner: Kobe Sanbashi K.K.
Remarks: Cruiser stern, one deck. Oil carrying capacity 93,000 bbls (42 gallon-type).

SPECIAL SUBCHASERs NOs. 38, 46, And 66

A Japanese dispatch was intercepted following the air raids of 29–30 April which reported sinking losses including SPECIAL SUBCHASER NO. 38 (CHA 38). It was reported lost on 30 April while towing a large landing boat south of Truk Atoll. The landing boat also sunk. This is most likely the "140-foot sub-chaser towing an empty barge toward Kuop Islands" described in the action reports. She was set afire by a thorough strafing attack by LANGLEY planes and was smoking heavily at a location "bearing 240 degrees true 10 miles from Kuop Islands." The pilots of subsequent strikes were unable to locate either the boat or the barge. The reported sinking location was 7°22'N, 151°45'E.

On April 5, 1944, two Navy B-24s flew a special reconnaissance mission over Moen Island and claimed to have sunk a destroyer in a bombing attack. The true identity of this vessel became known when a decoded dispatch stated that one B-24 attacked CHA 46 and destroyed her on April 5, 1944. Reference to the vessel appeared in messages one more time when her assignment to the Maizuru Naval District was cancelled. The reported sinking location of 7°26'N, 151°52'E indicates that she was lost just east of Moen Island. She appears to be one of the few wrecks not yet found at Truk.

The Dublon Island boat basin was bombed by eleven B-29 bombers of the 20th Air Force on August 7, 1945 while on a training mission. An intercepted radio message confirmed that CHA 66 was sunk by eleven B-29s on that date. The wreck of this vessel had not been identified by any known source and has probably never been found. Her sinking location was reported as 7°23'N, 151°53'E.

TECHNICAL SUMMARY:

Other Names: CHA 38, CHA 46, CHA 66
Type: Auxiliary Submarine Chaser (No. 1 Class)
Displacement: 130 tons
Dimensions: 85.3/18.3/6.5 feet
Machinery: 1-shaft geared diesel, 400 SHP.
Speed: 11 knots
Radius: 1,000 miles at 10 knots.
Complement: 23
Armament: One 7.7mm machine gun, one 25mm AA gun; 18–22 depth charges.
Built: 1943 onwards. A total of 200 auxiliary submarine chasers of this class were built by shipyards specializing in fishing vessels. It is not known at which shipyards the individual vessels were built. The following is a list of the shipyards and number of vessels of this class built in each:

Fukuoka Shipbuilding Iron Works, Fukuoka	(10)
Fukushima Shipbuilding Co., Matsue	(13)
Funaya Shipbuilding Co., Hakodate	(7)
Goriki Shipbuilding Co., Ujiyamada	(12)
Hayashikawa Heavy Industrial Co., Shimonoseki	(20)
Ichikawa Shipbuilding Co., Shizuoka	(16)
Jinen Shipbuilding Iron Works, Moji	(12)
Koyanagi Shipbuilding Co., Shizuoka	(12)
Miho Shipbuilding Co., Shimuzu	(13)
Murakami Shipbuilding Co., Ishinomaki	(8)
Nishii Shipbuilding Co., Ujiyamada	(13)
Saga Shipbuilding Iron Works, Takaoka	(18)
Shikoku Dock Industrial Co., Takamatsu	(20)
Tokushima Shipbuilding Co., Tokushima	(3)
Yamanishi Shipbuilding Iron Works, Ishinomaki	(17)
Marinewerft, Yokosuka	(1)
Yonago Shipbuilding Co., Yonago	(6)

The TACHIKAZE

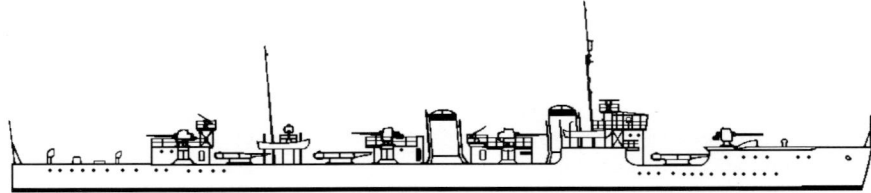

The destroyer TACHIKAZE was unintentionally grounded near the center of the southwestern reef of the Kuop Atoll just to the south of Truk on February 4, 1944 while apparently approaching on a course leading towards the South Pass entrance to the Truk Lagoon. The ship was hard aground and rescue vessels were unable to pull the DD free prior to the U.S. carrier strikes 12 days later. On the first day of the attacks, air groups from the Task Force came under medium to heavy AA fire from the DD while approaching or withdrawing from the south to and from their assigned target areas. BUNKER HILL planes initially mis-identified the ship as a TERATSUKI class DD. The TACHIKAZE was strafed by INTREPID and ESSEX FIGHTERS (Strike 2E); the ESSEX F6F pilots reported major damage to the grounded ship and attacked a picket boat and a small AK nearby. She was correctly identified later in the day as an "old DD of the MINEKAZE class" by COWPENS VF. Good photographs show the DD grounded bow-first straight on to the reef with a Daihatsu-type launch tied along her port side.

The grounded DD was finally assigned as a primary objective on the second day. She was the main target of ENTERPRISE VB planes on Strike 1BE. The ship was struck by three bombs which rocked the vessel enough to make it shift and slide off the reef into deeper water. U.S. intelligence learned the destroyer's identity following the interception of a dispatch which listed her position and reported heavy casualties from the bombing attacks and sinking.

Some attempts have been made to locate the wreck of the Tachikaze with negative results. She may have slid off the reef into very deep water.

The TACHIKAZE was one of 15 units of her class built between 1918 and 1922. Many of the units underwent conversions to other roles including minesweepers, patrol vessels, aircraft rescue ships, and one, the NAMIKAZE, was fitted out as a Kaiten-carrier. (Kaitens were 1- or 2-man midget submarines.) The destroyer was attached to the Combined Fleet; its main task was to perform convoy escort duty between Rabaul and Truk.

TECHNICAL SUMMARY:

Other Name: TATIKAZE (Kokutai spelling)
Type: MINEKAZE Class Destroyer
Displacement: 1,345 tons
Dimensions: 336.5/29.7/9.5 feet
Machinery: 2-shaft geared turbines, 4 Kampon boilers, 38,500 SHP.
Radius: 3,600 miles at 14 knots, 900 miles at 34 knots.
Speed: 36 knots (max)
Complement: 148
Armament: Two 4.7-inch guns, ten 25mm AA guns, two 7.7 mm guns; 2 torpedo tubes; 4 depth charge throwers, 36 depth charges.
Built: 1921 by Maizuru Kaigun Kosho, Maizuru

The TAIHO MARU

Attempts at locating this wreck following its initial discovery in 1973 had all ended in failure until a group of See & Sea Travel divers being led by the author found the wreck in May 1978. We were traversing through rough seas between Fefan and the west side of Uman Island when an overpowering skunk-like smell of oil was encountered. After several attempts at dragging an anchor, the wreck was snagged and all divers eagerly dove to investigate the new find.

The anchor had caught on the rudder of the wreck which was lying on its port side on a 140-foot bottom. Growth on the hull near the stern was not too heavy and certain letters of the ship's name were readable. Two letters (an "A" and an "H"), separated by a third unreadable letter, could be made out in the first part of the name. The "A" in the suffix MARU letters could also be seen. We swam along the upside of the vessel noting two holds with a mast in between that were filled with 50-gallon-sized barrels of oil or gasoline. Many of the barrels were spilled out on the floor of the lagoon. There was nothing but twisted and ripped metal beyond the forward hold; the midship structure and entire foreship were gone. Two divers swam nearly a hundred yards beyond looking for the foreship but it was not in the vicinity. The oil or gasoline carried on the ship can be dangerous to divers. Upon returning to the surface, I found that I had received a burn on my leg. One of the other divers had three or four quarter-sized burns also. It took nearly a month for my burn to heal even though treated daily.

The size of the vessel and the letters of the name visible on the hull indicated that the wreck may be that of the 2,827-ton TAIHO MARU. With the wreck showing evidence of having been blown apart by an explosion, it is possible that the TAIHO MARU was the ship reported west of Uman Island that was bombed, hit, and seen to explode at 1205 h by YORKTOWN SBDs (Strike 1DY, 16 Feb.). The ship was hit twice, once on the bow and once amidships; the explosion was reported to erupt amidships which corresponds exactly with the shipwreck described above.

The TAIHO MARU was one of 25 ships built as part of the Standard Type 1C Japanese War Standard Construction Program. These vessels were all 2,700-ton class cargo steamers.

TECHNICAL SUMMARY:

Type: Cargo
Configuration Sequence: M–F–M
Gross Tonnage: 2,827 tons
Dimensions: 321.4/44.9/20.8 feet
Machinery: Vertical triple expansion engine, single screw, 1,800 iHP.
Radius: 5,800 miles at 11 knots.
Complement: Unknown
Built: 1943 by Hitachi Jyuko K.K.
Owner: Osaka Shosen Kaisha

The TAIJUN MARU

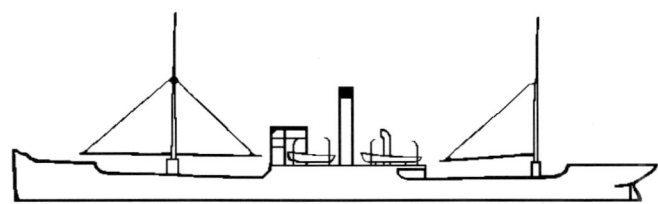

Little is known about this vessel except that it was reported by several references as being lost at Truk due to fires aboard on 11 April 1942. The wreck has not been found and identified to date.

TECHNICAL SUMMARY:

Other Name: TAIZYUN (Kokutai)
Type: Cargo
Configuration Sequence: M–F–M
Gross Tonnage: 1,274 (1,281 ?) tons

Dimensions: 228/33/18.7 feet
Machinery: Reciprocating engines, single screw, 88 NHP.
Radius: 1,550 miles at 7 knots.
Built: 1918 by Uchida Sanbashi & Co., Ltd., Yokohama
Owner: Hatiuma Kisen K.K.
Settu Shosen K.K. (Previous)
Remarks: One deck. Ship was also reported as sunk at at 6°49'S, 147°02' E by Army aircraft.

The TAIKICHI MARU

Monograph 116, The Imperial Japanese Navy in World War II, lists the 1,891-ton cargo vessel TAIKICHI MARU as being sunk by U.S. aircraft on 16 February 1944. A ship with a similar name, the DAIKICHI MARU, was included in a list of ships sunk at Truk in a message captured at Saipan. It is probable that these ships are one in the same due to the similarity in the names. The vessel was employed for civilian cargo duties by the Japanese.

A strong candidate for this ship is the vessel that was found at anchor west-northwest of Fefan Island that was definitely sunk but not identified. This vessel was described by the attackers as a 400-foot AO about 4,000 to 5,500 tons. The exaggerated tonnage estimate compared with the actual, 1,891 tons, is not untypical of those given by pilots engaged in attacks against shipping. The action reports consistently identify the ship as a tanker which in most cases indicates the ship had an aft-engine configuration. She could have been an aft-engine cargo ship; several of these ships were identified as AOs during the two-day attack at Truk.

The ship was initially attacked at approximately 0625 h by an SB2C from BUNKER HILL (Strike 3A) which hit the vessel with a 1,600-lb AP bomb and produced a large explosion and fire. She was the target of eight SB2Cs from BUNKER HILL on a later strike (3E) at about 1440 h; the ship was hit once amidships resulting in a huge explosion. ENTERPRISE planes (Strike 1EE) reported the complete disintegration of the ship.

Fathometer searches in the area have produced two large sections of the vessel lying on a 100-foot bottom. The largest section is that of the aft superstructure with the engine room and smokestack attached. Debris is lying all around the bottom including several air ventilators. The hull and deck plates are torn and blown askew from the explosion which tore the vessel apart. The second section found lies nearly 100 feet away from the first. This has been described as possibly a 40- to 50-foot section of the bow and forecastle, again with the hull and deck plating severely twisted and torn apart.

The TONAN MARU NO. 3

The Allied counter-offensive in the Central and South Pacific was spearheaded by the unrestricted warfare against Japanese shipping by U.S. submarines. Japanese transports and tankers were under a torpedo threat almost right at war's beginning. The success of a submarine patrol was not only measured in number of Japanese ships sunk but in total tonnage sunk. No wonder submarine commanders studied the silhouette of the TONAN MARU NO. 3 in the Japanese Ship Recognition Manual and dreamed of her coming into range of their torpedoes. At 19,209 tons, she and her sister ship, TONAN MARU NO. 2, were the largest tankers that Japanese had. They were in most cases twice the size or more than the average tanker. These ships had been used prior to the war as whale factories where total processing of the whales could be managed. These two whaling factories were turned over to the Japanese Navy and converted into fleet oil tankers.

In July 1943, Commander Dan Daspit, in the submarine U.S.S. TINOSA, was stationed off Truk with orders to intercept Japanese tanker traffic running between Palau and Truk. Japanese fleet messages were intercepted with details on TONAN MARU NO. 3 movements and the codebreakers provided the necessary information for TINOSA to intercept. The huge tanker was spotted heavily loaded making 13 knots on an easterly course on the morning of July 24th. At the time of contact, TINOSA had 16 torpedoes available having expended several already on enemy shipping. Daspit brought TINOSA to an attack position at a long range of 4,000 yards and fired an initial spread of four torpedoes. Two of the torpedoes appeared to hit and TONAN MARU NO. 3 was seen to stop dead in the water. Two more torpedoes fired caused her to belch smoke and settle by the stern with a port list but she still showed no signs of sinking. At this point, TONAN MARU NO. 3 was a "sitting duck," and with no anti-submarine ships or air escorts in sight, Daspit seemingly had all the time in the world to set up an ideal torpedo attack and finish the target at will. The tanker's deck guns prevented a surface approach so Daspit closed in for a torpedo attack calculated to sink the helpless ship. The next torpedo, fired from a position off the starboard beam at 875 yards range, made what looked like a normal run. The torpedo screws were heard (using sounding gear) to stop abruptly and a splash was observed at the aim point. No explosion was observed indicating the torpedo was a dud. Another deliberate torpedo was fired with no effect. Two more torpedoes were then fired with careful setups and no effect except that now the gun crews on the ship were firing at the periscope and torpedo wakes with machine guns and deck guns. It began to appear that the dream target was going to turn into a submarine commander's nightmare. Torpedo duds were going to rob Daspit and the TINOSA of one of the war's best submarine trophies. Daspit decided to get to the bottom of the problem and began an investigative firing procedure that would lend itself to determining the nature of the torpedo problems. Eight more torpedoes were expended over a period of several hours with checks and adjustments of each torpedo being made before it was fired from the tube. The best possible track angle was selected (90 degrees to the ship's beam) and eight hits were scored with no accompanying explosions. The torpedoes, fired at a 90-degree perfect position angle with a normal impact, failed to work against a 535-foot-long target that looked as big as a battleship. Daspit saved his lone remaining torpedo for analysis and later upon examination at Pearl Harbor, the torpedo was found to be in perfect adjustment. This was proof conclusive that the torpedoes indeed had problems and resulted in a cooperative effort to solve the torpedo problems that had been confirmed some 20 months into the war.

–National Archives Photo
TONAN MARU NO. 3 in the Panama Canal – 6/21/38.

The attack described had been the nearest thing possible to a laboratory test and provided proof that the Mark 6 contact exploder used in the Mark XIV torpedo was defective. With the evidence that Daspit provided and confirmed in tests of torpedoes fired at vertical cliffs on the island of Kahoolawe, Hawaii, followed by extensive impact tests, the Mark 6 exploders' firing pin was found to release properly but would strike the primer cap with insufficient force to set it off. If the target was positioned such that the warhead struck it a glancing blow, the exploder would work properly. Ships that had been hit previously by glancing blows at an angle were sunk while broadside hits would be duds.

For TONAN MARU NO. 3, help was on the way. A destroyer appeared near the time of the final torpedo firing and Japanese rescuers finally towed the tanker safely into Truk. The big one got away and TINOSA had to return to Pearl Harbor with a dispirited and disillusioned crew, but with the information supplied from the attacks on the "guinea pig" tanker, corrective measures were applied to the torpedoes and at last, U.S. submarines could go to sea with reliable torpedoes.

The TONAN MARU NO. 3 is believed to have been laid up for extensive repairs at Truk following the torpedo attack by TINOSA as the ship was damaged to such an extent that she couldn't be sailed to the Empire for repair without undue risk. Naval communications traffic intercepted by U.S. codebreakers reported her to be in the Truk area several times but never outside Truk. A captured list of ships sunk or damaged during the raids on Truk carried the TONAN MARU NO. 3 as "heavily damaged," but a second captured document (dated 26 February 1944) states that "Damage to ships is corrected as follows: TONAN MARU NO. 3 and UNKAI MARU NO. 6 were badly flooded. Although it was attempted to beach them, they finally sank."

Photographs taken the morning of the 16th show the large whale factory ship lying in the anchorage west of Dublon and north of Fefan Islands near the repair ship AKASHI and the other damaged merchantmen YAMAGIRI, KIYOSUMI, HOYO, and KENSHO MARUs. The photographs taken by planes which attacked the anchorage on both days of the raid show that TONAN MARU NO. 3 was set on fire by bombs early the first morning and then burned furiously throughout the rest of the day and the next. In photographs taken on April 29, 1944, her capsized hull was visible with a portion of the keel showing above water.

The TONAN MARU NO. 3 is most likely the ship mistakenly identified by BUNKER HILL pilots as the CVE ZUHIO in early morning attacks on the 1st day of the raids. Her location corresponds exactly with that reported for the carrier. She was actually much larger that the ZUHIO (19,209 tons versus 13,950 tons), comparable in length (535 versus 660 feet), and wider (75 versus 59 feet). In the early morning hour with low clouds hampering visibility, it is understandable how she could be mistaken for an escort carrier.

Following the attacks by BUNKER HILL planes, ENTERPRISE dive bombers (Strike 1BE) arrived over the anchorage and one division was directed to attack the largest ship (TONAN MARU NO. 3). Two bomb hits were scored near the stern flinging debris high in the air. The blasts blew out the sides of the ship and part of the superstructure. A portion of the starboard quarter was observed to be missing; she immediately began to settle by the stern. Attacks on the ship continued on February 17th with at least one bomb hit being scored by YORKTOWN SBDs (Strike 1AY).

The TONAN MARU NO. 3 was the largest ship sunk at Truk. Today, she should be a wreck diver's dream but it was not to be. After lying there upside down until after the war, she was raised by a Japanese salvage company given permission by the U.S. government as part of a repatriation-reconstruction agreement; the Japanese reportedly argued that the whale canning-processing equipment aboard was extremely valuable to them and that they couldn't replace this for nearly the cost of salvaging same from the wreck.

Remnants of the ship still remain; fathometer searches in the anchorage have produced sections of torn and twisted superstructure, one of the smokestacks (identified as being from TONAN MARU NO. 3 from the concentric circle stack markings of the ship's owner, Nippon Suisan K.K.) and other piles of metal wreckage in the area.

TECHNICAL SUMMARY:

Other Name: DAI-SAN TONAN MARU
Type: Naval Tanker (1943), ex-Whaling Factory Ship
Configuration Sequence: M–K–M–K–F
Gross Tonnage: 19,209 tons
Dimensions: 535/75/35.5 feet
Machinery: Reciprocating engines with exhaust turbines, twin screws, aft-engines.
Radius: 18,000 miles at 13 knots.
Complement: 90
Built: 1938 by Osaka Tekkosho, Osaka
Owner: Nippon Suisan K.K., Tokyo

The Tugboat Wrecks

The first of the two tugboat wrecks lies nearly 500 yards from shore with its bow facing the southern tip of Dublon Island. The location of this wreck is in an area where the water is murky and normally has a greenish hue. When descending, it is difficult to see any of it until you come into close proximity. The tug sits at a 45 degree list to the port side and lies at a steep incline on an underwater hill. The stern lies at 35 feet, the top of the bridge at 60 feet, and the bow at 85 feet. Entrance to the bridge can be made through a very narrow passageway. Inside are two small telegraphs flanking the wheel support structure. The silt here is very easy to stir up and visibility degrades very quickly. There are also entrances leading forward to some smallish compartments and below to the engine room but these are very narrow, making this area very difficult for divers to explore. A hatch on the foreship leads to a small hold. More narrow entrances lead to cabins which probably served as crew quarters.

The second, or shallow tugboat wreck, lies approximately 200 yards from shore on a 60-foot bottom opposite the Japanese landing craft wrecks on the west side of Dublon Island. This wreck, like the other, lies in greenish murky water. The top of the bridge at 35 feet is covered with a mossy algae growth and some orange-colored soft coral. There is a large searchlight mounted on the top of the bridge. Inside the wheelhouse is a binnacle with its compass and two speaker tubes attached leading to the engine room below. The binnacle is flanked by two horizontally-aligned telegraphs. After rubbing off the muck and growth on the face of the telegraphs, the control positions were found to be printed in kanji characters rather than the usual Romanized lettering. Several bronze light fixtures were lying in the muck on the floor of the wheelhouse. Further exploration led to an engine room with a very small entrance and another tiny room with small ovens for cooking. No armament was found on the wreck.

Prior to the first U.S. carrier strikes in February 1944, there were ten 15-ton tugs, three 800-ton tugs, and one 600-ton tug utilized by the Japanese Navy and assigned to the naval base on Dublon Island. Since there was no development of wharfs and piers to accommodate large ships due to the shallow coral reefs surrounding each island, the tugboats provided only limited maneuvering for large fleet ships in the Moen Anchorage and were mostly used for supporting the replenishment of stores and loading-unloading of supplies and equipment from the warships and cargo ships to and from shore. These tugboats were used in conjunction with sampans, water lighters, fuel barges, a single repair ship with crane (the AKASHI prior to the air strikes), a 2,500-ton floating drydock, and a multitude of small yard craft to carry out all logistical operations.

No record of the sinking of any of the 600- or 800-ton tugs is noted in available research material; however, three 10- to 15-ton diesel tugs were reported lost in attacks between April and July 1944. The two known tugboat wrecks are fairly large (over 100 feet in length) and are larger than the ones reported lost. There is no visible damage on the two wrecks that would have caused their sinking and it is possible that they were scuttled after the war by U.S. forces. There were two tugs at Truk at the end of hostilities and these may be the fore-mentioned vessels sunk off Dublon. The description of these is given below:

TECHNICAL SUMMARIES:

Ship's Name: FUTAGAMI
Type: HASHIMA Class Salvage Tug
Displacement: 625 tons
Dimensions: 131.25/31.8/10.2 feet
Machinery: Reciprocating engine (coal and heavy oil), 2-shaft, 2,200 iHP.
Speed: 14.5 knots
Complement: 59
Armament: Two 25mm AA guns, depth charges.
Built: 1939 by Harima Sanbashi Co., Aioi
Remarks: Tug was equipped with two 2-ton and one 5-ton derrick and salvage pumps. Japanese designation was "Kyunan-sen ken Eisen."

Ship's Name: EISEN NO. 761
Type: Tugboat
Displacement: 300 tons
Dimensions: 113 (o.a.)/22/10 feet
Machinery: Reciprocating engine (coal), 1,200 iHP.
Speed: 8 knots
Complement: 7
Armament: Unknown
Built: Unknown

The UNKAI MARU NO. 6

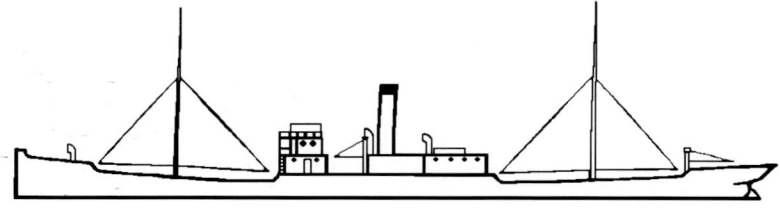

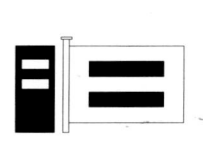

NAKAMURA KISEN K.K.

The wreck of the UNKAI MARU NO. 6, which was only discovered in July 1980, lies approximately 600 meters directly north of Uman Island on a line between Uman and Eten Islands. It was found by Klaus Lindemann using a fathometer and a war action photo showing the ship in proximity to the GOSEI MARU. Lying upright on the a 130-foot bottom, the 3,220-ton ship offers divers an interesting new wreck for exploration.

On our first dive, we descended past the forward mast directly into hold No. 1 at a depth of 115 feet where piles of shoes, gas masks, bottles, boxes, and lots of debris were lying about on the bottom. Up against a bulkhead, I spotted several stacks of china plates with the 5-point star insignia of the Japanese infantry on them. After a few minutes of sightseeing here, we swam upwards to the forecastle where my dive partner signaled to me to come see the lantern locker he'd discovered. Inside this small compartment were scattered several 2-foot-high bronze ship's lanterns. We photographed the lanterns and then swam forward to the 3-inch bow gun; the gun platform and gun itself were covered with a lot of marine growth and are very photogenic.

The No. 2 hold appeared to be empty of cargo as we swam over it towards the mid-ship superstructure and bridge. We found quite a bit of destruction inside the bridge. Besides having burned for a long time, the beams and walls showed signs of having buckled from explosions above. The rudder stand, the telegraph, and other equipment bolted to the floor of the wheelhouse had been knocked over to the floor. It was difficult to readily identify anything with all the collapsed decking, other debris, and the ever-present layer of muck. I did spot a strongbox lying in the debris.

Our Trukese diving guide, Cheny, had found the ship's bell previously and had disappeared over the side of the ship to the seabed where the bell lay in the sand. He then took a buoyancy compensator (BC) and tied it to the bell. He would have had a lot of trouble bringing it up to the deck level without using the BC as a lift bag. The bell was one of the largest I'd ever seen on a Japanese wreck; there was just enough sponge growth on it to prevent seeing whether the ship's name was etched on it.

The main deck-level cabins have been completely gutted by fire and there is little to interest the diver in the many small rooms. The charcoal and muck combination in these cabins is extremely filthy and discouraged our plans to search for artifacts. Just aft of the bridge superstructure, there is a single-level hold flanked by a kingpost. Two large air ventilators positioned just forward of the funnel have collapsed backwards toward the stern as has the funnel itself. The one or more bomb bursts which had caused the damage on the bridge were probably responsible for knocking them over. The funnel exhibited two 24-inch-wide metal bands; these are the stack markings of the Japanese owner, Nakamura Kisen K.K. The engine room can be entered through open hatches; there is not much to see besides the engines, a block and tackle, and assorted machinery. The whole engine room had been gutted by fire also. I could find no sign of a ship-builder's plaque.

The two large holds in the aft section appeared empty from above. A large unusual-shaped, squared mast was positioned between the holds flanked by huge winches. There was no stern gun; instead, there

–Naval Operational Archives Photo
The UNKAI MARU NO. 6 (foreground) is on fire and smoking heavily with an unidentified damaged auxiliary or harbor craft behind it.

was a double winch apparatus attached low to the deck. This was part of a steering mechanism where chains were connected from this machinery to the rudder below.

Divers will note many peculiarities of the ship's structure and configuration not seen in other Japanese ships sunk in the Pacific theater. This can be explained by the ship having been built in England instead of Japanese shipyards. The ship was originally named VENUS; she was purchased in 1911 by Japanese interests.

The UNKAI MARU NO. 6 appears to have been damaged and sunk by planes from ESSEX, BUNKER HILL, and YORKTOWN. She was initially attacked by ESSEX VT planes on the first day of the raids (Strike 2B); the ship was described as an 8,000-ton AK anchored two miles southwest of Eten Island. The TBFs scored bomb hits, one on the port side and the other on the port quarter. The ship was observed by a turret gunner to list to the starboard. She was reportedly damaged further during the "masthead attack" (Strike 1DY) by YORKTOWN VTs who scored one bomb hit (results not observed). The UNKAI MARU NO. 6 was then attacked about the same time by both YORKTOWN VTs (Strike 1EY) and BUNKER HILL VBs (Strike 3E). The YORKTOWN TBFs had two misses but two VB-17 planes released two 1,000-lb GP bombs at 1,500 feet altitude scoring one hit aft of amidships. A large fire was seen to break out pouring out black smoke from the ship described at this time as a 440-foot, 7,500-ton AK anchored between Eten and Uman. Four pilots and three gunners confirmed the bomb hit. The ship was swept by fire but was still afloat when ESSEX planes arrived the next day (Strike 2B). From the description given of this already damaged ship and her location, it appears that the VB-9 planes may have been the last to attack the ship. The SBDs scored two direct hits on the bow and bracketed the ship with three other bombs. The explosions were seen to lift the bow out of the water. She was still afloat when the planes departed.

TECHNICAL SUMMARY:

Other Name: VENUS (Original)
Type: Cargo
Configuration Sequence: M–K–F–M–K
Gross Tonnage: 3,220 tons
Dimensions: 331/49.2/21.8 feet
Machinery: Diesel engines made by Blair & Co., Ltd., Stockton, single screw, 288 NHP.
Radius: 6,100 miles at 8 1/2 knots.
Complement: Unknown
Built: 1905 by William Gray & Co., Ltd., West Hartlepool, England.
Owner: Japanese – Nakamura Kisen K.K.
Original – Unknown
Remarks: One deck.

The YAMAGIRI MARU

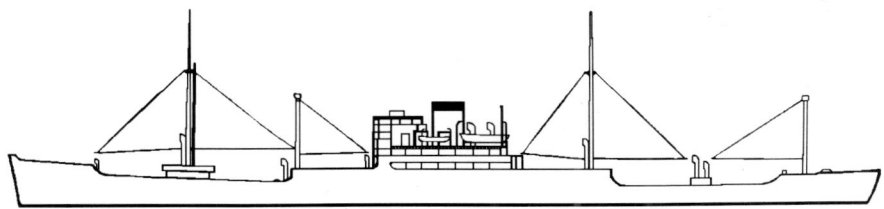

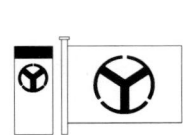

YAMASHITA KISEN KAISHA

There was no question that the pair of divers swimming ahead of us had run into something they didn't like. Something had scared them and they were swimming back in our direction fast while looking back over their shoulders like they were expecting something to be chasing them. When they swam up to my dive partner and I, they gave me what I thought was a hand signal for "shark." Earlier, as we had swum down the anchor line heading aft, we had encountered several large sharks that had circled us, appearing and then disappearing repeatedly in the bluish murky water. These sharks all seemed to be 6 to 8 feet long with heavy bodies. They had not yet come closer than 10 yards. We were used to seeing sharks on almost every dive while at Roi-Namur, and I was really curious as to what had scared the other two divers. We cautiously swam forward where the others had been and peered around the edge of the bridge of the shipwreck and found ourselves staring into the open mouth of a very menacing looking 7-foot-long barracuda. He was just lying motionless in the water with his mouth agape showing off an array of teeth that was incredible. Fortunately, he was just exhibiting normal barracuda behavior; I remember thinking that I wouldn't want to face him when he was mad or hungry. We skirted the great fish cautiously and swam towards the No. 5 hold aft where we had been told that we could find some large artillery shells.

The wreck we were diving on was the YAMAGIRI MARU. The 456-foot passenger-cargo vessel is lying on her port side north-northwest of Fefan Island with her bow facing towards the south end of Moen. She was sunk approximately one mile from shore on a 110- to 120-foot bottom. The wreck had been found by a group of island workers that were traveling by boat from Moen to Fefan. After noticing a large greenish-brown unnatural looking object in the water on their daily trips, they notified divers and she was shortly thereafter identified.

We found more than we had expected in the No. 5 hold of the wreck. Besides the artillery shells, there is lots of equipment and machinery located inside that had been separated on the port and starboard sides of the hold. After the ship had rolled over on its side while sinking, the contents of the hold were redistributed into an upper and lower level. I approached the upper level initially and looked over jumbled stacks of artillery shells. These 18.1-inch-diameter shells were the largest used by the Japanese Navy and were larger than any used by the Allies. The YAMAGIRI MARU had a load of these replacement shells for the largest of Japan's battleships, the 63,000-ton MUSASHI and the YAMATO. There were also what appeared to be loading equipment for the shells and heavy machinery including some large machined wheels. After exploring and shooting several photographs, I descended to the lower level at 90 feet where there was a stack of four more shells, two large air compressors on wheels, a furnace, and lots more unrecognizable machinery and equipment. The large air compressors might have been used to fill the 8,000-psi high pressure flasks in torpedo bodies. It was easy to spend the entire bottom time we had allocated for the dive exploring and photographing various items in this hold alone. After we left the No. 5 hold, we had time for a quick look into the aft hold (No. 6) where there was nothing but 50-gallon-sized drums.

On subsequent dives, the bridge was explored and found to be almost barren. A few of the ever-present beer bottles were all that could be seen. Almost everything else had fallen to the bottom where there was a 2- to 4-foot layer of muck, remains of burnt decking, and other debris. A large bronze ship's whistle is mounted on the forward side of the funnel; the whistle is barely recognizable as it is covered with heavy coral growth. This growth extends around the sides of the funnel and prevented our finding out if the Yamashita K.K. house stack markings were present.

The two layers of hatch cover beams over the No. 3 hold forward of the bridge supported some soft corals. The rest of the shipwreck with the exception of the area around the funnel was almost void of coral growth. There appears to be both bomb and torpedo damage in the No. 3 hold. The ship had been torpedoed on the starboard side; the hull shows a large gaping hole with a lot of twisted metal blown inward from the explosion. This may have resulted from a previous submarine attack on the open seas. The forward holds were empty of cargo. A large gun is mounted on the bow. The name of the ship in both Roman and kanji characters can be found on the exposed side of the hull.

The submarine U.S.S. DRUM was patrolling west of Mussau Island in the Admiralties on August 28, 1943 when she located a convoy in position 01°30'N, 148°35'E. She reported scoring two torpedo hits on a "5,000-ton freighter." The identity of the torpedoed ship was established only after the capture of two Japanese documents which reported that the sub's target was the YAMAGIRI MARU. The stricken vessel was taken back to Rabaul for repairs. Photographs taken by Allied forces between September 1 and October 1, 1943 showed a YAMAGIRI MARU class freighter lying down by the bow in Matupi Harbor, Rabaul. When Rabaul became the target for almost daily air raids in late 1943, the YAMAGIRI MARU sailed or was towed to Truk for completion of repairs.

The YAMAGIRI MARU can be identified from photographs of February 16–17, 1944 apparently damaged with her stern lying low in the water in same anchorage west of Dublon with other ships known to have been previously damaged and the repair ship AKASHI. YORKTOWN VT and VB planes attacked ships in that anchorage on

The 18.1-inch diameter projectiles in the hold of the YAMAGIRI MARU were destined for the guns of the battleships YAMATO and MUSASHI.

Strike 1EY on the 16th of February. The YAMAGIRI MARU, described as a "large AK anchored northwest of Fefan Island," suffered one close miss by the bomb-carrying TBFs and a hit and close miss by the SBDs. Three other AKs and an AO lying north and northwest of Fefan Island were also reported hit. A hospital ship (the HIKAWA MARU NO. 2) was reported in the anchorage also.

It appears that the YAMAGIRI MARU was not attacked again until the next day when 4VB from BUNKER HILL (Strike 3B) attacked the ship dropping one 1,000-lb and six 500-lb GP bombs from a 500-foot altitude. The target ship was described as being 550 feet long, approximately 13,000 tons. She was hit by one 1,000-lb and one 500-lb bomb. After the SB2Cs pulled out of their dives, a huge explosion erupted on the ship causing a large fire and black smoke up to 4–5,000 feet. It was felt that the fire and explosion gutted the ship causing heavy damage and probably sinking the vessel. Photographs taken later on the 17th showed a large oil slick covering the area in which the YAMAGIRI MARU had been located, and though clouds partially obscured the anchorage at the time, it was probable that the ship was no longer afloat.

TECHNICAL SUMMARY:

Type: Passenger-Cargo
Configuration Sequence: M–K–F–M–K
Gross Tonnage: 6,438 tons
Dimensions: 439.4/58.3/32 feet
Machinery: Diesel engines, single screw, 1,166 NHP.
Radius: 47,000 miles at 14 knots.
Complement: 45 (crew), 2 (passengers)
Built: 1938 by Mitsubishi Jukogyo K.K., Yokohama
Owner: Yamashita Kisen Kaisha, Kobe
Remarks: Navy Department transport. Two decks, cruiser stern, refrigerating machinery.

The YUBAE MARU

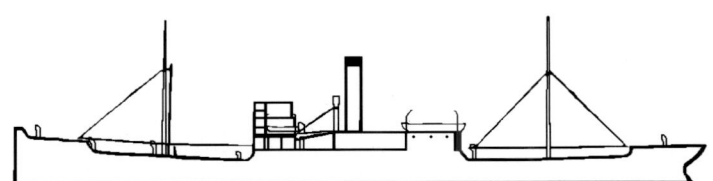

KURIBAYASI SHOSEN KISEN KAISHA

The YUBAE MARU arrived in Truk as part of an escorted convoy on the 10th of February. She was lying along the western shore of Uman Island not far from the southeastern tip of Fefan on the 16th when U.S. planes attacked the anchorage. It seems probable that the ship was attacked by both VT and VB planes from BUNKER HILL at about 1245 h (Strike 3D); she was hit by a 1,000-lb AP bomb and at least one torpedo. The ship was heavily damaged and starting to sink when the aircraft retired. Photographs show the ship sinking by the stern with her bow high and her whole after half submerged.

The wreck of the YUBAE MARU is one of the most recent finds at Truk. The ship is resting on her port side on a 120-foot bottom. Her identity was a mystery for some time until her name was finally found on the hull. China found aboard the wreck had the name "Sarawak" inscribed on several pieces.

TECHNICAL SUMMARY:

Type: Cargo
Configuration Sequence: M–K–F–M
Gross Tonnage: 3,217 tons
Dimensions: 305/44/27.3 feet
Machinery: Diesel engines, single screw, 279 NHP.
Radius: 9,600 miles at 10 knots
Complement: Unknown
Built: 1919 by Ishikawajima Sanbashi Co., Tokyo
Owner: Kuribayasi Shosen Kisen Kaisha
Remarks: Two decks. The YUBAE MARU received heavy damage from a submarine near Palau (07°30'N, 134°12'E) on 9 January 1943.

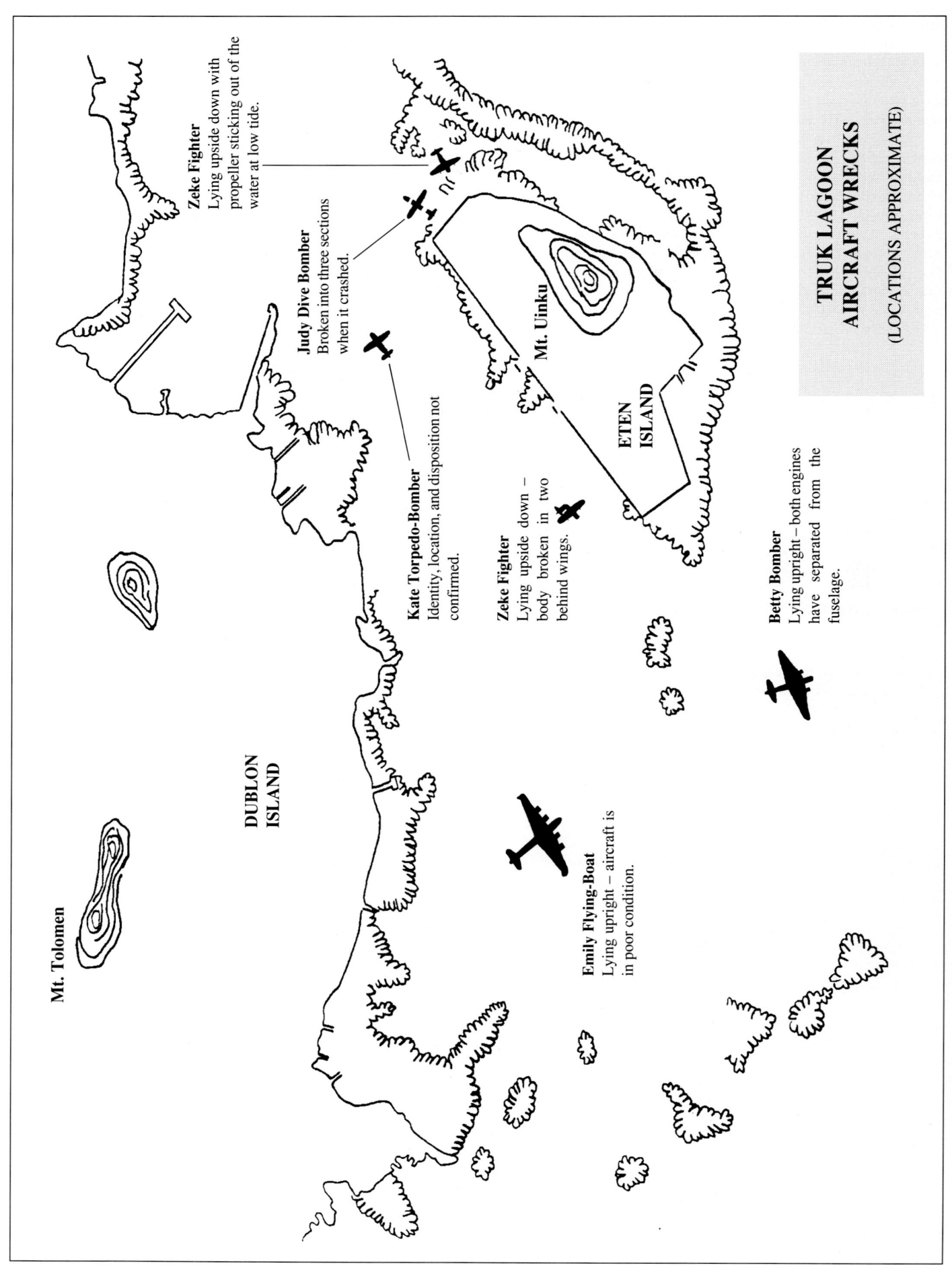

AIRCRAFT WRECKS

The Zeke Fighter Wrecks

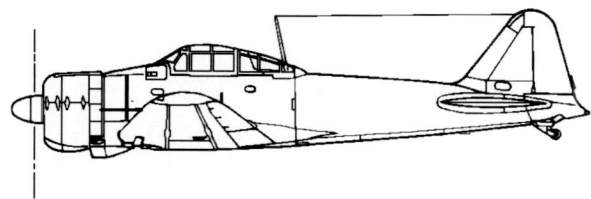

The wrecks of two airplanes lie approximately 100 yards off the northeastern end of Eten Island in shallow water. The first aircraft, with a single propeller blade protruding out of the water is a Mitsubishi A6M Navy Type 0 Carrier Fighter Reisen (Zero), known as a Zeke to the Allies. The location of the wreck is directly off the end of what was once the airstrip. The Zeke is lying upside down with its landing gear in the extended position indicating that it crashed while either taking off or landing. Aircraft action reports indicate that on 16 February 1944, many Japanese fighters were hit while attempting take-offs and some while landing. The plane has a large amount of algae and coral growth covering it. The rubber tires on the landing gear have disappeared due to physical deterioration or were destroyed in the crash. Machine gun barrels can be seen extending forward of the wings on both sides of the cockpit.

While traveling between dive sites during a trip in July 1972, one of the divers in our group happened to be lying on the bow of our dive boat looking down at the water below and just happened to see a light reflection off an object in the water near the southwest end of Eten. We investigated further and found a second Zeke fighter lying upside down facing toward Fefan Island. The body of the aircraft is broken in two about 2–3 feet behind the wings and the tail section is canted to the side. The wreck is nestled up against a coral head at an angle in about 35 feet of water.

Another Zeke is reported to be lying in 60 feet of water southeast of the site of the Dublon seaplane base about halfway between Dublon and Eten Islands. Few divers have ever been shown this aircraft wreck.

The last known Zeke found in the lagoon lies west of Param Island, about 500 yards off the end of the old airstrip. The Zeke crashed the water hard and broke into four sections in shallow water.

The Zeke fighter has become the symbol of Japanese air power for the Japanese themselves and their former enemies. More of these fighters were built than any other type of Japanese aircraft. The carrier-based Zekes spearheaded the attacks on American forces at Pearl Harbor and the the Philippines followed by further attacks on Wake, Darwin, and Ceylon. The Zeke was unstoppable the first six months of the war as it won victories over all Allied carrier- and land-based aircraft it encountered. The exceptional range and extreme maneuverability allowed it to "rule the roost" until more advanced Allied aircraft made their appearance towards the end of 1942. The weaknesses of the Zeke, the lack of armor and fuel tank protection, began to account for steadily increasing losses. Following the Battle of Midway in June 1942 when four Japanese carriers and their aircraft were lost, the Japanese offensive was essentially stopped and from then on, the Zeke was relegated to a defensive role.

The Zeke would do all right at low altitudes, but it was hopefully outclassed and was no match at higher altitudes for the modern Allied fighters such as the P-38 Lightning, the F4U-1 Corsair, and the Spitfire which were introduced in the Pacific Theatre. A Zeke with increased performance, the A6M5, was put into production and rushed to front-line units in 1943 in time to counter the new threat presented by the F6F Hellcat. These Zekes could hold their own in matching the performance of the F6F, but the American fighter maintained a superiority over the Zeke as it had a heavier armament and was more strongly built and better protected. The best of the Zeke fighters was probably the A6M5b which had better armament and was strengthened with armor and fuel tank protection. They were first delivered to fighter units on carriers to participate in the Battle of the Philippines, but were decisively defeated by the F6Fs in what became known as the "Marianas turkey shoot."

In October 1944, with the landings by U.S. forces in the Philippines, many of the Zekes were fitted with 551-lb bombs to be used in kamikaze attacks against U.S. ships. Later, the Zeke was still the mainstay of most fighter units even near the end when trying to defend the Japanese homeland.

Propeller blade sticking out of the water makes this Zeke (Zero) fighter lying off the northeast end of Eten Island easy to find.

Japanese Judy (Yokosuka D4Y) aircraft crashed with such force that wings and cockpit separated from the engine and tail section shown in the background.

The Judy Dive Bomber Wreck

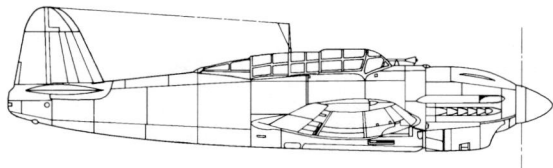

The second aircraft lying off the northeastern end of Eten Island about 50 yards from the Zeke with its propeller out of the water is a "Judy" or Yokosuka D4Y Suisei (Comet). This aircraft is located about 100 yards from shore slightly off to the side of the end of the airstrip on Eten. The plane crashed with such force that it separated into three sections: the engine and attached propeller, the fuselage with the cockpit, and the tail section.

The single-engined Judy was used by the Japanese Navy primarily as a carrier-based dive bomber and reconnaissance aircraft, but was also modified to operate as a land-based night fighter. Judys stationed at Truk during the initial U.S. carrier aircraft strikes were probably the carrier-bomber version; Judys present after April 1944 may have been the modified aircraft which was intended to operated in the night fighter role.

Production rights for the Judy were acquired from Germany; the plane was developed from the Heinkel He 118V4. The prototypes were actually powered by Daimler-Benz liquid-cooled engines imported from Germany while later production models used the license-built versions built by Aichi Kokuki K.K. The Aichi-built Judys were the fastest carrier dive bombers of World War II.

The Japanese carriers sent to intercept the U.S. Fleet heading to attack the Marianas in June 1944 had 174 Judys aboard which were part of the 1st, 2nd, and 3rd Koku Sentais. Most of these were shot down during the "Marianas turkey shoot." Later in the war, the Judy was used extensively as suicide bombers (kamikazes).

The Betty Bomber Wreck

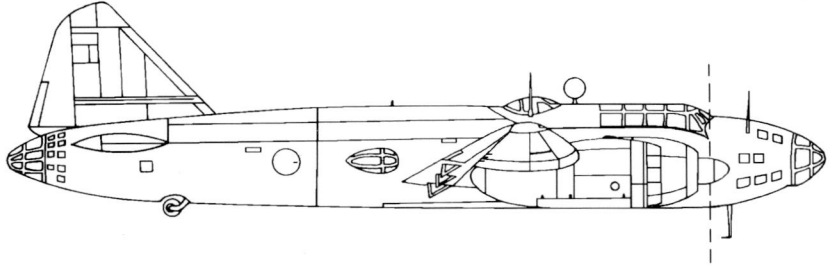

The Mitsubishi G4M land-based attack bomber, nicknamed "Betty" by the Allies, was the most famous of the Japanese bombers built. Produced in large numbers, the Betty was deployed in all Pacific war theatres and was utilized from the war's beginning to the end. The Japanese used the aircraft in many roles as it could carry torpedoes or bombs and some were provided with extra heavy defensive armament for "escort fighter" duties. This heavy escort fighter version, the G6M1, was designated a "wingtip convoy fighter" and was mostly used for escorting Mitsubishi G3M2s (Nells) on long-range bombing runs.

Early in the war, Bettys contributed to the elimination of American air power in the Philippines and the sinking of HMS PRINCE OF WALES and HMS REPULSE. In conjunction with Japanese carrier aircraft, the Bettys were involved in the Japanese attack on Darwin, Australia. In April 1943, Admiral Isoroku Yamamoto and his staff were flying two G4M1s over Bougainville when shot down by U.S. aircraft. Late in the war, a special version of the aircraft was built to carry the Ohka (cherry blossom) piloted suicide aircraft against American warships. After cessation of hostilities at war's end, the Japanese surrender delegation flew two Bettys bearing green crosses to meet with the U.S. command.

The long-range and load-carrying capability features of the Bettys were considerable, but the unprotected fuel tanks and lack of armor made them easy prey for Allied fighters even though they carried heavy defensive armament. When being attacked, the bombers often caught on fire easily and the aircraft soon became known as the "flying lighter."

The G4M2 model bomber was supplied to most front-line units starting in July 1943 and the Betty found at Truk was probably this type. This wrecked aircraft is located approximately 150 yards southwest of Eten Island lying upright on a 50-foot bottom. The aircraft has considerable damage which resulted from crashing into the water and the floor of the lagoon; the forward nose section is broken and canted downward due to impact. Both engines were torn from their mounts on the wings. Some damage may have resulted from the detonation of a 500-lb bomb 50 feet away from the aircraft by the U.S. Navy.

The Bettys on Truk were based on the Moen No. 1, Param, and Eten airfields. The wrecked plane was evidently flying from the north when shot down and now lies facing south on the bottom of the lagoon. When first seen in the murky water, the 65.5-foot-long and 19.5-foot-high aircraft is impressively large. The metal skin of the aircraft is relatively free from marine growth; the only coral or algae-type growth on the wreck is around the open cockpit area. Here you find some dull-colored soft coral and some hard coral growth. Entrance to the body of the plane can be made from the rear hatch on either side. Thirty-eight incendiary bombs were once removed from the aircraft as a safety precaution. The interior of the aircraft is interesting; the fuselage structure is intact and various equipment (including a radio), boxes, and debris lie on the floor. A saki and a French cognac or brandy bottle were reportedly found under a front seat of the airplane. Divers can exit through the aircraft through the damaged open cockpit. Two guns have been found on the wreck, a 20mm cannon from either the tail turret or beam blister, and a 7.7mm machine gun.

The Betty Bomber lies in murky water off Eten Island.

The Emily Flying-Boat Wreck

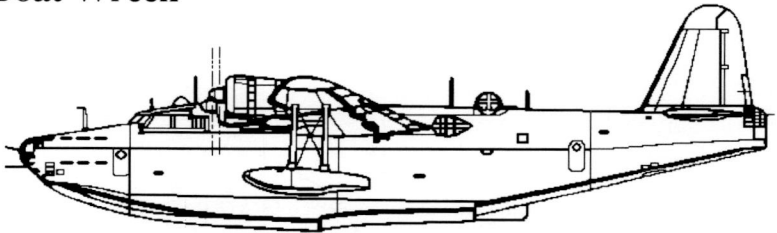

In 1938, the Japanese began designing a large four-engine maritime flying-boat with a maximum speed of 276 mph, a cruising speed of 207 mph, and a maximum patrol range of 4,500 nautical miles as a follow-on to the Kawanishi H6K (Mavis). The result was the Kawanishi H8K (Emily), which was superior to any other World War II water-based combat aircraft. The Emily combined impressive speed and long-range capabilities with extensive armor and fuel tank protection in conjunction with a heavy defensive armament to make it extremely successful in its intended reconnaissance role. It was also capable of carrying a heavy external load of two torpedoes, or eight 551-lb bombs, or sixteen 132-lb bombs or depth charges, thereby adding a flexibility that could be utilized in many combat roles.

In its first notable combat sortie of the war, two of the Emilys of the Yokohama Kokutai left Wotje in the Marshall Islands, made a rendezvous with a submarine at French Frigate Shoals to refuel, and then went on to make a bombing attack on Oahu. The aircraft were hampered by a heavy cloud cover over Honolulu and dropped several bombs which fell harmlessly into the Punch Bowl crater behind the city. A second attack, timed to coincide with the Japanese attack against Midway, had to be cancelled as the refueling submarine found that approaches at French Frigate Shoals had been heavily mined and U.S. forces were canvassing the area.

The Emily found several hundred yards off the southwest end of Dublon Island appears to have been sunk while moored. The tips of her propeller blades are straight; if she had been shot out of the air, the rotating blades would have been bent backward upon impact with the water.

Sunk in 50 feet of water, the flying-boat is in poor condition and appears to be deteriorating rapidly. The body of the aircraft is upside down with both the tail and the nose section separated from the body. The nose section is lying off to the side along one wing; it is smashed and broken apart. The instrument panel has been jerked loose from the cockpit and lies on the bottom near the nose. Heavy debris partially blocks entrance into the interior of the fuselage. Two of its huge engines with 4-bladed propellers have been separated from the wings completely. The pontoons and guy wires are lying askew on the bottom along the wings. The water in the area of the wreck is usually murky and photographers should take advantage of the mid-day sun.

The nose section of the Emily flying-boat lies on the bottom smashed and separated from the main fuselage of the aircraft.

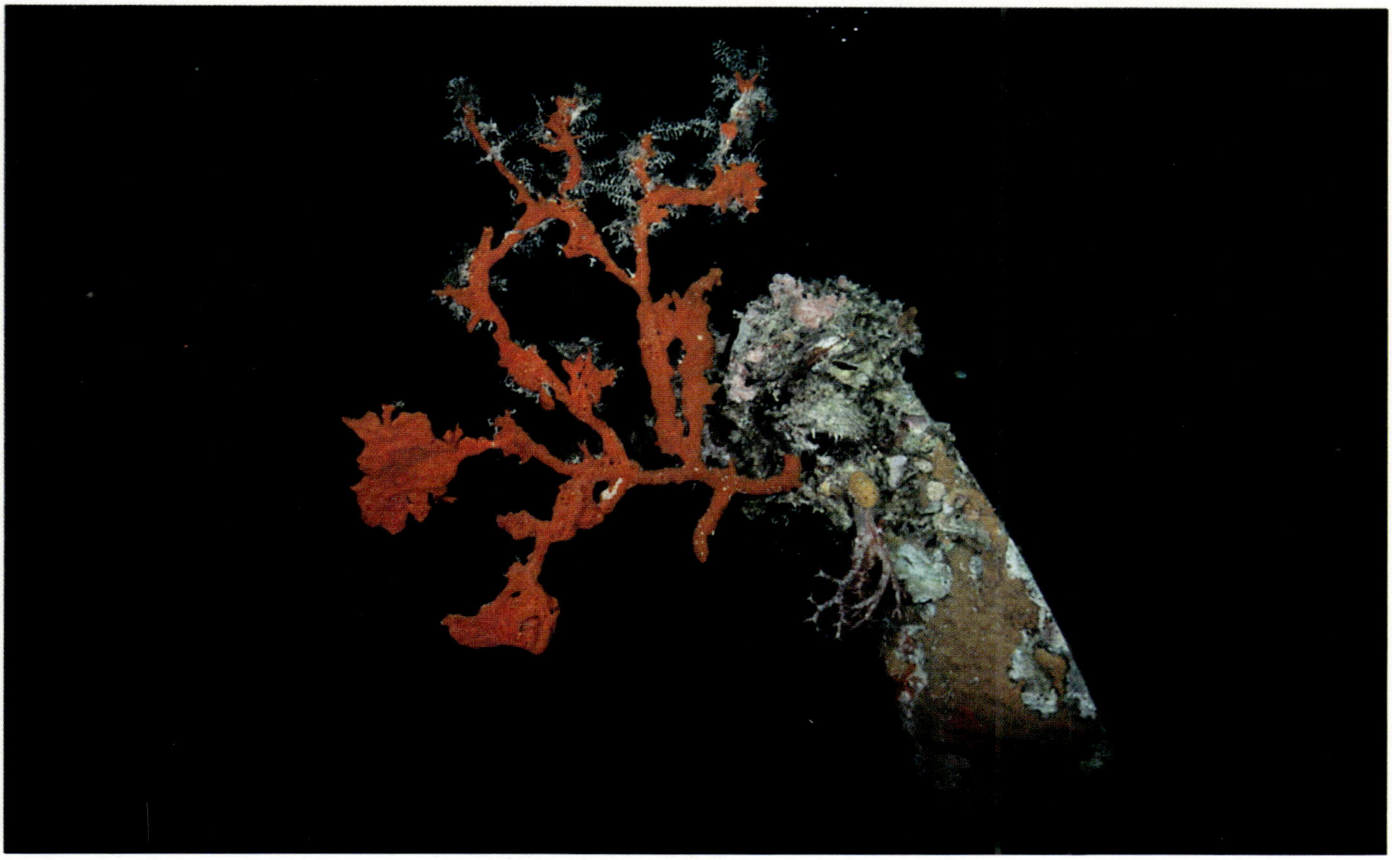

The tip of a propeller blade provides the support for a delicate orange sponge growth.

The Kate Torpedo-Bomber

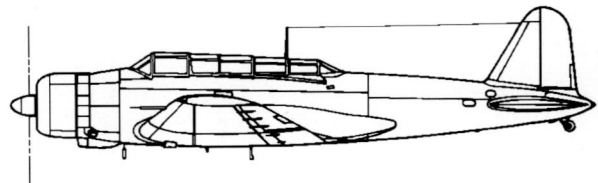

This aircraft wreck was reportedly discovered by members of the crew of the live-aboard dive boat THORFINN during the second half of 1988. The identification of the plane type has not been confirmed by this author. Information regarding this wreck was graciously provided by Carol Montgomery, one of the associate producers of SEA FANS Video Magazine.

The Kate (Nakajima B5N, Navy Type 97 Carrier Attack Bomber) is resting upright on a 110–115-foot bottom to the west of the channel marker mounted on the promontory of the shallow reef extending off the eastern end of Eten Island. The plane is in a deep-water channel between the south side of Dublon Island and the north (northeast) end of the Eten runway. In contrast to the other aircraft wrecks at Truk, this one is described as being in "pristine condition" with the only visible damage being several bullet holes in the fuselage. The cockpit of this intact three-seat single-engined plane is well preserved with the pilot's stick, gauges, and seat still remaining as it was when it went down over 44 years earlier. A center seat position was manned by the observer who was also responsible for navigating and aiming the bombs in level bombing sorties. The rear seat was occupied by the radio operator who also served as the gunner and a machine gun is still mounted with its front sight in place. This weapon is likely the standard flexible 7.7mm Type 92 machine gun.

The THORFINN's dive guides are attempting to be very careful not to drop their anchors on the wreck in order to maintain its good condition. Hopefully, this practice will be followed by others and divers will have a chance to see and photograph this magnificent wreck for years to come.

A total of 1,149 Nakajima B5Ns were built by Nakajima Hikoki K.K. at Koizumi, by the Dai-Juichi Kaigun Kokusho at Hiro, and by the Aichi Tokei Denki K.K. at Nagoya between 1936 and 1943. The Kate was widely used from land-based units in bombing operations in support of ground troops in China during the Sino-Japanese war. At the outbreak of the war with the U.S. and its allies, the Kate was considered to be one of the most modern and effective carrier-borne torpedo-bombers in the world. The plane was capable of carrying a single 800 kg (1,764 lb) torpedo or the equivalent weight in bombs. Some 144 Kates piloted by the elite of the Japanese naval aircorps were involved in the attacks against the U.S. Pacific Fleet battleships resting at anchor at Pearl Harbor on 7 December 1941. Japanese carrier-based Kates were also responsible for the sinking of U.S. carriers LEXINGTON, YORKTOWN, and HORNET within the next twelve months following the attack on Pearl Harbor. Allied forces encountered Kates extensively in the Solomon Islands campaign and later in the Philippines. The Kate was finally relegated to a secondary role after suffering heavy losses due to its vulnerability to enemy fighters because of its lack of protection for its fuel tank and three-man crew plus its light defensive armament. After being replaced as front line aircraft by the Jill (Nakajima B6N), the Japanese utilized the endurance performance of the Kate for anti-submarine and reconnaissance roles.

APPENDICES

APPENDIX A
JAPANESE SHIPS

Ship's Names

Many spelling differences appear in the Romanized spellings of the names of Japanese ships between various texts. There are two quite different common ways to convert written Japanese into Roman letters. This can be quite confusing as ship's names may be listed either way. The Hepburn conversion system, also referred to as the western or missionary convention, reflects the actual pronunciation much more closely than the official Kokutai convention, commonly used by the Japanese Navy in World War II. An example of this is the word for Roman letters. Romaji is the Hepburn spelling while Romazi is the Kokutai spelling. Roma means Roman; the ji/zi means the word characters.

The Japanese borrowed from the Chinese their basic set of several thousand characters called kanzi (kan means Chinese; zi again means characters). The Japanese also borrowed the Chinese spoken words which they added as an alternative to their own for that character. Each character has many different pronunciations depending on how it is used and how it fits with any subsequent characters. There are many characters with the same sound, just as there are words in English with the same sound, and it is troublesome in both languages. The Japanese found that the characters were not adequate to fully express their language, so they supplemented it with their own alphabet consisting of characters which are called kana. These kana are used to amplify the characters and to spell foreign words for which there are no characters. The kana, having a complete range of sounds, could also reproduce the sounds of the kanzi, although one always has the same problem as the spoken language as to precisely which kanzi is intended. The kana are an aid for the uninformed or uneducated reader. A Japanese newspaper will show the kana in fine print alongside each kanzi character so the reader can sound it and recognize the character. When one converts from kanzi to kana, one loses the precise meaning and Japanese themselves frequently must ask each other precisely which kanzi is meant (which they then draw on the palm of their hand with a finger). As you go from kana to Romazi, the precise meaning becomes even more blurred.

Each kana character in the alphabet can be considered by a Westerner to sound like a single Roman letter or a consonant-vowel digraph. The six kana consisting of single letters are the vowels A, E, I, O and U and an oddball character represented by a single letter N which is quite common, but can only end syllables. In Kokutai, the Westerner sees the digraphs as 14 consonants, B, D, G, H, K, M, N, P, R, S, T, W, Y, and Z, followed by the five vowels A, E, I, O, and U. A few combinations are impossible (YE, YI and WU); a few are archaic and only used in names (WE and WI); and some are becoming obsolete (WO is being replaced by O). In Hepburn, these are the same kana, but some are transcribed closer to their sound:

Kokutai	Hepburn
DI	JI
DU	ZU
TI	CHI
HU	FU
ZI	JI
SI	SHI
TU	TSU

The presence of C, F, or J in a Romanization is a clear indication that the Hepburn conversion is being used.

Conversion to Roman letters is not simply a problem of transliterating the individual kana; adjacent kana in a syllable can unite to yield a combined sound just as letters do in English. This is further complicated by the differences between Kokutai and Hepburn.

Kana (Kokutai)	Kokutai Romazi	Hepburn Romaji
SI YA	SYA	SHA
HI YO	HYO	HYO
TI YU	TYU	CHU

The differences in Kokutai show up with any Japanese syllable in which the vowel of the initial kana is "I", followed by the kanas A, O, U, YA, YO, and YU. These combine into 3 letters made up of the initial consonant, Y, and the terminal vowel (SI + YO = SYO, NI + YA = NYA, etc.). In this Kokutai conversion, the rule is simple. Hepburn is more complicated:

DY + vowel = JY + same vowel
SY + vowel = SH + same vowel
TY + vowel = CH + same vowel
ZY + vowel = JY + same vowel

Note that the first and last combine into the same three letters.

There are certain conversions in kana digraphs that affect both systems. For kana consisting of initial consonants and ending in U, the final U tends to be silent. For kana starting with T or D and ending in O, the final O becomes silent. The Yokosuka (YO-KO-SU-KA) Naval Base in Japan is Romanized in both systems as Yokoska. Fortunately, most of the peculiarities of both systems affect both Romanizations similarly.

To produce the sound of a double consonant in kana, the Japanese insert the kana TU, which is silent before the kana beginning with the consonant. All vowels can be either long or short. In using Romazi in either system, a long vowel is indicated by doubling it or putting a bar over it. In Hepburn, vowel length is sometimes ignored. The problem is much more complicated in kana. All vowels in individual kana are short. The vowel can be lengthened by adding a dash, but much more frequently by adding a second kana. Tokyo, the capital of Japan, is written in kana as TO-U-KI-YO-U; the U's make the O sound long. The Romanization becomes TOOKYOO or more commonly TŌKYŌ. Some kana combinations can yield quite unexpected results. For example:

$$WA + U = \bar{O} \text{ or } O\bar{O}$$
$$SE + U = SY\bar{O} \text{ (Kokutai) or } SH\bar{O} \text{ (Hepburn)}$$

Examples of actual ship's names which reflect translational spelling differences when converting from written Japanese to Roman letters are as follows:

Kokutai	Hepburn
DINGEI	JINGEI
YUDUKI	YUZUKI
HUMIDUKI	FUMIZUKI
SINKOKU	SHINKOKU
SYOEI	SHOEI
TIDORI	CHIDORI
TOYOTU	TOYOTSU
TYOKO	CHOKO
HUZIZAN	FUJISAN
TAIZYUN	TAIJUN

The above should illustrate some of the methodology in translating a ship's name from kanzi to Romazi. The main problem encountered, aside from Hepburn-Kokutai differences, is the pronuncication of the kanzi (incidentally, Japanese do not differentiate between singular and plural). For example, the KEMBU MARU can easily read as KENBU, KEMBU, or KENMU and possibly others without even getting into any Kokutai-Hepburn differences. It is nearly impossible to go from Romazi to kanzi. The Japanese think in kanzi and do not understand our problems.

The Japanese merchant vessels are given a name followed by the suffix MARU. Another problem is that the kanzi for MARU (丸) also means the digit 0 (zero). When and only when it is zero, it can be read as either REI (pronounced RAY) or MARU. When you see the character, it may or may not be a ship's name.

The Japanese merchant ships were named after many different things. Some names were taken from mountains. Direct examples include:

AMAGISAN MARU – Amagi-san is one of the principle peaks of the province of Izu.
FUJISAN MARU – The name comes from Mt. Fujiyama.

Some symbolic examples:

SANKISAN MARU – Dragon mountain
YAMAGIRI MARU – Foggy or misty mountain.

Ships were also named for foreign countries, cities, states, territories, and islands:

BRAZIL MARU
SAN FRANCISCO MARU
OREGON MARU
ALASKA MARU
LUZON MARU

Names of Japanese towns, cities, and districts (prefectures) were utilized also:

IKUTA MARU (town)
TATEYAMA MARU (city)
NAGANO MARU (district and city)

Some symbolic names referred to Japan itself:

AIKOKU MARU – Love of country
SHINKOKU MARU – Divine country

Some names were taken from rivers, seas, or oceans. Direct examples include:

GANGES MARU
PACIFIC MARU

Symbolic examples:

HOKUYO MARU – North sea
HOYO MARU – Rich or treasure ocean
UNKAI MARU – Sea of clouds
MOMOKAWA MARU – Peach river
HANAKAWA MARU – Flower river

Often, Japanese merchant ship's names were numbered. The common numbering system was used most often but the Japanese Navy used a stilted system. Examples are shown below:

Ship's Name	Common Numbering	Japanese Navy
UNYO MARU NO. 1	DAI-ICHI UNYO MARU	DAI-HITO UNYO MARU
HINO MARU NO. 2	DAI-NI HINO MARU	DAI-FUTA HINO MARU
TONAN MARU NO. 3	DAI-SAN TONAN MARU	DAI-SAN TONAN MARU
MISAGO MARU NO. 4	DAI-SHI MISAGO MARU	DAI-YOTU MISAGO MARU
SHOWA MARU NO. 5	DAI-GO SHOWA MARU	DAI-GO SHOWA MARU
UNKAI MARU NO 6	DAI-ROKU UNKAI MARU	DAI-ROKU UNKAI MARU
TAKUNAN MARU NO. 7	DAI-SHICHI TAKUNAN MARU	DAI-NANA TAKUNAN MARU
TOSHI MARU NO. 8	DAI-HACHI TOSHI MARU	DAI-HACHI TOSHI MARU
NISSHO MARU NO. 9	DAI-KU NISSHO MARU	DAI-KIU NISSHO MARU
SHONAN MARU NO. 10	DAI-JU SHONAN MARU	DAI-HITO SHONAN MARU
FUJI MARU NO. 11	DAI-JUICHI FUJI MARU	DAI-HITO HITO FUJI MARU
ETC.	ETC.	ETC.

Most of the larger Japanese merchant ships have their Romanized names on both sides of the hull near the bow with the corresponding Chinese kanzi characters placed above. The Romanized name is, of course, read left to right; the kanzi characters are read oppositely, right to left. This combination of names is sometimes found on the stern hull or fantail also. Japanese World War II destroyers and escorts generally had a number painted on both sides near the bow or amidships with the ship's name in the kanzi characters placed on the fantail. Large Japanese capital ships (battleships, carriers, and cruisers) apparently had no identifiers upon them.

The Japanese nomenclature for warships was structured (with some exceptions) as follows:

Battleships: Named after ancient Japanese provinces.
Aircraft Carriers: Named after dragons, phoenixes, and birds.
Heavy Cruisers: Named after mountains.
Light Cruisers: Named after rivers.
Destroyers (First Class): Meteorological names in poetic style... normally grouped in the following classes: moon, cloud, rain, wind, and wave.
Destroyers (Second Class): Named after flowers, trees and fruits.
Torpedo Boats: Named after birds.
Minelayers: Named after islands, straits, channels, and birds.
Submarines: Named after tides and currents.

APPENDIX B
JAPANESE NAMES

Japanese Map/Chart Names

GENERAL

Name on Map/Chart	Japanese Name
Secret	Hi
Ultra Secret	Gunki
Anchorage	Byochi
Road	Hakuchi
Point, cape	Hana
Rock	Iwa
River	Kaku
Harbor, port	Ko
Mountain	San
Cape, headland	Saki
Island	Shima
Reef	Sho
Channel, passage	Suido
Island	To
Bay	Wan
Mountain	Yama

KWAJALEIN ATOLL

Name on Map/Chart	Japanese Name
Kwajalein Island	Kuejierin To
Ebeye	Ebijie To
Loi	Rooji To
Gugegwe	Gugeegue To
Bigej Channel	Pigeji Suido
Bigej	Pigeji To
Meck	Meiku To
Enubuj	Eniibuuji To
Ennylabegan	Eniierappukan To
Gea	Kiiyo To
Gea Pass	Kiiyo Suido
Ninni	Niinii To
Gehh	Gae To
Legan	Anboo To
Ambo Channel	Anboo Suido
Eller	Erreppu To
Nell	Neru To
Tabik	Taabikku To
Tabik Channel	Taakikku Suido
Ebadon	Ebaden To
Boggerik	Yoruroppu To
Boggerlap	Bogarrappu To
North Pass	Kita Suido
Enneubing	Enibin To
Roi	Ruotto To
Namur	Nimuru To
Ennugarret	Enigaran To
Ennumennet	Enimanekku To
Ennubir	Enibuni To
Gegan	Gooankkan To

TRUK LAGOON

Name on Map/Chart	Japanese Name
Truk Islands	Torakku Shoto
Moen	Haru Shima
Dublon	Natsu Shima
Fefan	Aki Shima
Uman	Fuyu Jima
Eten	Take Jima
Udot	Getsuyo To
Eot	Mae Shima
Fala-Beguets	Kayo To
Tol	Suiyo To
Pata (NW part of Tol I.)	Mokuyo To
Polle (SW part of Tol I.)	Kinyo To
Onamue	Koyo To
Ulalu	Nichiyo To
Kuop	Kunto Shoto
Tarik	Hoshi Shima
Tsis	Usu Shima
Param	Kaeide Shima
Otta I.	Ota Shima
Mesagon I.	Masu Shima
Uijec I.	Uji Shima
Fanan I.	Hana Shima
Salat I.	Sara Shima
Mor I.	Uma Shima
Pis I.	Kita Shima
Faleu I.	Minami Shima
Tonelik I.	Ne Shima
Ollan I.	Aioi Jima
Northeast I.	U Jima
North Pass	Kita Suido
Northeast Pass	Nokuto Suido
Salat Pass	Sarshima Suido
Uligar Pass	Hanashima Suido
Otta Pass	Otashima Suido
South Pass	Minami Suido
Piaanu Pass	Nishi Suido

SELECTED BIBLIOGRAPHY

Belote, James H. and Belote, William M., "Titans Of The Seas," Harper & Row, 1975

Broadwater, John D., "Kwajalein – Lagoon of Found Ships," Three States Printing Company, Middlesboro, Kentucky, 1971

Crowl, Philip A. and Love, Edmond F., "The United States Army in World War II – The War In the Pacific – Seizure Of The Gilberts and Marshalls," Office of Military History, U.S. Army, U.S. Government Printing Office, Washington, D.C., 1955

Denfield, D. Colt, "Japanese Fortifications And Other Military Structures In The Central Pacific," Micronesian Archaeological Survey, Report No. 9, Saipan, C.M., 1981

Dickey, Capt. George L., Jr., "The End Of The Prinz," U.S. Naval Institute Proceedings, Annapolis, Md., August 1969

Fane, Richard P., "The Nomenclature Of The N.Y.K. Fleet," Nippon Yusen Kaisha, 1935

Francillon, R. J., Phd., "Japanese Aircraft Of The Pacific War," Funk & Wagnalls, New York, 1970

Grover, David, H., "U.S. Army Ships And Watercraft Of World War II," Naval Institute Press, Annapolis, Md., 1987

Hara, Capt. T., "Japanese Destroyer Captain," Ballantine Books, New York, 1961

Hashimoto, M., "Sunk," Avon Books, New York, 1954

Heinl, Robert D. and Crown, John A., "The Marshalls; Increasing The Tempo," Historical Branch, G-3 Division, HQ. USMC, U.S. Government Printing Office, Washington D.C., 1954

Ito, Masanori, "The End Of The Japanese Navy," English Translation, Norton Publishers, New York, 1962

Jane, Fred T., "Janes Fighting Ships 1944–45 (Corrected to April 1946)," Reprinted by David and Charles, Ltd., London, 1971

Jensen, Lt. Oliver USNR, "Carrier War," Pocket Books, Inc., New York, 1945

Jentschura, Hans Georg and Jung, Dieter and Mikel, Peter, "Die Japanischen Kriegsschiffe 1869/1945," J.F. Lehmanns Verlag, Munich, 1970

Joint Information Center – Pacific Ocean Areas Information Bulletin, "Dublon, Eten Islands," JICPOA 1944

Joint Information Center – Pacific Ocean Areas Information Bulletin, "Moen, Param, Tol Islands," JICPOA, 1944

Karig, Capt. Walter and Harris, Russel L. and Manson, Lt. Cmdr. Frank A., "Battle Report, The End Of An Empire," Rinehart & Co., Inc., New York, 1948

Karig, Capt. Walter and Kelly, Welborn, "Battle Report, Pearl Harbor To Coral Sea," Vol. I, Farrar & Rinehart, Inc., New York, 1944

Kennedy, Ludovic, "Pursuit, The Chase And Sinking Of The Battleship BISMARK," Viking Press, 1974

Lawson, R. C. (ed), "The History Of U.S. Naval Airpower," The Military Press, New York, 1985

Lindemann, Klaus P., "Hailstorm Over Truk Lagoon," Maruzen Asia, 1982

Lloyds of London, "Lloyds' Register Of Shipping 1944–45," London

Lockwood, Vice Admiral C. A., "Sink 'Em All," Bantam Books, 1984

Love, Edmund G, "The Hourglass – A History Of The 7th Infantry Division In World War II," Infantry Journal Press, Washington, D.C., 1950

Marshall, Lt. Col. S. L. A. , "Island Victory – The Battle Of Kwajalein Atoll," The Infantry Journal, Washington, D.C., 1945

Military History Section, Special Staff, General Headquarters, Far East Command, "Monograph No. 116, The Imperial Japanese Navy In World War II," U.S. Government Printing Office, Washington, D.C., 1952

Morison, Samuel E., "History Of U.S. Naval Operations In World War II, Vol III, The Rising Sun In The Pacific, 1931–April 1942." Little Brown & Co., Boston, 1951, Reprinted 1975

Morison, Samuel E., "History Of U.S. Naval Operations In World War II, Vol IV, Coral Sea, Midway, and Submarine Actions, May 1941–August 1942," Little, Brown & Co., Boston, 1951, Reprinted 1975

Morison, Samuel E., "History Of U.S. Naval Operations In World War II, Vol. V, The Struggle For Guadalcanal, August 1942–February 1943," Little, Brown & Co., Boston, 1951, Reprinted 1975

Morison, Samuel E., "*History Of U.S. Naval Operations In World War II, Vol. VII, Aleutians, Gilberts, And Marshalls, June 1942–April 1944,*" Little, Brown & Co., Boston, 1951, Reprinted 1975

Navy Department – Office Of Chief Of Naval Operations, "*Japanese Merchant Ship Recognition Manual,*" U.S. Government Printing Office, Washington, D.C., 1942

Navy Department – Office Of The Chief Of Naval Operations, "*O.N.I. 208-J (Revised) Japanese Merchant Ships,*" U.S. Government Printing Office, Washington, D.C.

O'Kane, R. H., "*Clear The Bridge,*" Rand McNally, Skokie, IL., 1977

Redford, Sam D., "*Truk's Magnificent Seven,*" Skin Diver Magazine, Vol. 23, No. 3, Petersen Publishing Co., Los Angeles, March 1974

Roscoe, Theodore, "*Pig Boats,*" Bantam Books, New York, 1958

Roscoe, Theodore, "*United States Submarine Operations in World War II,*" United States Naval Institute, Annapolis, Md., 1949, Reprinted 1972

Ruge, Vice Admiral Friedrich, "*Der Seekrieg, The German Navy's Story 1939–1945,*" U.S. Naval Institute, Annapolis, Md., 1957

Schmalenbach, Paul S. and Wise, Commander J.E., "*Prinz Eugen Album,*" U.S. Naval Institute Proceedings, Annapolis, Md., August 1969

Shaw Jr., H. I., and Nalty, B. C., and Turnbladh, E. T., "*Central Pacific Drive, History Of USMC Operations In WW II, V III,*" Historical Branch G-3 Division, HQ, USMC, Washington, D.C., 1966

Sherrod, Robert, "*History Of Marine Corps Aviation In WW II,*" Combat Forces Press, Washington, D.C., 1952

Tzimoulis, Paul J., "*Submarine,*" Skin Diver Magazine, Vol 21, No. 2, Petersen Publishing Co., Los Angeles, February 1972

U.S. Joint Army–Navy Assessment Committee (JANAC), "*Japanese Naval and Merchant Shipping Losses During World War II By All Causes,*" U.S. Government Printing Office, Washington, D.C., 1947

U.S. Office Of Air Force History, "*The Army Air Forces In World War II, Vol. IV, The Pacific…Guadalcanal To Saipan,*" University Of Chicago Press, Chicago, 1950

U.S. Office Of Air Force History, "*The Army Air Forces In World War II, Vol. V, Matterhorn To Nagasaki,*" University of Chicago Press, Chicago, 1950

U.S. Strategic Bombing Survey (Pacific) Military Supplies Division, "*Japanese Naval Ordnance,*" U.S. Government Printing Office, Washington, D.C., 1946

U.S. Strategic Bombing Survey (Pacific), Naval Analysis Division, "*The Campaigns Of The Pacific War,*" U.S. Government Printing Office, Washington, D.C., 1946

U.S. Strategic Bombing Survey (Pacific), Naval Analysis Division, "*Interrogations Of Japanese Officials,*" 2 Vols., U.S. Government Printing Office, Washington, D.C., 1946

U.S. Strategic Bombing Survey (Pacific) Naval Analysis Division, "*The Reduction Of Truk,*" U.S. Government Printing Office, Washington, D.C. 1947

Watts, A.J., "*Japanese Warships Of World War II,*" Doubleday & Co., Inc., New York, 1966

Whitehouse, Arch, "*Squadrons Of The Sea,*" Doubleday & Co., Inc., New York, 1962

Winton, John, "*The Forgotten Fleet, The British Navy In The Pacific 1944-45,*" Coward-McCann, Inc., New York, 1970

INDEX

A

AAF Transport Plane **48**
AIKOKU MARU (10,437 tons) 90, *97*, 111, 128, **129-132**, 156, 159, 161
AIKOKU MARU (35 tons) 35
Air Flotillas
    21st 76
    22nd 76, 135
    23rd 6
    24th 6, 76
    25th 76, 80
    26th 76, 110
AGANO 82, 106, 165
Aisek, Kimiuo 67, 146, 165, 166
AKAGI MARU 89, 91–95, 110, **132-133**
AKASHI 82, 87, 90, *92*, 106, 109, 110, 150, 154, 183, 184
AKIBASAN MARU 17, 20, **23–24**
AKIKAZE 89, 94, 98, 110
AKITSUSHIMA 86, 87, 90, 110
ALABAMA 17, 84
AMAGISAN MARU 96, 105, 111, 127, **133-134**
Army Organizations
    1st South Seas Detachment 6
    1st Mobile Amphibious Brigade 6, 130
    31st 78
    51st Independent Mixed Brigade 78
    52nd Division 78, 155
    69th Infantry Regiment 78
    150th Infantry Regiment 78
ASAKAZE MARU 14–16, 18, **24–27**
ASHITAKA MARU NO. 5 20

B

B–25 Bomber Wreck 63, *64*
BALAO 156
Base Forces
    3rd 6
    4th 6, 135, 153
    5th 6
    6th 6, 36, 41, 62
    8th 135
BATAAN
    Photographic Interpretation Report 117, 118
    Strikes 113
    Task Force Organization 112
BELLEAU WOOD
    Strikes 17, 37, 51
    Task Force Organization 12, 19, 84, 112
Betty Bomber Wreck **191**, *192*
Bigej Coastal Tanker **40–41**
Bigej Island 6, 8, 17, 37, 51
Bigej Island Fighter-Bomber **51**

BISMARK 29, 30
BUNKER HILL
    Air Intelligence Report 91, 101, 109
    Strikes 17, 23, 84, 87, 88, 91, 95, 96, 99, 101, 103–105, 108, 109, 133, 138, 142, 144, 145, 148, 149, 154, 159, 160, 165, 172, 175, 177, 180, 181, 183, 186, 187
    Task Force Organization 19, 84, 112
BURNS 17, 121, 122

C

CABOT
    Strikes 86, 89, 94, 112, 114, 133, 147
    Task Force Organization 19, 84, 112
Carlson Island (Enubuj) 26, 31
CATCHPOLE Operation 42
CHA–18 20, **37**, 41
CHA–19 20
CHA–20 110
CHA–21 20, 37, 41
CHA–25 20
CHA–28 20
CHA–33
CHA–46 **179-180**
CHA–66 **179-180**
CHA–38 118, **179–180**
CH–24 110, 121–123
CH–29 110, **135**
CHOKO MARU 14-16, 18, **26–27**
Clark, Rear Adm. J.J. 112
Combined Fleet 12, 72, 78, 80, 83, 112, 129, 170, 176
Convoy 3206 78, 99, 123–124
COWPENS
    Strikes 12, 88, 91, 95, 98, 101, 103, 121, 132, 133, 169, 180
    Task Force Organization 12, 19, 84, 112

D

DOLPHIN 7
DR Wreck **35**
DRUM 186
Dublon Island
    Description of 71, 73, 74, 80, *81*, 85, 91, *92*, *93*, *100*, 109, 110, 111, 113, 114, 116, 117, 119

E

Ebeye Island 1, 6–9, 14, 17, 20, 23, *49*, *50*, *51*
Ebeye Island Seaplanes **48–50**
EIKO MARU NO. 2 17, 18, **55–58**, 154
EISEN NO. 761 **184**
Eli Kanibu Island 77, 114

Eller Island 14, 20
Emily Flying-Boat Wreck 192, *193*
ENTERPRISE
    Strikes 7, 14, 16, 48, 84–86, 89, 90, 92, 95, 98, 101–104, 106, 109, 114, 135, 138, 140, 145, 150, 156, 158, 180, 181, 183
    Task Force Organization 12, 19, 84, 112
ESSEX
    Shipping Target Summary
    Strikes 13, 17, 84, 85, 87, 90, 93–94, 96, 99, 102, 104, 105, 108, 130, 133, 148, 149, 154, 159, 160, 161, 168, 172, 175, 180, 185
    Task Force Organization 12, 19, 84
Eten Island
    Description of 71, 73, 80, 76, *81*, 85, 91, *93*, 103, 109–111, 113, 114, 116, 118, 119, *173*

F

Faleu Island 77, 112–114
Fefan Island
    Description of 73, 76, *81*, *92*, 110, 111, 113, 119
FLINTLOCK Operation 18, 84
Fourth Mandate Fleet 5, 6, 12, 36, 41, 62, 72–74, 80, 83, *92*, 120, 154, 155
FUJI MARU NO. 11 46
FUJIKAWA MARU 14-16, 99, 108, 109, 111, 128, **135–138**, 161, 174
FUJINAMI 123, 124
FUJISAN MARU 82, 91, 98, 105, 106, 110, 128, 133, **138–141**, 154, 177
FUKUYOSHI MARU NO. 5 20
FUMI MARU 20
FUMITSUKI 82, 91, *100*, 110, **141–142**, 176
FUTAGAMI 184

G

GALVANIC Operation 12
G–Buoy Wreck **35**
GOSEI MARU 91, 105, 106, 109, 111, 127, *136*, **142**, 184
Gun-High Wreck 105, 106, **143**, 147, 157
Gilbert Islands 5–7, 12, 155
Ginder, Rear Admiral S. P. 17
Gugegwe Island
    Description 6, 9, 10, 17, 37, 38, *39*, 40
    Wrecks **37–38**, *39*
GYORAITEI NO. 10 110, **143**

H

HADDOCK 149
HAGOROMO MARU 83, 99, 110, 123, 124
HAILSTONE Operation 72, 84
HAKACHI 82, 110
HAKUSHUN MARU 111, **145**
HALIBUT 130
HALSEY, Adm. W. F. "Bull" 7
HANAKAWA MARU 83, 95, 98, 106, 109, 111, **143–145**, 154, 177
Hara, Vice Adm. Chuichi 72, 120
HARRISON 40
HARUSAME 89, 91-4, 98, 110, 133

HEIAN MARU 7, 72, 82, 87, *92*, *94*, 98, *100*, 105, 108, 110, 126, **145-147**
HADDOCK 149
Hermle, Gen . L. D. 120
HIE MARU 145, 147
HIKAWA MARU NO. 2 *88*, *92*, 94, 101–106, 141, 145
HINO MARU NO. 2 118, 127, **147–148**
HOKI MARU 83, 90, 111, 130, **148**
HOKOKU (10, 438 Tons) 129, 130, 156
HOKOKU MARU NO. 2 (36 Tons) 17
HOKUYO MARU 90, 99, 106, 108, 111, 128, **149**
Holden, Capt. Carl F. 84
Hopping, Lt. Cmdr. H. L. P. 7
HORNET
    Strikes 63, 112, 113
    Task Force Organization 112
HOYO MARU (8,691 Tons) 82, 83, 87, *92*, 98, *100*, 110, 126, 141, **149–50**, 154, 176, 183
HOYO MARU (2,930 Tons) 11

I

I–10 102, 110
I–23 11
I–169 7, 126, 147, **150-53**
I–174 114, 147
IKUTA MARU 6, 18, **27–28**, 154
IMPLACABLE 120
INMATE Operation 120
INTREPID
    Strikes 17, 84, 85, 87, 90–91, 94, 96, 99, 102, 123, 124, 130, 132, 133, 138, 180
    Task Force Organization 19, 84
IOWA 84, 121, 122, 124, 160
ISUZU 12–14, 18, 156

J

JINGEI 53
Judy Dive Bomber Wreck *190*, 191

K

Kaiten 73, 77
KASHIMA MARU 6, 36
Kate Torpedo-Bomber Wreck 194
KATORI 7–11, 82, 85, 87, 90–96, 98, 110, 121–123, 132, 133
KATSURA MARU 6, **41**, 62
KATSURAGISAN MARU **153**
KEMBU MARU 12–14, 18, **58–62**, 144
KENSHO MARU 55, 82, 87, 90, *92*, 99, 102, 105, 108, 111, 126, **154**, 176, 183
KIKUKAWA 128, **155**, 164, 166
KIKYO MARU 46
KIYOSUMI MARU 82, 87, 90, *92*, 98, 99, 102, 111, 126, 133, **155–157**, 174, 176, 183
Kobayashi, Vice Adm. Hitoshi 72
Koga, Adm. Mineichi 12, 72, 80, 84, 112
KOTOHIRA MARU **157**
KOTOBUKI MARU NO. 3 6, 20, 36, **41**
Kuop Atoll 95, 99, 101, 104, 106, 116, 180

Kurita, Vice Admiral Takeo 80
Kwajalein
    Further Preliminaries and Assault 12
    Initial Carrier Strikes 7
    Island Description 1, 6, 16–20
    Japanese Occupation of 5
    Kwajalein Today 1
    Miscellaneous Small Wrecks 35
    Northern Atoll Wrecks 53
    Southern Atoll Wrecks 23
    Southern Atoll Aircraft Wrecks 47
    West Reef Aircraft Wrecks 63

L

LANGLEY
    Strikes 112, 114–116, 158, 179
    Task Force Organization 19, 112
LEXINGTON
    Strikes 13, 58, 112, 114, 158
    Task Force Organization 12, 112
Lighter Wreck 127, 147, **157**

M

MAIKAZE 88, 90, 91, 93, 95, 96, 98, 110, 121–123, 132, 133
MANLEY 42
MASSACHUSETTS 17, 84
MATSUKAZE 89, 110, 141
MATSUTAN MARU 105, 106, 108, 111, 128, **158**
MEIHO MARU 46
Mellu Island Landing Craft Wreck **66**
Michiyuki, Rear Adm. Yamada 6
MIKAGE MARU NO. 18 14, *16*, 18
MINNEAPOLIS 12, 48, 84, 121, 122
MINSEI MARU 118
Mitscher, Adm. Pete 19, 84, 85, 112
Monzo, Rear Admiral Akiyama 6
Moen Island
    Description of 67, 73, 75, 85, 91, *92*, 101–103, 109–111,
        114–117, 119
MOMOKAWA MARU 83, 102, 105, 108, 111, 128, 154, **158-159**, 164
MONTEREY
    Strikes 17, 86, 89, 106, 108, 109, 114, 142, 144, 154, 158, 165
    Task Force Organization 19, 84, 112
Montgomery, Rear Adm. A.E. 12, 19, 112
Mugikura, Lt. Gen. Shunzaburo 78, 120
Murray, Vice Adm. George D. 120
MUSASHI 72, 80, 82, 186

N

N–Buoy Wreck **35**
N–East Wreck **36**
NAGANO MARU 87, 105, 111, 128, **159–160**
NAGARA 12–14, 18, 149, 150
NAGATO 30, 80
NAKA 12, 83, 87, 89, 90, 95, 101, 110, 156, **160–161**
Namur Island 1, *18*, 20
Nanko Area 73, *94*, 113–115

Naval Air Groups
    17th 73
    752nd 6
    753rd 6
    892nd 155
    902nd 73
    952nd 6
NEW JERSEY 84, 121, 122, 160
NEW MEXICO 48
NEW ORLEANS 12, 84, 121, 122
NICHIEI MARU 17, 20
Nimitz, Adm. Chester W. 7, 12, 19, 80, 84, 120, 156
NIPPO MARU 87, 111, 128, **161–164**
NORTH CAROLINA 17, 55, 57, 84
Northeast Island 77
NOWAKE 88, 91, 93, 95, 96, 110, 121–123, 132, 133

O

O–Buoy Submarine Chaser **36–37**
O–Buoy Wreck **28**
OITE 106, 108–110, **165–166**
OJIMA 128, 155, **166**
Ollan Island 78, 113, 114, 158
OS2U Kingfisher Scout Planes **47**
Ottu Island 78
OVERTON 42

P

Palau 6, 80, 112, 154, 182
PALAU MARU 35
Param Island
    Description of 71, 73, 76, 85, 95, 99, 112–114, 118, 119
PARAN MARU 17, 20
PATROL BOAT NO. 34 126, **166-167**
PERMIT 80
PETO 177
Phantom Maru **38**
POGY 23, 174, 175
Pownall, Rear Adm. C. A. 18
PRINCE OF WALES 29, 30, 191
PRINCETON
    Strikes 114, 115
    Task Force Organization 19, 112
PRINZ EUGEN **29–31**
PV–1 Ventura Wreck **47-48**

R

Rabaul 6, 7, 12, 49, 72, 73, 76, 79, 80, 110, 112, 135, 141, 180, 186
Reeves, Rear Adm. J.W., Jr. 17, 84, 112
REIYO MARU 87, 111,128, *131*, **168**
REPULSE 191
RIO DE JANEIRO MARU 88, 96, 101, 111, 127, **169–171**
RO–42 102, 110, 147
RO–60 **53–55**
Roi Island 1, 5–8, 12–14, 16, *18*, 19, 20, 27, 47, 52, 63, 72
RYUKO MARU 83, 99, 123, 124

S

Salat Island 77, 113, 114
SALT LAKE CITY 7, 30, 31
SAN FRANCISCO 12, 40, 51, 84, 113
SAN FRANCISCO MARU 90, 105, 108, 111, 128, 159, **171–172**
SANKISAN MARU 96, 98, 105,106, 111, 127, **172–174**
SAPPORO MARU 118, 126, **174**
SARATOGA
    Strikes 7
    Task Force Organization 19, 84
SCAMP 165
SCORPION 149
SEARAVEN 11, 105
SEIKO MARU 87, 90, 99, 108, 109, 111, 128, *131*, 149, 159, **174–176**
Shell Island Wrecks 38, **38**, *39*
Sherman, Adm. F. C. 17, 84
Shigeyoshi, Adm. 5
SHIGURE 89, 91-94, 98, 110
SHINHEI MARU 8, 11
SHINKOKU MARU 91, 98, 99, 106, 109, 110, 133, 154, 161, **176–179**
Shinohara, Cmdr. Shigeo 152
SHINSHO MARU 32
Ships of Eller Island **45–46**
SHOEI MARU 14, 15, 18, **28**
SHONAN MARU NO. 6 20, **41–45**
SHONAN MARU NO. 15 98, 110, 121, 123, 135
Sixth Submarine Fleet 11, 72, 147, 152
SKATE 165
Ski Area Dolphin Wreck **35**
Ski Area Wreck **35**
South Pass Wreck **41**
SOYA 82, 110
SPEARFISH 170
Spruance, Vice Admiral R.A. 7, 84
STEELHEAD 174–176
STURGEON 167
Sumikawa, Rear Adm. Michio 76, 80, 110, 120
SUTSUKI **166–167**

T

Tabik Anchorage 12, 13
TACHIKAZE 95, 99, 101, 106, 110, **180**
TAIHO MARU 111, 127, **180–181**
TAIJUN MARU 181
TAIKICHI MARU 87, 98, 99, 111, 126, **181–182**
Takagi, Vice Adm. Takeo 72
TAKEURA MARU 35
TAKUNAN MARU NO. 7 6, 13, 14, 18, **62**, *63*
TANG 113, 123
Taroa 6, 7, 17, 18
TATEYAMA MARU 14–16, 18, 27, **32–34**
TATSUHA MARU 99, 111, 123, 124
Task Force 8 7
Task Force 50 12, 19, 84
Task Force 58 17, 19, 23, 84, 112, 118, 130
Task Group 50.9 121–123
THRESHER 32
TINOSA 182, 183
TOA MARU 7, 9–11
TOKIWA 7–11
Tol Island
    Description of 73, 77– 79, 95, 106, 114, 116, 117
TONAN MARU NO. 3 82, 87, 89, *92*, 94, 98, *100*, 105, 108, 110, 126, *136*, 145, 150, 176, **182–183**
Tonelik Island 73, 77, 165
TRIGGER 147
Truk
    Army Operations 78
    Australian Reconaissance and Bombing Attacks 79, 80
    British Carrier Attack 120
    Fortifications – Reef Islands 77–78
    Island Description 67
    Japanese Surrender 120
    Major Island Installations 73–77
    Mysterious Truk 72
    Naval Operations 72
    Photoraphic Overflight 80
    Truk Lagoon Today 67
TSUKUSHI MARU 147
Tugboat Wrecks 126, **183–184**

U

UJI MARU 6, 19, **36**
Ulalu Island 77, 110, 114, 119
Uman Island 73, 76, 113, 114, 119, 127, 142
UNKAI MARU NO. 6 90, 99 105, 106, 108, 109, 111, 183, **184–185**
U.S. Army Concrete Barge **34**
ULTRA 23, 41, 177

W

West Reef Aircraft Wrecks **63–66**
Wotje 5–7, 18, 41

Y

Yamamoto, Vice Adm. Isoroku 72, 156, 191
YAMAGIRI MARU 98, 99, 106, 108, 111, 126, 154, 176, 183, **185–187**
YAMASHIMO MARU 14, 15, 18
YAMASHIRO MARU 35
YAMATO 72, 80, 186
YASUKUNI MARU 7–9, 11, 23, 147
Yawata Shima 78, 116
YMS 383 45, 48
YORKTOWN
    Strikes 7, 14, 17, 34, 45, 84–87, 90, 93, 95–96, 98–99, 102, 104–106, 108, 112, 113, 133, 145, 148, 150, 154, 156, 159, 171, 172, 177, 181, 183, 185, 186
    Task Force Organization 12, 19, 84, 112
Young, Cmdr. Howard L. 7, 8
YUBAE MARU 96, 98, 111, 127, 161, **187**

Z

Zeke Fighter Wrecks **189**, *190*
ZUHIO 87, 183
ZUKAI MARU 99, 111, 123, 124